Lancashire and Cheshire from AD 1540

A Regional History of England

General Editors: Barry Cunliffe and David Hey
For full details of the series, see pp. xii–xv

Lancashire and Cheshire
from AD 1540

C. B. Phillips and J. H. Smith

Longman
London and New York

Longman Group UK Limited,
Longman House, Burnt Mill,
Harlow, Essex CM20 2JE, England
and Associated Companies throughout the World.

Published in the United States of America
by Longman Publishing, New York

First published 1994

ISBN 0 582 49250 5 CSD
ISBN 0 582 49249 1 PPR

British Library Cataloguing-in-Publication Data

A catalogue record for this book is
available from the British Library

Library of Congress Cataloging in Publication Data

Phillips, C. B.
    Lancashire and Cheshire from AD 1540/C. B.
    Phillips and J. H. Smith.
        p.   cm. – (Regional history of England)
    Includes bibliographical references and index.
    ISBN 0–582–49250–5. – ISBN 0–582–49249–1
    (pbk.)
        1. Lancashire (England) – History.   2. Cheshire
    (England) – History.   I. Smith, J. H., 1928–.   II.
    Title.   III. Series.
    DA670.L2P48   1993
    942.7'1 – dc20   92–23399
                                                          CIP

Set by 3DD in 10/12pt Sabon Roman
Produced by Longman Singapore Publishers (Pte) Ltd.
Printed in Singapore

Contents

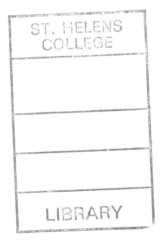

List of Plates

List of Figures

Acknowledgements

The following institutions have all been most helpful and courteous in making material available: the Cheshire County Record Office; Chetham's Library, Manchester; the Geography Department Library, Manchester University; John Rylands University Library of Manchester; the Lancashire County Record Office; the Manchester Central Library; the public libraries at Blackpool, Lancaster and Northwich; the Sydney Jones Library, Liverpool University; Tameside Local Studies Centre; and Wirral Metropolitan Borough Archives.

Similarly the following individuals have provided information or helped to solve problems: Viscountess Ashbrook, Owen Ashmore, Theo Balderston, Blackwell Barber, Fred Broadhurst, Duncan Broady, Mr & Mrs J. A. Day, Douglas Farnie, Charles Foster, Phyllis Giles, Ian Goodier, Edward Horton, John Horton, Stephanie Jackson, Beryl Johnson, Jean Johnson, Douglas Kaye, Evelyn Lord, Bob Millward, Michael Moores, Nigel Morgan, Norris Nash, Derek Nuttall, Jonathan Pepler, Chris Perkins, Michael Powell, Mike Rose, G. Saunders, W. J. Smith, Sarah Turner, Pat Walker and Ken Wood.

We could not have written the book without all those whose published or unpublished work is cited in these pages, to them our best thanks.

Additional thanks are due to: Dr N. J. Higham who allowed us to read his chapter on the later medieval period for the volume which will precede ours in the series; the General Editor, Professor David Hey, who provided encouragement and correction in just the right balance when reading our drafts; Mrs Barbara Smith who provided invaluable help with some of the maps and with the index; contributors to the Cheshire Parish Register Project for sight of Project data; the Department of Archaeology, Manchester University, who gave us photographic assistance; the Dean and Chapter of Chester and the Cathedral Verger for allowing us access to photograph part of Chester Cathedral (plate 1.5); and the staff of Longman Higher Education who turned our typescript into a book.

Readers should note that plates 1.3, 2.1, 2.6, 4.12, 5.5 and 5.11 are all photographs taken by us and plates 1.1, 3.6, 3.8, 4.1, 4.4, 4.13, 5.3 and 5.10 are reproductions from material in our possession.

The responsibility for any errors there may be is ours.

The authors and publishers would like to thank the following for their permission to reproduce copyright material: Jill Henderson (Mrs Bewley) for table 1.6 from her unpublished BA thesis (1979); Stephen Kenny for tables 3.12, 3.15, 4.9 and 4.10 from his unpublished thesis (1975); J. Lane and D. Anderson for table 5.8 from *Mines and Miners of South Lancashire* (undated); and HMSO for tables 5.15, 5.16 and the data used in figure 5.2 from Lord Redcliffe-Maud's *Report of the Royal Commission into Local Government in England, 1966–69* (1969).

Thanks are also due to the following for their permission to reproduce illustrative material: the County Archivist, Lancashire Record Office, for plate 1.4; Cheshire County Record Office for figure 1.3 and plate 2.4; Cheshire Museums for plate 4.6; John Murray (Publishers) for plate 2.5 from *Murray's Lancashire Architectural Guide* by P. Fleetwood-Hesketh; Lord Tollemache for plates 3.2 and 3.3; the Warden of Hulme Hall, University of Manchester for plate 3.7; Mike Williams and the Greater Manchester Archaeological Unit for plate 4.5; Catalyst: the Museum of the Chemical Industry, Widnes for plate 4.7; Wigan Record Office for plates 4.9, 4.10 and 4.11 from *Those Dark Satanic Mills* (Wigan, 1981); The Liverpool Daily Post & Echo for plates 5.1, 5.7 and 5.8; The Manchester Evening News for plates 5.6 and 5.9; Nigel Morgan for figure 3.2 from *Vanished Dwellings* (Preston, 1990); the Geography Department Library, Manchester University, for figure 5.1.

Whilst every effort has been made to trace the owners of copyright material, in a few cases this has proved to be problematic and we take this opportunity to offer our apologies to any copyright holders whose rights we may have unwittingly infringed.

General Preface and the General Editor's Note

England cannot be divided satisfactorily into recognizable regions based on former kingdoms or principalities in the manner of France, Germany or Italy. Few of the Anglo-Saxon tribal divisions had much meaning in later times and from the eleventh century onwards England was a united country. English regional identities are imprecise and no firm boundaries can be drawn. In planning this series we have recognized that any attempt to define a region must be somewhat arbitrary, particularly in the Midlands, and that boundaries must be flexible. Even the South West, which is surrounded on three sides by the sea, has no agreed border on the remaining side and in many ways, historically and culturally, the River Tamar divides the area into two. Likewise, the Pennines present a formidable barrier between the eastern and western counties on the Northern Borders; contrasts as much as similarities need to be emphasized here.

The concept of a region does not imply that the inhabitants had a similar experience of life, nor that they were all inward-looking. A Hull merchant might have more in common with his Dutch trading partner than with his fellow Yorkshireman who farmed a Pennine smallholding; a Roman soldier stationed for years on Hadrian's Wall probably had very different ethnic origins from a native farmer living on the Durham boulder clay. To different degrees, everyone moved in an international climate of belief and opinion with common working practices and standards of living.

Yet regional differences were nonetheless real; even today a Yorkshire-man may be readily distinguished from someone from the South East. Life in Lancashire and Cheshire has always been different from life in the Thames Valley. Even the East Midlands has a character that is subtly different from that of the West Midlands. People still feel that they belong to a particular region within England as a whole.

In writing these histories we have become aware how much regional identities may vary over time; moreover how a farming region, say, may not coincide with a region defined by its building styles or its dialect. We have dwelt upon the diversity that can be found within a region as well as upon common characteristics in order to illustrate the local peculiarities of provincial life. Yet despite all of these problems of definition, we feel that the time is ripe to attempt an ambitious scheme outlining the history of England's regions in twenty-one volumes. London has not been included – except for demonstrating the many ways in which it has influenced the provinces – for its history has been very different from that of the towns and rural parishes that are our principal concern.

In recent years an enormous amount of local research, both historical and archaeological, has deepened our understanding of the former concerns of ordinary men and women and has altered our perception of everyday life in the past in many significant ways, yet the results of this work are not widely known even within the regions themselves.

This series offers a synthesis of this new work from authors who have themselves been actively involved in local research and who are present in or former residents of the regions they describe.

Each region will be covered in two linked but independent volumes, the first covering the period up to AD 1000 and necessarily relying heavily on archaeological data, and the second bringing the story up to the present day. Only by taking a wide time-span and by studying continuity and change over many centuries do distinctive regional characteristics become clear.

This series portrays life as it was experienced by the great majority of the people of South Britain or England as it was to become. The twenty-one volumes will – it is hoped – substantially enrich our understanding of English history.

Barry Cunliffe
David Hey

This book is exceptional in the series in starting not at AD 1000, but at AD 1540. The decision to include the whole of the Middle Ages in the volume dealing with the earlier periods recognizes the peculiar history of Lancashire and Cheshire. The archaeological evidence is comparatively sparse, but the later evidence is unusually rich. From the sixteenth century onwards the region was transformed by the growth of its industries and it has therefore seemed sensible to divide our two volumes covering the region at that point, to reflect the special character of its development.

David Hey

A Regional History of England

General Editors: Barry Cunliffe (to AD 1000) and David Hey (from AD 1000)

The regionalization used in this series is illustrated on the map opposite.

* already published

1. The Northern Counties
2. The Lancashire/Cheshire Region
3. Yorkshire
4. The Severn Valley and West Midlands
5. The East Midlands
6. The South Midlands and the Upper Thames
7. The Eastern Counties
8. The South West
9. Wessex
10. The South East

Introduction

This volume in the Regional History series offers an introduction to the history of a region that comprises Lancashire south of the sands, Cheshire and that north-western part of the High Peak of Derbyshire that has long traditional ties with its western neighbours. The boundaries of the region have, of course, changed over time and they have always been permeable. Thus Chester's customs administration extended south to Cardigan Bay, nineteenth- and twentieth-century Liverpool drew both migrants and commuters from Wales, and in north-east and parts of east Lancashire the early textile trades looked east to Yorkshire almost as much as west to Manchester. Lancaster's urban influence was felt as much in Westmorland as in Lancashire north of the sands and, like the region's other ports, it formed part of an Irish Sea economy which embraced Wales, the south and east coasts of Ireland, the south coast of Scotland and the Earl of Derby's stronghold, the Isle of Man. Topographically too the region shared common features with its neighbours. To the east the high moors that hampered travellers were shared with Yorkshire, Derbyshire and Staffordshire and, in the south, the flat plain of the Cheshire cheese country, with its characteristic farming, does not stop at the county boundary. But the region we describe had a strong individuality which, in our view, sets it apart and gives it a unity as great as any other in the United Kingdom.

Within living memory the landscapes of the north-west have undergone remarkable changes. Physically the great multi-storeyed mills with their forests of chimneys and the rows of terraced cottages that dominated much of the region have given way to low-rise factories and high-rise dwellings, many of the latter now themselves being vacated and demolished. The region now takes on an appearance similar to the rest of modern England with new shopping centres and out-of-town supermarkets, leisure centres and car salesrooms, motorways and garages, individualized terrace cottages and 'executive' estates. The older people of the region have thus seen a change almost comparable to that of the late eighteenth and early nineteenth centuries, when their forebears saw a landscape of fields and woods, moors, meres and mosses

1

give way before the onslaught of those dominant features that are now themselves passing.

The economic landscape has also changed. Coal and cotton, long perceived as the 'natural' foundations of the region's economy, have virtually disappeared; engineering and the great public transport industries have declined; towns that knew only growth in the nineteenth century have gone into reverse and the rural retreats of yesterday have become vast rus-urban sprawls. The traditional religious affiliations of the region are in decline, though new ones have appeared, while each generation aspires to an education, culture and careers that its parents never knew. None of this is unique to the north-west but the changes of the last half-century or so struck the north-west early and with great force.

It has therefore become the task of modern historians, unlike that of their predecessors, to try to understand not only the growth of the region but also its decline. Histories of the north-west, written in its heyday, had a Whiggish flavour. They brought together the romance of that exotic import, cotton, the physical features of the region's landscape, and the perseverance and innovative skill of generations of Lancastrians and others in a celebration of the gigantic industry that dominated the region. Indeed the cotton industry and its many needs had fostered coal-mining, had fathered the chemical and engineering industries, had underpinned most of the transport developments of the region and been vital for the regional growth of the soap, glass and paper trades. Cotton and the north-west, with its human and physical resources, seemed to have been ordained by nature itself to come together for the benefit of the world. More recently, Douglas Farnie, in his work on the cotton industry, has pointed out that the advent and triumph of cotton was a complex paradox. It was an exotic fibre that transformed a backward and inward-looking region: it catered for the poor of the world rather than for the rich who had been the stimulus for earlier innovations; it took the north-west into a course of development that seemed permanent and undivertible but one that has proved to be relatively ephemeral. Its passing was not merely an event in the lives of a minority for it had been woven into the fabric of life itself and there were few parts of the region that were not disrupted by its demise. The passing of the great staples of the north-west leave a gap that is yet to be filled.

This book will necessarily have much to say about the rise and fall of the cotton industry and its social consequences but it also reflects continuities in many areas of life. It sets out to relate early industry to agriculture and landholding, then to follow each as they diverged with the coming of the factory system. Large areas of northern and western Lancashire, and of Cheshire, except in the Weaver and Mersey basins, remain agricultural with continuity especially marked in south Cheshire. We must also remember that the quintessence of modern foodstuffs, the potato, was established very early as a field crop in west Lancashire. The region knew not only textiles and the new industries that grew with them but also trades such as nail making and pewtering, felt hatting and glass making that were well established before the factories were built. The chemical industry of the nineteenth century grew out of the salt towns that had flourished since the Middle Ages and the coal-mines that had provided fuel before the Reformation.

The character of the region changed as industry waxed and waned. Chester remained a centre of local government and keeps its diocesan role, even if on a smaller scale. Lancaster had to give way to the new cities further south but now shows signs of greater aspirations. Migration and mobility produced new Lancastrians and Cestrians; political and religious attitudes often reflected economic circumstances and the recreations and culture of different groups and classes were circumscribed or extended by the opportunities open to them. Nevertheless there were attitudes and traditions that could survive even the most disruptive periods of innovation or hardship and this book will try to offer indications of them.

Much of the history of the region is still to be explored in detail – changes in family life, local surname study, the physical form and character of the industrializing towns in their early phases, the detailed study of immigrant groups and their relations with their longer established neighbours. But much work has already been done and this book, always intended as a work of synthesis, has the advantage of incorporating the findings of many modern scholars, both professional and amateur, which throw light on the region's history. The present authors owe these researchers a profound vote of thanks and hope that they will excuse the brevity of reference imposed by the size of the task. We have also undertaken our own researches, some especially for this book, but are conscious that we have not been able to discuss all the issues we would wish to include. For us, one of the benefits of writing this volume is that it has outlined an agenda for the local and regional history of the north-west. We hope that it will encourage others to extend our knowledge and deepen our understanding.

Chapter 1

1542–1660

In the Tudor and early Stuart period the north-west was a relative backwater in the English economy, though attempts by historians to describe it as backward need to be treated with caution. Its population in 1563, when it is possible to make the first cautious estimate, was some 146,000, roughly 4.7 per cent of the 3 million of England (excluding Monmouthshire). In 1664, when a second estimate is possible, it was over 240,000 or 4.6 per cent of England's 5.1 million (E. A. Wrigley and Schofield 1981: 531–3, for national figures). Population density was therefore low, even in 1664 (p. 135). The region was, in many senses, an old-fashioned society. It preserved its ancient gentry with strong local loyalties; it had few powerful incorporated boroughs; it maintained, especially in west Lancashire, a strong and persistent Roman Catholicism and elsewhere a belief in old traditions and superstitions. Behind this conservative screen there were, however, indications of change. Coal, salt and stone were a basis for new economic growth which was also supported by expansion of agriculture into moorland, mossland or woodland previously underused. The early growth of domestic industry was producing groups of small manufacturers and merchants who expanded the number of smallholdings, swelled the populations of upland parishes and unincorporated towns and provided eager listeners for puritan and radical preachers. It was not yet clear, in 1660, where these changes would lead, but there was already apparent a strong divergence between different parts of the region with the stresses and strains that were an inevitable consequence.

Population

There are no precise figures for the numbers of people in Tudor and early-Stuart Lancashire and Cheshire. The two dates of 1563 and 1664 mentioned above are significant because we can, with caution, estimate the region's population in each year (Thirsk 1959: 132, 183, 184). In 1563 families were counted chapelry by chapelry and parish by parish, grouped in rural deaneries. A few communities were returned with suspiciously rounded numbers. The figures for Lymm and Flixton parishes are very high, perhaps head counts rather than households. Similar uncertainties affect records of other areas of England (eg Goose 1985), while the hearth tax returns for 1664, too, have their problems for the user. They list names of heads of households, in townships grouped in hundreds. Many poor households were listed as exempt from the tax, but the very poorest seem to have been excluded from some records, thus in Middlewich 8 per cent were omitted (CRO, Middlewich parish records, P13/22/1, f.253). The 1664 returns can therefore give only a minimum figure for the population. The deaneries and hundreds had different boundaries, but the figures from 1664 can be regrouped to compare with the 1563 parochial returns (cf. Aldridge 1987; Walton 1987: 25).

The raw numerical data are set out in Table 1.1. The number of households rose from about 30,700 in 1563 to about 50,600 in 1664. When we try to convert numbers of households into numbers of people we have a major methodological problem: how many people comprised a household? Modern work confirms contemporary views that household size varied according to, for example, life cycle, wealth or poverty, or occupation. It has been argued that the average size did not change over time so that figures for mid-seventeenth-century size can be used for 1563; alternatively, it has been argued that household size was larger in times of population growth than in times of decline or stagnation. Using Wrigley and Schofield's national figures cited above, we might expect the average size to be smaller in 1664, requiring a lower multiplier, than in 1563, but evidence will be presented in Chapter 2 for continued growth in our region (Laslett and Wall 1972: 139; Arkell 1982, 1991; J. T. Swain 1986: 18). In the end, we have used a constant multiplier of 4.75 in Table 1.1: this gives a rough indication of the population of the region at about 146,000 in the mid-sixteenth century, rising to over 240,000 a hundred years later. On these figures the region's population rose about 64 per cent: Lancashire by 72 per cent, Cheshire by 56 per cent, and the fringes of Derbyshire grew even less. It is not necessarily the case that population change in our region would reflect that in the country as a whole, nor can the conclusions of Wrigley and Schofield's recent national sample study necessarily be applied to one region, but their calculations suggested growth of 68 per cent for the country as a whole between these years (E. A. Wrigley and Schofield 1981: 531–3).

Nationally the population was predominantly a rural one, but there was always an urban element, whose size depends on the definition of urban: if 2,500 people is taken as the lowest number to experience crowded urban living, then 18.7 per cent of the population lived in towns in 1700 (Corfield 1982: 6, 9). Chester was the only major city in the region in Tudor and early Stuart times, but its growth between 1563 and 1664 was a mere 45 per cent,

Table 1.1 Numbers of households, converted to people, in 1563 and 1664, arranged by deaneries

Deanery	No. of households in 1563	× 4.75 = people	No. of households[a] in 1664	× 4.75 = people	% increase 1664 on 1563
CHESHIRE					
Chester					
(exc. the city)	1,024	4,864	1,337	6,351	31
Frodsham	3,408	16,188	4,070	19,333	19
Macclesfield	1,371	6,512	4,409	20,943	222
Malpas					
(corrected for omission)	711	3,377	1,108	5,263	56
Middlewich	2,063	9,799	2,692	12,787	31
Nantwich	1,904	9,044	3,052	14,497	60
Wirral	1,085	5,154	1,509	7,168	39
Chester city	1,137	5,400	1,648	7,828	45
Cheshire total	12,703	60,339	19,825	94,170	56
LANCASHIRE					
Amounderness	2,541	12,070	5,615	26,671	121
Blackburn	2,657	12,621	4,169	19,803	57
Kendal (part)	525	2,494	694	3,297	32
Leyland	2,058	9,904	2,370	11,258	14
Lonsdale (part)	666	3,164	771	3,662	16
Manchester	4,835	22,966	9,147	43,448	89
Warrington	4,032	19,152	7,053[b]	33,502	75
Lancs total	17,314	82,371	29,819	141,641	72
DERBYSHIRE					
High Peak (part)	665	3,158	805[c]	3,823	21

Notes:
[a] All extra parochial areas, the rural portions of Chester city parishes, Rudheath lordship, Wirswall township (both Cheshire), and part of the parish of Mitton in Lancashire, are excluded. In 1664 in Cheshire these totalled at least 332 households, and in Lancashire 143.
[b] Some townships omitted in MS, therefore underestimates total.
[c] For 1670.

Sources: For Chester see Aldridge 1986. For Lancashire and Cheshire in 1563, BL Harleian MS. 594, ff. 97–102, 105, 108. For 1664, PRO, E.179/86/145 (supplemented by E.179/86/155, for 1674 to fill gaps) and G. O. Lawton 1979 for Cheshire; PRO, E.179/250/11 for Lancashire (our figures for Salford hundred differ significantly from those of Blackwood 1978: 7). Hearth tax records were examined on microfilm at the Cheshire and at the Lancashire Record Offices. Deaneries as given in Raines 1845; townships in Dodgson 1970, and *VCH. Lancs.* For Derbyshire in 1563: Riden 1978a; in 1670: Edwards 1982. See Figure 1.1.

contrary to Corfield's conclusion that the urban sector grew as fast as the national trend (1976: 229, 230–1). In 1664 Nantwich and Macclesfield were other Cheshire towns of 2,500-plus people while in Lancashire only Manchester reached this level. They constituted 15 per cent of the population of Cheshire, and 3 per cent of Lancashire; in addition there was an evolving network of some forty-two other towns (see Table 1.5, p. 31). We have no reliable population figures for the towns before then, except for Chester and perhaps Nantwich, which had populations of 5,400 and 2,100 respectively in 1563.

The geography of population growth in the region has some surprises. Figure 1.1 maps percentage changes in the deaneries by 1664, using 1563 as a base. Much of the region did not reach the 68 per cent projected national level of growth, but substantial portions did, and substantial areas had increased by proportions well above the national projection. In Cheshire an area of the Wirral and a belt in the south-east of the county achieved the projected level. Most of Macclesfield deanery outside the ancient parish of Prestbury grew by between 100 and 200 per cent, and Witton chapelry, centred on Northwich in the middle of the county, also exceeded 100 per cent, as did the parishes of Grappenhall and Warburton in the north of the county. (The maps on pp. 126–129 name parishes and chapelries.) The most spectacular growth, at over 200 per cent, took place in the vast parish of Prestbury, including the town of Macclesfield, and in the parishes of Cheadle and Alderley. Goostrey chapelry away to the centre of the county, and Nantwich chapelry and the parish of Baddiley in the south-east of the county also grew likewise.

Lancashire experienced high growth in the south of the county, along the coast, on the Mersey, in the centre around Warrington, in the east around Manchester and in the parishes of Bury and Bolton. Neither Rochdale nor Blackburn parishes reached the projected figure of growth, but Whalley in the east of the county did. The very highest growth occurred in the southern part of Amounderness deanery, to the north of the Ribble, and was especially marked in the western parish of Lytham and in the eastern parish of Chipping. This general picture contrasts with the stagnation north of the Ribble suggested by previous scholars, who laid emphasis on increase in the south of the county; Walton calculated growth in Salford hundred/Manchester deanery at 128 per cent, and thus the areas which stood out were the textile zones. The figures here presented will require some modification of our understanding of the links between population growth and economic development in Lancashire (Walton 1987: 25, following Blackwood's figures).

It is worth pointing out how mechanisms of population growth might account for these regional differences. Two explanations of changes in fertility have recently been advanced. In the first, the basic determinant of fertility was the age at marriage, which fluctuated according to prosperity or otherwise as measured by real wages, with the added constraint in a peasant society that a newly married couple needed land (E. A. Wrigley and Schofield 1981: 467). More recently Levine has offered two models: in his peasant model, which shared the assumptions that Wrigley and Schofield took,

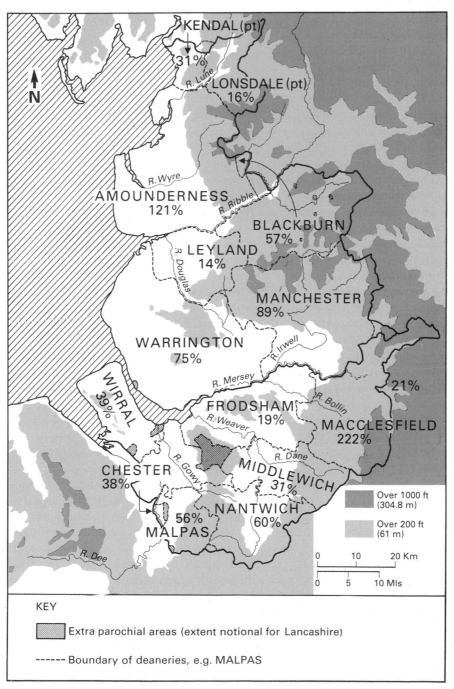

KEY

Extra parochial areas (extent notional for Lancashire)

------ Boundary of deaneries, e.g. MALPAS

Figure 1.1   1563–1664: estimates of population growth. (Sources: Table 1.1 and Figure 1.5.)

women married at twenty-six; in his proletarian model women married at twenty-three. Levine calculated that in the peasant model the population would double in 200 years, but in the proletarian model it would double in fifty-two years (Levine 1987: 78, 90, 91). Another basic mechanism of population change was migration. Recent work has argued that Chester sucked in people from the county, depressing population growth adjacent to the city. At the same time Cheshire people, in unknown numbers, emigrated to Ireland, especially in the mid-seventeenth century (Aldridge 1986: 13–15; Morrill 1974: 17). Population growth was accompanied by out-migration in Colne chapelry in the early seventeenth century (J. T. Swain 1986: 22). It seems likely that the increase in population produced new settlements in this period, as new land was brought into permanent use. Some of this extension can be demonstrated by documents relating to enclosure (see p. 28), but in other instances only topographical evidence of communities called greens and folds exists, whose frequently uncertain and hitherto ignored dating suggests sixteenth- and seventeenth-century origins. What is not clear is how far these new communities were fuelled by migration within the two counties, or by the housing of younger male children of existing local families.

Two of the reasons why growth in parts of the region may not have reached the levels observed nationally may have been the impact of crisis levels of mortality caused by disease and/or of famine (C. D. Rogers 1975a; J. T. Swain 1986: 22–5). We have identified as crisis years those years when burials were markedly in excess of decennial averages, though by using an average including a crisis itself such a method may depress the number of crises (cf. E. A. Wrigley and Schofield 1981: 647). The first widely observed mortality in parish registers came in the late 1580s: Frodsham (W & S), Cheadle, where (harvest year) burials in 1587 and 1589 were one-third and more above the decennial average. (The registers used are transcripts or counts made by the Cheshire Parish Register Project unless otherwise indicated. 'W & S' = E. A. Wrigley and Schofield 1981.) In Lancashire there were equally widespread increases in burials and in some Lancashire registers, for example Great Harwood, high mortality continued into the next decade (France 1938: 35), and the same was true in Great Budworth in Cheshire. In south Cheshire Wrenbury burials reached over half the decennial average in 1596 with peaks in December, and also in the following February (cf. W & S); there were swellings in Great Budworth's figures. In the north and east, whereas Mottram register shows mortality three times the decennial average, that of Cheadle suggests only slightly raised mortality, certainly not as high as that at the turn of the 1580s–1590s. In Lancashire the small parish of Radcliffe (W & S) escaped high mortality at this time, but not so neighbouring Rochdale (W & S), while in Aughton (F. Taylor 1942) burials in 1597 were 75 per cent, and in 1598 50 per cent above the decennial average and in the north of the region Whittington (F. Wrigley and Winder 1899) showed a similarly depressing trend.

The next outbursts of misery came in the years 1603–5. Plague struck severely in Macclesfield. Neston also suffered high mortality, as did Woodchurch and Heswall (Aldridge 1986). In 1605 in Manchester parish 1,053 people died of the plague, including about one-fifth of the population of Manchester township itself (Willan 1983: 30–2). There were other scattered parish-wide crises before the widespread horrors of the early 1620s. Burials, which topped the decennial average by more than 33 per cent in Cheadle, by 80 per cent in Rostherne, and by 300 per cent in Mottram, are examples. There was crisis mortality in one of Chester's parishes. In Nantwich, in the south-east of Cheshire, burials in 1623 and 1624 at 114 and 117 were up 40 per cent and 43 per cent respectively on a decennial average further swollen by the burial of 134 people in 1629. Indeed if the average of the previous decade was used, then the mortality in 1623 and 1624 would be up by 100 per cent. In Lancashire high mortality did not strike in every parish, but few were spared; there were 7,970 recorded burials in 1623 in the county, compared with between 2,000 and 3,000 in most years between 1611 and 1630 (C. D. Rogers 1975a: 11 and appendix).

The next two decades were punctuated by parish-wide crises; plague struck in small outbreaks in south Lancashire (France 1938: 85–6). The township of Barnton in the parish of Great Budworth lost sixteen people from the one village in April and May 1647 to an unknown cause. The last great mortality strike in these years came in 1657–8, a year of national crisis, which Wrigley and Schofield play down for north-west England. But two of their sample Cheshire parishes were affected, as were Cheadle, one-third up on the decennial average, and Great Budworth, where mortality was in a hairsbreadth of twice that average. Radcliffe in Lancashire showed prolonged heavy mortality in the late 1650s and early 1660s, while in Aughton in 1657 burials were two and half times the decennial average.

The widespread mortality peaks in the region might help to explain why its population did not grow even more, but they cannot account for geographical variations in growth. However, they may have had some effect on the timing of that growth. How constant or otherwise was the rate of change between the two dates? The scanty evidence on the timing of growth is contradictory. For early growth there is parish register evidence for Burnley from the 1560s and 1570s, with no growth in the early seventeenth century (J. T. Swain 1986: 22). By 1603 the population of the diocese of Chester had increased by about two-thirds of its 1563 level, according to a crude calculation based on the number of communicants in that year (Hollingsworth 1969: 83). For late growth there is the evidence of Bunbury's 1590 easter book, which contained 291 households liable to tithe, an increase of only 40 per cent on the 208 households in the 1563 list and well short of the 385 in the hearth tax returns (CRO, Crewe of Crewe MSS, DCR/27/3). The possibility of population growth later in the period is indicated for Lancashire in the years from 1611 to 1630, where despite the high mortality of the early

1620s, Rogers observed a county-wide surplus of baptisms (C. D. Rogers 1975a: 10, 17). Growth was neither late nor early in some parishes, just irregular; for example at Mottram in the hilly far north-east of Cheshire there was an early seventeenth-century surplus of baptisms, but overall they just exceeded deaths between 1580 and 1640 (Powell 1976); in the centre of the county Great Budworth, qualified by gaps in the register, saw a small surplus of baptisms, especially in the 1560s and 1570s, and from the mid-1620s to the mid-1640s.

This very small sample of aggregative studies supports the conclusion that growth occurred between the household counts of 1563 and 1664. The chronology and rates of change may have varied in different parts of our region, but there appears to have been growth to the late 1580s, when there were losses, followed by ups and downs until the mid-1620s when growth resumed only to be checked again in the 1650s. There is evidence, discussed in Chapter 2, that growth may have resumed or continued after 1660.

Landowning Society

The monarch was the head of the social order in Tudor and early Stuart England. Society was a hierarchy, firmly based on the wealth represented by the ownership of land. Though it was acceptable for landowners to have sources of income besides land, society was grudging in its recognition of urban status and wealth. The basic structure of landowning society remained constant into the nineteenth century and beyond. What had changed by at least the mid-nineteenth century, if not before, was the proportion of the country's wealth derived from land. In the seventeenth and eighteenth centuries trade became a serious rival to the landed interest, and, especially in our region, in the late eighteenth century the rise of the new manufacturing industries heralded the relative supremacy of other forms of wealth over landownership which was apparent after the mid-nineteenth century.

In Lancashire and Cheshire between 1542 and 1660 some of the extensive crown estates belonged to the Duchy of Lancaster, but when James I hunted in his royal forest of Delamere in 1617 he chased over land held directly by the crown. Crown estates were often let to and administered by local landowners on easy terms, useful patronage for the monarch. Below the crown the top strata of England's hierarchical social order were the peers, who numbered only 120 in 1641; in addition some 80 English men were ennobled in the peerage of Ireland, which contemporaries ranked inferior to the English peerage (Stone 1965: 99). Only eight lords were personally resident or influential in our region. The Stanley earls of Derby were pre-eminent in Lancashire, but they held large estates and major office in Cheshire too, though by the civil war their political influence in Cheshire had declined. Until the 1620s the region's only other resident peer, Lord Monteagle, descended from a younger son of the Derbys, lived in north Lancashire at Hornby castle. The Monteagle heiress married Lord Morley in 1581, and later the peerage was called Morley and Monteagle. The Talbot earls of Shrewsbury (later the Howards) dominated in the north-west of Derbyshire (GEC, *Complete Peerage*). The crown was an absentee landlord; similarly other peers such as Oxford and later Bridgewater (Wanklyn 1976: 14; Morrill 1974: 17) held large estates in the region, but did not live there. Derby and Monteagle also held land outside the region.

Stone (1965: 104–5) has argued that the creations of peers under the Stuart kings contributed to a decline in respect for the peerage because titles were sold, and because the new lords were indistinguishable from, or were the social inferiors of, families not ennobled, over whom they now took precedence as peers. The social order changed suddenly but respectably in our counties between 1624 and 1628, when in Lancashire one and in Cheshire three new Irish peerages were created for four families long seated in the region and among the most wealthy in the counties. Furthermore, Sir Thomas Savage of Rock Savage, Cheshire, was made a viscount, and in 1640 his son inherited the title of Earl Rivers. In Cheshire some families of equal wealth were not elevated, but no new lord rivalled the Stanley fortune, while Lancashire's new Viscount Molyneux could hardly have challenged the political power of the Earl of Derby in the county (GEC, *Complete Peerage*, *sub* Molyneux, Savage; Morrill 1974: 17; the eighth peerage, Gerrard, was created in wartime in 1645).

The group below the peers in the hierarchy were the gentry, and their top two ranks held the precisely defined titles of baronet and knight. There were few families headed by such men in the two counties at the start of the civil war: nine baronets in Cheshire and seven in Lancashire; six knights in Lancashire and five in Cheshire (Blackwood 1978: 10; GEC, *Complete Baronetage*; W. Shaw 1906; Wanklyn 1976: 157–9). As with the peers, so with these groups: were the new creations by James I and Charles I upstarts, or were they from families who would have been recognized as among the chief families of the counties? At least in Cheshire the titles seem to have been given to the latter group, and, indeed, it is argued that Charles I was so mean with honours in the 1630s as to have lost support in the civil war (Wanklyn 1976: 113). The status of esquire and gentleman, the two lower divisions of the gentry, was much less clear to contemporaries, merging with each other, and in the case of the gentleman with the wealthy members of the yeomanry in the status group below. This makes the definition of, and therefore the enumeration of, esquires and gentlemen difficult for historians. For us the difficulty is compounded because Blackwood (for Lancashire) and Wanklyn (for Cheshire) have used different definitions (Morrill 1974: 14; 1976: 18;

Wanklyn 1976: 136; Morrill 1979: 72). No enumeration of these groups is therefore offered here.

Another way of stratifying the gentry, which reflects landed wealth, is to distinguish between the county gentry and the rest, the parish gentry (Aylmer 1973: 179). The county gentry were the baronets and knights, and those esquires who were prominent office-holders in county government, though there were those who could not hold office for religious reasons. Historians recognize those families who provided justices as the county elite. At the start of our period, there were nineteen serving as Justices of the Peace (the most important office in local government) in Cheshire and, between 1529 and 1558, at least fifty in Lancashire (P. J. Turner 1974: 41; J. B. Watson 1963–4: 56–7). The Stuarts governed through ninety-three magisterial families in Lancashire, and eighty-one in Cheshire between 1590 and 1640 (Wilkinson 1983: 63–6; Higgins 1976: 34), not all of whom were on the Bench at any one time.

Of the Lancashire peers in 1642 the Earl of Derby had a landed income per year of over £6,000; of the Cheshire peers Viscount Cholmondeley's income totalled about £3,400. The richest of the Lancashire gentry, a baronet, received £3,240 a year, more than the lowest estimate of Lord Morley's income, while the humblest gentleman received only £8. Cheshire too had gentry with higher incomes from land than one member of the peerage; among baronets, incomes ranged from about £400 to over £2,000. Among thirty-three of the Lancashire Justices of the Peace in 1640 landed incomes ranged from £100 to over £2,000 (Blackwood* 1978: 13, 58, 69; Wanklyn 1976: 24, 390; Long* 1968: 31). Table 1.2 gives some examples of gross receipts of three landowners from all sources, and of the values of personal estates at death. Thus the equation between wealth and status was by no means rigid; there was a wide variation of wealth within any one status group. But status was not solely a function of wealth.

Table 1.2 Examples of gross annual receipts and personal estates of Lancashire gentry families

	Annual receipts (averaged over period) from land		Personal estate	
		£[a]		£[a]
Richard Shireburn, kt	1567–71	1,129	1594	4,240
John Cuerden, esq	—		1601	1,025
Richard Molyneux, bt	1605–13	1,825	1623	3,800
Thomas Southworth, esq	—		1623	259
Edward Moore, esq	—		1632	1,036
Thomas Walmesley, esq	1613–22	633		—

Note: [a] Figures rounded to nearest £.

Source: Long 1968: 32–8, 246–9.

Plate 1.1 Traditional style gentry building: Hall i' th' Wood, near Bolton. The date of the timber-framed part of the Hall is sixteenth century, Elizabethan or even later. The stone-built part is variously dated 1591 and 1648. This view predates the post-1899 restoration (Pevsner 1969, repr. 1979a: 91–2).

The gentry were recognized as such by their behaviour, the pattern of their spending on housing, dress and finery, and education, what the sixteenth-century commentator Sir Thomas Smith called 'the port, charge and countenance of a gentleman' (T. Smith 1583: 27). Social recognition came also with pedigree – a measure of how long a family had held land. The living style of the greater gentry stood out from their inferiors most obviously by their houses and their clothes. In Blackburn hundred even minor gentry houses became more obviously distinct from those of the yeomanry by the mid-seventeenth century (Pearson 1985: 6, 56). Modest manor houses built by the traditional timber-framed method were in scale far larger than anything the yeomanry could build (eg Plate 1.1). There is evidence of new traditions merged with the old, however, as early as 1545 when brick was used to make alterations by the knightly family of Southworth at Samlesbury Hall, and Renaissance patterns were early used on the woodwork at Smithhills Hall, Bolton, the house of a mere squire's family. The Davenports at Bramhall in Cheshire altered their late-medieval timber-framed house probably in the 1590s, flooring in the high roof space of some of the great rooms to make extra rooms, providing more chimneys for heat, and constructing an elaborately glazed long gallery. Pevsner and Hubbard are critical of the timber-framed buildings as conservative and naive in decoration, but J. T. Smith points to a socially convenient style of construction, with distinctive developments, such as in jettying, compared with timber-frames elsewhere (Pevsner and Hubbard 1971: 21–2, 257; Pevsner 1979a: 16, 385; J. T. Smith 1970a: 177).

Perhaps more ostentatious was the idiosyncratic style of Sir Peter Legh's new house of *c.* 1590 at Lyme Park in Cheshire embodying architectural styles which had emerged as recently as 1550. The more conventional house of the Hoghtons of Hoghton Tower in Lancashire was another in which old money plainly declared its position to all in the county. The Elizabethan mansion of Stonyhurst was built, in contrast, by the rising family of Shireburn, flush with the profits of high office under the earls of Derby, and the profits of Sir Richard Shuttleworth's office as a palatine judge in Cheshire helped to build Gawthorpe Hall in the Ribble valley. In Cheshire new ideas came back from London with successful gentleman lawyers in the medium of brick in 1615 at Crewe Hall (Plate 1.2) and Dorfold Hall (1616). Peel Hall near Runcorn demonstrated another route for innovation through the pocket of a successful Chester merchant-gentry family, the Hardwares (R. C. Turner 1987). If, as Pevsner observed, northern architecture 'was indeed exceedingly conservative in the seventeenth century', there were new ideas in circulation, and there was plenty of conspicuous consumption by landowners who altered or rebuilt their houses in our region, though few of these houses were notable for their style or building materials as, compared for example, with nearby Derbyshire (Pevsner 1979b: 21).

Inside the house, furnishings too were an expression of wealth. Sixteen 'chandeliers' gave plenty of candlelight in Nicholas Butler's house at Rawcliffe in 1577, where there were twenty feather beds and thirty cushions – enough for an esquire's family (Fishwick 1891: 148). The massive Jacobean four-poster bed at Gawthorpe Hall is as ostentatious as the hall itself. It is not only the number of items or their luxurious character that stand out in inventories of gentry furnishings, but also the range: at Bank Hall in 1632 ten of the rooms had a close stool or chamber pot; a few houses had musical instruments beyond a chapel organ, notably Rufford in 1620 and Lytham in 1634, and pictures and clocks were common (Ashmore 1958: 64–5, 82–3). Such items are very unusual in the inventories of yeomen.

There was an appreciation of how a gentleman or a husbandman should dress, though legislative attempts to specify the sorts of clothing each status group could wear failed. Clothing and jewellery displayed wealth and standing not only to one's inferiors, but to one's equals as well. Both men and women wore fine lace, precious metals and jewels, and on the whole such materials could be adapted as fashions changed. When Dame Anne Ratcliffe died in 1551 her gold filament for wearing with clothes was worth £50, and her gold chains £40, while eight rings and five other pieces together totalled

Plate 1.2 Innovative gentry building, in brick: Crewe Hall. Begun in 1615, completed 1636. The central bow is in the north side of the Jacobean house. A west wing was added around 1800, but this view of 1818 (from Ormerod 1882, III, facing p. 312) predates the nineteenth-century restorations (Pevsner and Hubbard 1971: 190–1).

only £7 10s. 0d. She had ten fine gowns to adorn herself, worth together £36, and she must have seen her reflection in some of the £45 worth of plate that she owned. At the same time, in 1556, a mere esquire, Thomas Tyldesley of Wardley had no jewels, his plate was worth but £9 16s. 8d., his wife's clothing £5 10s. 0d., and his own £5 3s. 0d. Sir Edmund Trafford and his wife had clothes valued at £400 in 1620, whereas the minor gentleman Edmund Jodrell left purse and apparel worth only £20 in 1630, and the widow of squire Ardern was clothed for only £26 13s. 4d. in 1619. Only a very few could cap displays of finery by alighting from a coach when they arrived at church or at the quarter sessions, but saddlery and horses, often worth more than the farm stock of a yeoman, figured in many gentry inventories (Piccope 1860, 1861; Ashmore 1958: 87, 89; C. B. Phillips and Smith 1985: 129; JRUL, Jodrell MS. 55).

Conspicuous consumption in clothing and building were neatly combined before the eyes of a gentry family's tenants every Sunday in church.

There too the form of the family's funerary monuments might display the wealth and finery of the family's past. The monuments to the Fittons at Gawsworth in Cheshire are justly famous, and most work of this nature was designed to reflect status: in 1579 William Massey of Burton wanted his executors to

> cause one conveniente tombe or monument of alabaster for my degree or vocation. . . . For the making thereof I give . . . xiii – vi – viii.
>
> (Crossley 1940: 102)

Again, Cheshire has been regarded as conservative in these matters, but it is interesting that the man who was paid £500 to make Queen Elizabeth's tomb in 1604 was making tombs in Chester later in the century, with the knowledge of London fashion in mind no doubt (Crossley 1940: 104–5). A major piece of ostentation, therefore, was the £662 14s. 6d. spent on his funeral and monument (£170) by Sir Thomas Walmesley of Dunkenhalgh in 1613 (Long 1968: 142–3).

If funeral monuments brought home to the tenantry the pedigree of their lord's family, the gentry themselves appreciated the long-established families of the two counties. In Cheshire perhaps more than in Lancashire there were small groups of families sharing the same surname who could trace descent from a common stock; at the 1580 herald's visitation there were nine Legh families, nine of the Masseys, seven Egertons, six Davenports and six Breretons (Higgins 1976: 33). Four-fifths of the greater gentry families of both counties had lived there as gentry before the Reformation. For those who did not rely on the unscholarly heralds for their pedigree, beyond mere genealogy, wealth provided the formal education and leisure time which allowed them to pursue the history of their family and county and its families. In Cheshire such practical involvement seems to have been confined to minor gentlemen, like Laurence Bostock, Sampson Erdeswicke (who also had major interests outside Cheshire), and William Vernon, and in Chester the urban gentry family of Holme had extensive knowledge of things Roman. It was to Sir William Dugdale of Warwickshire that Sir Philip Mainwaring unsuccessfully turned to commission a county history (Ormerod 1882: I, xxxix–xl; British Library 1808–12: 139, 338, 506, 2,014; *DNB sub* Erdeswicke; McKisack 1971: 179; W. T. Watkin 1886: 117, 165; J. Varley 1941; Fox 1956: 124–7). Henry Peacham's well-known conduct book besides proclaiming the need for an educated nobility and gentry, and advising on commonplaces such as heraldry, advocated the study of 'cosmography' and geometry (Heltzel 1962). Christopher Towneley, although a younger son and an attorney, with antiquarian interests in Lancashire, also assisted the researches of as many as five young astronomers and mathematicians, including the first observations of the transit of the planet Venus across the sun's disc by Jeremiah Horrocks in 1639 (Webster 1967; A. Chapman 1986).

18

Higher education for an eldest son did not need to culminate in any qualification; that was more necessary for younger sons, who would have to make a career independent of their family's land, or for the sons of the yeomanry. Nevertheless, perhaps two-thirds of the more wealthy Lancashire heads of gentry families in 1642 had received higher education (Blackwood* 1978: 17, 25).

The essential privilege of those of gentle status was that they did not labour with their hands, whereas their social inferiors did (T. Smith 1583: 27). The yeomen, husbandmen, rural artisans and labourers comprised the great bulk of the population, though it is impossible to enumerate each status group. The seating plan adopted at Acton church in 1635 is a good microcosm of the social order: the chief landowners, peers and gentlemen had the best seats at the chancel end of the south side, with the yeomanry and husbandmen occupying the rest (Livesey 1912). Scattered among them were some minor gentry, overlapping in status with the yeomanry, just as the yeomanry and husbandmen overlapped in terms of wealth (such overlap is not represented in Tables 1.2 and 1.3). At the back of the church was space for others to stand. A yeoman probably held some freehold land, whereas a husbandman was merely a manorial tenant. Our expectation would be that a yeoman was usually more wealthy than a husbandman. At the end of our period in Northwich hundred in Cheshire 38 per cent of husbandmen in the 1660 poll tax paid on landed estates valued at less than £5 a year, compared with only 2 per cent of yeomen, while 33 per cent of yeomen paid at values of £30-plus compared with only 6 per cent of husbandmen. All the labourers who paid the tax did so at the lowest rate (G. O. Lawton 1979: 13).

Schooling was available to the lower orders of society, though we have no details of the extent to which it was taken up. Rogers estimates that in the 1620s perhaps 90 per cent of children were not attending school at any one time. This was in spite of a rise in the number of teachers and schools in the two counties after the reformation (C. D. Rogers 1975b; Wallis 1969). Many children from the lower levels of society left home at an early age to take apprenticeship, or to be a servant in someone else's household. The yeoman who spent money to send his son to university made him upwardly mobile. Clearly, some yeomen had a knowledge of their pedigree for they tried, unsuccessfully, to register them with the heralds at their visitations, only for them to be rejected and disclaimed (Armytage and Rylands 1909: 1–4). Their consciousness of the family past was indicated by the wish to be buried with relatives, or under the family pew in church; bequests of heirlooms to descend with the family house demonstrated faith in the future of it too (Piccope 1860: 205; C. B. Phillips and Smith 1985: 1). The yeomen also spent considerable sums of money on new houses and alterations in this period. After 1600 those in the east of Blackburn hundred were building many new houses in which a medieval layout was adapted to give greater privacy. Apart from size, two facets of their houses contrast with those of the gentry: yeomen houses never became pure residences, for they usually retained industrial workshops in the building and they lacked external decoration (Pearson 1985). William Webb commented in 1621 that the yeomen of Cheshire were better housed than before, which may indicate the same process of expensive consumption in the south of the region (quoted in M. Campbell 1942: 63). Meanwhile on the Lancashire plain, cruck houses with clay walls were still being built in the later seventeenth century to produce houses of a very poor quality – perhaps because of a lack of materials (though there are some fine timber frames in the region) but more likely because of lack of surplus wealth to spend on conspicuous consumption (R. C. Watson 1957; R. F. Taylor 1966; J. T. Smith 1970b).

Table 1.3   Examples of the value of clothing in inventories of yeomen, husbandmen and artisans to 1650

					Clothing	Total of inventory
Christopher Bateson	Y	Caton	1588	E	—	£26 17s. 4d.
John Hall[a]	Y	Bramhall	1603	C	£1 0s. 0d.	£6 14s. 10d.
Hugh Hall[a]	Y	Bramhall	1603	C	10s. 0d.	£4 3s. 4d.
William Bentley	Y	Norbury	1612	C	13s. 4d.	£65 15s. 4d.
Raphe Rylands	Y	Culcheth	1633	E	£2 0s. 0d.	£208 8s. 10d.
John Cowper	H	Bramhall	1602	C	£2 0s. 0d.	£40 10s. 4d.
Thomas Cheetham	H	Bredbury	1605	C	£1 0s. 0d.	£125 18s. 9d.
Robert Cheetham	H	Bredbury	1613	C	£3 0s. 0d.	£92 0s. 0d.
Geo. Heyginbotham	H	Marple	1616	C	£1 10s. 0d.	£103 6s. 6d.
Thomas Beneson	H	Offerton	1617	C	£1 18s. 0d.	£61 9s. 4d.
James Downes	H	Outwood	1624	C	£1 6s. 8d.	£52 0s. 0d.
Ottiwell Heginbotham, tanner		Marple	1616	C	£2 10s. 0d.	£105 5s. 5d.

Notes: [a] These inventories suggest elderly deceased people.
　　　　 Y = yeomen.
　　　　 H = husbandmen.
Sources: C = Probate record in Cheshire Record Office.
　　　　 E = Earwaker 1893.

The value of clothing in the inventories of these people (and the surviving inventories are biased towards the more wealthy yeomen, husbandmen and craftsmen) was small, as the selections in Table 1.3 show. The yeoman Christopher Bateson did have two rings and a gold heart, but valued at nine shillings they were worth less than his dunghill, and the husbandman Thomas Beneson had a silver spoon valued at seven shillings. Most of the lower levels of society did not possess such luxuries.

Even these relatively humble people were adopting new fashions. In Lancashire, looking back to James I's reign, Adam Martindale remembered in his autobiography those yeomen's daughters who began to use 'gold and silver laces . . . about their petticoates . . . though the proudest of them below the gentry durst not have offered to weare a hood [and be] accounted an ambitious foole' (R. Parkinson 1845: 6). Over half a century before, Dame Anne Ratcliffe (see p. 16) had gold work to wear on her french hoods, a comparison which makes nicely the difficulty of reserving standards of dress for a particular status group.

The social order we have just been describing was not an unchanging one, though the major landowning families were regarded by contemporaries as remarkably stable because so many of them had long pedigrees; recent work has confirmed this view, especially in Cheshire where only 20 per cent of family pedigrees could not be traced back beyond the Tudors (Blackwood* 1978: 22–3; Morrill 1974: 3). By contrast, in counties such as Leicestershire, Norfolk or Hertfordshire from 60 to 85 per cent of gentry families cannot be traced back beyond 1500. However, the make-up of landowning society did change in our period: at the lower levels the number of copyholders in Barrowford and Roughlee in Pendle forest increased from thirty-four in 1539 to forty-seven in 1608 (J. T. Swain 1986: 71). In general, the yeomanry held a greater proportion of land in England than they had done in the late-medieval period. In part this may have been because the rising prices of produce meant greater profits for yeomen, though in our largely pastoral region the increase in prices and therefore profits was limited, and instead the profits of industry may have played a part. In the 1640s and 1650s yeomen may have been among those who made permanent purchases of land (Blackwood* 1978: 90, 118, 134).

For the gentry the dissolution of the monasteries and the civil war, which might have changed the make-up of landowning society, seem to have had only a limited effect. Historians are by and large persuaded that the English gentry as a group became more numerous, and owned perhaps twice as much land, by the start of the civil war than was the case a century earlier; and that much of their new land came from the church at the dissolution (Clay 1984: 143). But in Lancashire and Cheshire substantial amounts of monastic land remained in the hands of the crown, the new diocese of Chester and the ancient hospitals (Haigh 1969: 126; *VCH. Cheshire*, III). In Cheshire the Cottons of Combermere, the Brookes of Norton, and the Holcrofts of Vale Royal stand out as new owners of monastic property. Haigh argued that many of the established Lancashire families, including the Earl of Derby, who might have been expected to buy could not raise liquid capital. Nevertheless five existing major families, including the Holcrofts and Lord Monteagle, made substantial gains; two younger brothers, the London lawyer John Flete-wood, and Thomas Holcroft, who also acquired Vale Royal in Cheshire and whose elder brother was another beneficiary, founded their own line; and two obscure gentlemen became men of substance. A century after the dissolution the defeated royalists in Cheshire, with the exception of the Earl of Derby, suffered no major loss of lands. Derby suffered heavily in Lancashire too, but losses to the Derbys were not too damaging; in 1677 their rental income still exceeded £5,000. Among the Lancashire gentry between 1646 and 1659 more land was sold by non-royalists than by royalists, and most royalists quickly recovered land confiscated by the state. Nor is there evidence that the Lancashire parliamentarians benefited greatly from the upheavals (Blackwood 1978: 101, 147; Morrill 1974: 328–9; Coward 1983: 79).

The more usual changes in landowning society stemmed from marriage alliances, the failure of the male line of families, and voluntary sales, sometimes the consequence of an extravagant life-style. In Lancashire between 1600 and the civil war, at a conservative estimate twenty gentry families failed in the male line, thirty-five sold up due to economic pressures, and twelve moved out of the county (Blackwood* 1978: 21). The detailed work to detect and evaluate such changes over the whole period of this book has not been done, and is beyond the scope of this series, but two approaches are offered now, and in subsequent chapters. The first approach to changes in landownership is a sample study of the manorial and family descents given in the *VCH. Lancs.* (III; IV: 51–170), and in Ormerod (1882: III: 1–284). The samples used are the hundreds of West Derby (open to economic change emanating from the mining and industrial developments on the Lancashire coalfield and, in later chapters, from the port of Liverpool), and of Northwich (open to the influence of salt in the west and, later on, of silk mills in the east).

The *VCH. Lancs.* was completed before the First World War, since when much new material has come to light, and the genealogies for the sixteenth and seventeenth centuries in Ormerod (1882), though careful, need to be used with more caution than the later material, so that we should not make too much of these figures (Dore and Morrill 1967: 65). Continuity of ownership predominated, though less so in West Derby hundred, but the pattern of change indicated, which had not, of course, suddenly begun in 1540, represents the disappearance of families from the ranks of the gentry when the male line failed, or when debt forced them down the social scale (see Table 1.4). Thus in 1597 William Bradshaw of London tried in law to recover the estates which his ancestor had 'dissipated' some fifty years before (*VCH. Lancs.*, III: 295). While the new owners of properties in the sample included successful lawyers and a cleric, the overwhelming impression is the consolidation of these properties among existing landowning families, notably the Molyneux family of Sefton over the decades up to 1640, and the earls of Derby in the second quarter of the seventeenth century.

The second approach to landownership is to study individual families. Here, the Cholmondeley family of Cheshire provide an illustrative example. Sir Hugh, who died in 1597, had married Mary, daughter and heiress of Christopher Holford of Holford Hall. When Christopher died, Holford Hall passed to Lady Mary, after a long legal struggle with Christopher's brother, who kept other family estates. Lady Mary later bought Vale Royal abbey (from Thomas Holcroft, who died without a male heir), an old Grange of the abbey, and land at Leighton. Holford passed to the heir of the Cholmonde-

Table 1.4   Changing landownership in two sample hundreds 1540–1660

	Northwich		West Derby	
No. of properties in sample	68		111	
of which properties:				
1 poor data	−13		−6	
useable data	55		105	
of useable data:		(%)		(%)
2 owner family constant 1540–1660	39	71	57	54
3 owner family changed	16	29	48	46
properties in category 3				
3a owner's male line out	8	14.5	9	8.6
3b passed in marriage	1	1.8	3	2.9
3c sold	5	9	25	23.8
3d exchanged	—	—	1	1.8
3e don't know	2	3.6	10	9.5
	16		48	
3f changed hands more than once 1540–1660	3		8	

leys, who died without a legitimate male child, and settled it on his illegitimate son, creating the Cholmondeley of Holford branch. Lady Mary settled her purchased property on her fourth son, while the bulk of the Cholmondeley estates passed to her grandson by her third son. Lady Mary's marriage thus halved the property of the Holford family, and added to that of the Cholmondeleys, while her purchases created a new and substantial branch of the family at Vale Royal (GEC, *Complete Peerage*, *sub* Cholmondeley, and Delamere; Ormerod 1882, I: 672; and II: 638; Armytage and Rylands 1909: 128; Stewart-Brown 1934: 126–9).

The bonds which held men in place in society, and governed relationships between neighbours of differing status were not only rationalizations of wealth. There were also contracts between individual men which placed one in an inferior status to the other: the lord to protect and to promote his man's career, the inferior man to serve his lord as and when required. At the most straightforward, these ties were derived from the old feudal methods of parcelling out land, so that tenants-in-chief created subordinate tenants who owed them military service; it was the manorial tenants of these men who made up an army. Thus the Earl of Derby raised an army of some 2,000 men in 1557, of whom 700 were his own, and 1,300 were raised by the gentry, who were his feudal tenants. When the earl went to France as a royal ambassador in 1585 the whole retinue comprised 220 men, of whom about 38 were gentlemen from Cheshire and Lancashire, and 41 their servants (Coward 1983: 98, 150). For the bulk of the rural population obligations of this nature were reinforced twice a year when all tenants were supposed to attend the manorial court. At the beginning of the civil war in Lancashire and Cheshire men like Sir George Middleton or Sir Thomas Aston were still able to raise tenant armies for the king, though not all Stanley tenants were willing to serve (Blackwood 1978: 68; Morrill 1974: 64). A more distinct obligation was created by giving men a fee or annuity to serve, according to the terms of a written contract. This was called retaining, and some of the Lancashire gentry still practised it in the 1540s and 1550s, to the consternation of the crown, whose tenants were already retained when the stewards of crown manors tried to enrol them for military service (P. Williams 1979: 121, 238; Haigh 1975: 95–6). An especial loyalty to the head of the family was owed by the household, over and above their routine duty as financial or domestic officers. The Stanley household numbered 145 *c.* 1590; those of the gentry were of a much more modest size. In the early seventeenth century Sir Richard Molyneux kept a note of persons in livery which included members of six neighbouring gentry families (Blackwood 1978: 48).

One of the reasons why the earls of Derby were so powerful in the two counties was that they spent much of their time resident in them. So too did many of the major gentry families, though there were absentee landowners (e.g. below). Even so, the gentry were numerically thin on the ground and on as wide a definition as that adopted by Blackwood for Lancashire in 1642 they comprised only between 2 and 3 per cent of the population. Blackwood thought that the gentry were more densely distributed in the arable than the pastoral regions of Lancashire. Thus the township of Weeton-with-Preese had one esquire and two gentlemen resident, whereas the mossland districts of Bispham, Carleton, Marton, and Stalmine housed no gentry (Blackwood 1978: 6). In the large Cheshire parish of Bunbury in 1590 14 families out of 291 were of gentle status according to the easter book but two townships contained no gentry at all (CRO, DCR 27/3). The 1660 poll tax return for Northwich hundred of Cheshire, which probably also used a very broad definition of gentility, shows eleven townships without man or woman of gentle status. In one of them, Wymboldesley, an absentee Yorkshire gentleman was taxed. In four of these townships some authority may have resided in the resident clergyman, though only one of them, the Revd Henry Wigley, rector of Warmingham, was taxed as a wealthy man (G. O. Lawton 1979).

Men and women servants existed at all levels of society down even to the husbandmen. In 1634 Sir Cuthbert Clifton, in addition to servants in his own bedchamber, expected there to be four major officers in his service. The presence of a 'yeoman's chamber' in the inventory of Sir Edmund Trafford in 1620 suggests that at least some of his servants were regarded as the ancient companions of the knight, his yeomen. There were probably twenty resident servants at Rufford Hall in 1620; the Walmesleys of Dunkenhalgh paid wages for five women and nineteen men in 1617 (Ashmore 1958: 61–2). In 1584 the yeoman John Anyon of Bispham left two shillings to each servant in service when he died (Fishwick 1887: 121). In Bunbury in 1590 28 of the 291 households had servants, but there were only fourteen families of gentry status, not all of whom had servants, so that a number of the yeomen or husbandmen had a servant; the highest number in a household was six, but twenty households had only one servant (CRO, DCR 27/3). At the end of our period, in the middle of Cheshire, the wealthy husbandman Raph Holland, who lived with his widowed mother and brother, had five servants in his household in 1660 (G. O. Lawton 1979: 130). Thus at all levels of society there were those who lived in households because of a contractual relationship between servant and master. Though in some of the yeoman houses of the Blackburn district segregated accommodation was provided for servants which could be reached only by going outside the house, they were regarded as members of the family (Pearson 1985).

We should be wary of assigning too much power to the family as a social institution. Marriage need not indicate an intimate or friendly relationship between families, even in Lancashire and Cheshire where about two in every three gentry marriages were made within the two counties (Higgins 1976: 31; Blackwood 1978: 26). Disputes over wills and land between family members could consume wealth, as happened to the family of James Taylor of Stockport, whose relatives exhausted his personal estate in litigation in about ten years (C. B. Phillips and Smith 1985: 47, 77–9, 103). In the civil war four members of the Hoghton family of Hoghton fought for the king and one opposed him. Marriage alliances failed to deter men from taking the opposite side to their relatives (Blackwood 1978: 46). Neighbours and friends were other powerful influences on the individual and the family, and could be called upon to perform a variety of tasks. Thus the husbandman John Hamer of Shore Lanes appointed his 'trusty neyghbours and friends' as supervisors of his will (Earwaker 1893: 4); Robert Riddings, a minor Cheshire gentleman, gave all his goods to friends to avoid the consequences of an outlawry by a vexatious relative; the lawyer Richard Bradshaw, who died in London, arranged to be buried at the discretion of his friends (Piccope 1860: 126–7).

Agriculture

The great bulk of the population drew at least part of their income from the land, either directly husbanding the soil to produce crops or animals, or receiving rent from those who did farm. Peer and husbandman alike might enjoy some combination of farm income and rent; just as gentry produced foodstuffs for their own consumption and/or for market, so too the yeomen and husbandmen might work to subsist and/or to sell. Although there was a

25

national market for the farm produce of our region, and there was national legislation on such matters as the enclosure of fields or the wages of agricultural labourers, agriculture was organized within that localized legal entity called the manor. There it was subject to three influences: the relationship between manorial lords and their tenants; the organization of fields and farming routine by the manorial community; and the quality of the lands and the skills of the individual farmers, and we can look at each of these in turn.

Customary tenure regulated the rights and obligations of both manorial lord and tenant; we have already seen this relationship as one strand in the ordering of society. At least three major variants of customary tenure existed within our region: what was loosely called tenant-right in north Lancashire; customary leases in south Lancashire and parts of Cheshire; copyhold in east Lancashire and much of Cheshire (Blackwood 1966; Kerridge 1969; JRUL, Tabley estate court rolls, 1650s, and rentals 1583–1611, 1647–97). Although these forms of tenure were all distinctive there were common characteristics. The tenants paid an annual rent which was fixed, and therefore out of touch with prices and the value of the land. Under most forms of customary tenure a tenant's heirs had rights of inheritance. A new tenant paid a lump sum (a fine) to take his estate, and the amount of this fine might be negotiable; here was scope for a lord to increase his income, especially if all tenants also had to pay a fine when a new lord inherited.

Such fines had to be reasonable or the tenants could sue in the royal courts where equity held that one or two years profit of the land was a reasonable fine. Tenant-right in particular was plagued with disputes over fines; it is argued that such disputes turned tenants away from their royalist landlords to the armies of the parliament at the start of the civil war (Blackwood 1966: 31). The best solution was to make fines certain; indeed, the very uncertainty of customary tenures prompted some lords to challenge custom – tenants of the duchy in Pendle and in Trawden paid £1,796 in 1609, and the tenants of Colne over £525 in 1618 to confirm their customs under James I (J. T. Swain 1986: 64). At Glossop the Talbot tenants struggled for over twenty-five years against higher entry fines and twenty-one-year leases, even travelling in a body to London three or four times to present their case to the Queen and Privy Council. They held up change from 1580 to 1608 but finally they were forced to give way (Scott et al. 1973: 23–6). Other landlords however put no undue pressure on their tenants, believing that their role as lord should be a benevolent one; William Blundell of Crosby even gave established tenant families better terms than newcomers (Blackwood 1966: 20–1). Customary tenants also had to attend the lord's manorial court to which they were subject, and might pay further sums, for instance for commuted labour services (though so many days' work, for example carting, ploughing or weeding, was still demanded on some manors), or for a heriot when a tenant died (JRUL, Tabley rentals). In general, the advantage of such tenurial arrangements seems to have lain with the tenants as prices rose after

1540. In the early seventeenth century aggressive attempts by some landlords to replace customary tenure with leases, in order to give them greater control and flexibility in estate management, cost a substantial proportion of tenants large cash sums at a time when their income was adversely affected by bad harvests (Manning 1975: 135–9).

The acreage of customary land held by individuals was small; in central Lancashire many tenants held less than fifteen acres, though there was a group of more substantial farmers who held about sixty acres (Thirsk 1967: 87–9). However, those who owned small acreages could lease additional land from other tenants who did not choose to farm; the demesne land of a manor, for the exclusive use of the lord, was frequently let to men who were also customary tenants. Furthermore, all customary tenants, and the lord, had rights on the waste land of the manor, usually including grazing. While the quality of the waste was usually inferior to the cultivated lands of the manor, the demesne and customary lands could be intermingled and of the same worth.

It is clear that in the medieval period common field farming was widespread in both counties. The manorial court determined how the fields of these manors were used, and each tenant who held strips of land scattered through these fields had to grow the same crops as his neighbour; ploughing, harvesting and grazing were communal activities. The evidence as to which crops were grown, how often fields were fallow, and how the crops were rotated is very scarce, and open to contrasting interpretations. Some scholars have argued that some Lancashire common fields were never fallowed, but revitalized by the dung of cattle which grazed them for the half year between harvest and spring sowing; a more recent study suggests that the evidence for this intensive and exhausting use is inconclusive, and cites sparse evidence of alternative uses of fields in other parts of the county; different communities may have used their land according to their own local customs (Youd 1962: 22; Elliot 1973: 55–7).

It seems probable that common field systems never existed on every manor, while on some the process of *enclosing*, that is fencing-off an individual's land from that of his neighbours, had begun in the medieval centuries. The enclosure of common fields continued in piecemeal fashion throughout the years to 1660. At Garston in 1566 the lord of the manor enclosed all the town field, whereas at Lytham in James I's reign individual tenants made their own enclosures and farmed their land in severalty, while around them other tenants continued to cultivate in common. Communal farming persisted on many Lancashire manors long after the time-span of this chapter; arguments against rapid enclosure there in the sixteenth century and evidence of eighteenth-century common fields in Cheshire make it necessary to be cautious about the claim that enclosure was widespread before the civil war (Youd 1962: 40; Elliot 1973: 85, 90; Morrill 1974: 5). Youd associated the enclosure of common fields in Lancashire with enclosures made from manorial and forest wastes as characteristic of Tudor and Stuart Lancashire. Moss, heath, moor and forest were all cultivated for the first time in this period. In the south Cheshire parish of Acton in Elizabeth's reign Ravensmore was nibbled at by people who built houses, and by non-residents who cultivated it (CRO, DTW/Q/1). At Rainow on the higher ground in the east of the county a survey of 1611 showed forty-one copyholds and nine cottages established within a generation; more new holdings were carved there from the forest of Macclesfield in the 1650s (Laughton 1986: 23, 27). In Lancashire the disaf-forestation of Duchy lands on the Pennines in the early sixteenth century began a persistent extension of the cultivatable area, promoted by the Duchy itself (Tupling 1927; J. T. Swain 1986: 36–7, 63, 91–3). At Penwortham in the early seventeenth century the manorial lord drove some squatters off the waste (Sutton 1915: 36, 40). Harmony between lords and tenants, or sup-posed tenants, on enclosure was thus not total, but there does not seem to have been the widespread opposition characteristic of, for example, the Eng-lish Midlands. Both social strata, either by direct investment, or by tolerating enclosure in the manorial court, participated in the extension of farm land and made available to individuals the potential benefits of separated and/or consolidated holdings.

Most of Lancashire and Cheshire can be classed as pastoral vale country (Thirsk 1987: 38–9, 41–4). Parts of central and northern Lancashire are arable vale rather than pastoral vale, and in both counties there are small areas of wood-pasture land, and fringes of moorland. The advantage of this type of regional classification is that it neatly describes the landscape as well as explains the preponderant characteristics of the farming regime. Over time, such regions and their farming evolve; at any one instant in time, the exact detail of farming in physically distinct parts of the region can differ. Pasture land, with lush meadow and moss, dominated the west of Lancashire, penetrated the major river valleys, and was widespread in Cheshire. The glacial drift which covers most of that county changes unpredictably from sand to clay. In the east of both counties the extensive moorland lies on grits, and on limestone in areas of Lancashire and parts of north Derbyshire. The rewarding improvement of sandy soils with marl was well known in the two counties: 'he that marles upon sand intends to buy land', as Sir Richard Hoghton advised his son. James Bankes at Winstanley estimated that marling moorish ground cost five marks an acre, but it could then be let at one mark an acre. At Clitheroe, in different conditions, fields were limed (Long 1968: 90; Wanklyn 1976: 333–4).

The agriculture of this regime of varied soils, customary tenure, chang-ing field patterns and enlightened farmers was dominated by cattle (Thirsk 1967: 81–3; Kerridge 1967: 129–31, 144, 160–1, 166). The difference between, for example, south Cheshire and the Fylde of Lancashire lay in the different way the animals were farmed, and perhaps the extent to which arable provided human foodstuffs and cattle feed. Pastoral farming to produce cheese dominated in south and west Cheshire, which enjoyed the best reputation for Cheshire cheese, a delicacy famous by John Speed's time in the early seventeenth century. In north Cheshire the emphasis was on cows reared and fattened with others brought in on the good, late-growing grass; in the north-east in the forest of Macclesfield sheep, horses and pigs were additionally important. On the Lancashire Plain pasture and meadow were widespread, but there was extensive arable to feed both humans and cattle; in the north of the region the arable was more important, and here the agriculture was characteristic of the arable vale. As in north Cheshire, cattle were reared alongside animals bought in, in this case from up the Ribble valley, to fatten on the lush pasture. Between the rivers Mersey and Lune in the centre of the plain mixed farming stood out; between Mersey and Ribble, holdings were perhaps at their smallest as the availability of industrial and mining work allowed the support of more families than the land itself could accommodate. Finally, in eastern Lancashire and north Derbyshire cattle rearing predominated. Among small farmers in Lancashire dairy cattle were important, presumably for family food rather than for the market (J. T. Swain 1986: 47), while cattle rearing was the emphasis detected in the probate records of the larger farmers. Young animals were sold south and west to be fattened; sheep raised primarily for mutton were also fed here.

Major landowners received most of their landed income from rents, though many of them farmed part of their demesne, and produced on it more than was needed for domestic consumption. From Long's detailed examination of estate accounts, calculations show that rents, including the substantial fines permitted by customary tenure, averaged 54 per cent (Shireburn) and 48 per cent (Molyneux) of receipts on two estates. On the third estate (Walmesley), to which tithe rents made a substantial contribution, rental income never fell below 78 per cent. The complex supervision of demesne farming which the scattered nature of many gentry estates would have necessitated no doubt explains why some prudent landlords chose to farm only a small part of their demesnes. But demesne profits averaging 25 per cent (Shireburn) and 40 per cent (Molyneux) of receipts show a significant interest in the agricultural market.* The market was of course a difficult one, for the urban and therefore food purchasing, proportion of the region's population was small. On the other hand, cattle could be moved over a long distance to markets in the south of England. For the Shireburn estates *c.* 1570 cattle predominated, followed by grain sales; on the Molyneux estates in the years 1605–9 grain was important. It is impossible to suggest how the incomes of yeomen may have been divided between rents and farming, or how much of their farming was aimed at the market. Clearly in the production of cheese and cattle the national reputations of Cheshire cheese, and of both counties for cattle, suggest that much produce went to the market. But the extent to which arable was used for home consumption, whether for humans or ani-

* These calculations are based on figures in Long (1968: 246–9). The Shireburn figures (which may include non-Lancashire estates) cover the years 1567–71, Molyneux 1605–9, and Walmesley 1613–22.

mals, or what was purchased to meet such needs, is unclear. The small size of holdings and the importance of grain imports to the region suggest limits to self-sufficiency.

Small and large farmers in both counties were improving and extending their estates. Lancashire farmers of the period have been criticized for lack of interest in markets, and estate management in the county condemned as backward and conservative but this judgement seems to ignore the cattle trade, and a growing emphasis on dairying (Long 1968: 127). In Cheshire dairying offered little scope for innovation but the wide use of marl to improve the soil showed agriculturists eager to make improvement where they could (Wanklyn 1976: 336–7). There was only a limited role in the region for innovations which were chiefly directed at the improvement of more specialized arable and sheep farming.

Towns

The distinction between a small town and a large village is not easy to make today, and it was no more sure four centuries ago, in a society dominated by landowners. It has been argued that the distinctively crowded urban life-style could be experienced only by at least 2,000 or 2,500 people but this would exclude too many small places which both contemporaries and historians regard as towns (Corfield 1976; 1982: 6). Another analysis suggests five characteristics of towns: an unusually large population; specialist economic functions; influence outside town boundaries; a complex social structure; and a sophisticated political structure – the last two in contrast to the simple structure and politics of agrarian society (Clark and Slack 1976: 5). Table 1.5 defines and lists towns another way, according to the level of legal privilege enjoyed, though the categorization should not obscure important changes in urban status in our period.

Grants of privileges to towns were made by the crown; in Chester's case Henry VII's charter of 1506 gave it the ultimate status as a county, thereby excluding the jurisdiction of all the county officials (Justices of the Peace, sheriffs, etc.) from the town. No other town in the region enjoyed such independence (Weinbaum 1943: 10–12, 65–8). The incorporated boroughs listed in Table 1.5 were, by the end of the period, independent of county Justices of the Peace, but the sheriffs and deputy lieutenants had powers in them throughout (see Figure 1.2). By and large, the position of seigniorial boroughs rested on grants made in the distant past, and this was also true of some market towns, though the crown granted at least three new market charters, which simply allowed a market and its attendant courts to be held,

Table 1.5   Towns in the region[a]

County[1]	Incorporated[1]	Seigniorial borough[2]	Market[3]
CHESHIRE			
Chester[d]	Congleton	Altrincham	Sandbach[b]
	Macclesfield	Frodsham[b]	Tarvin[b]
		Halton	
		Knutsford	
		Malpas	
		Middlewich	
		Nantwich	
		Northwich	
		Over[a]	
		Stockport	
		Tarporley[a]	
LANCASHIRE			
none	Lancaster[d]	Bolton	Arkholme[4]
	Liverpool[d]	Chorley	Ashton-under-Lyne
	Preston[d]	Clitheroe[d]	Blackburn
		Hornby[4]	Bury
		Kirkham	Colne
		Manchester	Croston
		Newton-in-	Garstang
		Makerfield[d]	Haslingden
		Ormskirk	Leigh[c]
		Salford	Lathom
		Warrington	Padiham[c]
		Wigan[d]	Poulton-le-Fylde
			Rochdale
			Rufford[5]
			Whalley[c]
DERBYSHIRE (part)			
none	none	none	Chapel-en-le-Frith[6]
			Glossop[7]

Notes and sources:
[a] Unless marked [a] all towns were also market towns.
[b] Market noted as established 'lately' in W. Smith 1588.
[c] Evidence for a market in the seventeenth century only.
[d] A parliamentary borough; Newton, and Clitheroe for the first time in 1559 (Bindoff 1982; Hasler 1981).

[1] Weinbaum 1943.
[2] Beresford and Finberg 1973, and see also source 3.
[3] Leland 1535, III: 2–5, and V, 23–32, 223; W. Smith 1588: 119, 137–9; W. Webb 1623 for Cheshire. Leland 1535, V: 32 for Derbyshire. Leland 1535, II: 21; III: 5–11; V: 40–6; and Tupling 1936 for Lancashire. Cf. Everitt 1967: 468 and Dyer 1979: 124–8.
[4] The markets at Arkholme and Hornby may be the same one, see *VCH. Lancs*, VIII: 194 n61.
[5] For this see France 1985: 221.
[6] Riden 1978: 69.
[7] Coates 1965: 92–111.

in the sixteenth century. The presence of one or more fairs does not define a place as a town (cf. W. Smith 1588: 138–9).

William Harrison wrote that 'citizens and burgesses have next place to gentlemen' in the social order, though he was careful to emphasize that this applied only in towns (W. Harrison 1587: 115). In fact the burgesses or freemen were the only people allowed to run businesses in a town, but few of them were involved in town corporations. With a population in our period of about 5,000 (see p. 7), Chester after 1506 was governed by a mayor, twenty-four aldermen and a common council of forty, to whom were added the sheriff-peers (those men who had served the office of sheriff and now had no other post in the corporation). The mayor and those aldermen who had been mayor served as Justices of the Peace, and the city also had its own coroners, escheator and clerk of the market. Within the city walls a large area comprised the cathedral and the castle which were outside the corporation's jurisdiction (see Figure 1.3). While there were conflicts, for example between the city and the county, and the city and the cathedral, on the whole the fundamental rights of Chester were not seriously challenged in this period (Weinbaum 1943: 11; Johnson 1972: 204). All the other corporate towns faced challenges to their rights and privileges from neighbouring landowning families, or peers, and Congleton, Macclesfield, and Preston all got extra powers and confirmations of existing rights in new crown charters (Weinbaum 1943: 11–12, 67; Stephens 1970: 64–8; C. S. Davies 1961; Clemesha 1912).

To Liverpool, the root of whose government was a charter of King John, there were two main threats. The neighbouring Molyneux of Sefton family obtained a lease of the crown's rights as lord of the town, and proceeded to hold courts and collect market tolls. The town's other aristocratic neighbours, the earls of Derby, were generally more sympathetic to the townsmen, but claimed a veto over the election of the mayor. A permanent solution of the Molyneux problem did not come until after the Restoration, but at the fifth attempt between 1567 and 1626 the corporation got a new charter in 1626 by which the town 'may nominate and elect' the mayor (Muir and Platt 1906: 153–89; *VCH. Lancs*, IV: 15–16). Despite the emphasis on elections in these charters, it would be misleading to see in corporate towns anything more than the most embryonic seeds of democracy, given society's equation of social standing and wealth, and the calls on the time and money of the corporation members at the expense of their own livelihoods.

Among the seigniorial boroughs, in Stockport the Warren family certainly kept control of the town. About 1220 Sir Robert of Stockport had given his tenants there the essential freedom of burgage tenure and his charter set out the land and common rights attached to each burgage, and the power of the burgesses to mortgage, sell and bequeath the property, subject to acknowledgement of the lord's right, and his rent. Suit of mill and common oven was required, and civil and criminal jurisdiction was also the lord's. The

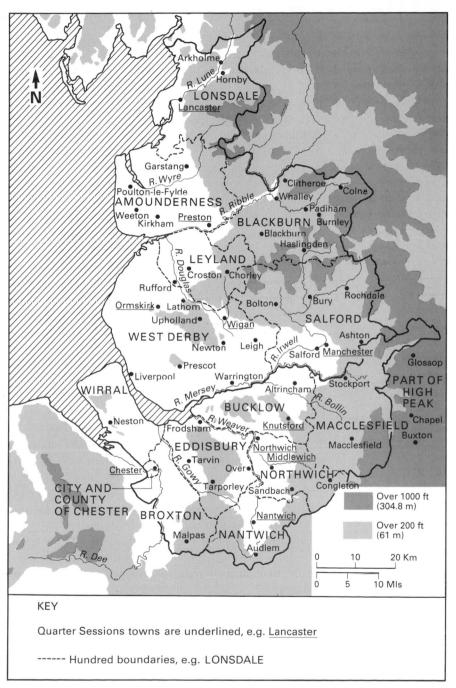

KEY

Quarter Sessions towns are underlined, e.g. <u>Lancaster</u>

------ Hundred boundaries, e.g. LONSDALE

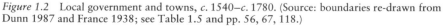

Figure 1.2 Local government and towns, *c.* 1540–*c.* 1780. (Source: boundaries re-drawn from Dunn 1987 and France 1938; see Table 1.5 and pp. 56, 67, 118.)

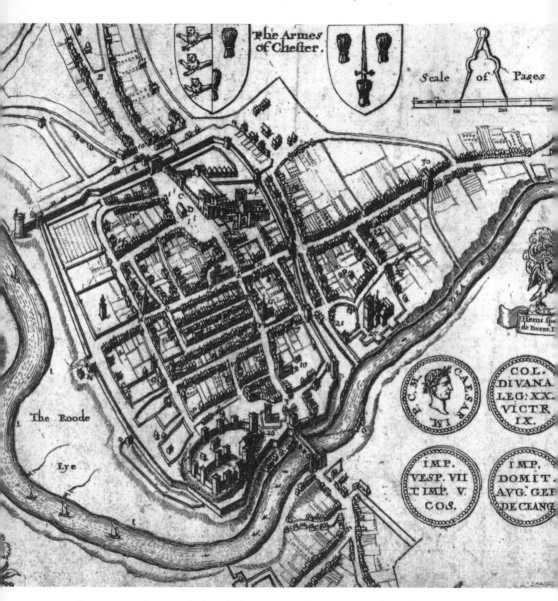

Figure 1.3 'The ground-plott of Chester'. W. Hollar's map, together with a prospect of the city of Chester, illustrated King 1656, between pp. 36 and 37. (Source: Cheshire County Record Office, original 1656 edition.)

burgesses were to elect a chief officer (mayor) each year, with the advice of the lord or his bailiff. The chief officer was confined to running the self-regulating aspects of economic and criminal jurisdiction for the townsmen, but through the lord's court. All these powers seem to have survived into the seventeenth century, although an élite group of wealthy aldermen with only a shadowy role had emerged by then. In Stockport the townsmen enhanced the role of their mayor and aldermen by making them supervisors of charitable funds (Phillips and Smith 1985: 59). In 1634 when Edward Warren wanted to improve law and order in the town by getting the crown to appoint a resident Justice of the Peace, he asked for his steward, rather than the mayor, to be appointed (Heginbotham 1877, II: 258; Morrill 1974: 6). There is little evidence of dissatisfaction with this system, and here and in Clitheroe and the much more populous Manchester (Weeks 1924–6; Willan 1980: 11–13) the more influential townsmen through their jury service had a not inconsiderable effect on the lords' courts. The absence of corporate powers avoided hosts of regulations and expenses without which the three towns appeared to be happily flourishing. Wigan too flourished, but conflict between the lords of the manor and the mayor and townsmen was virulent and recurrent. The lord of the manor chose the mayor from three men nominated by the burgesses, and both lord and burgesses kept courts, which allegedly infringed each other's rights. After three decades of irritation a settlement was reached in 1596, only to be discarded in 1617 for dispute to rumble on to the end of our period. In another dimension of seigniorial involvement in the town, the neighbouring Gerrard family always seem to have controlled the election of the town's two members of parliament (*VCH. Lancs*, IV; Hasler 1981, I: 192).

Six towns returned Members of Parliament (Table 1.5), and these seats, as at Wigan, provided opportunities for those peers and gentry whose ambitions were not fulfilled in the elections for the two counties, and in so doing forged links between town and country. In Chester the county gentry even became involved in town politics, and some served as mayor. Wigan, Preston, Liverpool and Clitheroe facilitated such connections by having a category of 'out-burgesses', or in Preston's case, members of the gild merchant (Weeks 1924–6: 59; Abram 1884). The gentry were also often urban property-owners. The Ardern family had houses in Chester and Stockport, and the widow Marie Ardern spent her last days in the family house in Stockport. William Swindells, a wealthy husbandman of the town, seems to have been the Ardern agent there. A younger son of the Wrights of Offerton also lived in the town, and other gentry families had houses there (Phillips and Smith 1985: 70–1, 122, 123; CRO; pr. Henry Wright, 1643). Town and country connections were further strengthened by younger sons of the gentry who became urban apprentices, as did the sons of yeomen and husbandmen.

The larger towns provided the widest range of skills, services and stock for customers from the countryside. Records of the admission of freemen provide the best, albeit imperfect, indicators of numbers following each occupation, but few Lancashire and Cheshire towns were corporate and thus kept such archives. In any case the number of freemen may not reflect the relative importance of one trade or another as employers of labour or generators of wealth (Pound 1981). Table 1.6 shows the numbers of freemen admitted to groups of trades in Chester between 1575 and 1625. The sophistication of Chester's trade structure was such that its freemen included goldsmiths making quality silver and gold vessels and perhaps jewellery. Its building workers included that relatively rare man, the plumber (a 'water leader' in 1587), and also carpenters specializing in housebuilding. By the end of our period silk-weavers, glaziers, apothecaries, stationers, musicians, instrument makers and farriers – all specialist workers – ranked among its freemen (Bennett 1906).

Table 1.6 Admissions to the freedom of Chester, 1575–1625 (in rank order)

Trade group	No. of freemen
Cloth	362
Leather industries	349
Food and drink trades	210
Distributive	184
Metal workers	153
Building trades	109
Yeomen/husbandmen (agriculture)	78
Gentlemen	62
Professions	13

Source: Henderson 1979: 35, based on Bennett 1906.

Liverpool seems to have had much the same range of tradesmen, without some of the more specialist trades (Twemlowe 1935: 1,184–7; Chandler and Saxton 1960: 370–1; Chandler and Wilson 1965: 469–70). Thus Chester had a goldsmiths' gild whereas Elizabethan and Caroline Liverpool had one goldsmith (Ridgway 1966: 14–32). When members of the Shuttleworth family of Gawthorpe Hall near Burnley were ill in the 1590s, it was Chester whence the physician came (Harland 1856: 85). Sixteenth-century Preston, if the gild merchant rolls are an accurate reflection, had a smaller range of trades than in the early seventeenth century; by 1622 such specialists as a watchmaker, a surgeon, a barber and two curious men termed 'medicus' had practised in the town, and between 1622 and 1642 three musicians had joined the gild (Abram 1884).

Despite the lack of freemen records, we know that Manchester and Nantwich had some specialist tradesmen, for example there was a stationer at Manchester in the early seventeenth century, and a specialist painter at Nantwich in 1572 (Earwaker 1888; Hall 1883: 101–2). Even the small market towns contained a range of occupations. Clitheroe tradesmen included wine sellers, shoemakers, tanners, butchers, smiths, a more specialist tallow chandler, a hosier and a yarn man, according to court records (Weeks, 1924–6, XLIII: 81ff). Probate records demonstrate in Table 1.7 that Stockport had

Table 1.7   Occupations from probate records for Stockport, 1578–1650

Cloth	woollen and linen weavers; shearman; tailor
Leather	tanner; shoemaker
Metal	cutler
Food	baker; butcher; innkeeper
Distributive	woollen and linen drapers; haberdasher; mercer; chapman
Building	carpenter; mason; glazier
Professions	apothecary; clergyman

Sources: C. B. Phillips and Smith 1985 (to 1619); CRO, Cheshire, probate records 1620–50.

people in each of the occupational groups present in Chester, though we have no idea as to how many practised these trades at any one time in the town.

Notwithstanding the range of occupations, there were some specialisms. Surprisingly, Chester has no reputation as a cloth producer, despite the fact that cloth-working freemen predominated. Its port gave it ready access to supplies of Irish hides, and it had an important leather industry (Woodward 1968). In Congleton too the leather industry predominated (Stephens 1970: 54). Macclesfield was already a button-making town (E. Swain 1984). The Lancashire towns such as Manchester and Bolton had growing reputations for cloth. Wigan developed as a specialist pewter town in the seventeenth century, and the three Cheshire wiches made salt. The townsmen themselves obviously consumed some of these manufactures, while their most distant markets could be international – Manchester cottons were exported through Southampton for example in the sixteenth century. But some of the demand for urban manufactures came from the surrounding countryside, even though there were rural manufacturing industries. There was certainly a qualitative difference between urban and rural manufactures of the same product, and towns did operate as complements to rural textile workers, providing finishing skills and distribution services (Thirsk 1978: 108). But towns had many more attractions than a range of manufactures.

To an extent people were funnelled into Lancaster because it was a bridging point over the Lune (Figure 1.4). A night's lodging for Daniel Fleming and his steward passing through Lancaster from Westmorland to London cost 2s. 4d., but 2s. 6d. for the horses, in 1652 (Magrath 1903: 30). The town hosted quarter sessions and assizes, the palatinate jurisdiction was based there and its castle was a county jail. It was also a port, had its own borough courts and market as well as the businesses of its freemen. All combined to attract outsiders. Similarly in most years the little market town of Knutsford was transformed into a centre of county business when the quarter sessions were held there. And of course Chester was pre-eminent as a regional capital whose legal and maritime powers extended into north Wales; people came to the heart of the diocese of Chester from all over Cheshire and Lancashire and parts of Cumberland, Westmorland and Yorkshire. It was also the assize town for Cheshire, and a quarter sessions town as well as having its own

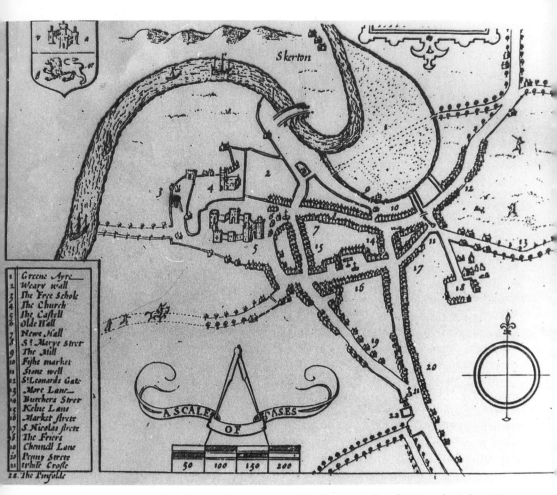

Figure 1.4 John Speed's map of Lancaster, *c.* 1610. (Sources: J. Speed 1611 and J. Arlott 1954.)

courts, market and port facilities and the lowest bridge across the Dee into Wales. All such functions brought business into the towns, over and above demand from the townsmen and with that business came the needs for food, drink, accommodation and entertainment. Chester races can be traced back to 1542 at least. If the gambling and loose women in Tuger Bold's house in early Stuart Liverpool were available to sailors, they could be enjoyed by countrymen as well. In 1647 there were no fewer than sixty-four alehouse-keepers in the borough, at least two of whom followed another trade as well (Chandler and Saxton 1960: 41; Chandler and Wilson 1965: 347–8). In the part of Nantwich that burnt down in 1583 there were seven inns – needed for the busy route between London and Ireland via Chester as well for locals (Hall 1883: 105). The half-timbered Crown Hotel (Plate 1.3) was rebuilt soon after the fire (Pevsner and Hubbard 1971: 287). In Clitheroe sixteen

Plate 1.3 The Crown Hotel, High Street, Nantwich. Rebuilt soon after the 1583 fire, which destroyed much of Nantwich, this half-timbered inn doubtless served as a meeting place for country visitors; there is a purpose-built eighteenth-century Assembly Room behind it (Pevsner and Hubbard 1971: 287).

people entered recognizances for good behaviour as alehouse-keepers in 1620 (Weeks 1924–6, XLIII: 93–4). There must have been somewhere in Stockport for Raphe Hunt, who died in 1599, to use his bowls (C. B. Phillips and Smith 1985: 26).

Chester was the most important port in the region and it imported from Ireland raw materials – sheepskins and cattle hides – much of which was consumed by its own leather industry, and wool and yarn which went chiefly to the Lancashire textile workers. Iron, wine, dyestuffs, salt and luxuries like figs, raisins and peppers came from Spain; similar cargoes came from France. In wartime, Chester's Spanish trade continued legitimately via Ireland. Chester also had a substantial trade with London, both overland and coastwise, supplementing the continental imports already mentioned, but also comprising fullers' earth and chalk for the textile industry. Occasional cargoes from the Baltic and Scotland arrived, and the port was an important distributor of imported grains in times of scarcity, but by comparison with other provincial English ports the overseas trade of Chester and Liverpool was unimportant in the early seventeenth century, by when Liverpool may have begun to rival Chester (Stephens 1969; K. P. Wilson 1969; Woodward 1970: 35, 131–3). Even in the sixteenth century Liverpool had been a significant importer of Irish raw materials, especially of linen yarn. None of the other small ports on the Lancashire coast had a significant foreign trade (Willan 1959: 87, 89; PRO, E190/1329/4, for Lancaster, 1607).

Much of what was imported was redistributed by sea to Ireland, and along the north Wales and Lancashire coasts (Willan 1938: 181, 184; Woodward 1970: 66–9). Chester also exported salt, foodstuffs, cheese and cereals, and manufactured goods, especially cloth. Surprisingly, for long under the Tudors, French salt was redistributed from Chester, despite the volume of salt sent overland from Nantwich. The two most important cloths in the sixteenth century were Kendal cottons to Ireland, and Manchester cottons to the continent. Chester then exported twice the volume of Manchester cottons that Liverpool did, but the latter may have caught up in the early 1600s. Merchants bringing these commodities to the town picked up imports for redistribution in their home towns. Liverpool's strength was in its coal exports, especially to Ireland, with some sent along the Lancashire coast.

By-and-large we have no records of the overland trade of the towns, and of who actually came to their markets and fairs. Some of Chester's Spanish iron imports went to south Lancashire (see p. 53). Sheffield hardware was exported via Chester (Woodward 1970: 18, 71). Given the low rates of tolls, Clitheroe's receipts of nearly £7 13s. 0d. on 22 July 1639 represents a significant volume of trade (Weeks 1924–6, XLIII: 109). In 1610 there were twenty-four butchers' stalls alone at Liverpool market (Chandler and Saxton 1960: 73). Ten visitors to Nantwich one day in 1572 came from six places close to the town, in social status they ranged from a gentleman down through husbandmen to a mere farm servant (Hall 1883: 101–2). Preston's market dominated the area within about seven miles of the town in the sixteenth century, and it had a significant pull within a fifteen-mile radius, in competition with other market towns (Rodgers 1956). Stockport men had connections with London, but local connections extended as far as Stone, Nantwich, Chester, Hope (Derbyshire), and Manchester (Wadsworth and Mann, 1931; C. B. Phillips and Smith .1985; probate records 1620–50 in the

40

Cheshire CRO). In north-east Lancashire trade connections over the Pennines with Yorkshire towns were probably as important as those to Manchester and the Lancashire plain (J. T. Swain 1986: 146). Gentry account books remind us that not all goods were bought locally, for the Shuttleworths often shopped in London, and the carriers of cloth overland to the London markets brought back a wide variety of goods (Willan 1976: 5, 12).

Industry

The thrust of mid-Tudor industrial legislation proclaimed industry for the towns and agriculture for the countryside; in practice there was little agriculture in towns but much industry in both town and country (Thirsk 1978: 108). The Wigan pewterer Gilbert Langshawe, whose stock of pewter moulds marks him out as heavily involved in the industry, had more capital in agriculture (30 per cent) than in his trade (20 per cent) according to the value of his inventory (M. R. Smith 1988: 20). The concentrations of manufacturing craftsmen in towns (see Tables 1.6 and 1.7 above) produced foodstuffs, metal and wooden products, leather and leather goods, and carried out some or all the stages of cloth manufacture. Many rural settlements had one or two such craftsmen – a smith, a carpenter and a shoemaker for example (G. O. Lawton 1979). Millers preparing foodstuffs and specialist clothworkers, as well as farmers who also worked textiles, were the most widespread of the rural manufacturers; there were important communities of nail makers in the rural Lancashire township of Atherton. There were rural industries which were quite different from those found in the towns: coal was mined in the countryside; the new, high technology, capital intensive iron-making, paper-making and glass-making industries were rural, but only of marginal importance in this period (Awty 1957; 1958; Langton 1979: 50). By contrast, salt manufacture was a distinctive Cheshire industry which was chiefly but not exclusively urban. Many agriculturalists, whether gentry or mere husbandmen, had more than one source of income, and industry was one common diversification of the family economy. Especially in textiles, but also in the salt industry and in coal-mining, it is not always clear whether a particular family was primarily engaged in agriculture or industry. The importance of the dual economy cannot be over-emphasized: at the lower levels of society a family with a non-viable agricultural holding could sustain itself through industrial activity; among the greater landowners, even a rentier interest in coal-mines or salt works broadened their economic outlook and created social respectability and political support for manufacturing. Textiles, leather, coal and salt were important throughout this period; the Chester

coopers and Lancashire nail makers will serve as examples of more specialized urban and rural industries; lastly, the hatting industry provides a good
example of a new industry appearing in both town and country.

Textile manufacture, of both linens and woollens, was long established
in the north-west in the mid-sixteenth century but it is difficult to quantify the
level of production or, in the case of linen, judge the quality of what was
produced. During the century that followed, the linen trade developed in
some western districts but further east it gave way to the weaving of cloths
uniting linen warps and cotton weft while the woollen trade, also drawn to a
lesser extent into mixed cloths, gradually withdrew to the eastern edge. There
were improvements to the woollen cloth trade but the entry of cotton
extended the range and changed the character of textile manufacture and the
development of smallware weaving brought some early concentration of
labour. By 1660 the linen trade and the formerly despised and deceitful
woollen cloth manufacture of the region had changed into a thrusting industry, keenly alert to new opportunities.

The linen trade remains rather obscure but there were marked differences between that carried on in the western belt of Leyland hundred and the
trade around Manchester. The western 'linen men' worked on a smaller scale,
used yarn from locally grown flax and probably dealt in a coarser cloth than
their Manchester counterparts. Flax and hemp were grown commercially in
west Lancashire and the Wigan area and, in smaller amounts, in many other
districts as many field names testify (Withersby 1990). Flax and yarn were
also imported from Ireland and the Baltic (Lowe 1972: 10–19; Kerridge
1985: 14). In 1569 when supplies of Irish yarn were threatened by a tariff it
was claimed that 4,000 people within the lordship of Manchester depended
on it (Lowe 1972: 11). The yarn took six months to bleach and Moston
bleachers carried out this process for much of the Manchester district (Kerridge 1985: 141). A great deal of this yarn was sold in small parcels. The
probate records of William Hollingworth of Matley in Longdendale, who
died in 1623, describe him as a yeoman but his debt book lists 103 people
who owed him £54 for flax and another eleven who owed £2 for hemp, all
living within a radius of a few miles of his home (CRO, pr. William Hollingworth, 1623). Linen weavers can be found across most of the region but
how their time was divided between weaving their neighbour's yarn to be
returned as domestic linen and how much in weaving for the wider commercial market is uncertain. The Chetham family of Manchester were selling
linens called 'Stopport' cloth in London in 1610 but it has left no evidence in
Stockport itself; this was presumably the cloth that sold for 1s. 3d. per yard
when the west Lancashire linens could fetch only 7½d. to 8½d. (Wadsworth
and Mann 1931: 14, 30; C. B. Phillips and Smith 1985; Withersby 1990: 45).
The prosperity of linen drapers such as Richard Nugent of Salford, who left
personal estate of £2,344 in 1609, suggests a buoyant market (Lowe 1972:

55). The linen men of the west also traded in the Midlands and the south independently of the Manchester network but they were less enterprising and may have put the more modest profits of their trade into farming and local money lending rather than into the expansion of textile working (Withersby 1990: 89).

The woollen trade is much better documented. Wool was produced in the region but the evidence for Colne, Pendle and Trawden suggests that as early as 1536, even on the Pennine edges, the cloth makers needed far more wool than the local flocks could supply (J. T. Swain 1986: 115). Flocks grew in size later in the century but most of the wool used in the region was imported. The bulk of the wool used was coarse and inferior and the sixteenth-century cloths made from it were not only narrow and coarse but also often notoriously poorly made, fraudulent or overstretched. Even so it was claimed that 10,000 people in Lancashire earned their living making friezes and cottons (woollen cloth with a raised nap) for export to France (J. T. Swain 1986: 108). Throughout the Tudor period attempts were made to improve cloth making by restricting it to towns, by enforcing seven-year apprenticeship and by preventing the making of inferior cloth or its overstretching after fulling. They had little effect on the cheap Lancashire trade and it may be that the poor quality of kersey exports was a local contribution to the national depression in trade of the 1620s and 1630s that resulted from the Cockayne project and the Thirty Years War (Lowe 1972: 81–95; J. T. Swain 1986: 126–7). There were also more hopeful developments. Better kerseys began to be made in Rossendale in the mid-1590s along with minikins, a new kind of cottoned cloth. 'Baizes', woven from both combed and carded wool, were introduced into Rossendale, Rochdale and Bury from about 1607. By about 1650 the region was producing better cloth though still cheap and made from the inferior wools that were being given up in other woollen areas (Kerridge 1985: 38–9).

The production of both linen and woollen cloth was the work of independent weavers and clothiers though both employed sons and occasionally daughters and non-family employees on the looms. In 1628 John Driver of Pasture in Pendle, a clothier, employed a weaver, Francis Hartley of Roughlee, who wove by the piece in Driver's house, where he was allowed meat, drink and lodging (J. T. Swain 1986: 115). Alexander Daniel of Stockport, who died in 1592, was unusual in that he owned five pairs of looms, linen and woollen, worked by his five sons and ran two cows and six sheep on his land (C. B. Phillips and Smith 1985: 6). This combination of weaving and husbandry was common across the region though Swain found increasing numbers of clothiers with few or no cattle in the Colne district after the 1600s (J. T. Swain 1986: 118). As Hollingworth's debt book illustrates, credit was widely used and a Duchy of Lancaster law suit of 1638 shows Colne clothiers selling their cloth weekly to Robert Walton of Marsden, some for ready money, some on trust (J. T. Swain 1986: 113). Neither linen nor wool have left strong evidence of 'putting out' or 'capitalistic' dominance of the trade during this period though there is a suggestion that linen weavers in Leyland hundred worked for wages (Withersby 1990: 36). There were however developments that heralded wider change.

One of the trades that migrated into the region in the sixteenth century was the weaving of smallwares on expensive Dutch or engine looms bought by small capitalists. These men were employing several weavers in their loomshops in Manchester by the 1660s (Wadsworth and Mann 1931: 103). The entry of cotton was even more portentous. In the second half of the sixteenth century it began to be used in the making of Milan fustians, cloth with a linen warp and a cotton weft. In the 1560s, 1570s and 1580s small parcels of fustians were exported from Lancashire to Ireland, in 1601 there was the first mention of a local fustian weaver, George Arnold of Bolton, and in 1600–1 twenty-two pieces of fustian were sent to Ireland from Chester. During the same period another cotton-linen cloth, check, began to be manufactured and in 1602–3 eight dozen Manchester checks were sent to Ireland from Chester (Lowe 1972: 76–8). By the early 1600s the woollen area was beginning to shrink towards the eastern Pennine edges, linen, canvas and sailcloth making were flourishing towards the western seaboard and on the Lancashire plain, with fustian making growing alongside the older linen trade, first in Bolton and Blackburn, then in Oldham, Middleton and the Manchester area (Wadsworth and Mann 1931: 245). The check trade meanwhile was growing in Manchester and west Lancashire. As yet there were still difficulties in spinning cotton strong enough for warp but some all-cotton cloth may have been woven in the Bolton district early in the seventeenth century, a small piece of such cloth having been found at Hacking Hall in a context of that period (Wadsworth and Mann 1931: 112).

Spinning was principally a by-occupation for women in and around the weaving districts but the new baizes of the early 1600s needed combed yarn for the warps, produced by full-time male combers and provided by specialist yarn masters. The Rossendale baize-makers used mainly Irish yarn until the late seventeenth century (Kerridge 1985: 157). Cotton intensified this shift to external control over the supplies of yarn and raw fibres to the weavers. The cotton used in England came from the Levant until 1628 when it began to enter from the East Indies and 1634 when the first West Indian cotton arrived (Kerridge 1985: 141). Eastern cotton came into London, West Indian at first to Bristol, then to Lancaster and Liverpool: supplies were limited and the Levant Company, who controlled that trade, sold to large merchants like Humphrey Chetham who then resold to chapmen and fustian makers in the north-west on three to six months' credit, often buying the woven cloth (Wadsworth and Mann 1931: 28–36). The fustian and check makers as yet kept their independence but the merchants were in a position of great power. In 1654 the weavers of Manchester and Rossendale complained that unlesse cotton woolle be brought downe to a much lower rate then nowe sould at, the manufacture of fustians will revert to Hamburrough, from whence, by our cheaper making than they, we gained it.

(Quoted in Kerridge 1985: 230)

Studies of Colne chapelry, Pendle forest and Rossendale have shown that the growth of textiles was associated with population growth, the inflation of food prices and a growth in the number of small landholders or the virtually landless. Sub-tenanting, even at high rents, enabled the cloth industry to grow on the poor lands in the east of the region while on the richer agricultural land it was less encouraged. In south-west Lancashire arable cultivation did not lend itself to textile working despite the local growing of flax and its linen industry remained untouched by the new expansion (J. T. Swain 1986: 196, 199–208; Tupling 1927: 70–97; F. Walker 1939: 55–61).

The textile trades could offer great rewards for families and individuals. Some founded dynasties, foremost among them the Mosleys, who bought the manor of Manchester in 1596 and the Chethams whose third generation representative, Humphrey, was able, before his death in 1653, to buy estates at Clayton, Ordsall and Turton Towers at Bolton and to found the school and library in Manchester which still bear his name. Others in the Manchester area were hardly less substantial such as John Hartley, who bought Strangeways, Henry Wrigley and Humphrey Booth of Salford and the Worsleys of Platt (Wadsworth and Mann 1931: 9, 29–36). Most of these great merchants had permanent connections in London, often relatives, and by the mid-seventeenth century much smaller merchants were also dealing through London factors.

Below these great merchants there was a growing group of lesser dealers who travelled to Chester and Ireland to buy wool and flax, bought local cloth for fulling and finishing and sold at the fairs or through their London connections. At a more local level John Abbott of Blackburn, who died in 1597, was described in his inventory (Plate 1.4) as a yeoman and had oxen, kine, horses, sheep and swine, but 'peece in the loomes' implies that he was making cloth near the time of his death. Wool, yarn, looms, 'tentors', shears and shearboards, and a dyehouse at home suggest involvement in all stages of cloth production, while the chest and cloths at Preston indicate that some of his output was sold there. His personal estate of £329 included £175 in debts owing to him, the fruits of dealing as well as manufacture (LRO, pr. John Abbott, 1597). Not all clothiers were as prosperous as Abbott but the growing trade provided opportunities for younger sons to stay at home and, perhaps, to marry earlier. It is unlikely that the Statute of Apprentices of 1563 (5 Eliz I c4. 5) was any more effective outside the boroughs than the Acts regulating the cloth trade and most country weavers may have learned their

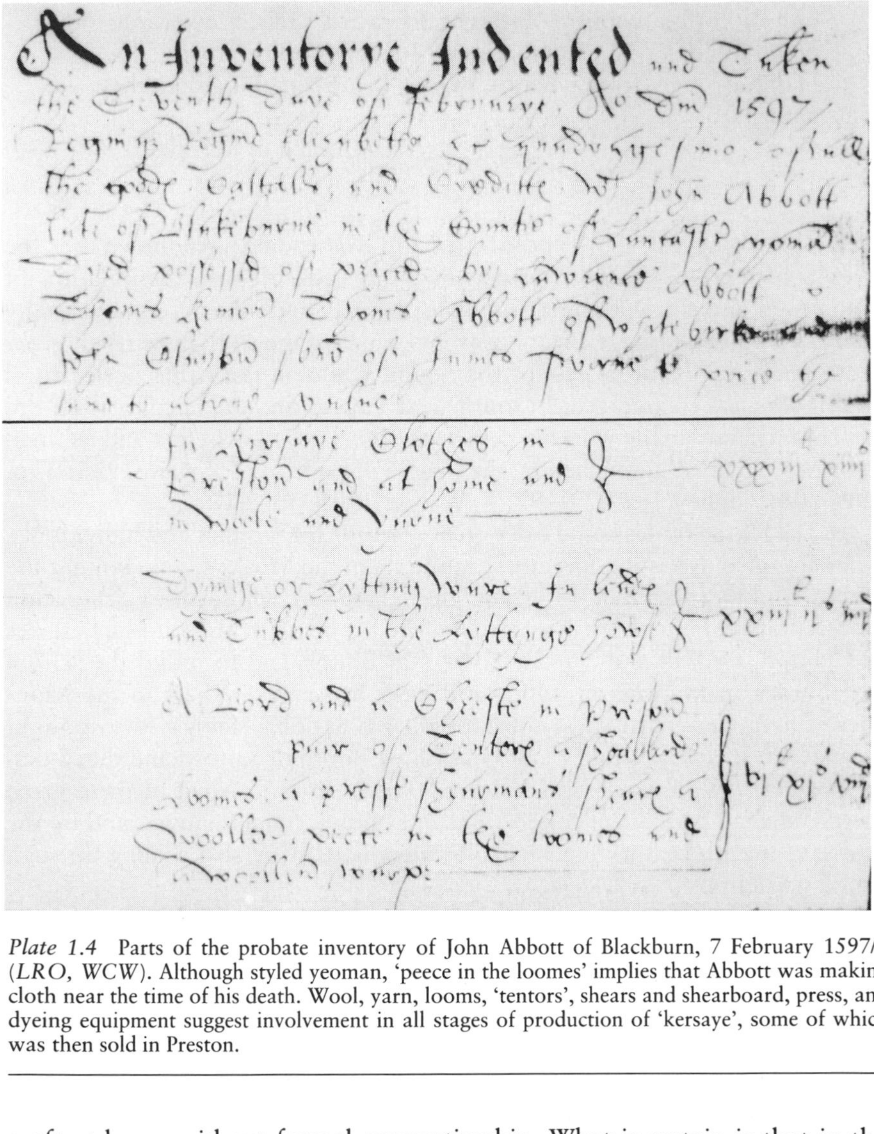
An Inventorye Indented and Taken the Seventh Daye of Februarye Anno Dm 1597

Plate 1.4 Parts of the probate inventory of John Abbott of Blackburn, 7 February 1597/8 (*LRO, WCW*). Although styled yeoman, 'peece in the loomes' implies that Abbott was making cloth near the time of his death. Wool, yarn, looms, 'tentors', shears and shearboard, press, and dyeing equipment suggest involvement in all stages of production of 'kersaye', some of which was then sold in Preston.

craft at home without formal apprenticeship. What is certain is that in the textile areas there was a growth of landless or virtually landless people, weavers, bleachers, dyers, fullers and shearmen who, with the button makers, colliers, hatters and other craftsmen lived in intimate contact with the countryside but were linked to it occupationally only by occasional field labour for the opportune wages of haytime or harvest.

The leather industry was scattered throughout the region but concentrated particularly in towns such as Chester, Clitheroe and Congleton (G. O. Lawton 1979; J. T. Swain 1986: 185–6; LRO, 1960, 18; Weeks 1924–6,

XLIII: 81; Woodward 1968; Stephens 1970). Markets and fairs and, in the case of Chester, access to Irish exports, provided raw materials in quantity, and townsmen and visitors alike bought the finished products. Tanned calf skins were also exported from Chester, leather was sold to rural shoemakers, while the Chester shoemakers may have sold shoes in bulk at Rothwell fair in Northamptonshire, and the glovers regularly sold leather to the London leather-sellers as well as sending small quantities of purses and gloves to Ireland. In Chester, masters in the leather trade, some employing up to six journeymen, were one of the two largest groups of freemen in the city, and a few were prominent as sheriffs and, more rarely, as mayor. The most wealthy leathermen were glovers in Chester, where in general the leather workers enjoyed a modest prosperity, as Table 1.8 shows. Woodward thought that as

Table 1.8   Wealth of Chester leather craftsmen 1591–1640[a] from probate records

Trade and date range	Range of values[b]					
	Trade goods				Total	
	£		% of total		£	
	max	min	max	min	max	min
Glovers (1601–38)	759	17	75	15	1,593	23
Tanners (1594–1638)	173	23	29	69	305	32
Shoemakers (1591–1640)	55	7	52	20	311	31

Notes:
[a] No account has been taken of inflation over these years.
[b] Figures have been rounded to nearest £ or percentage point.
Source: Selected and calculated from Woodward 1968.

many as ten of the craftsmen whose inventories he examined had a subsidiary interest in agriculture beyond a milk cow or an urban pig. By contrast, tanners in rural north-east Lancashire were primarily farmers, and none of the shoemakers' wills or inventories mentioned agricultural land (J. T. Swain 1986: 185–6). Nevertheless, one Colne shoemaker had accumulated money and gold worth £113 at his death, which would rank him among the more wealthy Chester men; elsewhere in rural Lancashire there were tanners of greater or equal substance than those of Chester (LRO, 1960: 15).

Coal was mined in Lancashire long before the Reformation but in the mid-sixteenth century there was greater activity in the search for coal and the sinking of mines (Mullineux 1973: 47). The coalfield itself runs in a thick belt across south Lancashire from Huyton and Prescot in the west to Manchester and Ashton in the east with extensions into north Cheshire and north-west Derbyshire. It also follows a great arc north-east from St Helens through Wigan, Burnley and Bolton to Colne then south again through Rochdale and Oldham (Ashmore 1982: 2–8). In Cheshire on the Wirral there is an extension of the north Wales field in the Neston area.

The most famous coal in Lancashire was undoubtedly the 'cannel' or candle coal of Wigan, the 'great myne of canale at Hawe' recorded by Leland in the sixteenth century (Leland 1535, V: 43). Roger Bradshaw of Haigh appears to have been the first entrepreneur to mine substantial amounts of cannel but his example was followed at Aspull where a second cannel mine was working by 1600 with an invested capital of £3,000 by 1626. The production of ordinary coal also grew rapidly with at least twelve collieries within five miles of Wigan by 1650, one of them at Shevington producing 1,500 tons by 1663 or 1664 (Nef 1932: 62–3, 378). The ordinary coal was sold locally but the highly valued cannel was carried up to fifteen miles overland to people who preferred it to cheaper local coal.

The south-west Lancashire field outside Wigan contained half a dozen manors with working collieries; Prescot manor yielded some 7,000 to 8,000 tons from 1594 to 1596 and others were probably at least as productive. The northern area centred on Burnley was also expanding and at Clayton-le-Moors one colliery was said in 1672 to show a clear yearly profit of £200 which suggests an output of about 6,000 tons. The south-west coalfield had a small but growing outlet through Chester and Liverpool to Ireland, coal exports through these two ports growing from 300 to 500 tons per annum in 1560–5 to 1,000 tons in 1595–1600 and 10,000 tons in 1635–40 when they appear to have reached a plateau (Nef 1932, II: 365). This market did not exceed the growing appetite of Manchester which, by the reign of James I, consumed over 10,000 tons per annum, mainly drawn from the manor of Bradford in east Manchester. As the town grew these pits were unable to meet the increased demand and in the later seventeenth century coal was being brought in overland from Worsley and Clifton to the west of the town (Nef 1932, I: 64). There was also mining in the Rochdale, Oldham and Ashton districts and between Manchester and Bolton where there were a dozen active mines. In addition to the principal areas there were minor ones such as Worth at Poynton in Cheshire where Thomas Mellor rented the mines in 1641 and wherever coal outcropped it was exploited by local gentry and others for their own use (Shercliffe et al. 1983: 14). Nef estimated the growth in the coalfield to be fifteenfold in the 150 years to 1700 but Langton's view that it was only 60 per cent in the south-west coalfield in the hundred years to 1660 may qualify this estimate (Nef 1932, I: 64; Langton 1979: 51). Certainly the growing use of coal did much to make up for the increasing scarcity and expense of wood. As early as 1526 James Roberts, an aged husbandman of Colne, deposed that neither he nor any other inhabitant had

> any nede in tyme past to get Colis for there fuell by Reason they hadde plenty of woode from the forests and turves at theyre liberty which now be decayed and Restrayned from them.
>
> (Quoted in Nef 1932, I: 160)

The right to coal belonged to the landowner and as it became more valuable old manorial customs under which freeholders or tenants could take coal from under their land came under attack. At Colne freeholders could dig for coal on their own land without seeking permission but in Haigh manor they had to pay 'certaine bonuses, presents and averages' for mining (Nef 1932, I: 306–7). Some copyholders lost their rights as at Burnley where, in 1527, 100 of the tenants who had 'enjoyed time out of mind sufficient cole for their fewell to be had from the coal pits of [the] waste' and who had just dug their winter coal were ordered to pay 3d. for every second fother to the farmer of the king's mines (Nef 1932, I: 315–17).

In 1550 the men who mined cannel and ironstone for Roger Bradshaw at Haigh called themselves husbandmen but by 1620, and perhaps before, the word 'collier' had taken on its modern meaning as a miner of mineral coal (Nef 1932, II: 136). We know little about the colliers. In 1600 at Worsley they were hired as individuals and paid a fixed wage of 6d. to 8d. a day and at Wigan in 1636 four miners were bound for twelve months, each man getting 2s. 6d. earnest money (Mullineux 1973: 51). Some worked on a contract basis like the four 'colers' who agreed to dig coal and cannel for the Bishop of Chester at Farnworth in 1637, finding their own tools and sharpening, candles and bellows and men to wind up the coal, the Bishop for his part providing baskets, ropes and a hovel and paying them 8d. for every quarter of coal dug (Nef 1932, I: 15–17). Work in the mines was irregular for most marketing and carrying took place in the summer and early autumn when the going was good and customers stocked up for the winter. The region's miners may have filled in these slack periods working on their own smallholdings or on other land since, even in the most intensively mined districts, they lived rural lives. Work in the mines was also dirty and dangerous, the Wigan area in particular being notorious for choke damp, fire damp and flooding. Techniques of mining showed some progress. Quarried outcrops gave way to horizontal day-eye or adit pits and the bell pits where coal was mined around the bottom of shafts to the safety limits of the unsupported roof. During the seventeenth century the shafts became deeper and wider areas were worked by the pillar and stall method in which the roof was supported by leaving areas of coal unworked. This was the practice at Bradshaw's colliery at Haigh. Flooding was a perpetual problem and at Worsley in 1647 they began a long campaign to relieve the mine of water by driving a sough from the workings to the valley. This was not an uncommon device in the coalfield but at Worsley it was to develop on an extraordinary scale (Malet 1977: 28).

The Lancashire coalfield differed from that of north-east England in that, apart from small exports through the region's ports, its situation confined it to selling by land. Coal from the pitheads was carried either in sacks of about 1 cwt on pack-horses or, where the state of the roads permitted it, in small two-wheeled carts holding from 7 cwts to 1 ton. A pack-horse could carry only 2 or 3 cwts and, as coal sales grew, great gangs of pack-horses were established within ten or so miles of each working colliery providing work and incomes for local husbandmen. By 1667 the streets of Liverpool could be described as much decayed by the 'frequent driving of carts laden with coal' and the road from Bradford to Manchester must have been similarly thronged with coal traffic (Nef 1932, I: 381–3). Carriers were reluctant to travel the roads after the first frosts and there could be other difficulties as at Preston in 1630–1 when plague stopped the carriers bringing fuel into the town (HMC 1894: 125, 46).

Although sea salt continued to be made with peat fuel on the north Lancashire coast, and perhaps also by natural evaporation in sunlight, the Cheshire wich towns of Middlewich, Nantwich and Northwich were the most important salt manufacturers in the region (Chaloner 1961: 59; R. Taylor 1975). Salt making was a straightforward industry. Brine from springs was piped to 'wich houses' where it was boiled in lead pans over wood-fuelled furnaces; there were four or six 'leads' per house. Precipitation was aided by small quantities of cow's blood, eggs and ale, and the crystals then drawn to the side of the pan, and loaded into cones called barrows, to dry adjacent to the flues of the furnaces; the salt was then ready for sale (Hall 1883; Calvert 1915; J. Varley 1941; Chaloner 1960).

Brine ownership was separate from salt making, brine being supplied only to the owners of wich houses in proportion to the number of leads they owned, the drawing being supervised by officers of the manorial courts leet of the towns (Hall 1883: 260–2; Calvert 1915). Most houses were owned by gentry families, who often held several, but yeoman families did own single wich houses (J. Varley 1941, 1944; Calvert 1915). By the late sixteenth century some wich houses were derelict or put to other uses, yet the brine owner still received his brine allocation for them. In Northwich, where there were four pans to the house, the Leycesters of Tabley had twelve leads of walling from 1599, that is three wich houses, but the site of one of them was by 1593 a man's home, so the Leycester allocation of brine was boiled in two wich houses, which they leased out. Up to 1660 the rent received for walling varied, but in most years it was about £14, plus 5s. 8d. for the salt house which had become a residence (JRUL, Tabley rental books, 1583–1611, and 1647–76; Cooke 1904).

Few gentry brine owners worked their salt houses, but most of the yeoman owners were active manufacturers. At Northwich in 1565 seventy-one individuals worked the wich houses, that is 'occupied' them, of whom ten, including only two gentry, owned some or all of the walling they used. Brine owners obviously leased out walling, but some active owners also leased additional walling, as the probate records of occupiers show.* There was a wide spectrum of involvement in manufacture, as Table 1.9 shows.

* CRO, Richard Robinson of Nantwich, 1582, 1603, 1608; John Moulton of Middlewich, 1616; William Sudlow of Witton, 1593; Raphe Pownall of Witton, 1606; Peter Paver of Northwich, 1609/10. For their identification as occupiers see Hall 1883; Calvert 1915; J. Varley 1944.

Table 1.9 Occupiers of wich houses

Northwich 1565[1]		Middlewich 1637[2]	
no. of individuals occupying (4 pans/house)	*no. of leads occupied*	*no. of individuals occupying (6 pans/house)*	*no. of leads occupied*
6	less than 2	1	10
10	2	5	12
1	3	5	18
21	4	1	20
18	6[a]	20	24
1	7		
4	8		
10	more than 9[b]		

Notes:
[a] One man had six and one-third leads.
[b] One man occupied 10, three 12, and one each of 18, 20, 22, 24, 26 and 28 leads.

Sources:
[1] Calvert 1915.
[2] CRO, Middlewich church-wardens' accounts, 1637 (P13/22/1).

Probate records show that wich house occupiers owned their own leads, valued at between eight and eleven shillings and bought their own wood. Barrows and measuring devices cost only a few shillings; those who worked as wallers obviously provided their own tools (CRO, inventory of Jane Broome, 1609). Most of the wich house occupiers were men: only two out of seventy-one at Northwich and four out of thirty-two at Middlewich were women. Walling, that is the raking-off of salt from the pans, was done by women like Jane Daniell, Margery Parker and Ales Whorrall, though this should not imply that all walling was done by women. The numbers of labourers and single women in the salt townships of Witton and Northwich in 1660, both heads of family and, apparently, servants, is no doubt a testimonial to the work provided by the salt industry. The cost of fuel was evidently a significant charge on the business, but if the Earl of Huntingdon's report in 1636 was accurate, wich house profits were at best £60 to £70 a year, with many worth only £30 to £40, but it was a rewarding pursuit for a yeoman (Chaloner 1960).

Two technical changes took place in the industry between 1540 and 1660. By 1636 pumps were in use to distribute brine at Nantwich (Chaloner 1961: 62), which would have perhaps saved on labour costs, at a small capital cost to the brine owners. Outside the wich towns, near Nantwich, Viscount Kilmorrey and Sir Thomas Smith had, by the 1620s, initiated the use of coal to boil brine in iron pans. In the towns themselves it was the occupiers rather than the gentry brine owners who replaced lead pans with iron ones and changed to coal for fuel, not without some initial resistance, at least in Nantwich, if we are to believe William Webb (1623 in Ormerod 1882).

The regional importance of dairying, of Irish Sea fishing, and of the maritime victualling industry must have stimulated the demand for salt. Population increase may have favoured the industry, except that it depressed the prices of dairy products relative to grains. Salt production in the wich towns was regulated by their courts leet, which controlled price, output and seasonality of production, all with the aim of maintaining a fair price for producer and consumer by matching supply with demand. The argument repeated by historians that Nantwich made salt for only twelve days in the year is based on a misreading of the court's rulings, and is a priori unlikely given that Northwich made salt from Palm Sunday to Christmas, and Middlewich from Ascension to Martinmas. If contemporary counts of the numbers of wich houses, showing a marked decline, are correct, they could reflect diminished output in response to strong competition from outside Cheshire, and also competition outside the wich towns from Viscount Kilmorrey and others, which was partly blamed for a decline in trade at Northwich in 1637 (W. Webb 1623 in Ormerod 1882; G. O. Lawton 1979: 172; Calvert 1915). Northwich court leet also blamed shortages of wood (and, by implication, high prices) for loss of profitability. Restrictions on output by courts leet would be a typical reaction to such problems. However, improved productivity consequent upon technical change may have led to decline in the number of pans, regardless of, or as a consequence of, pressure from competitors. Whatever the explanations of it, it seems clear that the Cheshire salt industry was changing rapidly in the middle quarters of the seventeenth century, threatening the wich towns and control by their courts.

Coopers were highly skilled craftsmen whose work was much in demand for the storage of wine and beer, salted meat and in the Cheshire salt industry as well as for domestic purposes. In Chester much of their trade came from the city, but their trading connections extended north-east to Ashton, east to Nantwich and south to Whitchurch in Shropshire (Salt 1983). Forty-one coopers became free in Elizabeth's reign, and a further ten under James I, so that the coopers were among the numerically large groups of freemen in the town, enough for their gild to have a distinctive role in the town's plays and pageants. In some ways the coopers typified the restrictive practices of an urban gild for, just as the city shoemakers' gild bought leather in bulk for its members at a fixed sale price, so too its coopers collectively bought both new and second-hand wood (Woodward 1968: 74). On the other hand, they clearly trespassed on the work of other gilds, but this was tolerated as there were no serious conflicts. Thus some coopers were also salters, others fishmongers, while one man, Thomas Tomlinson, carried on foreign trade on a significant scale (Woodward 1970: 33–4). Tomlinson avoided trouble with the merchants' gild by acting as a factor, and other coopers acted as porters for the handling of goods at the port. All this activity produced a modest prosperity, with surviving probate inventories totalling between £100 and £400, and clothing and household goods suggesting some comfort.

The rural nail-making trade concentrated in the township of Atherton was not regulated by gild, though apprentices were taken. Unlike the hatters and coopers, who both concentrated in the major towns, but were also to be found in the country, the nailers stayed close to their coalfield. Individual nail-makers had as many as three shops in separate market towns, markets which themselves were free of the regulation characteristic of corporate towns. By contrast Liverpool records emphasize that the nail-makers who sold there were but visitors to the market. The cold-short iron which was ideal for most nails came from Yorkshire, no doubt by pack-horse, while the tough iron for animal shoeing probably came from Spain, and through Liverpool rather than Chester. A nailer's smithy was often rented, when structure and hearth belonged to the lord, but the bellows, anvils and hand tools were the nailer's own. Arks to store nails in and a balance to weigh them were the other vital pieces of equipment. The most active might use water power to operate the bellows, and make spades, plough irons and scythes as well as nails.

When he died in 1582 Henry Walkden of Atherton anticipated that his three sons would continue to work in the family smithy, from which each would run his own business. Walkden had sold his nails from the smithy, or carried them to markets elsewhere, but in the seventeenth century nailers had shops and stocks of their own as far away as Preston, Manchester, Rochdale and Bury. Furthermore, some nailer families set up as ironmongers, especially in Warrington. These men not only supplied iron, but also sold nails, yet by the early seventeenth century were no longer themselves nail-makers. The capitalist nature of their business is shown by their willingness to rent out the use of a smithy for short periods of time. Sales from Warrington extended into Cheshire as far as Knutsford and Northwich (perhaps wholesale to dealers in these small market towns?), and to Lyme Hall in the east. However, Lancashire nailers found customers as far away as Denbigh to the south and Kendal to the north. The reward of this business was a fair measure of prosperity: several nailers left personal estate of £200 or over, and one, Robert Smith of Little Hulton, had over £700. Their historian makes little mention of any agricultural interest, though Richard Hampson of Westleigh had leases of land worth £20 in 1633; most probably the labour-intensive nature of their craft, and constant demand for the product made at least the most wealthy of them into specialists (Awty 1957).

One of the provincial centres to which the new felt-hatting trade spread from London in the mid-sixteenth century was Chester; the first feltmaker was recorded in the Freeman Rolls in 1550. During the following 100 years there were 135 admissions of hatmakers at Chester and the trade was clearly thriving, journeymen earning £5 per annum, a wage exceeded only by the smiths and carpenters and well above that of the weavers. The Chester feltmakers were members of and subject to the Skinners' and Feltmakers' Company which regulated apprenticeship, employment, wages, prices and marketing. Felt hats became increasingly popular, replacing the knitted caps which had been ordinary everyday wear. Hatting needed neither power nor machinery and could be carried on wherever there were people with the skills so long as they had access to raw material, fuel and water. Chester appears to have been the only north-western centre during the sixteenth century but early in the next century the trade began to spread, first to Liverpool, where the deaths of feltmakers are recorded in the 1620s and 1630s, then into Cheshire, at Nantwich, Congleton and Sandbach, and to other parts of Lancashire. By 1660 there was strong concentration at Chester with a wide dispersal of unregulated hatmakers across the region.

These early hatmakers worked either as individuals at home or in small hatshops close by unless they were journeymen in the Chester trade. They needed few rooms – a loft or garret for storing wool and fur and 'bowing' or preparing it for felting, a room with a fire and copper boiler for felting, proofing, dyeing and drying and a shop where the hats were finished, stored and sold. John Hind of Liverpool who died in 1623 and John Poole of Chester in 1637 both had 'shops' containing hats, bands and sundries. Poole had no fewer than thirty-eight dozen hats and fifty-eight dozen bands and the shop was furnished with a fine glass and a glass, brushes, a hanging candlestick, shelves, weights, scissors, presses, a 'hy stoole' and a 'loe stoole'. The interior of a retail hatter's shop was to remain very much like this for the next three hundred years. In addition to supplying customers in their own shops the hatters also supplied haberdashers, mercers and drapers in the north-west and north Wales. By the end of the seventeenth century they were also exporting through Chester (Bagley 1971: 139–40). Like their neighbours, the weavers, some of the hatters also engaged in husbandry, even in Chester, since theirs was a seasonal trade. Inside Chester the trade was tightly regulated but in the country outside it is possible that both apprenticeship and male monopoly of the trade might have been ignored (J. H. Smith 1980).

Government: Politics, Religion and Society

Lancashire and Cheshire were governed throughout this period as were other English counties. In each there was a triple framework – of civil control by

Plate 1.5 The Consistory Court of the Diocese of Chester, Chester Cathedral. The church courts were an instrument of social control, but also dealt with probate, and administered the fabric and estates of the diocese. The arrangements and furniture are those of 1636 (Pevsner and Hubbard 1971: 145).

the Justices of the Peace, of military control by the lord-lieutenant and his deputies, and of ecclesiastical government by the diocese of Chester, which embraced both. At local level the parish and township had their own officers – the churchwardens and constables, the surveyors of the highways, and after the passing of the Poor Law the overseers of the poor.

That some justices sat for both counties, and that the Earl of Derby was usually lord-lieutenant of both, did not bind their civil government together. The sheriff's role in each county was a vital but formal one in their legal administration, except when parliamentary elections were held, and until the ship money collections of the 1630s made sheriffs controversial figures. The manorial courts noted above also participated in local government. The forests of the Peak in Derbyshire and of Macclesfield (to the late seventeenth century) and Delamere (to 1812), in Cheshire, were subject to forest law (*VCH. Derbyshire*, II: 174; *VCH. Cheshire*, II: 178, 184). The routine connection between the privy council at the centre of government in London and the local governors was through the twice-yearly visits of the assize judges. As with many northern and western counties of England there were layers of authority intermediate between the Justices of the Peace of each county and the centre. Both counties were palatinates, which controlled the assize courts, and which provided a locally useful but anachronistic duplication of civil courts. For Lancashire the Duchy of Lancaster had limited but important functions as it appointed justices and ran parliamentary elections (Jones 1967: 370–1, 375; 1979: 192, 193; *VCH. Cheshire*, II: 40; PRO, *Lists & Indexes*, XL, 1914; Quintrell 1981; 1983).

In both counties quarter sessions were spread widely, but in Cheshire they never sat in the far north-east, where one wonders whether the Earl of Derby's influence made Macclesfield an unsuitable sessions town. Chester, Knutsford, Middlewich, Nantwich and Northwich were the usual quarter sessions towns, though the four meetings a year moved irregularly between them. In Lancashire quarter sessions met at Lancaster for Lonsdale hundred, at Preston for Amounderness and Blackburn hundreds and by turn at Wigan and Ormskirk for West Derby and Leyland, while for Salford hundred they were held in Manchester (see Figure 1.2); as in Cheshire, justices attended usually only sessions for their hundred. From at least 1578 onwards Lancashire's justices met (with the sheriff and assize judges) twice a year, which may have centralized some decision-making, in contrast with Cheshire, where inconsistent attendance at sessions destroyed policy-making, but where justices met monthly in their hundreds. It was one thing for magistrates such as Sir Richard Grosvenor to exhort the yeomen and minor gentlemen of the grand jury to perform their communal obligations, but another thing to find reliable men to serve as head constables, or to cope with the annual change-over of constables, the first line of authority (Cust and Lake 1981). Quintrell concluded that the enforcement of legislation was rarely checked at parish and township level in Lancashire. At county level Lancashire was no quicker than Cheshire in setting up a house of correction required under the Poor Law of 1576. One was built at Wigan for West Derby hundred in 1608 but was abandoned within ten years and that at Preston was not built until 1619. And Lancashire seems to have been slower than Cheshire in responding to the Book of Orders in and after 1631. Nevertheless the county rating system, which became more elaborate and flexible after the 1590s, seems to have worked well. The Cheshire county tax, called the mize, coped with most demands, including ship money, although at the very end of our period, and after the exceptional events of the 1640s and 1650s, there were complaints that taxation was out of line with land values (*VCH. Cheshire*, II: 50–4; Quintrell 1981: 7, 9, 24–6, 40–1).

The routine work of justices covered, among other things, licensing alehouses, crime, poor relief, wage regulation, and road and bridge maintenance; their discretionary powers were wide-ranging (eg P. Williams 1979). These responsibilities made their support of the tenor of central government policy vital, but the religious views of some men were unacceptable to London, though personal misbehaviour seems to have been tolerated. Thus

Sir Hugh Calveley was even put in the pillory in 1556 for violent feuding, a remarkable punishment for a gentleman, but he continued as a justice. In Cheshire rather more than in Lancashire the stable, elite group of gentry families providing justices was free from the influence of the Stanleys. In both counties Members of Parliament (MPs) were chosen from the same group of families. In the early part of the period in Lancashire, connections with the Stanley family dominated elections, while Cheshire favoured as MPs men linked to the central government. Such influences seem to have been more important than religious views in securing office: at the 1589 election in both counties recusants emerged as Members of Parliament, with one determined Protestant in Cheshire. There were usually men at least suspected of recusant sympathies on the Elizabethan Benches of both counties; such sympathies disappeared in Cheshire, but in Lancashire as late as 1639 justices who had become recusants some years earlier were dismissed (Wilkinson 1983: 53; P. J. Turner 1974: 99; *VCH. Cheshire*, II: 105–6; Hasler 1981, I: 186).

The secular law of the justices was only one arm in the attack on Roman Catholicism; alongside lay the Church of England and its courts. The new (founded 1541), impoverished, diocese of Chester extended beyond the region (Figure 1.5), but was centred in the cathedral city at its south-west extremity. Each of these facts weakening the established church was compounded by inept administration and, certainly under Bishop Chadderton, a lack of inclination to promote conformity (*VCH. Cheshire*, III). Yet Cheshire recusants were imprisoned in Chester castle, especially in the 1580s. In the 1590s the 300 or so recusants from all social strata, concentrated on the Wirral and in the south-west of the county, were only a minor threat compared with those in Lancashire, and in the next century recusancy was not a problem in Cheshire (Wark 1971: 134–7; Higgins 1976: 42). Cardinal William Allen, who led the missionary campaign against England from Douai in 1568, had first nurtured the old faith in the 1560s in the prosperous lowland west of Lancashire, and in the Ribble valley, where socially contented and self-contained communities were safely isolated (Bossy 1975: 92–4). By 1604 28 per cent of the communicant population of Prescot parish were recusant, and by 1642 221 out of 774 gentry families adhered to Rome (Haigh 1977: 51; Blackwood* 1978: 28). Largely absent from the pre-Armada plots against Elizabeth, Lancashire's Catholics were, at the end of her reign, in organized local revolt against Protestant landowners, government officials and ecclesiastics enforcing a variety of anti-Catholic laws (Leatherbarrow 1947: 146; Haigh 1975: 328–9). However, one of the supposed revolts, at Childwall in 1600, has been dismissed as the traditional behavioural response of the crowd, rather than as planned resistance or rebellion (Dottie 1983).

The Protestant state's church was threatened from its own flank by those who wished for more radical changes in liturgy than the 1559 church settlement had provided. In Chester diocese the bishops, with some support from London, were less concerned by Protestant Nonconformity than by

Figure 1.5 A–D: Evolution of the Diocese of Chester, from 1541. A: Diocese of Chester 1541–1847. (For full caption see p. 60.)

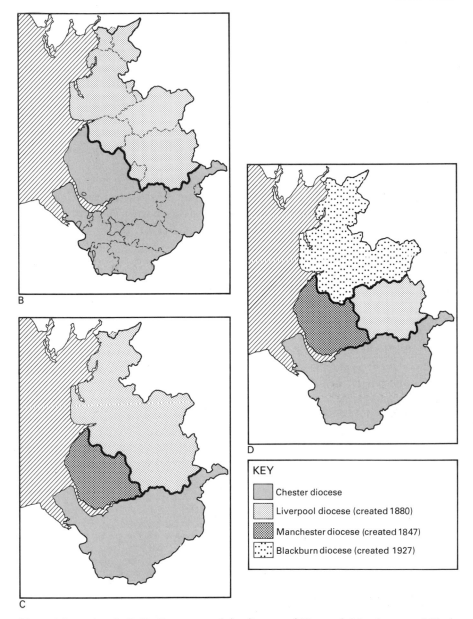

Figure 1.5 continued   B–D: Emergence of the dioceses of Liverpool, Manchester and Blackburn.

recusancy until 1633. Although clergy who omitted the sign of the cross at baptism, or who refused to wear a surplice were reported for these breaches, zealous Protestant preachers were employed in an attempt to convert Catholics to the reformed church, especially in Lancashire. At the same time, in the east of the diocese, and especially in south-east Lancashire and north-east Cheshire, Church of England clergy of predominantly Calvinist persuasion, with a leavening who refused to conform fully to the prescribed liturgy, became established. Alongside these, laymen of all ranks followed the more radical doctrines, spread perhaps by trade connections with London. Clerical and lay exemplars are the Rev Christopher Harvey, appointed to the popish Cheshire parish of Bunbury by the Puritan Haberdashers' Company of London, and the Puritan gentleman John Bruen, accused of iconoclasm over the smashed window image of St Andrew in his parish church of Tarvin, while the vicar of Rochdale, who did

> not refuse to wear the surplice but refers himself to unity seeking the quiet of the Church [ie congregation],

provides an example of clerical and lay alliance against that symbolically unreformed garment (R. C. Richardson 1972: 75, 123, 128).

In the light of evidence of organizational and financial deficiencies in the church, which weakened the work of individual ministers, of the personal failings of a few of them, and a question mark as to the appropriateness of the sermon as an evangelical weapon, the effectiveness of these preaching ministers is open to doubt (Haigh 1977). The argument can be extended into Stuart times. Certainly in Lancashire there is little evidence that Catholics were converted, while some conservative souls prepared to accept the compromises of 1559 were put off by Nonconformity. On the other hand, the preaching

---

Figure 1.5 Evolution of the Diocese of Chester, from 1541. The diocese as formed in 1541 was divided into a northern archdeaconry, of Richmond, and, to the south of that, the archdeaconry of Chester. A number of parts of this diocese are not mapped: in 1836 the ancient* Yorkshire deaneries of Boroughbridge, Catterick, Richmond and the Yorkshire parishes of the ancient deanery of Lonsdale were transferred to the Diocese of Ripon, and Mitton joined it in 1847; also in that year, and in 1849, the deanery of Bangor was given to the Welsh diocese of St Asaph; next, in 1856, the northern parts of the ancient deaneries of Kendal and Lonsdale, plus the ancient Lakeland deaneries of Copeland and Furness were joined to the Diocese of Carlisle. Population growth in the areas mapped in Figure 1.5 demanded new dioceses: first, in 1847, the southern parts of the ancient deaneries of Kendal and Lonsdale, and the ancient deaneries of Amounderness, Blackburn, Leyland and Manchester, plus the parish of Leigh, became the Diocese of Manchester. Then, in 1880, the diocese of Liverpool was created. Finally, in 1927, the diocese of Manchester was reduced to a manageable size slightly larger than the ancient deanery of Manchester with the creation of the diocese of Blackburn. (Sources: Redrawn from parish boundaries in D. Sylvester and G. Nulty 1958, R. S. France 1938 and Blackburn 1928; based on *VCH. Lancs.*, II: 100–1 and *VCH. Cheshire*, II, and F. I. Dunn 1987.)

* Different in area from modern deaneries of the same name.

exercises which, though proscribed elsewhere, were permitted in the diocese to improve clerical standards, probably served to promote radical clerics; they were usually held in predominantly Puritan areas into the 1630s and 1640s (R. C. Richardson 1972: 66–8).

Although some of them sympathized with the Puritans, and harried alehouses on occasion, Cheshire magistrates were notably less punitive over illegitimacy; there was not the same alliance between Puritan divines and justices to promote godly behaviour as existed in parts of Lancashire. There in 1616 one of the assize judges was swayed into approving a ban on ungodly behaviour such as Sunday sports. But he had been snared by the Puritan faction of the Lancashire JPs, and when James I came on progress through the county the following year he agreed to a new Book of Sports which endorsed many of the activities which the Puritans wanted banned: maypoles, bear or bull baiting, shooting, and dancing and other delights of the ungodly, even on the sabbath. Charles I re-issued this in 1632. It is difficult to take the measure of Puritan success in enforcing godly living. Between 1646 and 1658, in a favourable climate of Presbyterian and saintly rule, magistrates were much more active in prosecuting alehouses than they were under Charles I, or indeed than they were to be in the 1660s (Wrightson 1980: 34). It is tempting to conclude that the difference in performance reflects the frustration of the Puritans before the destruction of Charles I's monarchy in the civil war.

The struggle between the old, Catholic, communal society, and that based on household and church which the Puritans sought, was not only to do with liturgy, alehouses or Sunday sports. The Puritans associated superstition with popery, and reforming ministers, though not without some backward glances, attacked religious images along with the ancient array of ghosts, boggarts and fairies, and omens. They were, however, slow to give up their assent to the popular belief in witches, though it would seem to run counter to their view that God acted directly on human lives through general and special providences. In Cheshire only eleven persons were hanged for witchcraft between 1580 and 1709 but Lancashire, described by Thomas Fuller in the seventeenth century as 'the cockpit of conscience, wherein constant combats between religion and superstition', took place, gained a different reputation (Sharpe 1984: 61; R. C. Richardson 1972: 156). In 1612 the case of the Pendle Forest witches ended with the hanging of eleven-year-old Alison Device and her brother James, and eight more out of twenty accused people. The events which ended so tragically went back over fifteen years and were rooted in land disputes, family feuds, ungranted requests and unexplained misfortunes. Unusually a woman of substance and children were charged alongside the poor old women who were the normal focus of community anxiety or guilt (Seth 1967: 73, 83). Twenty-one years later seventeen witches were pardoned after the Bishop of Chester found that the story had been invented by a boy to save himself a whipping (K. Thomas 1971: 645).

The monarchy's financial extortions of the 1620s and 1630s were paid with grumbling in Lancashire and Cheshire. All the deputy-lieutenants' work can be regarded as further forms of taxation, to be set alongside other exactions. They mustered the horse and foot soldiers of the county militias, but they could hide most of their shortcomings from the privy council in London, though each county accumulated valuable magazines of weapons and ammunition. The lieutenancies also raised troops for continental wars and for service in Ireland, a difficult and expensive task, the success of which could be measured by London as the number of men who turned up at the rendezvous (D. P. Carter 1973). Ship money was initially collected without difficulty, but in the closing years of the 1630s both counties were reluctant to pay. Church affairs were transformed in the 1630s by the adoption at court and by the church authorities of arminian theology, with its emphasis on a priestly liturgy at the expense of lay influence. The godly Samuel Clarke, incumbent at Shotwick, where the church still has the seventeenth-century altar rails characteristic of arminian worship, was driven from his parish *c.*1630 (Richards 1947: 302; cf. R. C. Richardson 1972: 32). Four Puritan Cheshire clergymen were forced abroad by the arminian establishment of the Church of England, while many of the gentry were alienated from the church, though as late as 1640 they continued to prefer episcopacy to Presbyterianism (Morrill 1973: 150–5). From being radical members of a Calvinist establishment in the church, lay and clerical Puritans found themselves outside the tolerance, if not the theology, of Bishop Bridgeman of Chester and Archbishop Neile at York (Quintrell 1983: 71–2).

Historians of the civil war between king and Parliament which broke out in 1642 have found no clear correlation between allegiance in the war and opposition to the money-raising of Charles I's personal rule. Some religious radicals of the period, especially in Cheshire where egalitarian sentiment over landownership was linked with the radical preaching of Samuel Eaton, fought against the crown, but not all those opposed to Laud and his arminian church could turn against their monarch in 1642. After discussing hatred of the Earl of Derby (proposed by a contemporary apologist – Clarendon – as a cause of division), agrarian oppression by landlords, and local quarrels between individuals, a modern scholar has concluded that among the Lancashire gentry religion was the main division between the two sides in the civil war (Blackwood 1983: 117–20). For those who were Catholic an Anglican king who fined them for recusancy was a lesser evil than a Puritan Parliament. The most zealous parliamentarians were also ardent Puritans and clearly regarded the war as one against popery. However, each side included apparently middle-of-the-road anglicans. Only a minority of the gentry took part in the war, for many gentry (and plebeians) avoided joining either party. Nevertheless, 171 gentry supported the king in the first and second civil wars, more than the ninety-one who backed Parliament; another twenty-four changed sides. Of the loyalties of the merchants (except those who stood for the king in Chester), artisans, yeomen and the lower orders throughout the region we know little that is reliable. In Cheshire, in 1642–3, 139 gentry families fought for Parliament, but only 117 supported the king. There appears to be an economic difference: parliamentarians on the whole were drawn from the lesser landowners, the royalists from the county elite, but a few disgruntled religious radicals among the elite supported Parliament (Wanklyn 1976: 515, 517). (Note that Blackwood and Wanklyn defined civil war allegiance in different ways. The figures used are from Morrill 1979: 79.)

Much of the fighting in our strategically important region in the war was of little more than local significance. What such battles achieved by March and April 1643 was to ensure that, outside forces aside, both counties were controlled for Parliament, with the exception of a few scattered garrisons. Chester was astride a key route to north Wales and Ireland; it and Liverpool would permit seaborne reinforcement. Such reasoning might explain why Liverpool changed hands in the war, but not why Chester declared for the king, and why the civilian population supported the siege from November 1644 to February 1645/6. In the event, the royalists' success in holding Chester was of little strategic importance, except to hold one of a number of springboard garrisons from which operations could be mounted elsewhere in the north, for only insignificant reinforcements came from Ireland. The effect of the siege on the county, however, was probably to diminish moderate gentry opinion in Parliament's local councils, as the royalist troops in the city were a constant reminder of the need for a military solution to the war. The radical Sir William Brereton's position was thus enhanced, though it was his victories at Middlewich (1643) and Nantwich (1644) which established his leadership (Dore 1966; 1987). The west coast road to and from Scotland through both counties brought invading Scottish armies into Lancashire in 1648, to be defeated, with local help, by Cromwell's army at Preston and Warrington. Again in 1651 the Scots passed through the region on their way to defeat at Worcester (Woolrych 1961: ch. 8; Dore 1966: 76).

The counties played a broader role in the war, however, by their provision of troops to the king's army. Between September 1642 and April 1643 Lancashire sent eight foot regiments to the royal army, and two more when Rupert came into the county in May 1644; Cheshire too raised a number of regiments for the king's army in 1642 (Hutton 1980: 51–3, 55, 59; Dore 1966: 14). The extent to which the counties, part of what Parliament saw as the royalist north of England, provided officers and men for the king's army elsewhere in England should not be forgotten (Newman 1979). The removal of royalist troops from Lancashire was a major factor in Parliament's domination of the county after April 1643 (Hutton 1980: 60). For Parliament, Cheshire troops were a significant part of the forces who conquered Scotland and Ireland in the early 1650s (Dore 1966: 76).

Sir George Booth's rising in 1659 was one of the events which dealt the final blow to republicanism, and to its associated religious radicalism, and helped to bring about the Restoration of Charles II in 1660. The years from 1651 had seen many twists and turns in the attempts to establish a new government in England, Scotland and Ireland. Historians are turning with increasing interest to the problems of the 1650s. Perhaps in Cheshire there is some evidence for a rise in democracy at village level (Morrill 1974: 331). If that was so, however, there is little to suggest that the Restoration did other than try to return politics, government and the Church back to its pre-war state, with what degree of success we shall see in Chapter 2.

Such a bare chronology can do little justice to the details of nine years of warfare, and even less to the costs of war measured in family livelihoods interrupted by war service, men killed, houses burned (especially in the siege of Chester), crops stolen or damaged by soldiers – of whom Hamilton's Scots in 1648 were probably the worst – and animals, especially horses, taken (Woolrych 1961: 173). Taxation by both sides increased; this was especially true of parliamentary taxes imposed from the centre of government in London. The defeated royalists had their estates sequestered and lost income. Nor can much of the reader's time be taken up with the impermanent changes in local government that warfare necessitated. The commission of the peace remained the basic administrative machine; committees to run the war in each county, to sequester and to control money were created by Parliament. In both counties the social standing of the families involved as Justices of the Peace or as committee-men was significantly lower than before the war, a reflection of the support for the king among the leading gentry, and, of course, their exclusion once the war was lost (Blackwood 1978: ch. III; Morrill 1974: 82–9, 224–5). Only one newly prominent family that had supported Parliament made its way in the commission of the peace after the Restoration – the Duckenfields in Cheshire (Dore 1966: 97; Blackwood 1978: 101).

Conclusion

The growth in population in the region from 1540 to 1660 was based both on the expansion of settlement and agriculture in the large and under-populated parishes as exemplified in the hill country of the east and on the Cheshire plain and on the growth of mining and bye-occupations, especially textiles. It is therefore unremarkable to find substantial population growth in Blackburn deanery, in part of which population doubled with the growth of textiles, in Manchester deanery where textiles were even more flourishing, in War-rington deanery where coal, metal-working and textiles were growing together, and in Nantwich deanery where the salt industry supplemented dairying for cheese. Most of this growth was set in rural areas which, never-theless, housed an increasingly industrial people who were to some degree beyond local manorial structures based on the land, and who provided for their children with cottages, looms and tools rather than sending them out to service. Dynasties of great merchants had emerged and yeoman/clothiers and their like were already amassing capital which could be turned to trade or land as circumstances dictated. It is tempting to see in these localities later developments of the eighteenth and nineteenth centuries in embryo, but the competitive drives and pressures that produced growth could also have over-whelmed the nascent industries. Furthermore, population growth was not confined to the textile areas. Some of the agricultural parishes of south Cheshire were also growing rapidly, and the massive expansion of numbers in Amounderness deanery poses an as yet unsolved problem. Much growth took the form of new farmsteads or the development of scattered rural sub-hamlets based on new or existing farms. Great landed estates such as those of the Cholmondeleys or the Stanleys are also a reminder that not all the wealth of the region lay in industry.

Chapter 2

1660–1780

Population

The eighteenth century saw the beginnings of a period of marked population growth in England which lasted into the twentieth century. Parts of eighteenth-century Lancashire and Cheshire played an important part in industrial change in this period, and whether that change is regarded as gradual or revolutionary in its pace, population growth was a vital component of it. Modern research suggests that the population of England had dipped below 5 million in the 1670s, and did not regain its 1660 level until the first decade of the eighteenth century. Thereafter it increased, by 36 per cent from 1660 to 1780, from just over 5 million to just under 7 million; three-quarters of that increase took place after 1740 (E. A. Wrigley and Schofield 1981: 532–4). More people lived in towns. By 1750 five provincial English conurbations had populations in excess of 20,000, and the proportion of England's population living in towns of 2,500 plus was about 23 per cent (Corfield 1982: 8). Unfortunately for our region the sources for population change in these years are fragmented and difficult; they do, however, suggest some departures from the national picture just outlined, although the basic trends are similar.

The first discrepancy is apparent by 1690, when seventeenth-century calculations of the population of Lancashire and Cheshire based on the hearth tax suggest that numbers of households had increased by between 23 and 31 per cent in Cheshire, and by between 20 and 40 per cent in (pre-1974) Lancashire (Glass and Eversley 1966: 216–19). Some credibility is given to these estimates if the 500 or so young people sailing for the Americas from Liverpool each year about 1700 include surplus people in an increasing local population (Clemens 1976: 213–14). About 1720 Bishop Gastrell's figures for families in each parish (south of the Ribble) suggest that in Lancashire the growth indicated by *c.*1690 may have been concentrated in parts of the county (Raines 1845).* Thus, by comparison with 1664, the numbers of

---

* These and subsequent percentage changes give a probably unjustified impression of precision to Gastrell's figures, which were presumably collected for him by the clergy. Our estimates of change are based on only those parishes for which figures for 1664, in Gastrell's MS, and for 1778, exist. It is not impossible that figures for the missing parishes could upset the suggested trends. For them to do so in Cheshire, there would have to have been phenomenal growth in Macclesfield deanery and in that town.

Table 2.1 Population figures 1664–1801

Source		High Peak (part)	Cheshire	Lancashire
1664	Table 1.1	3,382	94,170	141,641
1690	Glass and Eversley 1966: 218	—	121,562	237,315[a]
	× 4.75	—	114,257	190,960[a]
1750	Kay in Poor Law			
	Commissioners 1836: 303	—	131,600	297,400[a]
1801	Census			673,486[a]
1801	Census, see Table 3.2	12,852	191,751	655,075

Note: [a] Figure for the pre-1974 county, not comparable with p. 134.

households in Warrington deanery had increased by a massive 60 per cent by *c.*1720, and in Manchester deanery by only 24 per cent, and in Blackburn deanery (parish of Whalley only) by a mere 13 per cent. In Leyland deanery and in Cheshire outside the major towns of Chester and Macclesfield the number of households was at a similar level to that reached in 1664. Thus, by *c.*1720, Cheshire followed the national trend, from which it may have deviated earlier, but parts of Lancashire showed significant increase in contrast to the suggested trend.

It would be unwise to estimate the proportion of our region's people who were urban from the *c.*1720 figures for the smaller towns include rural parts of parishes. Gastrell's figures suggest that Macclesfield and Nantwich, Prescot, Warrington, and Wigan may have exceeded 2,500. Chester's population (measured by households) dropped from the 7,828 of 1664, before increasing by more than 10 per cent to about 8,700 people in 1728 (Aldridge 1986: 36). Manchester and Liverpool both grew rapidly, Manchester more than doubling its 1664 population in Gastrell's estimate to over 2,000 households or about 9,500 people (Wadsworth and Mann 1931: 509). Liverpool's growth in the early eighteenth century may have been even more rapid than Manchester's: by 1720 its population was estimated at 10,446 (Percival 1774: 57).

We can next measure population levels in 1778. In south Lancashire, between the time of Gastrell's estimates and those made in 1778, population growth was most marked in the textile deaneries of Blackburn (161 per cent) and, especially, Manchester (287 per cent).* In this south-eastern deanery growth was three times that of Warrington deanery (93 per cent), which itself had grown more than two-and-a-half times the 36 per cent projected for the whole country by Wrigley and Schofield. The growth rate for Leyland deanery was nearly twice the projected average. Between 1664 and 1778 in those northern deaneries of Lancashire not included in Bishop Gastrell's figures, growth in Amounderness was 79 per cent and in Lonsdale 32 per cent; but in Kendal there was a 12 per cent drop. In Lancashire south of the Ribble

---

* These and subsequent growth rates are calculated on a 1664 base.

67

growth from *c.*1720 to 1778 exceeded growth from 1664 to *c.* 1720, in line with, though at a much higher rate than, the trends of Wrigley and Schofield. In Cheshire, by contrast, the highest growth from *c.* 1720 to 1778 was at 57 per cent in Macclesfield deanery, closely followed at 50 per cent by Middlewich deanery, two deaneries with important industrial areas. Chester deanery (excluding the city) even showed a small decline. The growth in other deaneries ranged from 7 per cent to 24 per cent. In the whole of the county, growth averaged only 24 per cent between 1664 and 1778, but, as Wrigley and Schofield projected, growth in Cheshire was higher in the later rather than the earlier part of our period.*

The 1778 survey gives broad support to other sources of information about town population levels. The 1782 directory of Chester gives a population of 14,700 (Dyke 1949: 243). Most of the other Cheshire towns were omitted in the 1778 survey or their populations are concealed by rural elements in the parish. Nantwich seems to have declined in size, but Stockport had for the first time become a sizeable town; its population may have reached 5,000 in 1779 (S. I. Mitchell 1982: 43). A survey of 1786 is supposed to have counted 7,000 people in Macclesfield (C. S. Davies 1961: 145). Population growth in urban Lancashire was massive. Manchester and Salford were estimated at 17,101 and 2,738, respectively, in 1758. According to a contemporary, Dr Thomas Percival, increase was marked from about 1765, reaching 24,386 and 4,765 respectively in a 'census' of 1773–4. The Revd J. Aikin also thought that growth in Warrington (population about 8,000 in 1778) was faster in the early 1770s than it had been in the two previous decades. Liverpool's population was estimated at 34,004 in 1770 by another of Percival's contemporaries. Bolton town had 1,500 houses in 1778, and Bury had about 500, marking the emergence of more distinctively urban settlements in the textile districts outside Manchester. Unfortunately we have no figures for the older centres of Preston and Lancaster from the 1778 survey (Percival 1774: 54, 55; Percival 1775: 322; Aikin 1774: 438; Wadsworth and Mann 1931: 510–11; CRO, EDV/3).

A distinction between the population history of the two counties is clear by 1780. Population increase in Lancashire far outstripped the national average projected by Wrigley and Schofield. Cheshire on the other hand failed to reach the level of the national model. By the end of the period covered in this chapter, massive growth seems to have taken place in some communities though not in others: in the economically contrasting deaneries of Manchester and Amounderness growth took place in all the parishes in observation bar one, but in the whole of Cheshire the population levels of fifteen parishes declined between 1664 and 1778, and another fifteen showed no significant change.

---

* The growth rates are calculated on a 1664 base. The absence of much of Macclesfield deanery from the sources may understate growth in that area, and in the county as a whole.

Little research has been done to fill out the bare chronology of population change suggested above. By this period parish registers are more difficult to use for demographic purposes because of Dissent (Gautrey 1980; Percival 1775: 322; Aikin 1774: 438). The registers of the parishes of Wybunbury (south-east Cheshire), Warton (north Lancashire), and of the chapelries of Rossendale (central Lancashire) all show stagnation or low growth early in the period. A rise in the number of marriages, and of children per marriage, with a surplus of baptisms over burials is evident at different dates. In Rossendale it began in 1716 and accelerated again after 1765; in Wybunbury and Warton growth began *c*.1740 and accelerated towards 1780. It is worth emphasizing the persistence of scattered mortality crises, though they were less severe than those before 1660. In Rossendale they struck in 1672–6, 1683, 1700 and 1712–13, and a further ten times in the period of growth from 1716, the last as late as 1776 (Wyatt 1990; W. King 1976; Speake 1970). In the Lancashire parishes of Aughton and Radcliffe (F. Taylor 1942; Clayton 1923), and in the Cheshire parishes of Cheadle, Rostherne and Weaverham (counts by Cheshire parish register project) similar disasters are apparent, especially in the mid-1680s, the late 1720s, the early 1740s and in the 1760s, though the precise years vary from locality to locality. Epidemic disease, local famine and trade slumps could still play a significant role in the level of mortality (W. King 1976: 160).

The causes of population change in this period (according to Wrigley and Schofield) were the same as in the sixteenth and early seventeenth centuries, namely more marriages and a decrease in the age at marriage that produced more children. They discount the significance of work showing that improved diet, environment and medication reduced mortality in the eighteenth century. Levine's emphasis on the importance of lower ages of marriage in industrial communities such as existed in parts of Lancashire and Cheshire (see p. 10) remains apposite. In rural Wybunbury, Rossendale, and perhaps Warton modest population growth, and a surplus of baptisms over burials in the third quarter of the eighteenth century, suggest emigration from these areas (Wyatt 1990: 7, 10; W. King 1976: 145; Speake 1970: 64). Country people from these parishes may have moved to the larger towns, though in some areas they may have moved to work in the coal-mines, the early silk mills, and into domestic spinning and weaving. As long ago as the 1830s James Kay Shuttleworth considered that there must have been net migration into Lancashire to account for the levels of population observed by the early nineteenth century (Poor Law Commissioners 1836: 304). If Wrigley and Schofield's national population growth rate is applied to John Houghton's population estimate for 1690 (Table 2.1, p. 67), then by the time of the 1801 census Lancashire's population should have been about 407,000, that is some 265,000 below the actual level. This discrepancy could be evidence of migration into the county though, equally, it could merely indicate the inappropriateness of Wrigley and Schofield's national calculations to the specific circumstances of Lancashire. Walton (1987: 83) was dismissive of in-migration as a cause of population growth in the county. Nevertheless, to explain the number of papists in their parish, the Manchester College clergy in 1778 pointed to a numerous Irish, that is migrant, community in the town, while Irish surnames in the Liverpool directories from 1766 on suggest the presence of migrants. In the eighteenth century Cheshire magistrates were clearly used to returning Irish vagrants across the sea (CRO, EDV/3; T. Burke 1910: 27; Bennett and Dewhurst 1940: 203, 224–5).

Landowning Society

The ranks of landowning society were the same in 1780 as they had been in 1660 (see p. 12), though the term 'gentleman' was so widely used that it probably no longer indicated a member of the landowning gentry (eg Tait 1924: 120–63). As a consequence the term 'esquire' was probably more widely used by the less wealthy gentry in the last quarter of the eighteenth century than in the mid-seventeenth (Beckett 1986: 33–5; cf. Mingay 1963: 26). Although the terms 'husbandman' and 'yeoman' persist through this period, by as early as 1764 the leaseholder Robert Swindells of Offerton called himself 'farmer', a sign of the new, commercial attitudes to agriculture which were promoted in the eighteenth century (CRO, Will, pr. 1764). Wealth and status were, as before, still roughly equated: thus in 1677 the Earl of Derby's landed income was some £5,300 which would place him in the top income bracket of landowners according to Gregory King writing in 1688; in 1779, despite the 1717 division of the estate, the Derby rental was some £7,809, plus some £2,000 in casual sales (Laslett 1983: 32–3; Mingay 1963: 26; Coward 1983: 210; LRO, DDK 1806/51). In 1680 the Leycester of Tabley rental in Cheshire totalled £657, by 1779 it was £6,331 (JRUL, Tabley MSS, rental books, 1647–97; 1758–97); as baronets the Leycesters ranked in the upper group of landowners according to both King and Colquhoun. With an income of only £978 in 1761 Ralph Leycester of Toft is an example of a minor gentleman (JRUL, Leycester of Toft MSS, LT. 705). William Swindale of Torkinton, yeoman, with a net income from his estates of £24 in 1765, fits easily into the category of lesser freeholders, that is, a non-gentle stratum of society (CRO, Will, pr. 1765). Nowhere is the imprecision of income statistics greater than in relation to the very bottom of society, the labourers. On the Egerton of Tatton estate from 1756 among a regularly employed labour force working a six-day week, most men day labourers received a shilling a day, boys and women 8d. What is not clear is how this translates into a family income, nor what land a family might have. The farm servant who lived at the farm might, like those employed by Thomas Furber near Nantwich in 1767, receive five guineas a year plus board and lodging; female servants would get at most half of that rate; by 1780 men received £8 (C. S. Davies 1960: 80, 83). The great inequalities of wealth between the different ranks were presented, for example, in the expectation of Sir Thomas Aston in 1734 that his tenants would vote as he directed (*VCH. Cheshire*, II: 264). On the other hand, a squire like Nicholas Blundell had close contact with the daily lives of his tenants. At Shrovetide he ate pancakes in the homes of humbler neighbours and ended the day with a pancake supper and dance at the hall, with Henry Kerfoot, miller and one of the district's four fiddlers, providing the music. Blundell visited his tenants, drank with them at the alehouse, sometimes treated them when they were sick and prayed with them after funerals, for most, like him, were Roman Catholic. He was generally tolerant of his workpeople and servants but strict to prosecute them when theft could be proved (N. Blundell 1968–72, *passim*).

The individual families in the local hierarchy were constantly changing, for society was no less mobile than in the preceding centuries. Blackwood's prognosis for the Lancashire gentry at the Restoration was one of decline, and therefore of change in landowning society, whereas Morrill has emphasized continuity in Cheshire. Elsewhere in England historians have noted that the frequent failure of the male line was a major cause of social mobility. The accumulation by a few gentry and peers of very large landed estates was a contrasting trend; in 1660 in our region perhaps only the estates of the Earl of Derby approached this category. Richard Pares long ago drew attention to examples of fortunes from trade with the West Indies ploughed into land, a phenomenon associated with the rise of Liverpool. Lower down the social scale, national estimates of the proportion of land owned by the yeomanry peak in the late seventeenth century, but there is evidence (see pp. 78–9) of change in their regional position by 1780.

The detailed work to detect and evaluate such changes has not been done, but some preliminary trends can be gauged for the gentry and peerage from a sample study (outlined above, p. 22) of the ownership of some 156 properties held in 1660 by some 83 families. Twenty-six families remained as landowners throughout the period; in addition, heirs inherited through a female line who took the family name, as in the case of the Moretons of Little Moreton in Cheshire in 1763, so that one-third of the families lasted through to 1780. Four of these made significant additions to their estates by inheritance through female heirs, two by inheritance and by purchase of more estates, and three by purchase alone. Thus the Blackburnes of Orford in Lancashire purchased Hale in 1733, acquired Risley in 1736 and bought the manor of Warrington in 1769. The Molyneux earls of Sefton were a second major element of stability among the landowners of West Derby hundred, while the succession in 1736 of Sir Edward Stanley of Bickerstaffe, bt, sixth cousin of the tenth earl, as eleventh Earl of Derby, with many of the family estates, was probably the most dramatic example of the accident of inheritance at work (GEC, *Complete Peerage*). The Derbys over the decades had lost estates by inheritance, and even sold some; now the new earl found that most of the lands had gone to the heir general of the tenth earl, the Duke of Atholl, and only Knowsley and the old entailed Lancashire manors were left to support his transformed status (Bagley 1985: 134). A minor gentry family, the Percivals of Allerton, struggled on throughout this period, though heavily indebted. The Chorleys' Walton estate was confiscated after the 1715 rising. Not all the landowning families who lasted through to 1780 were thus as well off as they had been in 1660.

The affairs of the Leycesters of Toft and the Grosvenors of Eaton (two families outside our sample) demonstrate the complexities which lay behind the demographic and the economic survival, or failure, of landed families. Ralph Leycester's annual income from land in 1761 was £978, nett of taxes. Of this, £286 was committed to servicing the interest on debt (almost wholly resulting from the purchase of more land) and £262 to financing settlements on his sisters and seven children. This left him with £430 clear, but with his siblings and younger children provided for. The whole arrangement took care of the present needs of the family, accumulated cash for the support of younger children, and, through the settled estates, guaranteed the future descent of land within the family, and so the settled estates could not easily be sold. A problem would arise if Ralph's wife outlived him, for a dower estate of £403 a year was settled on her. Were Ralph's son to inherit while his mother was still alive, her jointure estate of £403 would cripple his income. At this point the son might be forced to pay off debts. The capital value of the unsettled land would pay off the debts (mostly incurred in its purchase), and leave a small surplus. If that surplus was re-invested in land, then Ralph's heir would have an income of just £54 a year. Of course, once his mother died, then his income would rise as her jointure estates reverted to him. Leycester's position was a dramatic example of the unpredictable potential of longevity, of the financial penalty of having to provide for two generations of children, and, in so far as Leycester had seven himself, of rearing too many children. Yet events were to prove the need for spare, younger sons, for the eldest son died without a male child, according to Ormerod (JRUL, Leycester of Toft MSS, LT 705). The marriage of Sir Thomas Grosvenor (d. 1700) to Mary Davies, which brought with it property in what were to become some of the wealthiest areas of London's west end, together with additional purchases in Cheshire, and lucrative lead royalties in north Wales, contributed to the increase in Grosvenor revenues, from £4,500 a year in 1676 to £22,000 in 1742 (GEC, *Complete Baronetage*; Baskerville 1980: 60; Mingay 1963: 56–7).

Not all were as lucky or as careful as Ralph Leycester: thirty-five families in our sample failed in the male line; their demises were scattered over the whole period. Other families sold their estates and passed into obscurity. Sometimes these agonies were prolonged: the Wolfalls of Wolfall first mortgaged land in the 1680s, yet did not finally sell until 1744. But the spendthrift Samuel 'Beau' Byrom, lord of part of Prescot, got through his estate in twenty years. Sometimes more than one cause or occasion brought about a sale, and consequent social mobility, thus when Earl Rivers' line died with him in 1736 his Cheshire manor of Shipbrook did not pass with his other Cheshire estates, but was sold to pay his debts (GEC, *Complete Peerage*). While some of the lands of these unfortunate families were added to the estates of existing families, as when Peter Shakerley received part of Lees (Cheshire) through his wife in 1748, other properties passed to, or were bought by, scions of existing landed families or even newcomers to landowning society. The younger son of a duke, and of a minor Shropshire gentleman, acquired estates in their own right (Ormerod 1882, III: 122; *VCH. Lancs.*, III: 136). A mariner and three families of merchants from Liverpool bought property in West Derby hundred, merchants from Dublin and Manchester bought estates in Northwich hundred (*VCH. Lancs.*, III: 30, 172, 352; Ormerod 1882, III: 45, 114, 120); a Chester lawyer acquired Ormskirk, while a Wavertree lawyer bought the neighbouring lordship of Litherland. Lawyers from distant Manchester and nearby Nantwich acquired estates in the east of Northwich hundred (Ormerod 1882, III: 212, 251). Some Lancashire land was held by Cheshire families, and vice versa (eg *VCH. Lancs.*, III: 352; IV: 114, 120, 139, 149), but other estates passed to absentee landlords who lived in Staffordshire, Shropshire, north Wales, Warwickshire, Leicestershire and Hertfordshire (eg Ormerod 1882, III: 22, 45, 86; *VCH. Lancs.*, IV: 109). Not surprisingly, some of these owners resold their estates to buyers based in the region (eg Ormerod 1882, III: 45).

Such acquisitions, whether by the newly landed or by long-established families like the Grosvenors, brought about social mobility. The Grosvenors were promoted up the ranks of landowning society from baronet (created 1622) to baron in 1761, at the instance of William Pitt. When the last daughter of Peter Venables, styled Baron of Kinderton though not a peer, died in 1715 his lands passed via his niece to the Vernons of Sudbury in Derbyshire, and in 1762, no doubt for political purposes as well, George Venables-Vernon joined the peers as Lord Vernon, Baron of Kinderton (GEC, *Complete Peerage*). The merchants and lawyers who purchased landed estates became esquires as they moved into the landowning hierarchy, and some existing families moved up the social scale: the Molyneuxs became earls of Sefton, though still in the Irish peerage, in 1771 (GEC, *Complete Peerage*). New baronetcies were created for the Duckinfield of Dukinfield (1665), Cotton of Combermere (1677), Clayton of Adlington (1774) and Horton of Chadderton (1764) families (GEC, *Complete Baronetage*).

The social and intellectual life of landowning society, like its make-up, was both constant and changing. Sir Peter Leycester of Tabley published a history of his own county in 1673, and collected more material besides. His university and legal education in the 1620s and 1630s helped to produce a widely read man well capable of documenting the legal charges he gave to grand juries at quarter sessions (Leycester 1953). A century later Dorning Rasbotham, the chairman of Manchester quarter sessions, was also an eminent county historian (*DNB*). Like Leycester, Rasbotham had other interests, but whereas Leycester wrote epilogues for some of Shakespeare's plays performed in his own house, Rasbotham wrote his own, commercially successful, plays for Manchester theatres. The newly confident and expanding professional classes also figure in county history. While Drs Edward Williamson and William Cowper were Chester physicians and younger sons of minor Cheshire gentry families who collected historical material, Dr Gower, who proposed in 1771 to write a history of Cheshire, was a doctor of medicine and a clergyman, but not a landowner (Ormerod 1882, II: 751–2; *DNB*). Landowners continued to be men of science: Lord Grosvenor was a Fellow of the Royal Society (FRS), and a century earlier Richard Legh of Lyme had brought home to Cheshire a barometer, 'a device to know the weather by' (Newton 1917: 282).

But there were intellectual innovations: the grand tour of Europe became fashionable for the sons of the more wealthy: the fifth Duke of Bridgewater found it difficult to manage abroad on his allowance of £2,000 a year. His visit may have inspired his canal building; it certainly taught him an interest in painting (Malet 1961: 24–35). The tenth Earl of Derby's patronage sent a young artist to Italy, and was repaid in pictures for his internal decor as Knowsley was further altered and rebuilt. Housebuilding remained a form of ostentation: expensive work was almost always going on at Lyme, where the innovative work of Leoni *c.*1720 is now most praised by architectural historians (Pevsner and Hubbard 1971: 26, 260). Other than Lyme, few houses of this period in either Lancashire or Cheshire are of great remark; in north-east Lancashire building more often took the form of updating the decoration of existing houses, until late in the century. The south portico, among all the rebuilding at Knowsley in the 1720s and 1730s, was of national significance in architectural history, and so too, though half a century later, was Heaton Park near Manchester (Pearson 1985: 118; Pevsner 1979a: 23). The most elaborate ostentation was Mow-cop, a castellated folly and a very early piece of architectural medievalism, built by the Wilbrahams of Rode in 1754, soon after they finished their new family house. The Georgian houses (eg Ramsdell Hall, Plate 2.1) that are scattered over Cheshire indicate a measure of prosperity among the greater landowners (Pevsner and Hubbard 1971: 28). Equally elaborate was the internal decoration of these mansions: the stucco at Townley Hall in 1725 marked new taste (Pevsner 1979b: 25). Outside the house carefully attended gardens took in new plants

---

Plate 2.1 Georgian brick: Ramsdell Hall, Cheshire.

and trees, and new patterns of colour; at one time the lake adjoining Lyme house was to be graced with a statue. Peter Legh of Lyme baulked at paying his gardener £80 a year, but when he died in 1762 Admiral Hore of Appleton near Warrington (another instance of the penetration of the new professionals into landed society, who built his house on 'the pattern of a ship') valued his gardener enough to grant him a £20 annuity (Newton 1917: 282, 283, 314, 375; Rylands 1897: 130, 131). Nicholas Blundell's diary is full of references to the planning and execution of work in the garden, and perceptive comments on the flowers and fruit produced. Plate and jewels and clothes of course remained a constant sign of wealth in the probate records of this period as before. Coaches appeared more often and were not only expensive to buy, but also required six or so horses to pull them and incurred heavy costs for new teams and for ostlers' services on a journey. The Leghs of Lyme took theirs to London in the 1660s, Sir Thomas Grosvenor bequeathed his to his wife in 1701, while four years later Dame Mary Calveley's coach was to be draped in mourning at her funeral; in the mid-eighteenth century, however, Admiral Hore preferred to dash around in a post chaise. Towards the end of our period even a Macclesfield industrialist owned a private carriage, a chariot (Newton 1917: 229; Rylands 1897: 59, 65, 132; Chaloner 1952: 81).

More mundane social behaviour is revealed in diaries and letters. Nicholas Blundell's religion excluded him from politics and administration above the parish vestry, but his dining room was well used by a succession of relatives and neighbours, and members of the professions, Catholic and Anglican clergy, physicians and lawyers; Blundell and his family returned visits just as frequently. He drank and bowled (and bet) with the same mixture of society, and might, less frequently, join the Earl of Derby or Lord Molyneux at Ormskirk races (N. Blundell 1968–1972, *passim*, esp. 1972: 148–174). Richard Legh, with Lord Derby, was apparently instrumental in formalizing Newton races around 1680. His son, Peter, was a regular correspondent with his friend Sir Francis Leycester of Tabley and drinking companion of other gentlemen of Jacobite persuasion (Newton 1917: 304, 367–77).

Some of the new intellectual ideas were spread by schoolmasters, whose occupation had become one of the respectable professions. For much of England the Restoration brought an end to educational expansion, but decline was less marked in the north-west. Indeed, in Cheshire eight new grammar schools were founded between 1660 and 1700 as well as twenty-three other schools; in Lancashire at least forty-eight, principally elementary schools, were founded or substantially re-endowed between 1660 and about 1720 (Hodson 1978: 52; Raines 1845, *passim*). Fifteen of these schools had been founded by community subscription before 1725 and one, Hale, out of the township's stock, though at least three were subsequently endowed by wealthier patrons. In Cheshire the last grammar school foundation was that at Halton in about 1725 and in Lancashire Bilsborough was endowed in 1718, and Ormskirk re-endowed in 1721. If children lived at a distance from the parish school, dame schools, like that at Marsden in 1720 where a poor woman taught some small children, or itinerant teachers had to suffice. Dissenting children wherever possible attended schools like Priestley's or Samuel Eaton's at Congleton (where Robert Clive was a pupil) while the children of wealthy Catholic families such as Squire Blundell's were sent abroad where they could be secure in the faith (N. Blundell 1968: 72, 173). In the 1660s and 1670s the two counties had sent more students to university than the English county average. By 1778 only 5 per cent of children in Cheshire were attending school (the towns recorded particularly low attendances). For most children school was a very brief episode in their lives; at Wrenbury free pupils were allowed only two years. In 1778 only half of Cheshire's grammar schools were teaching Classics. Poor rural schooling forced many Cheshire boys to attend Manchester Grammar School where the tradition still flourished (Hodson 1978: 52, 57). Many grammar schools began to charge fees, like the private schools which prepared pupils for Oxford or Cambridge. There was some improvement, but the stimuli to the new literature, science and technology courses which some thirteen schools were offering by the end of this period came mainly from the towns (see pp. 113–14).

Farming was still more important than schooling for yeomen, who owned horses rather than coaches: in other words the scale of their wealth remained as proportionately small in this period as in the sixteenth and early seventeenth centuries when compared to that of the gentry. Yet yeomen too spent on plate, albeit only a few spoons, were anxious to maintain the past of their families by bequeathing furniture heirlooms or heraldic rings and were proud of such status symbols as their increasingly expensive and complex clocks: Thomas Oldham had an eight-day clock when he died in 1755 (Rylands 1897: 29, 31, 34, 46; CRO, Thomas Oldham of Offerton, pr. 1755, Robert Dodge of Offerton, pr. 1765). Valuations of houses are rarely given but the inventory of Isaac Gee, a flax man, of Werneth in 1708 valued his cottage at £6 out of a total personal estate of £36 2s. 3d. His mare was worth £5 10s., his cow £3 15s., his pair of looms £3; apparently his cottage was a humble affair (CRO, Isaac Gee of Werneth, pr. 1708). New housing may have been built as much out of necessity as from a desire to impress. But in Trawden 'good stone houses' were clearly built by yeomen whose inventories totalled more than the average for the community (Pearson 1985: 109; CRO, William Oldham of Brinnington, pr. 1734, inv. total £581). Even where houses were not new, increasing comfort was both created and reflected by the more specialist use of rooms, so that the Brinnington yeoman John Shuttleworth had a 'dining room' listed in his inventory of 1689 (CRO; cf. Thirsk 1985, II: 655). New building at yeoman level did not take place everywhere: in north-east Lancashire there was little new built in the middle quarters of the eighteenth century, and in south Lonsdale the evidence is for yeomen rebuilding their houses in the latter half of the seventeenth century rather than in the 1700s (Pearson 1985: 118–25; M. E. Garnett 1988). The eighteenth century, with a peak in the 1770s, was a period of marked building activity of all types in Cheshire, which no doubt included yeomen's houses; the relatively new style of building with brick extended down to small houses in this century. Nevertheless, such houses might be of a one-cell design, with only one hearth, perhaps for a husbandman or rural artisan rather than for a yeoman (Machin 1977: 36; McCaig 1977: 84, 86, 100).

Agriculture

Tenurial relations changed little in the first hundred years or so covered by this chapter (see pp. 26–27). Thus in northern and eastern Lancashire, customary and copyhold estates which were tantamount to freehold continued; leases on the Lancashire plain differed little in effect, and also continued to be granted after 1780 (Beckett 1986: 185). In Cheshire leases for three lives, into which new lives were inserted on payment of a fine, had provided the same sort of long-term security for tenants. Even under these conditions, holdings did not always stay in the same family. In Aston-by-Budworth *c.* 1750 only four out of forty-two three-life leaseholders had inherited from people who were tenants before 1700, although one of the four had descended by inheritance since 1572 (Foster 1992). Many of the holdings worked under these tenancies were small: on the Lancashire plain and in Cheshire they varied between ten and fifty acres. In a distinct, and according to one authority misleadingly untypical, minority of townships, fields were still cultivated in common, as at Warton in north Lancashire, or at least partly in common with some enclosed parcels among the strips, as at Witton in the centre of Cheshire (Thirsk 1985, I: 59, 60, 149; C. S. Davies 1960: 55–7; M. E. Turner 1980: 35–6). Some common field agriculture may have persisted into the nineteenth century, but around the middle of the eighteenth century in Cheshire the old tenures, and any boon services, rents in kind and heriots which were due, began to be replaced, and rack rents, that is annual tenancies determined by twelve months' notice on either side, were adopted; when tenancies were completed the number of farms could be reduced, so that farm sizes became larger. As a consequence, some families may have left the land, or become labourers. On the central Cheshire manor of Nether Tabley in 1757 there were twelve 'old rents', that is leases for three lives, by 1777 only seven, and to continue what was essentially a slow-moving story, by 1796 only two old rents were collected. A calendar of all such leases in being was made in 1772, when the oldest Nether Tabley one was dated 1729; its terms were long out of kilter with the rising Cheshire rents of the late eighteenth century. Apparently no more were granted on the estate after the existing ones expired. Similar changes of tenancy took place in the north-east near Hyde between 1742 and 1768, were apparent at Dutton, in the west of the county, by 1764, and began on the Dorfold Hall estate in the south-east in 1779. Engrossing of holdings was apparent at Nether Tabley; a similar reduction in the number of holdings was apparent at Dutton, and on some of the Macclesfield estates of the Earl of Derby in 1774. And there were similar changes among free-holders: at Crowley in 1690 there had been fifteen owner-occupiers of farms, but by *c.* 1750 this number had fallen to only one (JRUL, Tabley MSS, rental book 1756–97; C. S. Davies 1960: 21, 31, 33, 39; Foster 1992).

Another cause of a reduction in the number of holdings may have been enclosure of the waste, which was such a vital adjunct to the small acreages worked (Thirsk 1985, I: 60, 149). Parliamentary enclosure had minimal impact in this period, though in Lancashire beginning in 1677 and in Cheshire from 1765, there were some such enclosures. No common-field arable was enclosed in this way, but some waste was thereby reorganized (Tate 1978: 78, 148). However, enclosure also took place by less formal means, though there was a ready recognition by such poor-rate payers as Viscount Cholmondeley, after an enclosure at Little Budworth (Cheshire) that wastes helped the poor and kept the rates down. On the higher ground of east Cheshire and Lancashire land was brought in from the waste in small parcels, for example in Macclesfield forest after the Restoration there was a spurt, followed by no enclosure between 1685 and 1714 whereafter enclosure began again, increasing in frequency after 1750. Enclosure around Maccles-field was often for industrial rather than agricultural purposes (C. S. Davies 1960: 8, 18, 70–1). In Cheshire and south Lancashire the peat mosses and meres were prime targets for improvement, and the ready availability of marl with which to improve the moss soil was a further attraction; work on these sites was common after 1750 (Thirsk 1985, I: 64–5; C. S. Davies 1960: 73).

Dressing newly enclosed soil might show immediate improvement, but marl on clay land soon lost its effect; some overmarled Lancashire ground was re-dressed with lime. Devoid of limestone, farmers in central Cheshire and the Lancashire plain could improve their grass that way only with high transport costs. Cheshire fields in the east where the rock outcropped were limed, and as the River Weaver Navigation made waterborne transport of limestone cheaper, so its use became more common in mid-Cheshire. But because the ground was often poorly drained, lime was not everywhere a success (Thirsk 1985, I: 64–5; C. S. Davies 1960: 113, 114). Nightsoil from the little market town of Knutsford was purchased by the Tatton estate (C. S. Davies 1960: 117).

The agriculture carried on across the region was characterized by locally consumed arable and an emphasis on dairying (Cheshire and parts of south Lancashire) or stock rearing (Lancashire plain and Pennines); there was surprisingly little sheep farming, especially given the importance of wool textiles in eastern Lancashire. The acreage of hemp and flax contracted to north-east Cheshire and to north Lancashire. Barley, oats, wheat, peas, rye and vetches were all grown, but the growing urban centres relied on corn dealers supplied with grain from the south-east, a tendency exacerbated in any sort of poor local harvest; nevertheless, in the last decade of this period supply was sufficient for grain prices in Preston to drop. A bad hay harvest put the animal food supplies at risk, while the dependence on cattle for either stock or dairy made the region vulnerable to cattle plagues. In Cheshire the grazing was good enough to make even clover relatively unattractive, for it appears in few probate inventories. Innovation in dairying and grassland management was, as in the rest of the country, minimal. In both counties crop innovation too was limited: nevertheless, by 1680 Wigan had a specialized potato market following the introduction of that vegetable to England as a field or cottage crop in west Lancashire in the mid-seventeenth century. It was grown in both counties, but because it attracted the poor was disapproved of by some landlords who allowed tenants to grow for their own table only. Herds were small according to inventories: for Lancashire Hey has calculated that the median number of cows per holding dropped from nine in the second half of the seventeenth century to seven in the first half of the next century; in Cheshire it fell from twenty-two to sixteen, though farms may have concentrated on the dairy rather than stock rearing. In Cheshire, and especially in the south, cheese was pre-eminent: overall five out of six inventories showed involvement in cheese (Thirsk 1985, I: 59–64, 151–3; II: 508; Mingay 1989: 159, 348).

Initially cheese went overland to London, or perhaps down the Trent and by sea, or by sea from Chester and Liverpool to London or Dublin. Imagine boats carrying between 189 and 330 tons of cheese, the range of cargoes from Chester and Liverpool in 1722! Cheese was attractive to provision agents as well as for the home table. Improved transport up the Weaver helped make the price more competitive. Contemporaries valued Cheshire cheese over its main competitor, from Suffolk, to the extent of a 60 or 70 per cent price premium; towards 1780 Cheddar and Stilton cheeses commanded higher prices than Cheshire. London factors who tried to beat prices down, as well as men in the local specialist markets of Frodsham and Warrington, could be bypassed by the farmer who marketed his own cheese directly to other provincial centres, or even to London. Nevertheless, difficult price data show that cheese prices had increased in 1780 by perhaps a quarter on mid-century levels (Thirsk 1985, II: 33, 467, 486–8; Mingay 1989: 114, 116, 253). The concentration on cheese let competing dairy interests into the local market, with Welsh and Irish butter consumed at least in the towns by 1780 (Mingay 1989: 209, 250, 338).

There was a clear contemporary understanding of the limits to such forms of improvement as the use of marl, but, equally, there is evidence of an obvious determination to invest in farming techniques. Overall, to the success of such measures must be added the skills of Lancashire and Cheshire men in marketing their foodstuffs and animals, the price premium that some products came to enjoy, and the generally more favourable commodity price structure for pastoral farmers. The Irish cattle Acts cut out one source of competition for stock breeders and rearers between the 1680s and 1759. After 1750 the demand for foodstuffs in the newly urbanizing north continued to provide support for farming (Thirsk 1985, II: 355, 508).

There were, however, problems for tenants and landowners alike. Market-price fluctuations or cattle plagues could leave tenants with no income to pay their rents. Estate revenues dropped as arrears of rent mounted, and tenants either absconded from their farms, as when cheese prices were low *c.*1707, or had to be helped by their landlord, as Lord Molyneux's steward advised in 1750, after they had lost their animals to the plague, lest good tenants be lost to the lord (Thirsk 1985, II: 79, 231, 360, 487; Mingay 1963: 56). Even in the last decades of our period, when agricultural prices were rising, Sir John Leicester's farm rental showed arrearages of £710 in 1757, when £1,500 was collected, and of £1,437 when £5,790 was collected in 1777 (JRUL, Tabley MSS, rentals 1756–97). At worst, the capital value of land fell. In these circumstances those landowners who drew an income such as the Grosvenors' £3,000 a year from north Wales lead mines, or from salt, or coal, or iron, or textiles would bless the benefits of diversification (Mingay 1963: 57; Beckett 1986: 227; see also p. 86). Flexible and credit-worthy estate settlements were another important weapon in the landowner's armoury, as well as sound management and an element of luck.

Of course, like Charles Cholmondeley of Vale Royal, they might find that entrepreneurship could also go wrong. Cholmondeley's fortunes were organized by a strict settlement, and this had to be altered by Act of Parliament to allow his trustees to lease and sell land to pay his debts when Cholmondeley got into £12,000 worth of financial trouble. Cholmondeley was a Member of Parliament for Cheshire, and therefore frequently absent from his estates, so he must have relied upon his agents to manage them for him. In his own estimate the problems lay partly in inherited debts, and partly in debts he contracted himself in an ill-fated iron-making partnership based on a furnace built on his own estates. There was, as Cholmondeley wrote, no 'extravagance of my own' involved. Here was a man deserving of success, well connected in national affairs, a willing entrepreneur in the exploitation of his estates. All was negated by his lack of commercial judgement or expertise. He worried himself sick over these matters: 'the melancholy state of them hath really as often almost turned my head and my resolution hath failed me'. The solution was a reorganization of his family settlement, the base of every gentleman's fortune (JRUL, unlisted Brooke of Mere MSS).

Transport

By 1780 improvements in roads, and in river navigation, with the construction of canals, had changed the transport infrastructure of the region out of recognition compared with 1660; this achievement is summarized in Figure 2.1. Coastal shipping, the other vital means of internal transport, is best dealt with alongside foreign trade (see pp. 108–12). For the second half of the seventeenth century main overland routes through Lancashire and Cheshire are known from maps and road books, such as John Ogilby's *Britannia*. Other routes including most of the old pack and prime ways on lower ground have long been lost but the salt industry in Cheshire generated three major routes to the east which can still be identified by the names of features; these ran through Macclesfield via Whaley Bridge and Winnats Pass to Sheffield, through Buxton to Chesterfield and through Stockport, Mottram, Woodhead and the Etherow valley into south Yorkshire (W. Harrison 1886; Crump 1939: 237–48). It is difficult to be certain about the quality of these early roads, though clearly the direct roads carried wheeled traffic, albeit slowly, and there is evidence that other, less important roads, such as the road from Clitheroe to Bury and Manchester, were also used by wheeled vehicles (HMC 1894: 50.136). The cross roads within the two counties were either lanes between enclosed ground, hollow ways or causeways. Some highways appear to have been pack and prime ways, wide soft haulage ways for carts with a hard narrow causeway alongside (HMC 1894: 193.629).

Celia Fiennes saw the best and worst of local roads in 1698. Between Chester and Prescot, in the country round Lancaster and from Rochdale to Manchester, she rode in good lanes between hedges that gave evidence of enclosures. She also found good 'gravel ways' around Preston and on a very pleasant road on the downs from Manchester to Northwich. In West Lancashire however she found 'deep stony ways' and missed visiting Ormskirk for fear of Martin Mere, 'it being neare evening and not getting a guide I was a little afraid to go that way it being very hazardous for Strangers to pass by it' (Fiennes 1947: 184, 188, 222–4). Around Lancaster she was pleased to find direction posts with hands at all crossways, a rapid response by the justices to

Figure 2.1 Investment in communications on the eve of the factory system, *c*. 1780. Even in the infancy of the factory system Manchester had established itself as the major communication centre of the region though travel and carriage to the south involved either westward diversion or the crossing of the southern Pennines. Warrington remained the major crossing place over the Mersey. Chester still looked resolutely to London. Areas such as the Wirral, the Fylde, Rossendale and west Lancashire were largely unimproved. To the north the crossing of the sands provided a hazardous short-cut to north Lonsdale. (Sources: Redrawn for Lancashire from W. Yates 1786, J. J. Bagley 1956 and T. W. Freeman et al. 1966; redrawn for Cheshire from P. P. Burdett 1777 and D. Sylvester and G. Nulty 1958.)

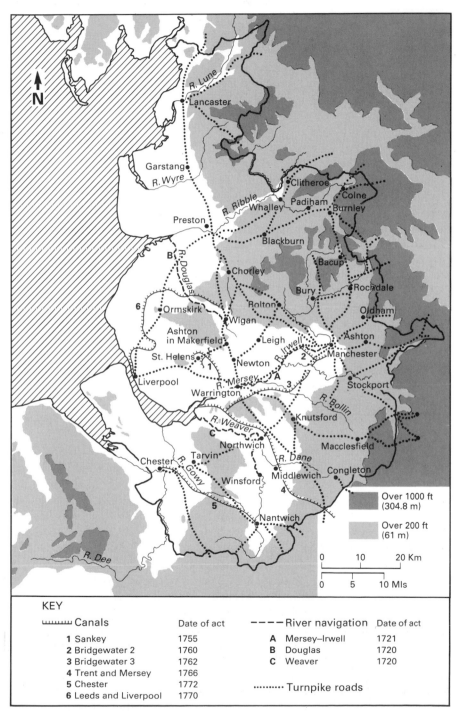

N

R. Lune
Lancaster

Garstang
R. Wyre

R. Ribble
Whalley
Clitheroe
Padiham
Colne
Burnley

Preston

Blackburn

B
R. Douglas
Chorley
Bacup

Bury
Rochdale

Bolton
6
Ormskirk
Oldham

Ashton in Makerfield
Wigan
Leigh
Ashton

St. Helens
Newton
Manchester

1
Liverpool
R. Mersey
A
Stockport

Warrington
3
R. Bollin

R. Weaver
Knutsford

C
Northwich
Macclesfield

Chester
Tarvin
R. Dane

R. Gowy
Winsford
Middlewich
Congleton

5
4

Nantwich

R. Dee

Over 1000 ft
(304.8 m)

Over 200 ft
(61 m)

0   10   20 Km

0   5   10 Mls

KEY

〜〜〜Canals   Date of act   ―――River navigation Date of act

1 Sankey   1755   **A** Mersey–Irwell   1721
2 Bridgewater 2   1760   **B** Douglas   1720
3 Bridgewater 3   1762   **C** Weaver   1720
4 Trent and Mersey   1766
5 Chester   1772   ·········· Turnpike roads
6 Leeds and Liverpool   1770

the Act of 1697 which authorized their erection. During the early 1720s Daniel Defoe was able to use the Postmaster-General's cross post roads from Chester to Liverpool and Warrington and on east to Manchester, Bury, Rochdale and Halifax. The journey from Rochdale over Blackstone Edge was dangerous even in August for a sudden snowstorm blotted out all but the mark of a road or hollow way over the steep hills and the eight miles from the Edge, all uphill and downhill, that took them on to Halifax (Defoe 1724–6: 486–90).

The emphasis on causeways suggests that the pack-horse was a major means of carrying goods within the region and probably for much movement outside until the roads were turnpiked. In 1697–8 there were 89 licensed chapmen who owned 243 licensed horses in a band of country stretching across south Lancashire, north Cheshire and the West Riding of Yorkshire, far more than in any other region in England. Macclesfield was the leading centre with thirty of the thirty-two men trading from there employing eighty-two horses, some of the men having strings of five horses (Spufford 1984: 18–20). The horse-chapmen were soon to decline but a more lasting enterprise was that advertised by James Pickford in the *Manchester Mercury* in August 1756. The Pickfords are reputed to have begun carrying stone at Goytsclough in the seventeenth century and may have graduated to general carrying to the south of England by 1730. By 1756 they had six wagons with teams of nine draught horses for each wagon based at their Poynton, Cheshire, home. They carried from Manchester to London, following the 1724 turnpike from Manchester to Hazel Grove then diverging through Congleton to join the road south from Carlisle in Staffordshire en route to London. By 1788 their London service left daily except on Sunday (Turnbull 1979: 15–23).

Most heavy carriage between the north-west and London was by coastal vessels. In the 1680s William Stout of Lancaster travelled to London with other Lancashire shopkeepers, a journey of five days, and stayed at the Swan with Two Necks, where the Lancashire carriers lodged. But the goods he bought in London were carried to Lancaster by sea (Willan 1976: 93–4). When privateers restricted this route during the French wars of 1689–97 merchants had to depend more on the roads. Wartime trade seems to have extended the activities of the coal carters of south-west Lancashire who carried coal from the Wigan area to Cheshire where it was discharged, the carts then being loaded with salt and cheese for London. Groceries and other imports were brought north on the return journey but with rates of 60s. to 100s. per ton between Lancashire and London only goods worth at least £220 per ton would bear this cost (T. Baines 1867, II: 45–7). The first stage coach services from the north-west were the Chester coaches of 1655–7 (Crofts 1967: 125) using the Chester–Nantwich road; but there seems to be little evidence for any Lancashire coaching service until the mid-eighteenth century, apart from a brief period in the 1660s when there was a London–

Preston coach. The Lancashire connection began again in June 1757 with the twice weekly Warrington flying stage coach which made the London journey in three days at a cost of two guineas inside and one guinea outside (T. Baines 1867, II: 105).

The direct roads were the first to be improved by turnpike trusts. In 1705 the Barnhill and Hatton Heath section of the Chester–Whitchurch road was turnpiked and in 1724 the second great route was improved with the turnpiking of the Manchester–Buxton road. By 1750 both roads between Manchester and London as well as the Chester–London road were turnpiked for most of their length. Hard on the heels of the Manchester–Buxton Act there were three Acts, the first of which linked Liverpool with the south-west Lancashire coalfield, the other two improving the main road north from Warrington to Preston. The first of these improvements was extended by further Acts in 1746 and 1753 linking Liverpool, Prescot, Ashton-in-Maker-field and St Helens. During the 1730s it was the turn of the Pennines when three routes from Manchester into Yorkshire were turnpiked. Although there were fifty-five Acts of Parliament to turnpike the region's roads, route survey-ing only gradually improved: the 1724 turnpike route of the Manchester–Buxton road at Disley in Cheshire rose from under 600 feet to over 1,000 feet in just over one mile at Higher Disley before dropping again to under 600 feet where it crossed the River Goyt at Whaley Bridge. Not until after 1800 was this entire line abandoned as a turnpike in favour of a new line following a bend of the Goyt at a steady height of about 600 feet with very little added distance.

It was obstacles to navigation that hindered river traffic. During the late seventeenth century while Chester worried about keeping the Dee navigable, the salt, cloth, and, especially, coal interests of the region turned their atten-tion to other, potentially more useful rivers (Willan 1937: 65–7). In 1698 it was said that 2,000 tons of goods were carried between Manchester and Liverpool each year and by 1721 land carriage between the two towns amounted to £1,500 per annum (Hadfield and Biddle 1970: 15). In that year an Act was passed to improve the River Mersey to Manchester by locks, cuttings and a towpath from Warrington to Manchester. Work on the river began in 1724 and in 1734 the Mersey 'flats', sailing boats which could be bow-hauled by teams of men when necessary, could get to Manchester where the undertakers built a big open quay and warehouse; a projected branch for coal from Worsley was not built (Malet 1977: 32). The Old Quay Company as it came to be called, although limited in the tolls it could charge, eventually made a handsome revenue from its near monopoly of warehousing on the navigation in Manchester. In the 1750s a rival carrier, the Salford or New Quay Company, built its own quay and warehouses upstream of Quay Street on the Salford side of the river.

Lancashire coal and Cheshire salt were expensively led or carted, trans-shipped, then unloaded in order to bring them together. Four Bills to improve the Weaver between 1710 and 1720 all failed. Cheshire landowners who feared disturbance, brine producers who believed that the lower transport costs would offer more benefit to the Liverpool dominated rock salt producers, and the existing land carriers, all opposed them (Willan 1936: 46–7). Nevertheless the 1721 Bill to make the Weaver navigable to Winsford, and the Witton Brook navigable to Witton, passed. An unusual feature of the Act was that after repayment of the undertakers' costs any balance left after maintenance should be paid to the county of Chester to maintain public bridges and to repair roads near the river, any surplus still remaining to be spent on roads elsewhere in the county.

The River Douglas which ran north from Wigan to the Ribble estuary was an obvious route to supply coal to north Lancashire and, after an abortive attempt in 1713, an Act was obtained in 1720 and money was raised to begin work. Finally, in 1742, the navigation was open from Wigan to the estuary. Some thirteen years later the southern part of the same coalfield at Haydock and Parr was opened up on the initiative of the Common Council of Liverpool by means of a cut constructed along the line of the Sankey Brook. Coal from this source was being advertised in Liverpool in 1758 and before 1780 the cut was open to St Helens (Hadfield and Biddle 1970: 60–4, 42–8).

Coal also provided the motive for a new venture at Worsley. The Sankey canal threatened Worsley's sales into Cheshire, while Manchester and Salford, relatively close by, were obtaining their coal from the east of the two towns with the heavy cost of land carriage of up to and sometimes beyond ten miles. The Duke of Bridgewater, who was lord of the manor, saw the opportunity; in November 1758 he petitioned for an Act permitting him to build a canal from Worsley to Patricroft and, after amendment, into Manchester at Castlefield, south of the Old Quay. The Duke, with the vital assistance of his agent John Gilbert and engineer James Brindley, astonished the country with a level canal that ran from the depths of Worsley Delph, floated 39 feet above the Irwell on Barton aqueduct (Plate 2.2) and crossed the unstable Trafford Moss. By 1780 the Duke was selling 400 tons of coal each week in Manchester at the statutory price of 4d. per hundred. Even at this price the canal quickly showed its value; in 1760 the Duke's two mines on Walkden Moor had made a combined profit of £406 which trebled after the opening of the canal in 1765 to £1,421 in 1769 (Malet 1977: 92). In 1766 the Bridgewater Canal began a passenger service between Worsley, Castlefield and Lymm.

Even before his canal was open to Manchester the Duke was casting covetous eyes at the Liverpool–Manchester trade. In 1761 he mounted an attack on the inefficiency of the Mersey–Irwell company in relation to the

---

Plate 2.2 Barton aqueduct on the Bridgewater Canal 1795. This engraving, from Aiken 1795, shows that feature of the canal that most impressed the public at large. The spectacle of narrow boats passing over the river inspired a respect that verged on awe.

large and growing volume of traffic, claiming that he could cut the cost of carrying from 12s. per ton to 6s. and avoid tidal problems. His new canal would alternatively save merchants the 30s. or 40s. per ton that it cost by road. After a long struggle with Sir Richard Brooke of Norton Priory, the canal was opened through to the Mersey in 1776. Even before it was completed the Mersey–Irwell company reduced its rates and in 1779 its owners sold it (Hadfield and Biddle 1970: 29, 36). There was one final link to be made. In 1766 the Act was passed for the Trent and Mersey, a narrow canal, which joined the Bridgewater at Preston Brook for the descent to the Mersey and gave access, via the Staffordshire and Worcester (passed on the same day) not only to the Midlands but also to Bristol and the Severn. It was completed in 1777.

Industry

There were few new industries established in the north-west in the period under review, the most significant perhaps being copper and the newly re-established glass industries, both of which are dealt with in Chapter 3, and calico printing, which moved north to take advantage of the new cloths being produced there. The industries that were present in the region in 1660 grew and prospered. Coal and cotton showed the greatest growth but other trades were also making progress. All benefited from the great transport improvements of the period which broke down the isolation of the region and of most places within it. Turnpikes and canals not only served existing centres of trade and manufacture, but also created new ones in town and country alike. Industries remained small in scale by comparison with modern concerns, even in coal-mining or metal-smelting, glass or paper making and in textiles the domestic system based on the family was dominant until the 1770s. Nevertheless there was growth in the size of units in coal-mining and, with improving spinning technology, in textiles before the powered factories of the late 1770s and 1780s were built. Technology was changing many trades during these years. In paper making Hollander beating engines began to replace simple stampers during the 1740s, silk throwing and spinning showed the way to powered factory concentration at Stockport in the 1730s and the sequence of inventions in the wool and cotton trades produced water-powered spinning by 1780. These changes increased the capital necessary to set up and maintain extractive or manufacturing concerns. By modern standards the capital needed was modest but it was rising rapidly beyond the few pounds that would set up a hatter or weaver and circulating capital was also rising with increased production and turnover.

Water was becoming crucially important. Corn mills and fulling mills using water for power had coexisted quite happily but the proliferation of bleach works, dyers, print works, hatters, paper mills, breweries and others who all sought clean water which they could foul for their neighbours downstream did not promote harmony. Nor did the search for power as paper, silk and cotton mills began to join battle to control streams and rivers by the building of weirs or to buy rights to collect water and impound it for their own use.

The textile industry showed the greatest growth and change. The London links and export markets pioneered by the Chethams and others remained strong and clothiers and chapmen continued to travel to fairs to sell cloth and to export but another market came into existence. In 1700 the first Liverpool slaver, the *Liverpool Merchant*, delivered 220 slaves in Barbados and later in the same year the *Blessing* was fitted out for the Gold Coast, Ouidah and Angola. This trade developed on the basis of mixed cloths imitating Indian fabrics which were much in demand in West Africa where they could be used for the purchase of slaves. By 1752 the Liverpool slaving fleet was eighty-eight strong and could carry over 25,000 slaves. This African trade, which grew to take in exotic imports of cotton, dyestuffs and timber from the Americas from the proceeds of slave sales there, reached substantial proportions. It was at its peak in 1769 when the exports of cloth for this market were worth £98,699 out of a total of £211,606 for all exported cotton piece goods (Fryer 1984: 35–6; Wadsworth and Mann 1931: 72n, 146).

One Manchester merchant who illustrates this link between the slave trade and the north-west is Samuel Touchet. Touchet, the son of a successful linen dealer and manufacturer who died in 1744 leaving £20,000, followed the traditional pattern of acting as London partner to his brothers who manufactured in the north-west. In 1751 he and Joseph Hague, who had moved to London from the parish of Glossop, were called as witnesses in a House of Commons inquiry into the state of the linen trade, since both were involved in linen manufacture in the areas round Stockport, Blackburn and Preston. To their surprise however the weavers' greatest complaints were directed against the control which the two merchants had exercised over the import of raw cotton into London for several years, a monopoly which the weavers claimed had given the two men profits of £20,000 or £30,000. Much of this cotton had been used as weft, probably with a woollen warp, in weaving a cloth called anabasses, a blue and white striped loincloth (Wadsworth and Mann 1931: 243–8). It was through cloths like this that the money generated by the slave trade flowed into the cottages of the north-west bringing work and wages to spinners and weavers who knew little of events beyond their townships.

From 1701 to 1774 legal prohibitions and duties directed against Indian cloths in the interests of the older British fabrics hampered the development of the British cotton trade. Exports of cotton piece goods however grew steadily from £7,853 in 1719 to £14,324 in 1739 and then, in a series of great leaps, to over £100,000 in 1759 and over £300,000 in 1779, two-thirds of this in Europe. The import of raw cotton followed the same path, rising from 1 million pounds weight in 1710 to over 5 million pounds in the 1770s (Wadsworth and Mann 1931: 170). By 1750 cotton cloth manufacture in the United Kingdom was largely concentrated in north-west England and Lanarkshire in Scotland, both areas with previous linen manufactures.

The early importation of cotton into England was through the Levant Company into London where Touchet and Hague made their cotton corner. American and West Indian cotton began to enter England through the west coast ports of Bristol, Lancaster and Liverpool very early in the eighteenth century but it was not until about 1750 that Liverpool took the lead. As it did a new class of cotton dealers, the Manchester jobbers, came into existence, dealing only in raw cotton while in the export of cloth foreign-based agents took over from the travelling supercargoes. In the home trade the 1740s saw the emergence of 'riders out' who travelled the country with patterns and samples in search of orders rather than carrying batches of cloth to the fairs like earlier clothiers and dealers (Aiken 1795: 184).

It was the merchants of London and Liverpool who created the markets but they depended upon the skill and adaptability of the region's weavers. Both spinning and weaving were domestic trades, carried on in people's homes, until late in the eighteenth century but the networks through which orders and materials became finished cloth were increasingly complex. At the apex there were great merchants like the Mosleys in the seventeenth century or Touchet in the eighteenth and below them lesser merchants and drapers, flaxmen, wool broggers, chapmen and others who had a role in the movement of raw materials, yarn or grey or finished cloth. In both the wool and linen trades weavers could continue to work independently for local customers or wider markets, buying the raw fibre for local spinning or yarn from broggers or flaxmen, weaving the cloth and contracting with bleachers or fullers to finish it before taking the cloth back and selling it. Linen weavers who looked for more fashionable markets wove spots, stripes or diaper cloths and needed both knowledge of the market and patterns and gearings for their looms; they were more dependent upon the merchants. Those who wove cloths containing cotton suffered a further loss of independence. The number of dealers in cotton was restricted until American cotton broke the Levant monopoly; since many weavers worked on credit they could easily fall into debt to the merchant who controlled their local supply and become little more than piece-workers (Wadsworth and Mann 1931: 78–91).

Manchester apart, where the smallware trade required more expensive looms, most weavers worked in the country rather than the town, dispersed in farms and cottage settlements. They normally learned to weave on their fathers' looms and set up their own when they married, preferably on a holding with some land. Their independence has already been questioned and it is possible that some Lancashire weavers were little more than employees in the seventeenth century but it was later that many drifted into that relationship known as 'putting out'. This was most marked in the weaving of cloths that included cotton and was well developed by 1700 with masters, drapers and merchants providing the fibre or yarn for weavers to weave at home on their own looms and then receiving and paying for the woven pieces. Cotton wool, wool and flax were also put out for carding or combing and spinning on the same basis both by masters and by weavers who did not have enough hands at home to do the work for them. Large merchants increasingly operated this system from their own warehouses; others worked through their own agents, independent middlemen or country manufacturers. The weavers were not employees. They worked their own looms in their own homes though they might be provided with healds and gears for the looms; they could work or play as they saw fit and could change masters as they chose subject to the laws governing embezzlement and the finishing of work (Burn 1780, IV: 118–53). Many had smallholdings, crofts or gardens on which they grew food or kept a few animals. Like their counterparts before 1660 their lives were a mixture of agriculture and industry in which every member of the family had a role but perhaps the agricultural element was diminishing as weaving grew more profitable.

However, specialization was developing within the region. By 1750 the linen industry remained strong in west Lancashire especially in heavy sailcloths while mixed linen-cotton cloths were made in south Lancashire and adjacent parts of Cheshire with the woollen trade continuing along the Pennine edge. More important changes were taking place further north where the Bolton weavers had begun to produce new, heavy fustians with cut and raised patterns, and also thicksets followed by cotton velvet, velveret and, finally in 1776, velveteen. The Blackburn area was also producing cotton cloth in plain weave for printing and the scale of operations there is demonstrated by two brothers who, in 1736, were paying 3,000 persons and had 600 looms working for them. Another exotic fibre began to assume prominence during this period when the region's first silk-throwing mill was built at Stockport in 1732. This followed the example of the pioneering mill built by Thomas Cotchett at Derby in 1702 and its later expansion by the Lombes (Nixon 1969: 180–6). The Stockport mill, in its turn, stimulated others to build silk mills on the Carrbrook in Stockport and within a few years Congleton and Macclesfield were also centres for the new manufacture (Wadsworth and Mann 1931: 173, 211, 277–8, 305).

The spinners and weavers were highly adaptable and their flexibility extended to fibres as well as weaves; probate records show weavers' homes containing looms for both wool and linen and one Gorton chapman, Samuel Bennyson, who died in 1686, had looms, Dutch or smallware looms and a knitting frame (Meadowcroft 1976: 51–2). There were few restrictions to hamper the weavers in the sparsely peopled countryside and, despite efforts by the gilds or corporations at Liverpool, Preston, Wigan and Lancaster to restrict outsiders and by the lord of the manor of Manchester to impose tolls on incoming goods, the trade remained free from corporate regulation (Wadsworth and Mann 1931: 61–70).

The evidence of the county Agricultural Reports of the late eighteenth century for the region agrees with modern studies of Rossendale and Blackburn in suggesting that many weavers were independent and prosperous. Common to all these sources are indications that there was great subdivision of holdings where manufacture was well established with more weaver families able to buy or lease land, build cottages and workshops (Plate 2.3), and settle into the rising expectations of their little mixed economies (J. Holt 1795; Pilkington 1789; Wedge 1794; Holland 1808; Tupling 1927; Pearson 1985).

Looking back a century later Lancashire writers such as Brierley and Waugh could portray this domestic system in idyllic terms but the scales were increasingly weighted in favour of the merchants and master manufacturers. It is significant that the first weavers' combination that has been traced is the Manchester Smallware Weavers' Society, established in or before 1747, by weavers who were employed on looms owned by small capitalists in an urban situation. In 1758 the Manchester masters threatened this and other weavers' unions with prosecution but in the same year there was a great strike of check weavers in Manchester, Ashton, Oldham, Eccles and the surrounding villages. The strikers wanted a return to the price lists and piece lengths of the 1730s and recognition of their society but after the prosecution of some of their number for illegal combination they were forced to give up their 'box' and return to work. A similar prosecution in 1760 brought to an end the worsted smallware weavers' combination in Manchester but both there and in the countryside legal action might do no more than drive union activity underground (Wadsworth and Mann 1931: 340–75). The friendly societies which were rapidly growing in number in the later eighteenth century could provide excellent cover for the discussion of trade matters. The object of combination was not only the raising of prices paid for weaving; the most skilled weavers wanted enforcement of the Statute of Apprentices which would limit the number of journeymen seeking work. The plain weavers of the countryside may not have shared this view. After the 1750s the masters' opposition to such enforcement was increasingly supported by both Parliament and the courts, not only in textiles but also in other trades.

Whatever the tensions between weavers and those who paid them it

---

Plate 2.3 Plan and elevation of James Brandwood's house at Turton, 1807. This house and loomshop, one of many designed and built by Brandwood at the turn of the eighteenth century, combines the vernacular with the functional. It also shows the weaver's house when that trade was close to its greatest prosperity and largely divorced from agriculture. The house cost £200. (Source: W. J. Smith 1977.)

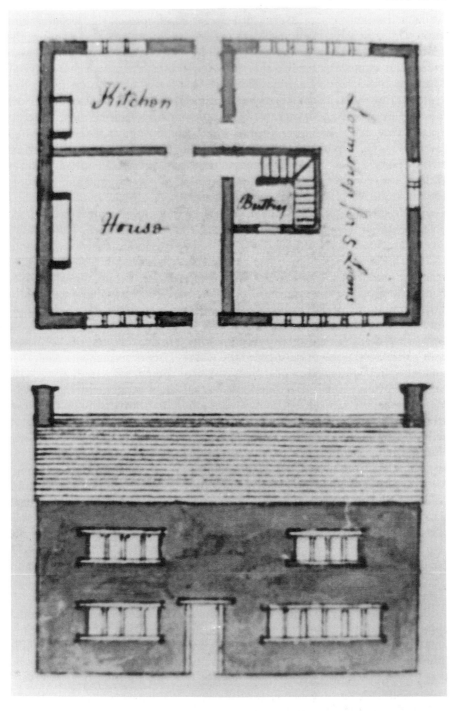

seems reasonably clear that by 1780 the condition of the weavers had improved during the century, perhaps a continuation of a seventeenth-century trend. The masters were in no doubt that weavers' incomes had risen too much, citing as evidence their unwillingness to work on Monday, St Monday to the weavers, or on 'bearin whom' day when many spent the day 'fuddling' in the alehouse on the way home from taking their cloth to the master's warehouse. Masters were equally unhappy about the spread of luxury in weavers' homes typified by the consumption of tea and wheaten bread (Wadsworth and Mann 1931: 390–1). But the trade was prosperous and weavers, no less than merchants and putters out, were entitled to order their own lives: the more thrifty were investing in houses, land and the tools of their trade.

The technology of cloth manufacture had changed only slowly in the seventeenth and early eighteenth centuries, the major advances being draw-boy looms for fancy weaving and Dutch or swivel looms for weaving tapes and smallwares. In 1733 John Kay of Bury made a more fundamental change when he patented the fly-shuttle which made it possible to weave double-width cloths and also weave more speedily. By 1737 the woollen weavers of Rossendale were producing double cloths but its wider diffusion in the woollen trade was very slow. It was not introduced into the cotton trade until the 1750s but then became very successful in producing better cloth with less weft yarn. Its wide adoption speeded the weavers' work to such an extent that they outstripped the ability of their traditional spinners to supply them with weft. John Kay never received the rewards to which he was entitled and was met by hostility and riot by the weavers when his shuttle was first demonstrated in Lancashire but they were great beneficiaries of his inventiveness. A second Kay device, the drop box, which enabled the weavers to change shuttles easily further increased the efficiency of the weavers.

Kay's disturbance of the balance between weavers and spinners stimulated the inventiveness of his contemporaries. Kay himself devised a multi-spindle spinning machine in the 1740s but it was never adopted, Lawrence Earnshaw of Mottram in Longdendale is said to have invented another in 1753 but destroyed it for fear that it would ruin the poor and James Taylor of Ashton-under-Lyne patented a third in 1755 but it never gained acceptance (Aiken 1795: 467; Wadsworth and Mann 1931: 473–5). The later eighteenth century however saw a series of inventions that progressively increased the flow of yarn although the full effects were not felt until after 1780.

The first successful introduction was the jenny, a hand-powered machine invented by James Hargreaves, a weaver near Bolton, between 1764 and 1767. Initially the jenny had eight spindles but by 1780 eighty-spindle machines were common. Intended for spinning cotton it was quickly found that its soft, thick yarn was suitable only for weft in that trade and it was used much more widely in woollen weaving. Nevertheless by 1769 weavers and others were installing jennies in their cottages and some were teaming together jennies and another innovation, hand-turned carding engines, in small workshops. These workshops provided slubbings or weft for the cotton weavers. The carding engines and jennies were more expensive than the old hand cards and single wheels but they offered greater productivity and higher earnings and the small early machines could be operated by young people. It had needed the output of five or six spinners to keep one weaver at work before Kay's fly-shuttle, more after it; the jenny solved the problem of cheap and plentiful weft. By 1764 the spinner working a twenty-four spindle jenny could earn 8 to 9 shillings a week against the 5 shillings to 7s. 6d. of the single spindle spinner. As jennies spread and spindles increased jenny wages fell to between 4 and 6 shillings by 1780 when the machines were growing to a size beyond the strength of children. Hand spinners by this time could expect no more than 1s. 6d. to 3 shillings a week. (For this and what follows see Wadsworth and Mann 1931: 403–503.)

The use of jennies in conjunction with carding engines began to change the structure of the cotton industry but before it could take full effect it was overtaken by a further invention, patented by Richard Arkwright in 1768. As in the case of Hargreaves and the jenny there has been long controversy over the origins of the water frame, especially in relation to the machine invented by Thomas Highs of Leigh, but it was Arkwright who obtained the patent and the rewards. Arkwright's machine, like one invented by Lewis Paul in the Midlands thirty years before, used rollers in pairs to draw and twist the yarn which was then wound on to bobbins by means of flyers. The process was continuous, unlike that of the jenny, and the machine was harnessed first to horse power then water. Arkwright's first water-powered spinning mill was built at Cromford in Derbyshire in 1771 and by 1775 he had successfully applied power to every stage in the spinning process. A Lancashire man, he had developed his machines outside his native county but that was where their greatest effects were to be felt.

The improvements in spinning were not yet at an end. During the 1770s Samuel Crompton, while jenny spinning and weaving at Hall i' th' Wood, near Bolton (see Plate 1.1, p. 15), was experimenting with yet another machine. This combined roller drafting with twisting and winding on multiple spindles set on a travelling carriage. This machine, the mule, was hand-powered and intermittent, with spinning and winding two separate operations, but by 1779 Crompton could produce fine, strong, even yarn suitable for fine muslin weaving. The curiosity aroused by his fine weaving drew attention to his fine spinning and the machine on which he accomplished it; his attempts to keep it secret were in vain.

The introduction of jennies may have been resisted for there were riots at Blackburn in 1768 and 1769 and at Bolton in 1769, the 1769 riots resulting in the destruction of houses at Oswaldtwistle and Blackburn by weavers. Ten years later, in September 1779, when there was a wave of attacks on mills, a pamphlet referred back to the earlier troubles as an outright attack on jennies by a mob which feared they would take the bread from the poor. It is uncertain whether this refers to 1768, 1769 or both years but it does suggest that the rioters intended to destroy and prohibit all jennies. The ten years that followed the 1769 riots saw the continued spread and increase in size of jennies, the erection of carding and jenny shops and the invention and exploitation of the water frame. Following the success of the Cromford mill Arkwright had gone on to build or license fifteen or twenty similar mills, among them the first in Lancashire at Birkacre near Chorley, where he rented a newly built mill in 1777. Spinning had begun its migration into the powered mills but in 1779 there were widespread riots and attacks on them. The disturbances started in the area between Bolton and Wigan in September with attacks on carding and spinning water mills, followed in October by the destruction of Arkwright's Birkacre mill, where a rioter was killed. In the same month mills were attacked and damaged or destroyed in the Blackburn and Bolton districts, Stockport millowners prepared to defend their mills and the merchants and manufacturers of Manchester requested military assistance. When the military arrived they were quartered at Manchester, Liverpool, Preston, Wigan, Blackburn, Bolton and Stockport. By the end of October the rioters had dispersed and peace was restored. Arrests had been made and some rioters were imprisoned, the longest sentences handed down being for two years (Rose 1963–4: 60–100; Fitton and Wadsworth 1958: 79–80).

The riots of 1779 were directed against powered mills and hand jennies of over twenty-four spindles; the rioters were largely male and none of those arrested were spinners, most being weavers, colliers and labourers. Their defence of small jennies strongly suggests that they either owned them or were concerned about their wives and children losing their occupations. What they were defending was not an ancient craft but an innovation of only ten or fifteen years; the casualties of the first technological change had been the women, children and young people remote from or unable to take advantage of the small jennies. Hand carding and spinning had been a small but vital addition to the wages of their agricultural or labouring husbands, fathers or sons.

The growth in the linen trade in the late seventeenth and eighteenth centuries increased the areas of land given over to bleaching and the amounts of cloth lying in them for the weeks that were necessary for the processes. Parliament, faced with the problem of securing this valuable property, introduced the death penalty in 1745, felony without benefit of clergy, for croft breaking or the receiving of cloth worth 10 shillings or more (18 Geo 2. cap 27). The long bleaching process itself was under examination however and in 1750 the use of sulphuric acid instead of buttermilk in souring cut that stage from one week in the croft to between 12 and 24 hours. A few years later Manchester bleachers were adding lime to the bucking stage in order to speed it even though this was illegal under Elizabethan legislation (Sykes 1925: 9).

The spirit of improvement was beginning to change the ancient craft. Some of the Lancashire bleachers of this period founded long-lasting concerns. Peter Ainsworth of Halliwell near Bolton opened his bleachcroft there in 1739, founding a firm that joined others from the eighteenth century in the Bleachers' Association of 1900 (Sykes 1925: 66–9).

From the mid-eighteenth century printing on cloth, that is calico printing, which had begun in London in 1619 on imported Indian bleached cotton, started to shift to the north-west where printing cloth (though not yet all-cotton) was now being made and where both labour and land were cheaper. The first calico print works in the region may have been that of the Claytons at Bamber Bridge, founded in 1764, but Chadkirk in north Cheshire also lays claim to primacy and the Manchester burial registers record that on 4 September 1763 there was the burial of 'John, son of William Jordan, Callique Printer, Little Green'. What is clear is that the first enterprise in the region was quickly imitated so that by 1773 there were two cotton or calico printers in Manchester and six firms printing on linen or silk, sometimes combined with cotton. There were also two print cutters and engravers. Until 1774 the trade was held back by legal prohibition and after that date printed cloth was still subject to duty. Nevertheless Raffald's Directory of 1781 indicates a rapid growth with eight cotton or calico printers and thirteen unspecified printers as well as seven print cutters and engravers in Manchester with a further nineteen firms printing in the country districts that looked to the Manchester market (Turnbull 1951: 23–5).

This early calico printing was carried on either as a specialist trade or in association with manufacturing as can be illustrated by the Peel family. Robert Peel the elder was first a printer then combined it with spinning and weaving at Brookside mill near Blackburn before 1768. His son, later Sir Robert, was in a similar partnership at Bury and another son, William, began printing at Church works in 1772. The combination of manufacturing and printing did not always succeed; the firm of Livesey, Hargreaves near Preston was founded in 1776 but its combined manufacturing, printing and banking did not save it from failure in 1788 while some specialized printers such as Rumneys survived until the end of the nineteenth century when they entered the Calico Printers' Association (Turnbull 1951: 73–8, 437).

Printers, like bleachers, needed plentiful supplies of pure water and this took precedence over both the supply of labour and accessibility to transport. Corn mills such as those at Bury in 1772 and later at Turton and Ainsworth and woollen mills like those at Church Bank and Irwell Springs made suitable sites. But most printers were forced to look for new sites on cloughs or river banks where they had to cohabit with all the other users and struggle with them for their water. All cloth printing before 1783 was carried out by pressing engraved wooden pattern blocks on to the pieces of cloth, each pressing introducing one colour and design from the block face. The print-works needed designers, block cutters and printers, the latter assisted by 'tierers', young children who kept the colour trays filled and gave general assistance. Wages were good although working days were long; most printers were time-served men but there are occasional references to women printing, the earliest being Livesey, Hargreaves of Mosney near Preston, who had women working 40 of their 150 tables before they failed in 1788 (Turnbull 1951: 72).

Felt hatting had become established at Chester before 1660 but after that date it gradually moved east through mid-Cheshire into Lancashire, especially the Ashton and Oldham districts, and into north Cheshire where Stockport became the centre. Chester itself kept a hatting industry but by the 1750s it was in decline and overshadowed by the buoyant growth in greater Manchester. The feltmaker-retailer system which the Chester Company sought to protect by its regulations was superseded by new forms of organization so that Chester lost not only its trade but also its journeymen, who could see more prospect of independence in the free atmosphere outside its walls. The trade was not only moving, but also growing. Probate records for hatters in the two counties run at about five per decade from 1660 to 1730 but from 1760 to 1780 there were ten per decade and from 1780 to 1790 thirty-three records.

As the trade grew the hatmaker-retailer gave way to the manufacturer. In 1712 Thomas Malbon of Congleton still had his workhouse with the tools and a shop with a counter, chairs, shelves and hats. In 1721 Josiah Lancashire of Salford had no shop but he had a bow garret, two 'planking' workhouses for felting the bodies and a 'finishing' house for blocking, ironing and shearing the hats. Daniel Higham, who died in Stockport in 1798, shows a further stage in the development of the trade. He had rooms for storing fur and wool, for dyeing and for finishing, and a warehouse for the finished hats. He had no planking rooms or kettles and it is clear that he was putting out wool and fur to bodymakers, taking back the bodies and finishing on his own premises. Almost all his hats were of one kind, 'youth's hats', which he probably sold wholesale to the large hatting houses in London.

The hatters' wills tell us a great deal about these craftsmen. Many owned or leased their own homes and workshops. William Bertenshaw of Openshaw, who died in 1686, possessed two dwelling houses, a hatshop and a shippon for three lives under George Legh of High Legh. Zachariah Peacock of Denton owned in 1791 two dwellings at Hooley Hill and another four at Crown Point with at least one hatshop. Many kept up a connection with the land. Families like the Hackneys of Congleton in 1703 or the Denton Bertenshaws of 1762 had feltmaking in progress as well as cattle with cheese presses, husbandry gear and horses. In 1703 John Hackney left personal estate of £100, John Bertenshaw left £224 in 1762 – respectable indications of prosperity. Daniel Higham, the specialist hatter, had no involvement outside his trade but he left £408. Their wills also show them as members of friendly societies and building clubs, further indications of prosperity.

Although small by the standards of cotton, hatting too needed ancillary trades and workers – carders, furcutters, woodworkers and smiths in a variety of metals. They bought wool from local broggers as well as fur, wool, dyestuffs and proofing materials via London or Liverpool. They also needed the more local work of the blockmakers, who made the wooden blocks on which the hats were shaped; twelve of them left probate records in the eighteenth century, ten in Liverpool and two in Chester. The other specialists, small groups of hatband makers, lining cutters and bow string makers were concentrated in the Manchester area, though there were also hatband makers at Bosden and Macclesfield late in the century. Retailing was carried out either through the retailer-makers of the Chester system or by mercers and haberdashers with a few specialist hat retailers appearing late in the century (J. H. Smith 1980).

The extractive industries of the region shared in its economic growth. Salt boilers at Northwich still used cordwood for boiling after 1660, but iron pans heated by coal were spreading through the wich towns (Burgess 1989: 39). Salt works outside the towns, worked for or leased from great landowners, were competing with those in the towns (CRO, DCH). At Nantwich salt boiling was already in some decay when a dispute in 1696 ended the traditional distribution of brine and damaged production still further; and tax debts added to the industry's problems. By the second decade of the eighteenth century many of the works were derelict (Hall 1883: 263–4; Twigg 1989). Technical developments were few in the Cheshire brine industry; there was some fuel economy by changes in furnace and chimney design and also improved quality by the addition of alum to the brine (Calvert 1915: 85–116, 121). There were, however, worrying problems with subsidence in the Northwich district after 1750 (Calvert 1915: 305).

Rock salt had been discovered at Marbury in 1670 but was neglected and in the 1690s only four or so pits were at work. Nevertheless, in the 1690s it was being refined on the Mersey and Weaver estuaries and at other coastal locations in England, promoted from 1694 to 1696 by a favourable tax regime (Barker 1951: 91). Mid-Cheshire brine boilers perceived this as a threat and thus after 1699 took a less favourable view of the Weaver Navigation Bill than did the 'rockmen'. Brine boilers paid carriage to and from Northwich: coal inwards from Lancashire and salt outwards to Frodsham, where it was sold and shipped. Rockmen sent rock salt outwards to sea water refineries at Frodsham (1694) or Liverpool (1696) or Dungeon near Hale in Lancashire (1697), all closer to Lancashire coal, and sold salt from the refinery (Barker 1951: 86–7). Rough calculations for the early eighteenth century suggest that rock salt carried to Frodsham cost about 12s. 2d. a ton with coal there perhaps 7s. 10d. a ton: it took one and a half tons of coal to make a ton of salt from brine, giving a total cost of £1 3s. 11d. plus labour and site charges. The cost of a ton of white salt brought from Northwich to Frodsham was £1 2s. 6d. (Barker 1951: 86; Willan 1951: 3–4). The two trades continued side by side suggesting that initially neither had much advantage over the other, though the rockmen's transport costs would be reduced more significantly if the Weaver became navigable (cf. Barker 1951: 84, 86).

From its opening in 1732 the Weaver Navigation depended largely on salt and coal, which comprised 79 per cent of its cargoes in the first year and 64 per cent in 1753 (Willan 1951: 39–40). By 1778 there were only two works of five pans each working at Nantwich, which was not served by the Weaver. Development of salt works at Winsford was slow (Willan 1951: 31; Calvert 1915: 731). In contrast Northwich had sixty-three operators in 1780 and was the prime salt town, with Middlewich second; the rock salt mines in the vicinity of Northwich further boosted its position (Calvert 1915: 74, 597, 600, 633, 685; Willan 1951: 27).

In 1675 Lord Brereton estimated the entire production of the Cheshire field at 27,000 tons per annum (Calvert 1915: 282). There are no complete figures for a century later but in 1769–70 nearly 34,000 tons of white salt was shipped down the Weaver and in 1770 some 23,336 tons were exported from Liverpool and a further 6,810 tons sent to Ireland; 32,518 tons of rock salt moved down the Weaver in the same period with 7,626 tons of rock salt exported and 12,276 sent to Ireland (Calvert 1915: 283; Willan 1951: 213). There was also an unknown quantity of salt transported overland. Thus an expansion in white salt was matched by production of rock salt and the triangular links between Liverpool and Cheshire salt and Lancashire coal had been established. The African, Baltic and Dutch markets were added to new West Indian and American outlets (Barker 1951).

Demand for iron salt pans helped the growth of Cheshire's iron industry. There were small amounts of bloomery smelting in Rossendale before 1660 but direct evidence of blast furnaces does not appear until 1658 at Church Lawton in Cheshire though there are claims for a furnace at Holme Chapel near Burnley *c.* 1588. The first of the region's refining forges, which made the brittle pig-iron output of a blast furnace into malleable bar-iron for sale, was at Tib Green on the Cheshire–Staffordshire border in 1619 (Ashmore 1982; Awty 1958 (1); Schubert 1957: app. IV).

By 1660 however there were good foundations for growth. The shift from wood to coal in salt boiling left landowners looking for new wood customers and there were many demands for iron – for salt pans, for nails and for the iron distribution centres of Chester and Warrington. Nailers wanted an iron called coldshort, made from Staffordshire iron ore, and by 1670 furnaces were established at Church Lawton, Doddington and, perhaps, Street. (For these and what follows see Awty 1958.) Four forges and a slitting mill associated with these furnaces were in action by 1677 and the Street furnace became a plate mill for salt pan production about 1702. In a second burst Vale Royal and Disley were built in the 1690s and Holme Chapel near Burnley was in blast by 1700. There were other forges and slitting mills at Wigan in the late seventeenth century. Carr furnace was built near Wigan in 1720, also associated with a forge and mill; there were forges and mills at Great Sankey, Lymm, Bidston and in the Chorley area in the eighteenth century (Langton 1979: 178).

The partnerships that operated much of this plant were nationwide in extent and significant sums of money were involved. In 1662 the stock in one mill was worth £2,227; in 1699 a consignment of nails sent to London sold for just under £1,000 and the Foley partnerships in Cheshire *c.* 1700 had a capital of £21,426 on which 10 per cent was earned. Four Cheshire land-owners were also involved but it is uncertain whether they were more than rentiers or suppliers of fuel.

The south Lancashire and south Cheshire iron industry was rooted in nail making but Wigan and the south Cheshire furnaces also used Cumbrian ore so that they could send tough pig-iron to the south Midlands. In iron for nail making there was competition with Yorkshire partnerships but increasing home consumption and, from the mid-eighteenth century, exports to the West Indies and North America improved markets (Langton 1979: 179). Partnerships from the south of the region in their turn competed in Cumbria and there were also furnaces at Leighton and Halton in the north of the region, though they are best considered as part of the Cumbrian iron industry (Fell 1908; Awty 1977; Marshall and Davies-Shiel 1969: 122). All these furnaces made Lancashire and Cheshire a growth zone in the industry while it declined elsewhere. Carr furnace seems to have changed in 1759 from char-coal to an early and unsuccessful coke furnace and there was another coke smelter at Dukinfield in Cheshire in 1775 (Riden 1978b: 38–9; Langton 1979: 178; Riden 1987: 29).

The most important non-ferrous metals worked in the region were copper and brass. Lead working in Rossendale depended on local ore but the earliest copper smelter in the region, that at Warrington in 1717, used Cornish ore brought to cheap coal and a good market (Ashmore 1982; T. C. Barker and Harris 1954: 75; Langton 1979). Even Charles Roe's smelting works at Macclesfield was probably sited there because of local coal supplies; later he and his partners used water-powered sites some miles to the south of Macclesfield for rolling and milling and for brass manufacture. The Alderley Edge ore was disappointing in quantity and ore was brought first from Coniston in Cumberland, later from Cornwall, even when his Parys Mountain mines on Anglesey were working. By 1780 these mines were making a profit of £15,000 per annum for Roe. He moved his smelter from Macclesfield in 1767 when a proposed canal was blocked by the Duke of Bridgewater. His works at Liverpool took coal from Warrington and from his own mines in north Wales. Calamine for brass making and copper pig and ingots went up the Weaver or later the Grand Trunk canal to be finished in the east Cheshire works. Roe's business was enormously successful and survived his death in 1781 (Chaloner 1950b: 141–4; 1952: 52–65). Competitors built a smelter at Garswood in 1772 and in 1780 what was to be the biggest works in English copper smelting was put up at Ravenhead at the end of the Sankey navigation (T. C. Barker and Harris 1954: 76–7; Langton 1979: 180–1).

The smelting, forging and slitting plants did not directly employ much labour though they needed ancillary suppliers of coal, wood and ore as well as carters, seamen and dockers for transport. The craft industries were mainly small scale; the famous Peter Stubbs in 1776 employed only one apprentice and one part-time journeyman in his file business (Ashton 1939: 6). Black-smiths, whitesmiths, clockmakers, locksmiths, watchmakers, toolmakers, brasiers, pewterers, tinkers and instrument makers were to be found all across the region. There were concentrations in large towns like Chester while Stockport, then a small market town, had at least two watchmakers in the 1690s (Dyke 1949; CRO, wills of Roger Hough, pr. 1691 and Francis Newton, pr. 1694). Nail makers were concentrated on the south Lancashire coalfield as earlier (see p. 53); other specialists were grouped in and around Wigan, Prescot, Ashton-in-Makerfield and Warrington where they depended upon imported raw materials (Ashton 1939: 2; F. A. Bailey and Barker 1969). Thus the Wigan pewterers obtained tin from Devon and Cornwall and the Warrington toolmakers used Sheffield steel (Hatcher and Barker 1974; Ashton 1939: 7, 37–9). These craftsmen exported their products to the rest of England – parts and tools to Birmingham, watch parts to the high fashion trade. Wigan was unfortunate: its reputation for fine pewter, second only to that of London, was of no avail once earthenware and china made it un-fashionable (Hatcher and Barker 1974: 285; McKendrick et al. 1982: 10, 12). By the late eighteenth century the skills of many of the metal craftsmen were being enlisted in the building of textile machines.

Increasing population and a growth in industrial coal consumption stimulated production in the Lancashire coalfield but there is disagreement between historians over its timing (see Nef 1932; Langton 1979). The most recent estimate suggests an output of some 80,000 tons in Lancashire in 1700 rising to 350,000 tons in 1750 and 900,000 by 1775 (Flinn 1984: 26).

The increase in demand in the eighteenth century changed the nature of mining in the region. Shafts deepened from a normal 100 feet before 1700 to 400 or 500 feet in mid-century as at Arley Mine at Parsonage Colliery, Leigh (Ashmore 1969: 101). Winding was still generally by horse whims or gins but Nicholas Blundell recorded in his diary in 1719 'the new engine which is to draw water from one of the cole pits' at Whiston, a Newcomen engine, probably the first in Lancashire (Ashmore 1969: 109). Later in the century Boulton and Watt engines were also introduced into the coalfield. Soughing continued to be used as a means of dewatering and at Worsley from 1760 the soughs developed into the underground canal system along which the fifty narrow boats or 'starvationers' of 1766 could each carry eight tons of coal to the Bridgewater Canal (Malet 1977: 85–92). Another underground canal was constructed in the mines at Standish in the late eighteenth century; at

Wet Earth colliery, Clifton, James Brindley built between 1752 and 1756 an elaborate drainage system which provided water power for a wheel to pump the mine (Banks and Schofield 1968).

Collieries, especially those in areas of increasing demand, grew in size as did Prescot Hall and Whiston in south-west Lancashire following the construction of the Weaver Navigation in 1732. At Worsley, the duke's coal-mining activities expanded greatly after the Bridgewater Canal reached Manchester in 1761. Between 1762 and 1765 in the midst of his purchases – land for docks at Liverpool, land on the canal route and the building of the Brick Hall at Worsley, the duke bought Wardley Hall in Salford and other mining rights from Lady Cholmondeley. Between 1762 and 1764 he was advertising for colliers as far away as north Wales and by 1783 some 207 miners and 124 drawers were working at the Worsley pits (Malet 1977: 80–2). An American refugee recorded in 1777 that the colliers each turned out one ton of coal a day for a wage of 2s. (*VCH. Lancs.*, II: 358).

Until 1768 underground working was carried on by pillar and stall but in that year John Mackay advertised for colliers to work longwall at his pits at Parr, and by the 1780s some of the Worsley pits were also working longwall, backfilling with stone and slack. Longwall working had been first introduced in Shropshire and incomers from there seem to have worked in the Lancashire longwall pits (Ashton and Sykes 1929: 31).

Pits did not grow in size or depth all over the coalfield, with Wigan, for example, seeing a growth in the number but not in the size of pits (Langton 1979: 43). In mining the shallower seams as at Orrell where there was good coal at 6, 11 and 14 yards, shafts were sunk 30 to 100 yards apart and were worked by small groups of colliers, four in the 1760s (D. Anderson 1975: 63). Before the end of the eighteenth century however at the larger collieries shafts were being sunk 150 to 200 yards apart with paired roads driven for drawing, drainage and ventilation (D. Anderson 1975: 60–1). These deeper and larger pits posed new working problems in ventilation, where furnaces replaced fire buckets, and in haulage, where women and girls were brought in to supplement the labour of boys. At Orrell colliery there were women and children underground hauling the 150 pound baskets in 1776. Betty Hodson from that coalfield left the pit in the 1790s when her manager recorded that

> she was as good a girl as any alive and was both beloved and
> protected by the colliers, who were sometimes quarrelsome when
> relaxing over their cups, but howsoever, they would never let anyone
> say improper things or offer harm to a woman in the pits.
> (Quoted in D. Anderson 1975: 133–4)

The long development of mining appears also to have produced a strong family tradition with sons following their fathers, as is shown in the Haigh accounts

1 October 1773; by paid Charles Lowe for training and instructing his son for a Drawer £1 11 6d.

(Quoted in Ashton and Sykes 1929: 156)

At Haigh in 1765 the five pits at work in the colliery were described as Matthew Lowe's Pitt, Henry Lowe's Pitt, Peter Lowe's Pitt, Thomas Lowe's Pitt and William Lowe's Pitt (Ashton and Sykes 1929: 156). As the collieries expanded, this close family connection was weakened by incomers and the growth of longwall working which broke the link between individual colliers and their drawers. Colliers continued to be bound during the eighteenth century, usually for periods just short of a year, but some were employed for shorter periods. Runaway miners who broke their bond were sought as indicated in the Worsley accounts

1771 Mar.1. By pd. Thomas Speakman and John Walker Bill of Expenses in 1769 and Decr. 1770 seeking Colliers who had deserted from the works £4 1 4d.

(Quoted in Ashton and Sykes 1929: 86)

Miners' wages appear to have been higher than those paid to labourers, ranging from 8s. to 10s. 10d. a week in the 1750s and 1760s when labourers' wages were around 6s. with 15s. paid to men driving levels (Ashton and Sykes 1929: 146–8; D. Anderson 1975: 24). Work was irregular, however, with some pits at Wigan closing for up to a month at Christmas and colliers there working normally only four or five days a week on average through the year in the 1770s. Some mineowners provided cottages for their men, principally in relatively small groups, one of which at Smithills Dean, Bolton, was recorded in 1969 (Ashmore 1969: 117). In general however industrial development and the thickening of population that resulted moderated the isolation of mining communities so that the purely pit village was less common in the region than in most mining areas. Miners acted together in disputes but they often lived in close association with weavers and others and joined them in their campaigns.

The organization of mining and the marketing and carrying of coal were transformed by the transport changes of the eighteenth century. The Mersey–Irwell Navigation, open to Manchester in 1734, seems to have had little effect on colliery development or coal prices in Manchester, leaving the way open for the Duke of Bridgewater. The Weaver and Sankey Navigations of 1734 and 1754 however shifted the focus of mining to south-west Lancashire, stimulating not only salt boiling but also the glass and soap trades on the Mersey (Langton 1979: 42–3). The Douglas Navigation of 1720 had stimulated colliery growth in the Wigan district so that in 1748 Wigan coal brought by way of the Douglas was advertised by the Kendal press and called by the town bellman. In the 1770s the Wigan district and, to an even greater extent, the Orrell coalfield were opened up still further by the Leeds–Liverpool Canal which was open, by way of the Douglas, from Liverpool to Wigan by 1774 (D. Anderson 1975: 12).

Merchants and landowners benefited greatly. Liverpool merchants were involved in the promotion of the Douglas and Sankey Navigations and the Leeds–Liverpool Canal brought heavy involvement of wool men from Bradford, Yorkshire not only in canal promotion but also in the leasing of mines in the Orrell coalfield. This capital was used for exploration, for shaft sinking, for drainage and, initially, to purchase or lease land at vastly increased values where coal had been proved. In the mid-eighteenth century a valuation of estates round Orrell showed that in three of them the land was valued at from £1 to £3 15s. per Cheshire acre (the measure used); one seam of coal found on one estate, Atherton's, raised its value to £80 per Cheshire acre and a neighbouring estate with coal proved was valued at £70 per Cheshire acre (D. Anderson 1975: 46). The profits of industry were flowing through many channels.

Towns

Some communities which we recognized as towns before 1660 lost that status during the time covered by this chapter; Over's status as a market had been dubious even before 1660. Cheshire seems to have acquired a new market at the village of Neston, on the Wirral, and perhaps at Audlem in the extreme south east of the county (Thirsk 1985, II: 417; JRUL, Brook of Mere, NRA list, p. 169). Eighteenth-century lists of markets give twelve (1720) or thirteen (1784) in the county (Thirsk 1985, II: 411; W. Owen 1786: 8–9;* 1784). Weeton in Lancashire received a new market from the king in 1670, but does not appear in late-eighteenth-century lists of markets, which name some twenty-three places (W. Owen 1786: 35–7; 1784; Tunnicliffe 1787; Tupling 1936: 109; see also Figure 1.2, p. 33). Some of the older market towns swelled to a much greater size without any change in their legal status. In Derbyshire, the developing spa of Buxton did not fit easily into any of these categories of town. In both manorial (market) towns and corporate boroughs urban life was divided by religion; in parliamentary boroughs political parties produced some exciting, even riotous elections, often an extension of county politics. Town life was also characterized by squabbles over legal rights and powers, which in some instances were a continuation of, or differed little from those investigated in the previous chapter..

* Some obvious gaps in this list, which Owen warned needed to be checked, have been filled by reference to W. Owen 1784.

In later-eighteenth-century Stockport, with a population in excess of 3,000 by about 1750, the lord of the manor, Sir George Warren, was perhaps old fashioned, if hard headed, in enforcing his market rights, and requiring suit of mill of the townsmen, but up to date when he turned the castle into a manufactory (communication from P. Giles 1992). In Manchester, although the court leet under an absentee landlord had become a more independent oligarchy, the scale of population growth meant massive problems. We can best measure them at the very end of the century, when streets had to be widened and property demolished to make way for new streets. By the 1780s the court's powers were in a state of desuetude (Redford 1939, I: 195). Those wealthy enough to have a practical interest in town government were split by religious differences between Church of England and Dissent, while Church of England worshippers were themselves split between high and low church. Attempts to replace the court leet with more effective means of government failed because they would have in effect excluded dissenters: in 1731 a parliamentary Bill to deal with the poor was lost, and in 1763 moves to incorporate the town came to nothing. Two Acts of Parliament which were passed proved not very effective; for example the powers in the 1765 Act to compel householders to clean the streets outside their houses were rarely enforced, and the Manchester Improvement Act of 1776 achieved no more; however, both avoided religious discrimination among the commissioners who were to execute them.

When he visited the town in the early eighteenth century, Defoe thought that Manchester deserved a better form of government, presumably by a corporation. Yet corporations too were uncertain of their constitutions and conscious of lacunae in their privileges. In 1698 Chester reverted to its previous practice of filling vacancies in the corporation by co-option rather than by popular election. Liverpool, like Stockport, had to face an assertive feudal seigneur, but in 1672 Liverpool sidestepped its outstanding difficulties with the Molyneux family (see p. 32) after a new quarrel about the Viscount's lordship over the town wastes. The town leased the manor for £30 per year and in 1777 the corporation bought the rights absolutely (Muir and Platt 1906: 98–100). A lease of the castle from the crown, and of Liverpool tower, extinguished troublesome liberties where the corporation's writ did not run. However, the creation of Liverpool as a parish by Act of Parliament in 1699 brought into being a vestry which was to disagree with the corporation over the treatment of the poor. Neither were corporate towns immune from pressures exerted by great landowners. For the years after the Restoration, Mullett has argued that the earls of Derby, with crown support, attempted to maximize landowners' influence in Liverpool, Preston and Lancaster, partly as a punishment for urban support for Parliament in the civil war, and partly out of a countryman's distrust of towns. But in the eighteenth century Lord Strange (son of the eleventh Earl of Derby), who lived at Patten house in Preston, was content to make that town his power base (Bagley 1985: 140), while in Chester the Grosvenor family established strong control over parliamentary elections. Sir Thomas (d. 1700) and Sir Richard (d. 1732) had lived hard by the city at Eaton Hall. Sir Robert Grosvenor, at least before 1748, was more of an absentee and his electoral influence suffered. After that he paid much closer attention to the city, though short of Lord Strange's intimacy. Chester freemen should also have been in a gild; Grosvenor's vehicle for influence was the Innkeepers' Company, whose annual dinner he attended (Weston 1971: 35). Grosvenor representation via Chester must have eased the pressure from eligible gentry for one of the two county seats (Baskerville 1980). Before the end of the seventeenth century, towns had become useful institutions again, even allies of the landed gentry. But in un-enfranchised Nantwich in the early eighteenth century the aim of country landowners seems to have been much more simple: to keep down the poor rates which free-spending townsmen charged on rural dwellers' property in the town (Hall 1883: 207–28). However in Macclesfield, another town with no parliamentary representation, such men were involved in the corporate oligarchy. Under its new charter of 1684 120 burgesses comprised the lower level of the two-tier corporation. In the eighteenth century countrymen helped to swell this number to 280 (C. S. Davies 1961: 81). It was not merely parliamentary boroughs that attracted outsiders.

Political division between Whig and Tory entered a variety of issues. The dispute over the power of the Common Council in Liverpool (which tended to be Tory dominated and oligarchic) *vis-à-vis* the powers of the Assembly of freemen (in which Whigs were more numerous) continued until the Reform Act of 1832. The Tories obtained a charter from Charles II in 1678 which enhanced the Council's position by removing the right of the freemen to elect the mayor. William III's charter of 1695 still left unresolved the constitutional position of the Common Council, and some eighteenth-century mayors attempted to govern without a Council, only for another mayor to summon a Council meeting that promptly excised from the record the decisions of the Assembly made without the Council (Muir and Platt 1906: 118–32; Mullett 1973). In Chester Whigs supported Bills to improve the navigation of the Dee, while there was a suspicion that the Tories under Grosvenor were at best lukewarm because the estates of rural Tories were adversely affected (Baskerville 1980: 71–80).

Corporate towns still regulated their economies with the aid of gilds. In Lancaster attempts to interfere with the gild structure for political ends were resisted in James II's reign. About 1711 the Chester tanners solicited help from the county MPs to resist a tax on leather and to try to prevent the export of bark, and as late as 1726 the Chester stationers compelled a printer in the town to join the gild. In Wigan in the 1720s gilds were still prominent in artisan organization. The Chester gilds lasted well into the nineteenth century, but when a charitable bequest made them rich during the second half of the eighteenth century, entry became more restricted and their economic influence atrophied (Groombridge 1952: 101; Langton 1979: 98; Nutall 1967: 52–3). Unregulated wholesale trade in urban markets was more obviously in decline now than under the early Stuarts, and corn dealers rarely operated in the open market in 1780 in Cheshire (S. I. Mitchell 1982: 48). If gild and corporate rules did have any constricting effect on town economies, that pressure fell away in the 1700s. The internal excise and international customs duties were probably more effectively administered, despite smuggling, than any town-based regulations, and it is to the seaborne trade of the region's ports that we must now turn.

Parkgate, a landing place as much as a port, joined the list of the region's ports in the 1680s, and helped to stimulate the emergence of Neston as a market town (Place 1989; Willan 1938; R. Craig 1963: 105n). Liverpool invested significant sums in docks to improve ship handling (see Figure 3.1 and Plate 3.5 for the cumulative effect, pp. 168 and 167). Chester struggled against the silting of the River Dee, and a channel cut in the 1730s and 1740s maintained access to the city, as Boydell's picturesque engraving of 1749 claims (R. Craig 1963: 100–3; see opposite). The Irish trade was always important in the 'foreign' going trade of our region, and it comprised roughly three-quarters of Chester's overseas trade throughout the eighteenth century. Hides and tallow were constant imports, with Irish linens noticeable in the third quarter of the eighteenth century. The important role of Dublin merchants is emphasized by transhipped cargoes of wine and tobacco, which arrived in the port from Dublin. Chester sent coal to Ireland in return for these commodities; its other major exports were lead and its by-product litharge. There were some years in which grain went abroad, others in which it was imported, especially after 1765, from Holland and the Baltic (R. Craig 1963: 106, 109, 111, 117–19, 123–5). For Liverpool the most important commodity sent to Ireland was salt, which until the early decades of the eighteenth century, under technical and transport changes in the salt industry (see p. 99), plus the collapse of north Wales salt refining, used to go via Chester. Ships from Lancashire ports exported Irish provisions to the West Indies, often preserved in Cheshire salt (R. Craig 1963: 116; M. M. Schofield 1961: 143).

Though Lancaster's foreign and coastal trade increased in the eighteenth century, to which the new customs house designed in 1764 (Plate 2.5) paid elegant tribute, Liverpool far outshone it and the other Lancashire ports of Preston and Poulton (M. M. Schofield 1946: 21, 31; 1989: 242, 249ff). The American and West Indian trade of Liverpool grew from almost nothing in the 1660s. Between the 1670s and 1697–1702 the average weight of

---

Plate 2.4 'A South prospect of the city of Chester'. J. Boydell's engraving was published in 1749, and shows ships at the city, and the lowest bridge over the River Dee, to north Wales. The large church to the right is St Johns.

Plate 2.5 The new Customs House, Lancaster.

annual imports of tobacco increased nearly ninefold, the sugar averages more than doubled; tobacco nearly doubled again by 1727–30, and perhaps doubled again in 1738–50, while sugar averages rose by two and half times by 1727–30 and perhaps trebled again by 1738–50 (Clemens 1976: 212). In the late seventeenth century the colonies needed labour, and Liverpool merchants could supply indentured servants at a time when London and Bristol were finding this difficult. Liverpool's connections by salt with Irish victuallers were vital at a time when planters concentrated on cash crops, or when Indian wars disrupted mainland farming. The ability to supply food and labour gave the Liverpool merchants their entry into the established colonial trade of their metropolitan and provincial rivals. In the frequent wars of this period, Liverpool's route to the west was north around Ireland, away from the worst attacks by enemy warships and privateers (Clemens 1976: 213–16). It is unclear how important the slave trade was to Liverpool's commerce, though there was some slaving in the seventeenth century (C. N. Parkinson 1952). But when the demand for slaves increased because of an upturn in the demand for colonial products in Europe in the 1730s, Liverpool merchants increased the supply of slaves more effectively than those of Bristol or London, and thereby captured more of the commodity trade (Clemens 1976: 219). But, while some merchants, like William Davenport or Christopher Hasell, specialized heavily in slaving, others appear not to have engaged in it at all, for example Christopher's son Edward Hasell (D. Richardson 1976: 63–4, 65; E. M. and M. M. Schofield 1989: 87, 102). Not only did the Liverpool men fight their way into the market, but also once there, efficient factorage ensured better availability of cargoes and a quicker turnaround for their ships than for those of other ports. Factors in the colonies and their merchants at home combined to direct trade to colonies where the need for imported slave labour, due to high mortality, was constant, and which were highly integrated into the English market. At home in Liverpool in the 1730s and thereafter, mercantile partnerships enabled a bigger scale of operation in Africa, and could better stand the difficulties involved in remitting home profits (Clemens 1976: 220–1). Their entrepreneurship in developing the port's hinterland industries, or in making efficient transport connections, or in buying in export cargoes of textiles, not only in Lancashire but from Westmorland as well, is noted elsewhere (pp. 89–90), but was no less important because it ensured full holds for outward voyages.

Equally important for the region was the coasting trade. Cheese shipments to London through Chester, and to a lesser extent through Liverpool, seem to have been dominated by the London cheesemongers, whose near monopoly of the trade some farmers tried to break with their own direct marketing (see p. 80). Chester and Liverpool also distributed coal coastwise. The main difference between the two major ports seems to have been the importance of lead for Chester, at least in the eighteenth century, and the growing dominance of Liverpool as the distributor of salt. At first this trade was mainly along the west coast of England, but by the fourth decade of the eighteenth century shipments went to the east coast as well. Liverpool seems also to have distributed earthenware. Brought into the region were luxury foodstuffs, such as spices, and domestic goods, from London, while Bristol sent tobacco. Liverpool redistributed tobacco and sugar, some of which also came down the coast from Glasgow and Lancaster. Iron, cotton wool and dyestuffs were the chief raw materials on the cargo lists. The coastal trade of

Liverpool had doubled between 1689 and 1737, while that of Chester, though at first fluctuating, increased in volume in the third quarter of the eighteenth century (Willan 1938: 181–2, 185–6; R. Craig 1963: 115–16).

Seaborne trade in general stimulated shipbuilding all along the coasts of the region, and in turn that involved textile workers in sailmaking, especially on the Mersey and around Kirkham and Poulton. Compared with Liverpool, one of the weaknesses of Chester's trade seems to have been the importance of Dublin and London merchants, and, indeed, Liverpool men in the limited new world trade. Also, by comparison, Chester failed to develop an industrial hinterland. Some Chester men did invest in industry like the merchant Daniel Peck, who *c.* 1700 was involved in coal-mining in north Wales, where he also refined salt and smelted lead (Chester City RO, Daniel Peck's letterbook). Liverpool's success was based on the way its merchants developed interests in the commodities they handled, and improved transport to and from the port for these items. Liverpool merchants, such as members of the Blackburne family (also landed proprietors), invested in coal and salt production (see p. 86). Raw items such as sugar shipped to the port were processed in the area, and the goods needed to buy slaves for example, or to provide necessities and comforts for American colonists, could be bought in the port's hinterland. The growth in trade and industry were interdependent, in contrast for example with Whitehaven, where the coal and new-world trades compare well with Liverpool's, but where industry in the hinterland failed to develop (eg M. M. Schofield 1986; T. C. Barker and Harris 1954; cf. Beckett 1981: 202–7).

The growth of urban populations (see p. 68), the involvement of the rural gentry in urban government and politics, the development of both new and existing manufactures (see p. 102), the role of some towns as ports, and improvements in transport focused on the towns (see p. 85), all served to increase demand for retail shopping and urban services. Thus while small market towns enjoyed a local hinterland, that of the larger towns extended across whole counties: Chester supplied Macclesfield and Ruthin, and its newspapers were delivered in south Lancashire while Manchester's reach extended well into east Cheshire. The townsmen had to compete as always with professional men who worked in the countryside, and with itinerant tradesmen both at and outside of fairs. In Chester from the 1760s onwards shopkeepers were extending and making more attractive their retail premises, where goods direct from London, and therefore including the latest fashions not only in clothes but also in household items, could be bought. In 1757 Thomas Ledsham's book shop in Chester dealt in over 1,000 volumes. At the end of the period covered in this chapter Chester was well provided with milliners and drapers and tailors. There were premises in Manchester called shops selling toys (ie metal goods and trinkets), and glass and china (S. I. Mitchell 1984: 268, 276, 277; Raffald 1772).

Alongside the new retail emporia the familiar blacksmith and inn, exemplars of service industries, remained. The equally familiar forms of credit were widespread in the economy (eg Pressnell 1956: 19, 319), with the town courts to enforce payment. By the end of the period of this chapter banks have emerged, usually out of the dominant trades of a town. One of the members of an early Manchester bank was a check maker, while at Liverpool merchant houses were the birthplaces of banks; Preston, Chester, Liverpool and Manchester all had them (Pressnell 1956: 20, 25, 49, 390). There was, however, still some suspicion of them, as for example, when in 1761 the Weaver Navigation trustees preferred to borrow from individuals rather than from a Chester bank (Pressnell 1956: 389). New forms of transport bought new services: the chairmen (Sedan chairs), porters and packers in Manchester, or the three coach hirers and two coach builders in Chester. Chester had an organist whereas Manchester had an organ-builder, and provided for both pleasure and for pain with musical instrument makers and surgical instrument makers respectively; there were dancing masters in both towns. (Raffald 1772; Dyke 1949). The specialist gardener in Chester, Manchester and Preston is evident quite early in the eighteenth century, and Preston was one of the first towns in England to develop walks where socialites could promenade and display (Borsay 1977: 583). Even the supposedly old-fashioned gilds played their part, at Chester in the later seventeenth century by putting up the prize money for one of the Roodee races (Groombridge 1952: 100).

Education was a service by no means exclusive to towns, for there were many country schools. Neither was urban education only the concern of dissenters, though their influence was disproportionately large. Dissenters, numerous in the region, were barred from the universities and the major professions and, though they clung to classical training for their ministers, the laity who increasingly looked to trade and industry for their living began to seek a more directly useful form of education. For boys, entry into commerce could be as expensive as sending a child to the universities (eg Aiken 1795: 183–4). Indeed, it could be the equivalent of a university education in economic prospects and, as trade grew, useful knowledge as well as money could open the way to a commercial career. It was the dissenters who responded to this demand. Their early schools, like the Quaker school at Stockport in 1706, reflected a desire to remove their children from Anglican influence or worldly pressure and were not radically innovatory in their curricula. Towards mid-century however peripatetic speakers began to deliver courses of lectures and demonstrations. Richard Kay of Bury attended at least twelve sessions in June and July 1741 of a wide-ranging afternoon course in natural philosophy (ie physics) taken by Dr Rotheram of Kendal at Manchester. He wrote in his diary 'Mr. Rotheram's Performance and Apparatus have been very entertaining and I hope will be useful' (Brockbank and Kenworthy 1968: 63–6). A similar course, for ladies and gentlemen, was advertised in the *Chester Courant* in November 1749 (Robson 1966: 83).

During the 1750s the deaths of the three principals of dissenting academies elsewhere in England opened the way to the establishment of Warrington Academy, based on subscriptions mainly from merchants and others in Liverpool, Manchester, Birmingham and Warrington. The new academy, which opened in 1757, was principally intended for the training of dissenting ministers but two of the three academic tutorships were in mathematics and natural philosophy, and in languages and *belles-lettres*. Although it flourished only from 1757 to 1783 Warrington left a profound mark on the region. Its enlarged and modern curriculum included modern languages, English literature, history, natural history, physics and chemistry as well as classics and divinity. Its tutors were men of note, especially Joseph Priestley who joined it from his Nantwich school and ministry in 1765. Its students, boys, came from both Anglican and dissenting backgrounds and included laymen as well as ministerial candidates. Of the 400 or so students three, Drs Percival, Aiken (see p. 68 for their contribution to the study of the region's population) and Barnes became highly influential in the region's life; one, T. R. Malthus, at the academy only in its last year, had a much wider impact. Former students founded the Manchester Literary and Philosophical Society and the Manchester Academy, tutors founded the Liverpool Academy of Art and presided over the Warrington Circulating Library of 1760. (See W. Turner 1957 for the history of the academy.) The town grammar schools were not untouched by the new spirit. Macclesfield, described by Hodson as Cheshire's outstanding improving school, obtained a private Act of Parliament in 1774 to permit the teaching of modern languages (Hodson 1978: 54; Robson 1966: 64). Manchester Grammar School taught book-keeping, mathematics and French from mid-century but only as paid extras on the half-holidays from Latin and Greek and in defiance of the founding statutes (Graham and Phythian 1965: 33). Young ladies, excluded from the old grammar schools, were equally unwelcome at the new modern ones; increasingly in the eighteenth century their path lay through private boarding schools which inculcated the skills and manners necessary for entering society. However, money was a prerequisite for such schooling, and its impact was limited to the children of the more wealthy.

There were other intellectual interests to be catered for in towns besides those of children. And, just as with clothes or such consumer items as fine china, there was some imitating of London. For example, there was a Drury Lane playhouse in Liverpool in 1749 or 1750 where London actors performed a summer season (Darcy 1976: 8n). Manchester too had a theatre, and a concert hall capable of seating 900, which had emerged by 1765 from a small informal gathering of musicians. A circulating library had started in 1757 (Frangopulo 1962: 38). Informal literary discussions in the 1750s in Liverpool led to the formation of a subscription library with 109 members in 1760. Lancaster, Rochdale and Warrington all established libraries within ten years. In Liverpool the Academy of the Fine Arts stuttered to failure by

1775, but in Manchester the Literary and Philosophical Society founded in 1779 was to go on to great things. Manchester too seems to have lacked a taste for art, though there were plenty of commissions for portrait painters in both cities, including at Liverpool Joseph Wright of Derby. Merchants were more numerous than professional men among these intellectual pioneers (Darcy 1976: 21–9, 65). However, clergymen, physicians, surgeons and apothecaries (both Chester and Manchester founded hospitals in the 1750s) and lawyers were present in most towns, and in quantity in the larger ones; there were no fewer than thirty attorneys in the 1782 Chester directory. The interconnection between different services is well illustrated for the early eighteenth century by the notary Henry Prescott, who was deputy-registrar of Chester Diocese, and a great patron, with some of his clients, of Chester inns (Addy 1987: viii, xv). Churches and courts still played their part in attracting visitors to Lancaster and Preston as well. Indeed, clergymen had more opportunities as new Anglican churches were built in Liverpool, Manchester, Macclesfield and Preston to cope with those in the rising populations who did not attend chapel. We can add schoolmasters, surveyors, mathematicians and government officers to the list of urban professionals. The breadth of urban interests and entertainments widened significantly before 1780, and moved closer together with those of the landed elite (see p. 74); equally with retail outlets, and professional and craft services, they made towns intellectually and economically vital, as well as socially attractive places to go to. In Chapter 3 we shall see the pace of such developments accelerate.

As manufacturing and trading towns grew in numbers of people, and as their economies became more varied and complex, so the buildings of the towns changed. Certain types of houses became associated with particular occupations and the trade in manufactures in particular moved from open market place or private shop to prestigious public halls. Manchester's first Exchange was built in 1729, Liverpool's in 1749–54. Official buildings also declared status: Liverpool erected a succession of Customs Houses, while Lancaster built a fine Customs House in 1764 (see Plate 2.5). By the end of the period some of the smaller textile towns had established cloth halls, such as Colne's 1775 Piece Hall of twenty-three bays.

The physical growth in existing towns in the region was generally unplanned and haphazard, but at Ashton-under-Lyne the fifth Earl of Stamford planned a new town west of the old parish centre and south of the old road to Manchester in 1768. The new layout, depicted later as in Figure 2.2, was based on a gridiron with a broad, straight east–west spinal street, Stamford Street, running through the centre from a polygonal circus in the east to a wider square in the west with a new church closing the east–west view. In the older towns, the unified facade, so successful in Bath, made an early regional appearance at Abbey Square in Chester in the 1750s, though it was some time before it was followed elsewhere in the region. Urban prosperity was revealed in new building materials: brick-built houses began to emerge in

115

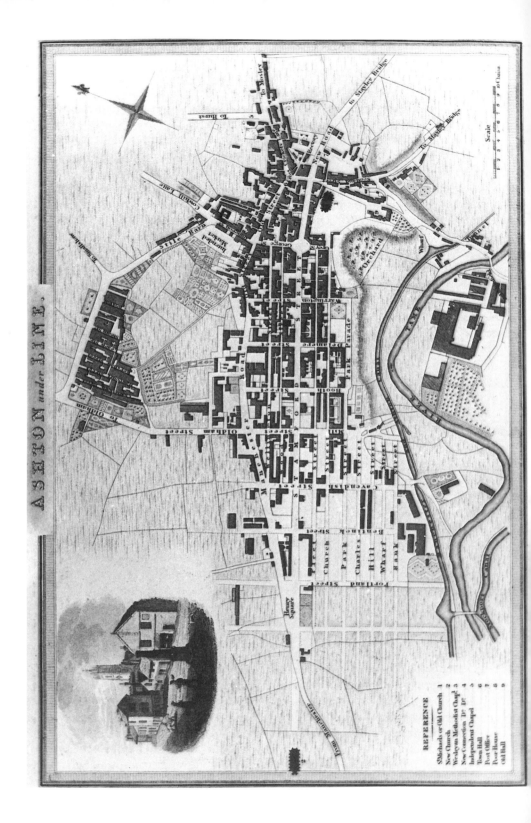

ASHTON under LINE.

To Mossley

To Staley Bridge

To Hurst

To Staley Bridge

Scale
1 2 3 4 5 6 7 8 9 10 Chains

New Road

Rectory

Scotland

Wharf

Orchard

Stile Karr

Herald's Market

Cornhill Lane

George Street

Warrington Street

Park Parade

Booth Street

Delamere Street

To Saddleworth

Road

Old Bridge

To Oldham

Oldham Street

Cavendish Street

Bentinck Street

Portland Street

Henry Square

Church Street

Park

Charles Street

Hill Street

Wharf Street

Bank Street

Peak Forest Canal

TAME

REFERENCE

S.Michaels or Old Church	1
New Church	2
Wesleyan Methodist Chapel	3
New Connection D.º D.º	4
Independent Chapel	5
Town Hall	6
Post Office	7
Poor House	8
Old Hall	9

Manchester as early as 1700. Inside houses, room use developed; the new and showy role of the parlour indicates an increase in casual visiting as transport improved and rude overnight hospitality gave way to greater politeness. Aiken describes how this change affected Manchester.

> In 1708 the act passed for building St. Ann's Church, which in a few years was followed by the square and streets adjoining, where was displayed a new style of light and convenient rooms. . . . The front parlours however were reserved for company only: and the family usually lived in the back parlours. This fashion continued to our own times, and in small houses subsists in some degree at present.
>
> (Aiken 1795: 186)

Later, the houses of the well-to-do might become showcases for the new consumer fashions. Of the lower quality urban house we know little, particularly in those burgeoning textile towns where successive waves of nineteenth-century development washed away the physical evidence.

Government: Politics and Religion

The basic structures of local and ecclesiastical government described in Chapter 1, shorn only of the prerogative Council of the North, continued throughout this period. On occasion that normally passive peculiar, the Duchy of Lancaster, became of political significance because of the chancellor's power to issue the commission of the peace for the county. Thus in the aftermath of the Glorious Revolution the chancellor, lord-lieutenant and Privy Council in London clashed over the composition of the Bench of JPs (Glassey 1979: 278–80, 291–4). Duchy administration continued to make Preston a centre of government, while the palatinate remained based at Lancaster. In Cheshire the Palatinate Court of Grand Session served as the assize, and its equity jurisdiction was active until the later part of George III's reign, though a decrease in volume of administrative records suggests decline elsewhere in the palatine Exchequer (*VCH. Cheshire*, II: 56–8). In both

Figure 2.2   Ashton-under-Lyne, 1824. In the 1760s the fifth Earl of Stamford cut a wide, new street south and west of the old town centre. The old church of St Michael at the eastern end of the street was to be balanced by a new church at the west end. The grid of streets north and south of the new one produced what was in effect a new town but, although some substantial buildings dignified Stamford Street itself, the growth of the cotton industry swamped any idea of an elegant residential quarter. (Source: E. Baines 1824–5.)

counties the lieutenancy became a political post, changing much in the aftermath of the Glorious Revolution as first Whig, then Tory, magnates were appointed. The recurring appointment and dismissal of a member of the Stanley family from the post marked a major change in that family's role in Lancashire; they also lost the lieutenancy of Cheshire (Glassey 1979: 277). Although some 1,200 men had mustered as the Cheshire militia in 1684, sixty years later in 1745 the Earl of Cholmondeley, the lord-lieutenant, reported that there were no men, arms, or cash to field an effective force against the Jacobites (*VCH. Cheshire*, II: 74). Later in the century new militia forces were raised (Western 1965: ch. 6).

The Justices of the Peace remained the backbone of local government, but it would be misleading to write of smooth continuity in the magistracy. In Cheshire the buildings in which quarter sessions were held decayed and were not renewed, so that sessions ceased to be held at Middlewich after 1723, and at Nantwich and Northwich after 1760, leaving only Chester and Knutsford. Though there were fewer sessions, there were more justices: in Cheshire in 1675 there were forty-four, and ninety in 1720, a number which declined a little in the later part of the century; in 1715 a proposed commission for Lancashire totalled fifty-nine. Compared to the continuity of membership in earlier periods, only one of the justices of Lancashire in 1716 had served continuously since 1688; another contrast was the increasing number of clergymen who served as justices (Glassey 1979: 15, 291, 293; *VCH. Cheshire*, II: 61, 62). The range of business dealt with by the JPs was as large as ever, with considerably more time being spent on examination of disaffected persons, whether in respect of the anti-monarchist plots of the 1660s, the Jacobite threats of the 1690s against King William, or those suspected of opposing the government after the 1715 rising, or even in the 1720s. As grain prices rose in the 1750s and 1760s, so the justices found themselves dealing with food price riots, particularly in the large towns like Manchester; as early as 1736 the grand jury at Chester sessions were recording grain prices. (Bennett and Dewhurst 1940: 213; S. I. Mitchell 1982: 50–1, 60; Redford 1939: 141–6).

Although the diocese of Chester was re-established with the Stuarts in 1660, the denominations which had emerged in the intellectual maelstrom of the 1640s and 1650s did not disappear. At first the news of the Restoration was greeted with general rejoicing in the north-west not least by the Presbyterians who saw themselves as principal agents in the King's return. On 24 May 1660 Henry Newcome preached in Manchester's Collegiate Church on the text 'And he bowed the heart of the men of Judah, even as the heart of one man so that they sent this word unto the king. Return thou, and all thy servants'. By 23 April 1661, the occasion of the Coronation, Warden Heyricke's sermon sounded a sombre note of warning, and his anxieties were fully justified. Presbyterianism, which had been strong in Cheshire and had officially dominated Lancashire, not only in its religious but also in much of its secular life, rapidly lost its power and most of its influence once its parochial basis had been destroyed. The last classical meeting of Lancashire Presbyterians was held on 14 August 1660, the Book of Common Prayer, candles, organ and choir reappeared in the Collegiate Church in November of that year and in September 1662 Heyricke himself preached in a surplice, 'a standard bearer fainteth' (Halley 1872: 367). The Act of Uniformity in that year forced 100 dissenting ministers in Lancashire and at least sixty-four in Cheshire and north Derbyshire out of their parishes. John Angier at Denton, who had been episcopally ordained but refused to conform, remained undisturbed with the support of the local gentry families of Holland and Hyde until his death in 1677 but his nephew, who attempted to succeed him, was ejected. Most of the ejected ministers held to their beliefs and carried on ministering to their adherents who supported them by voluntary offerings. Others were forced to adopt a second occupation. William Bagshawe, ejected from Glossop in 1662, was fortunate in that respect. He returned to the family home at Ford Hall and was able to devote himself to that travelling ministry of houses, fields and barns which made him the 'Apostle of the Peak'; his successor James Clegg had to be both farmer and doctor. Devoted service of this kind enabled Presbyterianism to survive until the Toleration Act allowed the building of chapels in 1689 but in the eighteenth century the ministry was drawn to Unitarianism and many succeeded in taking their congregations with them. Cross Street chapel in Manchester, where the Trinitarians seceded in about 1750, became the leading north-western centre for the Unitarians; in Cheshire, Dean Row, which had the largest dissenting congregation of 1,309 in 1718, followed the same course. The Independents, who were strongest round Samuel Eaton's pioneering centre at Dukinfield in north-east Cheshire drew closer to the Presbyterians as they shared common sufferings, hopes and anxieties in the late seventeenth century but they proved far more resistant to Unitarian ideas so that a chapel like that at Chinley (Plate 2.6) in Derbyshire, founded by William Bagshawe, moved quietly into Independency in the mid-eighteenth century. Quakers and Baptists, though they caused much concern, were not present in very large numbers. By 1715 the Protestant Nonconformists had forty-three congregations in Lancashire with some 18,000 hearers, the largest groups being in Manchester, Liverpool and Bolton (Halley 1872: 436). In Cheshire too it was the textile hundred of Macclesfield that harboured Protestant dissent with over 58 per cent of Cheshire Nonconformists (Hodson 1978: 39).

From the Declaration of Indulgence in 1672 to the collapse of the Jacobite rebellion of 1745, religion dominated politics in the north-west. The restored Church of England was strengthened by a gradual accession of gentry from Puritan families, including even Henry Booth, the second Lord Delamer, but that 'whiggish' wing of the Church was matched in strength by High Church fervour in much of south Lancashire, especially in Manchester where a Tory populace carried Stuart loyalties into Jacobitism after 1688.

Roman Catholicism, weak in Cheshire where it was largely confined to the Wirral, remained strong in Lancashire, particularly in the north and west, and potentially threatening because many of the gentry families and their tenants maintained the old faith (Hodson 1978: 44).

The gentry of both counties were politically divided throughout this period. The national parties of Whig and Tory were often split and fragmented at Westminster, so that the term 'party' has to be used with caution. The words 'Whig' and 'Tory' were not in use in Lancashire until Anne's reign, though the term 'Whig' was used in a letter about Cheshire politics in 1682. Either party could be fragmented. Thus in Cheshire in the early eighteenth century the Tories were split into a group who supported the Hanoverian monarchy, a second group dissatisfied with both the Stuarts and the outcome of the Glorious Revolution, and a third group (including the Leghs of Lyme and the Grosvenors) who were on the fringes of Jacobitism. The unity of the Cheshire Whigs on the other hand was split because of the reluctance of the Earl of Cholmondeley to subordinate himself to the Booth earls of Warrington (*VCH. Cheshire*, II: 118–26; Glassey 1987; Henning 1983: 151). By mid-century party divides were less energetically celebrated.

Gentry politics were fought out in three main political arenas, two of which also involved the lower orders of society. Each of the arenas was closely interrelated with the others, though they are here treated separately. First, the composition of the lieutenancy and the magistracy was ruthlessly changed by the dominant party under the Stuarts and early Hanoverians. In so doing, Charles II and James II defeated their own ends, upsetting potential supporters whom they removed from office, and insulting them because their replacements were often men whose social status was noticeably below that normally required for such office. Men who may not have wished to attack the king in 1688, were unwilling to do anything to support him, and once William III was in power, qualms over the legitimacy of his rule were of no effect. The second arena was the parliamentary election for the two county seats, which also brought in freeholder tenants; those towns with parliamentary franchises became an extension of the conflict (see over); the clergy also took on an electoral role (Baskerville 1987). Vigorously fought under Charles II and James II over issues which amounted to the preservation of the Church of England against the Romanist aspirations of the Stuarts, the outcome in Cheshire was victory for the Whigs, who sat for Cheshire until 1702. But other issues and influences, of local interest, were at work in parliamentary elections: Whigs and Tories took sides over the appointment of the recorder

---

Plate 2.6 Chinley chapel. The chapel was built in 1711 by the north Derbyshire Presbyterians who had gathered around William Bagshaw, but the congregation later became Independent. Later alterations converted separate doors for men and women into windows, made a new doorway, and added a gallery, but it still preserves its pulpit on the north wall and a wealth of box pews.

of Wigan in the 1690s. In Cheshire they divided over the navigation of the Weaver. Between the Restoration and Glorious Revolution in Lancashire the Stanley and Gerard families disputed elections. After 1688, the Stanley family normally returned one, Whig, Member of Parliament in Lancashire, which circumscribed electoral opportunity in the county; the Jacobites managed to return a member of the Shuttleworth family in every Parliament between 1712 and 1758. Preston in particular reflected county issues in its parliamentary elections (see p. 106), while Newton and Clitheroe were pocket boroughs, though Clitheroe's result could not be guaranteed before the 1720s; county gentry families were involved in elections in Liverpool and Lancaster (where the Kirkby family of Furness was dominant in the late seventeenth century). In the latter part of our period contested elections were unusual in both counties. Only a small number of individuals and families served as Members of Parliament, so that there was a remarkable continuity of personnel. The Shuttleworths in Lancashire were paralleled by the Cholmondeleys of Vale Royal; Charles Cholmondeley sat seven times for Cheshire, and was a sitting member when he died, to be replaced by his son Thomas (*VCH, Cheshire*, II: 115; Glassey 1987: 49–52; Henning 1983: 286; Namier and Brooke 1964: 315–22; Sedgewick 1970: 269–72).

On occasion a few of the gentry and peers took a third, direct, form of political action. Monmouth's visit to Wallasey races in September 1682 was a triumphal occasion supported by Delamer and others who wanted to exclude a Catholic heir to Charles II. While the Duke supped in Chester the loyalist gentry rallied in Delamere Forest as they did again in 1683 to celebrate the failure of the Rye House plot. Cheshire's enthusiasm for Monmouth however fell short of rising in his support in 1685 though Delamer was suspected of complicity and spent six months under arrest before being cleared in January 1686. In 1688 he took the lead in raising the north for William of Orange, declaring not only for himself but also for the Earl of Derby, rallying his Warrington, Manchester, Ashton and Cheshire tenants on Bowdon Down and seizing arms as far away as Edgbaston Hall (HMC 1894: 198–202). Bowdon Down figured again as the setting for a great rally in June 1689 when, in an echo of the Good Old Cause, an immense army met there with contingents from all over Lancashire and Cheshire under familiar names, Birch of Ordsall, old Colonel Dukinfield and 'Blakley Lyon led by Captain Leaver of Olerington and Sam Dickinson' (HMC 1894: 222–3).

It was now the turn of the high Tories and the Catholics to suffer investigation of plots, real or imaginary, and to hope for another landing that would restore the 'rightful succession' and High Church power. Informations given by two agents, John Lunt and George Wilson, in June 1694 implicated a large number of Protestant and Catholic peers, gentry and clergy in Lancashire and Cheshire in Jacobite plots but trials at Manchester and Chester failed to elicit evidence and the ten men accused were discharged (Hodson 1978: 20). The 1715 rising showed that the 1694 plot, however dubious, was not remote from reality. Catholic gentry who joined the Jacobites at Lancaster and Preston included members of the families of Townley, Tyldesley and Dalton, all named in 1694, though many others lay low. Ten of the leading Cheshire Jacobite gentry, more cautiously, decided at Ashley Hall, by the casting vote of Peter Legh of Lyme, not to rise, agreed to have their portraits painted and took comfort in a romantic Jacobitism which again failed to ripen into action in 1745, again by the casting vote of another Peter Legh, emulating his father. The Lancashire Jacobites were less cautious. Not only did old Catholic families like the Townleys turn out in 1745 but also some 500 Manchester men marched with Charles Edward south to Derby, then north again to Carlisle where the Manchester Regiment surrendered. The heads of Syddall and Deacon, two of the eleven Manchester men executed, displayed on poles on the Exchange provided a sad postscript to the high hopes of St Andrew's Day in November 1745, when the Prince attended a great service in the Collegiate Church and his troops marched to the muster through streets bright with tartan (T. Baines 1867, Div III: 101–2).

By the 1740s a hundred years of dispute and dissension, wars and rumours, plot and counterplot had left the north-west with a declining body of dissenters, clustered mainly but not entirely in the industrial areas, with quiet islands of Catholic gentry, their kin and tenantry, above all in north and west Lancashire and with a Church of England split by faction as in Manchester, where Whig St Ann's and the Tory clergy of the Collegiate Church sustained a long feud. The Church itself had been enfeebled by the loss of devoted if heterodox ministers in 1662 and, on a smaller scale, of non-jurors in 1688, their replacements often being of a lower calibre. Pastoral care was weak and in the huge parishes of the region with their growing populations the Church had done little to reach out to Nonconformists or the indifferent or to inspire nominal Anglicans with more than destructive zeal. Perhaps the time was now right for a simple religious message that asked hearers to look inward once again and to judge themselves rather than others.

The first stirrings of evangelical revival in the north-west were felt in the late 1730s and early 1740s when David Taylor, a former servant of the Countess of Huntingdon, and Benjamin Ingham, an excluded Anglican priest, began preaching in the hamlets and villages of the Cheshire–Derbyshire border with forays into south Lancashire. It was Taylor's preaching that converted John Bennett, a Chinley pack-horse carrier, in 1741 and his societies in Lancashire and Cheshire provided the earliest hearers for John and Charles Wesley in 1744 and 1745 (E. A. Rose 1975: 24–5; 1982: 68–9). Other laymen and women had also been at work and during the 1750s and 1760s many of their societies were drawn into the Wesleyan network though the revival of the Baptists, Independents and other sects and a defection of some congregations to the Moravians produced confusion and rivalry. Despite set-backs however the influence of the Wesleys grew, surviving a breach with Bennett in 1752, and the Methodists went on to build new societies and integrate them into their 'rounds' or circuits. They met great opposition. At Altrincham in 1750 they were pelted with rotten eggs, potatoes and dirt, Rochdale greeted them with 'multitudes of people, shouting, cursing, blaspheming, and gnashing upon us with their teeth', and 'the lions at Rochdale were lambs in comparison with those at Bolton' while Oldham was even worse (E. A. Rose 1982: 71–5). But by 1801 they had spread their message from east to west across the region, had chapels in most of the towns and could claim 1.64 per cent of the population of Lancashire south of the Ribble and 1.76 per cent of the population of Cheshire as members (E. A. Rose 1982: 86).

Changes in the Distribution of Wealth

It is difficult to establish the levels of wealth, or of poverty, which resulted from the demographic, agrarian and industrial changes in town and country-side between 1660 and 1780 discussed above, or to compare them at the beginning and end of the period covered in this chapter. There is no quantifiable evidence of wealth, so we shall concentrate on poverty. Exemption from the hearth tax in 1664 can be used as a measure of poverty in each parish. Such a measure understates the poor (see p. 6), and the willingness to record the exempt may vary from hundred to hundred, but the present argument assumes that any understatement is constant. At the risk of indicating a spurious exactitude that the data and methodology may not support, the proportion of exempt households in each parish has been ranked, and the parishes represented on Figure 2.3 in quartiles of that rank; those parishes with the highest proportion exempt were the poorest, those with the lowest proportions exempt were the richer parishes.

The richer Cheshire parishes were concentrated in the west of the county, in a strip from Shocklach in the south to Ince in the north. Dairy farming was important here, especially in the south of this area and, no doubt, the wealth of nearby Chester must have permeated the country. There were a few other parishes with a notably small proportion of exempt households scattered over the county. At the other end of the scale, there was an apparently patternless scattering of parishes in the centre of the county with a notably large proportion of exempt. These included Northwich and Nantwich where the salt works required numbers of wage labourers in an industry made unstable by internal competition and technological change (see pp. 51 and 99). The Wirral, isolated from much of the region, stands out as a poor area with all but two of its parishes appearing in the upper half of the rank. Although Prestbury (excluding Macclesfield chapelry), Gawsworth and Mottram in Longdendale parishes appear in the bottom two quartiles of the ranking, the rest of the north-east of the county ranked at the (poor) top. The distribution of rankings in Lancashire is much more concentrated than in Cheshire. South-east Lancashire, dominated by textiles, ranked at the (poor) top, while south-west Lancashire where coal and agriculture were important, ranked in the bottom (least poor) half. Agriculture predominated in the west, and textiles in the east, of central Lancashire, which ranked chiefly in the upper middle quartile, above most of the parishes north of Garstang which ranked in the lower middle quartile.

Nationally collected figures for poor law expenditure in the year ending at Easter 1776, divided by 1778 estimates of households per parish (see p. 68), give a per household expenditure on the poor, to relieve sickness, unemployment, old age, and pay the legal costs of settlement and removal; we have assumed that expenditure on a pauper is roughly constant across the region. These figures have been ranked and mapped (Figure 2.4) in the same way as the hearth tax data. In 1778 in Lancashire the textile areas appear to be less poor than the mining and agricultural regions, though gaps in the record fragment the picture. Thus the major urban centres of Lancashire and north-east Cheshire are not in observation. In the rest of Cheshire no clear geographical pattern is apparent, except that much of the Wirral appears in the bottom half of the ranking.

Figures 2.3 and 2.4 and the two ranks of data from which they are derived provide a basis on which to estimate changes in the geographical distribution of wealth by 1780, though, obviously, they do not indicate the time-scale of any such changes. The tax records for 1664 and 1775–6 are not of course of the same type, and we are on less certain ground when we use them to make comparisons, which for some parishes are prevented by gaps in the evidence. With all its shortcomings, and putting aside those parishes from the 1664 ranking which do not appear in the 1778 ranking, the available material presents two contrasting pictures, particularly at the top and bottom of the ranks. In Lancashire, of the ten parishes ranked in the top quartile in 1664, nine are in the bottom half of the 1778 rank; while seven from the bottom quartile in 1664 are in the top half in 1778. The same inverse correlation is present in Cheshire, though less distinctly; thus eleven of the top twenty 1664 parishes are in the bottom half in 1778, and sixteen of the bottom quartile in 1664 are in the top half in 1778.

If economic resources had remained undeveloped since 1664, it might be expected that those parishes in which population growth was highest between 1664 and 1778 would be the poorest. But of course there had been industrial, commercial and agricultural development and in both counties many parishes, such as Bolton-le-Moors (+300 per cent), Audlem (+126 per cent), and Mottram in Longdendale (+140 per cent), at the top of a ranking by percentage population change 1664–1778, appear at the bottom of the ranking of poor law expenditure. In Lancashire it would seem (allowing for

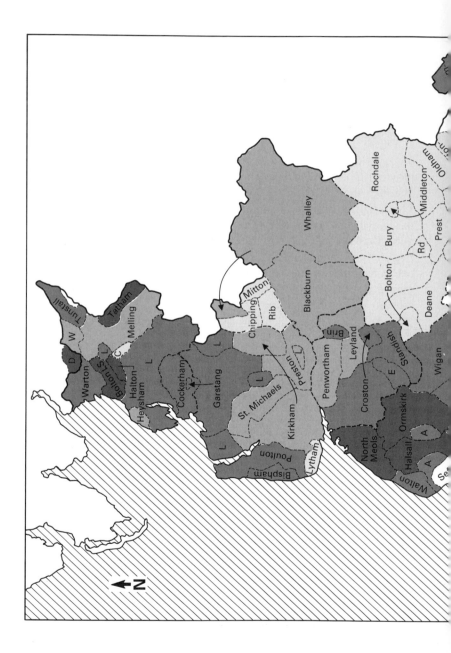

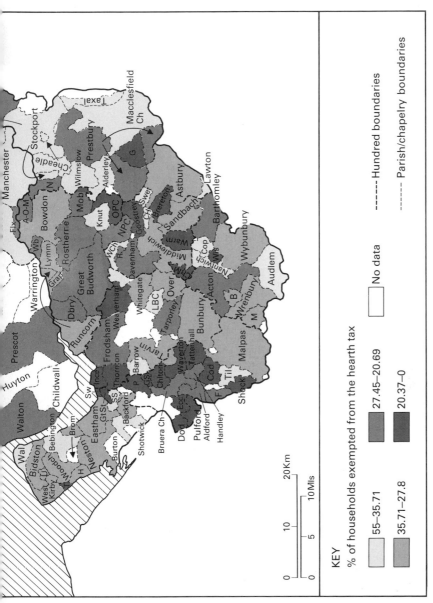

Figure 2.3 Estimates of the distribution of poverty, *c.* 1664, Lancashire and Cheshire.

KEY

% of households exempted from the hearth tax

- 55–35.71
- 35.71–27.8
- 27.45–20.69
- 20.37–0
- No data

------ Hundred boundaries

------ Parish/chapelry boundaries

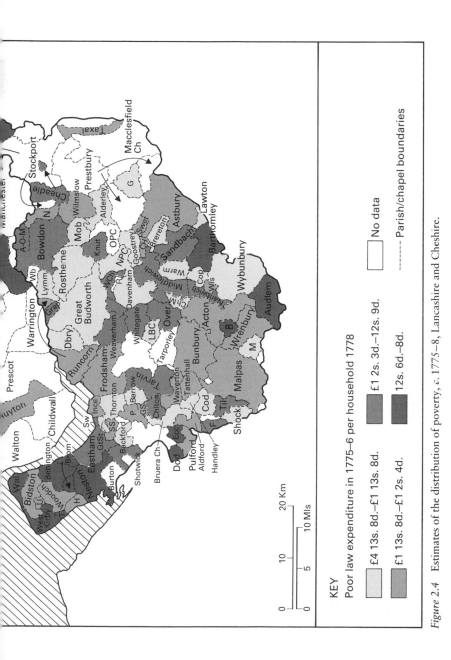

KEY

Poor law expenditure in 1775–6 per household 1778

- £4 13s. 8d.–£1 13s. 8d.
- £1 13s. 8d.–£1 2s. 4d.
- £1 2s. 3d.–12s. 9d.
- 12s. 6d.–8d.
- No data
- ------ Parish/chapel boundaries

Figure 2.4 Estimates of the distribution of poverty, *c.*1775–8, Lancashire and Cheshire.

Abbreviations used in Figures 2.3 and 2.4.

parish/Chapelry

Cheshire

Ashton-on-Mersey	A-O-M
Baddiley	B
Bromborough	Brom
Christleton	Chlton
Church Coppenhall	Cop
Church Hulme Ch	CH
Church Lawton	Lawton
Church Minshull	Ch M
Coddington	Cod
Daresbury Ch	Dbry
Dodleston	Dod
Eccleston	Ecc
Farndon	F
Gawsworth	G
Grappenhall	Grap
Great Stanney	Gt St
Guilden Sutton	GS
Heswall	H
Knutsford Ch	Knut
Little Budworth Ch	LBC
Marbury	M
Mobberley	Mob
Mottram-in-Longdendale	Mottram-in-L
Nether Peover Ch	NPC
Northenden	N
Over Peover Ch	OPC
Plemstall	P
Rudheath Lordship	R
Shocklach	Shock

Stanlow	Sw
Stoke	SS
Swettenham	Swet
Thornton-le-Moors	Thornton
Thurstaston	T
Tilston	Til
Upton	U
Wallasey	Wal
Warburton	Wb
Warmingham	Warm
Wistaston	Wis
Witton Ch	WCh
Woodchurch	Woodch

Lancashire

Ashton-under-Lyne	Ashton-U-L
Aughton	A
Bolton-le-Moors	Bolton
Bolton-le-Sands	Bolton LS
Brindle	Brin
Claughton	C
Dalton	D
Eccleston	E
Flixton	Flx
Lancaster	L
Poulton-le-Fylde	Poulton
Prestwich-c-Oldham	Prest
Radcliffe	Rd
Ribchester	Rib
Whittington	W

Sources: Figure 2.3, see Table 1.1; Figure 2.4 P.P. 1803–4 (175) Abstract of Returns to 43 Geo. III *c.*144.
Note: Maps drawn from parish boundaries in Sylvester and Nulty 1958 and France 1938. Some Cheshire boundaries are slightly modified by Dunn 1987.

the lacunae in the evidence) that poverty was less of a problem in the textile areas in the south and east of the county than on the coalfield in the south-west. Although there were good wages for miners working full time, and work for women and boys in the coal industry, was there perhaps more work for all the family in textiles than in coal, giving higher family incomes and less poverty in the east? Was there more sickness on the coalfield, and did the costs of removal bear heavily on the poor law expenditure? One might have expected Lancashire's agricultural areas to benefit from the great increase in demand for foodstuffs from the county's rising population. This is by no means clear in Penwortham, but the central parishes, at least as far north as Cockerham, seem to have done so. Scanty wage evidence suggests that, whereas lower wages were paid in north as opposed to south Lancashire in the early eighteenth century, by the 1760s that differential had disappeared (Gilboy 1934: 175). Yet in the north of our region there were still high per household levels of poor expenditure, in some parishes, though migration from such parishes as Warton (see p. 69) may have kept expenditure down. In Cheshire too, despite specialization and rationalization in farming (fewer holdings (see pp. 78–9) therefore more landless labourers but no marked population increase), poor law expenditure in the agricultural west, where there was no industry, was high in some parishes. Was transport good enough yet to connect the farmers to the towns, or had the farmers fastened onto the local as opposed to the London foodstuffs market yet (Mingay 1989: 243)? In the industrial centre, Nantwich had become a market rather than a salt town, and the zeal of its property owners against high rates (see p. 107) appears to have paid dividends in per household poor expenditure. Northwich, now the centre of a buoyant salt industry (see p. 100) also seems in 1778 to be less burdened by the poor than in 1664.

By 1780 southern Lancashire had begun to sever its ties with the past. But the north of the county and Cheshire, with the probable exception of Stockport and Macclesfield, still had more links with the past.

Chapter 3

1780–1860

Population

In south-east Lancashire and north-east Cheshire and the High Peak the growth of the textile trades during these years changed the character of family life, encouraged immigration and transformed a predominantly rural, traditional and semi-independent population into one which was urban, wage earning and dependent upon the decisions of a small elite. The old society was typified by that which John Higson recorded at Droylsden in 1859

> The land of the township generally, excepting Clayton Hall, is broken into small sized farm holdings, which consequently are sub-divided into diminutive fields and enclosures. The fields were formerly smaller than now. . . . Before the extension of the cotton business the cottages were far outnumbered by the farmsteads, and the inhabitants were engaged in an admixture of trade and agriculture. The farming department which only supplied milk and butter for the dairy, was considered least remunerative, and, therefore, neglected in favour of the buckhouse, the plank and the loom.
>
> (Higson 1859: 71)

But the old society Higson described could not long survive the massive population growth which resulted from industrial development. The varied commercial and industrial growth of Manchester and Liverpool saw these cities spread into new suburbs. But in much of Cheshire and northern and western Lancashire, population growth was smaller and slower than in the industrial regions; by 1861 some communities, such as Rufford or Tatham, show no significant increase on 1801 levels (see Table 3.1). Nevertheless, rural population density increased (as Table 3.2B shows) though it was in the towns (Table 3.19: see p. 189) that problems associated with overcrowding developed.

Unlike the figures for 1778, the 1801 census does allow (see Table 3.1)

Table 3.1 Population levels in 1664 and 1801, by deaneries

Deanery	1664 × 4.75[a]	1801	% change 1664–1801
CHESHIRE			
Chester city	7,828	15,052	92
Chester[a]	6,380	9,852	54
Frodsham	19,333	38,412	99
Macclesfield	20,943	65,961	215
Malpas	5,263	7,266	38
Middlewich	12,787	22,738	78
Nantwich	14,497	19,644	36
Wirral	7,168	10,757	48
	94,199[b]	189,682	101
LANCASHIRE			
Amounderness	26,671	59,987	125
Blackburn	19,803	82,806	318
Kendal	3,297	4,444	35
Leyland	11,258	30,461	171
Lonsdale	3,662	3,500	−4
Manchester	43,448	281,290	547
Warrington	33,502	191,327	471
	141,641	653,815	362
DERBYSHIRE			
Part of High Peak hundred	3,823	12,852	236

Notes:
[a] Note the exclusions in Table 1.1; in 1801 these, at least, totalled 2,000 people in Cheshire, and 1,260 in Lancashire. There are marginal discrepancies between the deanery figures as calculated here, and the hundred totals in the 1801 census.
[b] Differs from Table 1.1 to include Priors Hey EP, which is also included in the 1801 figure.

Sources: For 1664 see Table 1.1 (p. 7). For 1801 *VCH. Cheshire*, II: 207–37; *VCH. Lancs.*, II: 332–49; *VCH. Derbys.*, II: 192–4.

almost complete geographical comparison with the population levels of 1664. The 1664 and 1801 figures confirm as widespread the growth suggested by the partial figures of Bishop Gastrell, and of 1778, already considered. Between 1778 and 1801 some parishes grew at a lower rate than earlier in the eighteenth century. Between 1778 and 1801 some actually evidence a decrease, due probably to out-migration, but only in Chester, Amounderness and Lonsdale deaneries was it notable. Overall between 1664 and 1801 the proportion of growth was much higher in both counties and the High Peak than the 69 per cent growth projected for the whole country by Wrigley and Schofield. In fact Lancashire's population increased in this period by 360 per cent, more than five times their national figure (E. A.

Table 3.2   A: Population Growth 1664–1801–1831–1861, by hundreds

	1664	1801	1664 to 1801	1831	1801 to 1831	1861	1831 to 1861	1801 to 1861
CHESHIRE			%		%		%	%
Chester city	7,828	15,052	92	21,344	42	31,110	46	107
Broxton	8,883	13,064	47	16,415	26	18,499	13	42
Bucklow	14,901	28,768	93	42,942	49	62,762	46	118
Eddisbury	10,593	17,851	69	26,891	51	30,339	13	70
Macclesfield	20,563	65,180	217	146,478	125	199,426	62	206
Nantwich	13,329	17,637	32	23,072	31	34,292	49	94
Northwich	12,274	23,455	91	38,149	63	59,552	56	154
Wirral	7,377	10,744	46	19,100	78	69,448	264	546
	95,748	191,751	100	334,391	74	505,428	51	164
LANCASHIRE								
Amounderness	18,639	39,618	113	69,987	77	130,728	87	230
Blackburn	22,563	88,503	292	168,057	90	286,955	71	224
Leyland	11,258	30,461	171	48,338	59	58,622	21	92
Lonsdale	12,911	25,015	94	32,415	30	35,426	9	42
Salford	43,952	281,404	540	612,414	118	1,112,951	82	296
West Derby	32,999	190,074	476	380,078	100	769,020	102	305
	142,322	655,075	361	1,311,289	100	2,393,702	83	265
DERBYSHIRE								
Part of High Peak	2,964	12,852	334	23,411	82	39,125	67	204

Wrigley and Schofield 1981: 532, 534). Looking forward from 1801 (Table 3.2), and using the more convenient unit of the hundred, by 1831 the population of Lancashire doubled; it took another decade for the same proportional increase to appear in Cheshire. In fact in some parts of Lancashire population doubled by 1821, with the exception of suburban Liverpool this was confined to the textile areas: Clitheroe and Habergham in the north-east, townships around Manchester, and individual townships in Middleton, Prestwich and Rochdale. By 1831 eight of the townships in the massive ancient parish of Whalley had doubled, as had Blackburn, while further south, Bury and Bolton with, to the west, Preston, Chorley and areas around Horwich, showed the same degree of increase. In the south-east the whole of the ancient parishes of Middleton, Rochdale, Prestwich, Radcliffe and Ashton-under-Lyne, and much of Manchester parish including both Manchester and Salford towns, had also doubled. Chorlton on Medlock grew the most in Manchester, from 675 in 1801, to 2,581, 8,209 and 20,569 in the successive census returns to 1831. The population of Toxteth, largely incorporated into Liverpool in 1835, had increased sixfold between 1801 and 1831, from 2,069 to 12,829; the old Liverpool borough itself had doubled by

Table 3.2   B: Population Density 1664–1861, by hundreds

	Numbers			Density (person/acre)		
	1664[a]	1801	1861	1664	1801	1861
CHESHIRE[b]						
Chester city	7,828	15,052	31,110	2.57	4.96	10.24
Broxton	8,883	13,064	18,499	0.12	0.17	0.24
Bucklow	14,901	28,768	62,762	0.14	0.28	0.61
Eddisbury	10,593	17,851	30,339	0.12	0.19	0.33
Macclesfield	20,563	65,180	199,426	0.14	0.44	1.35[c]
Nantwich	13,329	17,637	34,292	0.16	0.21	0.40
Northwich	12,274	23,455	59,552	0.17	0.32	0.82
Wirral	7,377	10,744	69,448	0.06	0.09	0.56
	95,748	191,751	505,428	0.14	0.27	0.72
LANCASHIRE						
Amounderness	18,639	39,618	130,728	0.12	0.25	0.83
Blackburn	22,563	88,503	286,955	0.12	0.48	1.56
Leyland	11,258	30,461	58,622	0.13	0.35	0.68
Lonsdale	12,911	25,015	35,426	0.09	0.19	0.25
Salford	43,952	281,404	1,112,951	0.19	1.22	4.83
West Derby	32,999	190,074	769,020	0.13	0.73	2.97
	142,322	655,075	2,393,702	0.14	0.62	2.26

Notes:
[a] For the 1664 figures there are slight differences between Tables 3.1 and 3.2, due to rounding.
[b] The acreages used for Cheshire were taken from the 1871 census returns.
[c] The acreage includes those parts of Stalybridge and Stockport boroughs in Lancashire.

Sources: For 1664 see Table 3.1. For 1801–1861 *VCH. Cheshire*, II: 207–37; *VCH. Lancs.*, II: 332–49; *VCH. Derbys.*, II: 192–4.

1831. Table 3.3 gives some idea of the emergence and growth of major towns in the area, though problems of boundary definition can give rise to differing figures as the table shows. Population continued to increase after 1831, and the new town of Fleetwood (with 2,833 people in 1841) emerged. But by 1861 it was only the suburbs of the major towns which had doubled again, while some of the rural townships in the north and west had doubled their 1801 populations. In all, over 60 per cent of Lancashire's population was probably urban.

The story was much the same in Cheshire: dramatic population growth was confined to the textile areas, and to the emerging town of Birkenhead, opposite Liverpool on the Mersey estuary. Textiles in the north-east extremity of the county no doubt helped Macclesfield and Mottram townships to double by 1821, as well as some of the townships around Stockport (Plate

Table 3.3   Major 'town' populations 1801–61 (cf. Table 3.19)

	1801	1811	1821	1831	1841	1851	1861
CHESHIRE							
Altrincham	1,692	2,032	2,302	2,708	3,399	4,488	6,628
Birkenhead	—	—	—	2,569	10,777	30,804	46,130[a]
Chester city	15,052	16,140	19,940	21,344	23,115	27,766	31,110
Congleton	3,861	4,616	6,405	9,352	9,222	10,520	12,344
(Crewe)[b]	—	—	—	—	—	4,571	8,159
Dukinfield	1,731	3,053	5,096	14,681	22,391	26,418	29,953
Hyde	—	—	—	7,144	10,170	11,569	13,722
Macclesfield[1]	8,743	12,299	17,746	23,129	24,137	29,648	36,101[c]
Macclesfield[2]	11,000	15,000	21,000	30,000	33,000	39,000	36,000
Nantwich	3,463	3,990	4,661	4,886	5,489	5,579	6,225
Northwich[d]	3,524	3,770	4,470	5,085	5,470	6,005	6,262
Runcorn	1,370	2,060	3,103	5,035	6,951	8,688	10,063
Stalybridge MB	—	—	—	—	—	20,760	24,921
Stockport MB	—	—	—	—	—	40,175	40,843
township	14,830	17,545	21,726	25,469	28,431	30,589	30,746
Stockport[2]	17,000	21,000	27,000	36,000	50,000	54,000	55,000
Wallasey parish	663	943	1,169	2,737	6,261	8,339	10,723
LANCASHIRE							
Ashton-u-L[1]	*c.* 6,000			*c.* 14,000			33,917
Blackburn	11,980	15,083	21,940	27,091	36,629	46,536	63,126
Bolton[e]	24,195[f]	31,295[f]	41,195[f]	46,506[f]	49,763[f]	60,391[f]	69,326[f]
Burnley[1]	3,918	5,405	8,242	10,026	14,224	20,828	28,700
Burnley	3,305	4,368	6,378	7,551	10,699	14,706	19,971
Bury[1]	9,152	13,302	13,480	19,140	25,000	31,262	37,563
Bury	7,702	8,672	10,583	15,086	20,710	25,484[f]	30,397[f]
Lancaster borough[g]	9,030	9,247	10,144	12,613	14,089	14,604	14,487
Liverpool town	83,250	105,516	141,487	205,964	286,487	375,955	443,938
Manchester town	76,778	91,130	129,035	187,022	242,983	316,213	357,979
Manchester[2]	75,000	89,000	126,000	182,000	235,000	303,000	339,000
Oldham[1]	21,677	29,479	38,201	50,513	60,451	72,357	94,344
Oldham	12,024	16,690	21,662	32,381	42,595	52,820	72,333
Ormskirk	2,554	3,064	3,838	4,251	4,891	6,183	6,426
Preston	11,877	17,065	24,575	33,112	51,131	68,537[h]	81,101
Prescot	3,465	3,678	4,468	5,055	5,451	6,393	5,136
Rochdale[1]	8,542	10,753	14,017	19,041	24,423	29,195	38,114
St Helens[i]	—	—	—	—	—	15,000 –18,000	18,000 –32,000
Salford MB[1]	—	—	—	—	—	85,108	102,449[f]
Salford	13,611	19,114	25,772	40,786	53,200	63,423[f]	71,000[f]
Warrington	10,989	11,738	13,570	16,018	18,981	20,800	24,050[j]
Wigan borough	10,989	14,066[k]	17,716	20,774	25,517	31,941	37,658

Table 3.3   Major 'town' populations 1801–61 (cf. Table 3.19) (*continued*)

Notes: 'Suburban' growth is not included in this table nor are those developing towns which achieve status later in the century.
[a] Figures include Tranmere township after 1831.
[b] Monks Coppenhall township.
[c] These figures from T. Baines 1867 are the census totals for Macclesfield township, except for the 1861 figure; B. R. Mitchell's figure appears to include (two) other townships.
[d] Castle and Witton townships added into Northwich figure.
[e] Bolton figure comprises Great and Little Bolton.
[f] Figures complicated by boundary changes.
[g] Lancaster includes the castle.
[h] Cf. 1851: 70,000; 1861: 83,000 in B. R. Mitchell 1988: 26.
[i] T. C. Barker and Harris 1954: 374.
[j] Warrington MB (created 1847) contained 2,723 people in Cheshire in 1861, query excluded from this figure.
[k] 14,066 in T. Baines 1867.

Sources: Unless noted otherwise figures are for townships, sources as for Table 3.2.
1. From T. Baines 1867.   2. Rounded totals from B. R. Mitchell 1988: 26–9.

3.1). There was marked growth in all these townships by 1831. At the western end Bidston parish was home to much of the new Birkenhead, and its population doubled by 1831, nearly trebled again by 1841, and again by 1851, while there was similar growth in neighbouring Wallasey and in Tranmere (Bebington parish). The population of Birkenhead township itself in 1861 was fourteen times its 1831 level. In Cheshire as a whole just over half the people can be safely classified urban dwellers.

There is little doubt that high marriage and birth rates, though accompanied by comparatively high death rates, helped to create this growth in population. Lancashire was notable for high marriage, birth and death rates, higher than any other county in the 1830s and 1840s, when it had a shorter life expectancy and a younger population. Fertility rates in the county were higher than the English average until 1851 when they fell more quickly than in other counties to 0.599, below the national average of 0.625 (Fleischman 1985: 267–78). Marriage, whether 'common law' or formal, appears to have been entered into earliest in the great towns but people may have married two or more years earlier in the country mill areas. Marriage remained the basis for most heterosexual relationships and, despite contemporary head-shaking, there is no real evidence to suggest that women in the mills were any less moral than those who were not. Indeed the country mill often took over the moral role of the village. In 1828 a mill girl at Sidebottom's mill at Haughton Green who kept company with a married man was treated to 'rough music' and pushed in the mill dam by her workmates (*Stockport Advertiser* 14 February 1828). Mill girls also consistently returned lower rates of illegitimate pregnancy than servants or girls in other occupations (Hewitt 1958: 58, 61).

Migration also played a part in the region's growth. Dr Kay writing in 1836 thought that annual immigration into (pre-1974) Lancashire had been 4,000 between 1750 and 1801, 4,500 from 1800 to 1811, 8,800 from 1811 to 1820 and 17,000 per year between 1821 and 1831 (Poor Law Commissioners 1836, app. B, no. 11: 185). The 1851 census demonstrates the extent of inward movement. The population of Lancashire and Cheshire was then 2,460,265, of whom 1,903,772 had been born in the two counties, 217,000 in other parts of England, 213,500 in Ireland, 76,000 in Wales, 31,000 in Scotland and 10,900 abroad. Those in that census born in the two counties included, of course, the children of parents who were immigrant so that the real degree of incomer influence is understated.

The region's economic growth drew large numbers from Ireland in a flow that began before the potato famine and perhaps reached its peak in the years before the cotton famine. Total numbers of Irish-born in the two counties at census times grew from 213,500 in 1851 to 245,442 in 1861 then fell back to 224,000 in 1871. Table 3.4 (over) shows the numbers of Irish born in 1861 in the two counties and in the two major towns of the region.

Manchester and Liverpool were magnetic for immigrants. If the population aged twenty or over is counted separately it becomes clear that traditional Lancashire was giving way in both towns to a new blend of people and cultures. In 1861 only 50 per cent of Mancunians over twenty had been born in Lancashire; in Liverpool the percentage was 37. Even these Lancashire-born percentages include the children of earlier migrants from all over the British Isles as well as a few from abroad. The larger cotton towns preserved a greater measure of that 'Lancashire' character that survived most strongly in the smaller textile and mining centres of north and east Lancashire and the rural parts of both counties but Manchester and Liverpool were already cosmopolitan by 1860. The Irish were both the largest and, because of religious difference, the most identifiable of these incoming groups. Their influence on the region, especially on Liverpool, was the subject of debate even before the potato famine and the influx that followed it merely added fuel to fires already smouldering.

Many Irish emigrants with resources used Liverpool only as a staging post on their way to America's urban opportunities. Those who stayed in England, the 137,519 who remained in, or passed through, Liverpool from November 1846 to May 1847 for example, were mainly poor and undernourished, many of them victims of disease (T. Burke 1910: 84). They settled in the poorest quarters to do the least desirable work, were sometimes imported as blacklegs in trade disputes and often attempted to live, in the

Plate 3.1 Stockport in 1818. This view appears to be from the north-west with the old church of St Mary prominent on the left and the newer St Peter's on the right. The clustering of spinning mills on the river is very marked. (Source: Ormerod 1882 III: facing p. 794.)

Table 3.4   Irish born in Lancashire and Cheshire 1861

	Number	%
Cheshire		
Total population	505,428	
Irish-born	28,613	5.6
Cheshire-born	344,644	68.1
Lancashire		
Total population	2,393,702	
Irish-born	216,829	9.0
Lancashire-born	1,760,228	73.5
Liverpool (borough)		
Total population	443,938	
Irish-born	83,949	18.9
Lancashire-born	246,989	55.6
Manchester, Salford and Chorlton Registration Districts		
Total population	519,202	
Irish-born	54,378	10.4
Lancashire-born	340,063	65.4

Notes: The Irish settlement was at its greatest in Liverpool but Birkenhead registration district with 14.5 per cent Irish-born was close behind. Stockport at 11.2 per cent was more favoured by the Irish than Manchester but the coal, cotton and engineering towns to the east and north had lower percentages – 7.4 at Bolton, 5.2 at Oldham, 4.7 at Rochdale, 4.9 at Haslingden, and, further north, 5.8 at Blackburn, 2.7 at Burnley and 1.8 at Clitheroe. To the west, Preston had 8.3, the Fylde 5.7 but Lancaster only 3.6 while in Cheshire, Chester with 6.3 had more Irish than Macclesfield with 4.9.

Source: Calculations based on House of Commons, Parliamentary Papers, 1863, vol. LIII, part II.

congested slums of the industrial towns, the rural lives they had known at home. They could not with safety rely on poor relief since they had no settlement in England: 3,660 people were removed to Ireland by the Manchester poor law authorities as early as 1826 and in 1847–8 24,529 were sent back to their native parishes from Liverpool. It is not surprising that these early generations of incomers included some who were volatile and intractable, given to heavy drinking and casual violence with only the support of a devoted and overworked clergy holding many fast to the Catholic faith. They also brought with them their aspirations for Ireland and had little interest in English politics other than a fixed hostility to authority whether that of the landlord, the excise man or the police. The reaction of the native Cestrians and Lancastrians was equally predictable. Nurtured on Low Church Anglicanism and Nonconformity, most feared Rome as a foreign threat provoking religious hostility while Irish nationalism stimulated the English nationalism that lay not far below the surface of the radicalism of the region. Industrial workers and labourers also resented the low-wage competition of the Irish and the changes they brought to working-class neighbourhoods. Even the old Catholic families of Lancashire viewed the incursion with concern. They had long settled to peaceful coexistence with their Protestant neighbours and had no desire to be disturbed by assertive Catholicism.

The Orange Order had early English connections in Manchester in the 1790s and it spread across the region, especially in the textile towns. Irish disruption of Orange processions took place during the early years of the nineteenth century and there were frequent disturbances in the Irish quarters of the major towns. The 1830s were marked by fierce battles between English and Irish labourers on the North Union Railway at Preston and on the Chester and Birkenhead Railway. Skirmishes at Sunday School processions in Ashton-under-Lyne in the 1830s were followed in 1852 by riots at Stockport but the religious divide was at its greatest in Liverpool where it dominated local politics until the third quarter of the twentieth century (see Redford (1926, Second edition 1964), Engels (1845), Faucher (1844), Burke (1910), Neal (1988), T. Shaw (1902), Heginbotham (1882), Manchester Statistical Society Reports 1834, 1837).

For native and migrant alike the transition from the old society was prolonged and could be painful, the old and the new coexisting side by side until late in the century. In 1833 the two boom towns of Stalybridge and Dukinfield had 38 steam engines providing power for 8,542 operatives spinning and weaving but eight years later at Moston, only two or three miles away, 56 of the 125 heads of household were hand-loom weavers, mainly working silk, 37 were farmers and none was a mill worker (Hill 1907: 67; Ward 1905: 9–23). The population of Stalybridge had grown from 140 in 1749 to over 20,000 in 1841, over 3,300 of them Irish Catholics but in Moston the 125 families of 1841 were virtually all Lancastrian both by birth and origin. What drew the newcomers was, of course, the mill wages which could be earned by both sexes from a comparatively early age.

In general mill wages seem to have fallen irregularly to 10s. 6d. in 1810, to 9s. 2d. in 1850 then recovered to 13s. 9d. in 1870 though, of course, these averages conceal great disparities of age, skill and sex. Over roughly the same period the wages of hand-loom weavers had fallen from an average of 20s. in 1806 to a notional 6s. 3d. in 1860 while local agricultural wages had hovered around 12s., higher by two or three shillings than the national average (G. H. Wood 1910: 128; Fleischman 1985: 183). Despite growing numbers of hand-loom weavers who needed support and the heavy burden of the Irish, many of whom arrived in the region penniless and stayed to become the most marginal part of the labour force, Lancashire consistently recorded the lowest poor rates of any English county (see Appendix 3.1, pp. 213–18). Expenditure per head was 4s. 4d. in 1801 against a national average of 9s. 5d., 4s. 4d. against 9s. 11d. in 1831, 3s. 6d. against 6s. 2d. under the New Poor Law in 1841 (Fleischman 1985: 332). Millowners, as might be expected, were in no doubt about the prosperity of the factory workers; the Gregs' report to the Manchester Statistical Society in 1833 claimed that wages in cotton would be regarded as positive opulence in the agricultural districts (Ashton 1934: 17–18). Indeed incomes were clearly higher for mill families than for most in the working class but they could be irregular as trade boomed or slumped while continuous improvements in machinery affected piece-rates and added to the workers' uncertainties.

The population increase is also remarkable because of the high levels of child mortality that obtained. In Manchester mortality under five was 50 per cent in 1789 and in 1842 57 per cent for the infants of the working class and in Preston, a year later, 55 per cent of the children of operatives died under five compared with 38 per cent of those of tradesmen and 18 per cent of those of the gentry and the professional classes. Manchester kept its high rate, close to 50 per cent, from 1859 to 1869 though of 132 children born to Quaker parents only 17 died under five (Cruickshank 1981: 25, 62–4). Abortion and still births were common, infanticide was all too frequent and 'Godfrey's Cordial' and other opiates produced slow decline, convulsions and death for many hapless babies. The sanitary shortcomings of the towns, overcrowding, poor feeding and neglect provided a seed bed for infections which many parents met with fatalistic resignation or with herbal or patent remedies of little value. But it was not poverty as such that killed the children. Poorer rural counties such as Dorset and Wiltshire had lower infant mortality as did the rural areas of the north-west and it is significant that trade distress lowered rather than raised the infant death rate. It fell in the depression of 1842 and again during the Cotton Famine when families who had lived well were forced down to poor law standards (Hewitt 1958: 102–20). Contemporaries believed that it was a combination of increased parental sobriety and care and fewer mothers working that produced this improvement.

Landowning Society

The impact of industrialization on landownership was profound. The 1861 census, at the end of the period covered by this chapter, heightened public concern about the ownership of land, for its confused occupational data arguably underestimated the number of landowners. In 1872–3 an investigation of landownership was undertaken for Parliament, and the data from that offer a good insight into the impact of industrialization on landownership.

The new Domesday survey of 1872–3 listed, county by county, the names and addresses of owners, the amount of land they held, and its gross estimated rental (GER). Only about 16 per cent of families in Lancashire (pre-1974) and about 21 per cent in Cheshire owned any land at all, as Table 3.5 shows. In the nineteenth century, an income of £1,000 a year roughly

Table 3.5   Landownership in 1873 (excluding waste)

	Below 1 acre			1 acre plus		
	acreage held	*no. of owners*	*GER (£)*	*acreage held*	*no. of owners*	*GER (£)*
Cheshire	4,664	17,641	1,005,788	597,554	6,029	2,011,434
Lancs.[a]	14,811	76,177	6,537,595	932,652	12,558	7,340,681

Note: [a] Pre-1974 county.
Source: Great Britain 1875: 15.

equated with an estate of 1,000 acres, marked the bottom level of the land-owning aristocracy (F. M. L. Thompson 1963: 112). If we abstract names with either £1,000 a year or 1,000 acres the 1873 returns show a distribution across the region as in Table 3.6. A few examples will illustrate the sorts of problems which the data in Table 3.6 contain. The Earl of Derby was the most wealthy individual landowner in the two counties with £156,735 and the most wealthy Cheshire individual was the Duke of Westminster with £29,249, but Westminster's high-income holdings in London were not included in the 1872–3 survey. While entries such as that for Amalgamated Cheshire Salt may reveal something of the nature of land use, most entries merely give the owner's name, and no indication of use. Rents higher than £5 an acre appear to indicate industrial, commercial or urban housing use, though many of the suburban owners did not give the size of their plots. Table 3.6 can therefore tell us next to nothing about land use.

As industrialization progressed so more land came to be held by companies for manufacturing, mining, gas works, docks, railways and canals. Urbanization too occupied more and more of the region's soil, as did government concerns in the form of, for example, workhouses. For our sample hundreds of Northwich in Cheshire and West Derby in Lancashire (see p. 22), Table 3.7 shows that land was no longer the domain solely of a landowning aristocracy and its tenants living largely on the rents and profits of farming. Liverpool Corporation had the highest GER in Lancashire, followed by the Mersey Docks and Harbour Board, and by two railway companies. The impact of the new industrial and residential circumstances is most clearly indicated by the group of owners of between 5 and 100 acres and by the Liverpool area landowners. (Liverpool was not peculiar in this respect, for the old parish of Manchester returned 186 owners valued at over £1,000 GER, of whom just 11 held more than 100 acres.) In Wigan an acre of Henry Woods' forty-nine acre estate was worth over £69, while in Kirkdale John Orrell's five acres were worth over £342 each. In the centre of Liverpool itself

Table 3.6 Distribution of Lancashire and Cheshire landowners with GER of £1,000+ or 1,000+ acres

Hundred	No.	Acreage	GER (£)
CHESHIRE			
Broxton	11	29,477	54,227
Bucklow	31	48,100	150,577
Chester city	13	7,343	27,790
Eddisbury	15	49,417	72,361
Macclesfield	82	71,771	241,000
Nantwich	16	67,536	111,900
Northwich[a]	39	61,168	177,027
Wirral	30	16,298	94,735
Out of county	69	87,932	341,580
Totals	306	418,932	1,271,287
LANCASHIRE			
Amounderness	40	69,224	164,923
Blackburn	73	69,355	219,098
Leyland	32	47,396	114,258
Lonsdale S	31	51,852	75,069
Salford	453	55,052	1,490,677
West Derby	292	145,630	2,238,087
Out of county	149	124,783	858,652
Totals	1,070	563,292	5,160,764

Note: [a] There is some confused use of Northwich as an address. Cf. Table 3.7 for an alternative total.

Source: As Table 3.5 (land outside the region owned by residents of the region omitted).

an individual's land could be valued at £1,300 or £1,500 or £2,500; the Exchange Building Company's one acre, and of course the buildings on it, were given a GER of £41,978. Plots in the residential Toxteth Park were put at over £1,000. Northwich Hundred was not entirely agricultural land, for there were salt works and textile factories, for instance at Congleton, but only in one case did these produce the very high revenue on low acreage characteristic of Liverpool and widespread in West Derby. Over the region as a whole, there were clusters of high-value holdings in Blackburn hundred, and of course they were commonplace in Salford hundred. Even in low-rented Lonsdale and Amounderness hundreds (in the north of the region) one iron company at Carnforth stands out, as well as the low acreage and high-value land at Blackpool. In Cheshire it was Macclesfield and Wirral hundreds which had the most small-sized estates with large revenues: there were three holdings in Stalybridge worth over £1,000 an acre, and there were others in Dukinfield, Stockport and one in Macclesfield itself. The new town of Birkenhead had

Table 3.7   Landowners with £1,000+ GER in West Derby and Northwich hundreds

	West Derby	Northwich
Acreage of individual owners		
1,000+ acres	38	18
100–999 acres	25	14
5–99 acres	40	1
Liverpool & area less than 5 acres	117[a]	
Other towns less than 5 acres	12	
Companies	49	1
Local government	3	1
Uncertain	8	
	292	35[b]

Notes:
[a] Includes the many entries for this area which omit the acreage.
[b] See Table 3.6.

Source: As Table 3.5 note [a].

eight high-value holdings. The wide acres and rich rent rolls of the aristocracy were however still to be found in every hundred, even Salford, where the Earl of Ellesmere's lands, and those of Sir Humphrey de Trafford represented the old landed society.

In the nineteenth century an income of £1,000 a year, roughly equated with an estate of 1,000 acres, marked out the landed gentleman; above £10,000 we enter the titled aristocracy (F. M. L. Thompson 1963: 112). The social distribution of land based on the 1872–3 new Domesday is set out in different ways in Table 3.8. If we accept inclusion of the family name in

Table 3.8   Landownership by size of holding in 1873

% of total county acreage (less waste) held by each category					
[a]	Ches.	Lancs.	[b]	Ches.	Lancs.
Peers	14	24	Great estates (10,000+ acres)	35	24
Great owners	26	23	Greater gentry (3,000–10,000)	16	12
Squires	11	14	Squirearchy (1,000–3,000)	11	14
Greater yeomen	10	14	300–1,000	10	13
Lesser yeomen	9	12	100–300	9	12
Small proprietors	13	17	1–100	13	18
Cottagers	0.77	2	no figure given		
Public bodies	4	3	no figure given		

Notes:
[a] Bateman 1883 (pp. 502, 505).
[b] F. M. L. Thompson 1963 (pp. 32, 114, 115, 117).

Burke's *Landed Gentry* (1871 edition) as evidence of gentle status, then we might have to include in the gentry of Lancashire and Cheshire families whose estate size or income level does not match Thompson's criteria. Thus Nathaniel Eckersley of Standish Hall appeared in Burke, but on the new Domesday his estates were listed at 453 acres, though worth £4,968 in GER. In short, more than one factor determined social status, and the use of other sources to list the names of gentry families would give a different list from that out of Burke (Beckett 1986: 38). In our region the ancient gentry no longer contained so many knights, while the hereditary title of baronet might be given to those with less land than long-established gentry families, like Sir Thomas Moss of Roby Hall, whose estate was listed at only 110 acres, albeit worth £1,559 GER. Indeed contemporaries like Sir Edmund Burke were concerned to make the point that an Englishman did not need a title to be a member of the nobility, in contrast to European nobilities. Was there, too, a more noticeable number of heads of gentry families with at least an auxiliary professional income: clergymen, lawyers and a few serving or retired naval and army officers (E. Burke 1871: eg 154, 354, 450)? The development of public and utility companies offered the gentry opportunities to diversify their investments. For example in the 1840s James France of Bostock Hall received about £300 per year from railway shares and about £1,000 from other shares, as well as £500 in interest payments – a long-used source of income for landowners. At £1,800 such income totalled very roughly one-fifth of his rental income of £8,042 in 1842 and £9,716 in 1849 (JRUL, Eng. MS 1132,* cited in C. S. Davies 1960: 100). London urban rents were, of course, a large element in the income of the Grosvenor family. As early as 1779 about 5 per cent of the Earl of Derby's revenue had come from his Liverpool estates; by 1835 this had increased to 30–40 per cent (LRO, DDK/ 1805/51, 107). Landowning interests in new towns such as Southport were even more lucrative, in the case of the Heskeths reviving their depressed fortunes after 1850 (G. Rogers 1981: 9).

Landowning society continued to absorb new families, while families disappeared as their male lines failed, or, less commonly, sold up under economic pressure. Cheshire in particular enjoys a reputation among scholars for continuity among its great landowners (C. S. Davies 1960: 13; *VCH. Cheshire*, II: 115, 144; cf. Scard 1981: 17). In fact there was considerable fluidity in both counties among landowning families. In the 1871 edition of Burke's *Landed Gentry* 38 per cent of families could first be identified with a landed seat in the nineteenth century, 35 per cent in the eighteenth. Commonly, the head of a new landowning family was the younger brother of an existing family. Others could trace their origins back to soldiering, to the West Indies trade, and to the cotton industry. Men of commerce spread

---

* This anonymous MS. is attributed by the Library to Bostock Hall, so it is probably written either by or for James France, who died in 1869.

throughout the region; on the north Lancashire plain in the mid-nineteenth century 'the old landed families [would] soon be unable to compete with the fortunes of the men of commerce' (quoted by G. Rogers 1981: 70). In our sample hundred (for sources see p. 22) of Northwich the newly accumulated estate of the France-Hayhurst family had the highest GER, and their history illustrates many of the causes of change among the landed elite. In the late eighteenth century a mercantile suburban Liverpool family, they purchased the manor of Bostock, property in Lach Denis between 1835 and 1859, and made more purchases shortly before the 1872–3 survey. They also inherited property, including in 1872 the Harper's manor of Davenham, which itself had already followed a tortuous descent typical of some properties in the hundred. The male line of the Holfords of Davenham had failed in the 1780s and the manor had passed via a female heir to the Ravenscroft family, who in turn had sold to a Liverpool merchant William Harper in 1795; he settled it on his daughter's husband, who took the name Harper. The history of the West Derby family of Scarisbrick of Scarisbrick is an even more complex example. At the end of the eighteenth century the family changed its name to Eccleston and took the Eccleston estate; there was a further addition in 1807 when the Wrightington estate of the Dicconson family was inherited. The family then divided its estates in 1809, a younger son taking the Dicconson name and Wrightington estate. The eldest son sold Eccleston, but died without a male child, so the younger son inherited Scarisbrick, changed his name back to Scarisbrick, and acquired the manors of Bold and North Meols in 1843. He died unmarried in 1860 when the different family elements of his estate passed via female heirs, again retaining the family name, or to his illegitimate children.

Other old families, such as Stanley of Hooton, Bold of Bold and Molyneux of Hawkley, disappeared from the ranks of West Derby hundred's landowners. Significant estates passed to absentees such as the Bretherton family, or to Lord Lilford. And of course some of the ancient properties were sold up and fragmented under the pressure of urbanization and industrialization: a salt works had been built at Garston before 1823, when the estate was split up in sales to land companies; Chorley was fragmented in 1824, and the Hardshaw estate too was dispersed. Liverpool merchants were involved in such buying and selling.

In contrast, Lawton of Lawton or Twemlow of Twemlow were demographically stable, ancient, landowning gentry families. The continuity among such families meant that about one-third of the properties in the Northwich hundred sample were held in 1872 by the same male lineage as in 1780. Equally, of the 104 properties in the West Derby hundred sample, 46 remained in 1872 with their 1780 lineage; those families had also acquired a further four properties. Controversy raged in the nineteenth century over the alleged accumulation of more and more land in the hands of fewer families; indeed the Earl of Derby intended the 1872–3 survey as a weapon in that argument. Table 3.8 (p. 145) shows the effect of such accumulations: 51 per cent of Cheshire was held by landowners in Thompson's top two acreage brackets. In England, 71 per cent was the top figure and Cheshire ranked sixth, just behind neighbouring Shropshire. Only 36 per cent of Lancashire was similarly held – a marked difference between the two main counties of our region. The willingness of creditors to fund land purchases and high levels of debt, and of the large estates to sell some land to liquidate debt when and if pressed, kept estate acreages at least constant or even growing (G. Rogers 1981: 9, 62). Among the two sample areas studied here, the great estates (10,000 acres plus) apparent in 1872–3 belonging to the Earl of Derby, or the Blundell family, or the Seftons, were already great a century earlier, while the accumulation of the France-Hayhurst estate in Northwich hundred right at the end of the period, and the splitting-up of the Bridgewater estate after the third Duke's death in 1795, are both reminders that the growth and fragmentation of large estates was not restricted to any particular time span. Nor was it restricted to place, as the out-of-county figure in Table 3.6 proclaims. Within the region, for those families like the Grosvenors whose holdings were concentrated, there were others like the Wilson-Patten family who held land in Warrington in the south of Lancashire and in Garstang in the north (Bateman 1883: 485; C. S. Davies 1960: 13; Scard 1981: 18–19).

The Grand Tour of the eighteenth century had taught young men the culture of Europe, and such expeditions no doubt continued. William Farrington may not have sailed in the Pacific, but his library contained a copy of *Cooke's Voyages*; his international interests are confirmed by such volumes as *View of Manners in France*, or the *Antiquities of Herculaneum* (LRO DDF, list of goods at Shaw Hall 1795). In the 1830s the Grosvenors went to Europe as a family, and for at least part of the 1860s the Leghs of High Legh were resident in France (Huxley 1967: 7–8; JRUL Cornwall Legh MSS, engagement diaries). If some parts of landed society in north-west England had almost become cosmopolitan, it was also more metropolitan, travel of course aided in the latter years by the railway. For the great families the London season, and involvement with Parliament, were long-standing connections between capital and provinces; the Grosvenors, the Derbys and the Cholmondeleys had London houses and moved from one to the other; indeed Lord Cholmondeley also had a house in Norfolk (Huxley 1965: 58; Bagley 1985: 151–2; Scard 1981: 15). Hugh Lupus Grosvenor, the first Duke of Westminster, spent little of his boyhood in Cheshire, being schooled in London and at Eton, then Oxford University, and holidaying in Scotland and abroad (Huxley 1967: 5–19). But connections with the capital were and became more varied than schooling or the season: Sir Thomas Hesketh was a member of Boodle's Club by 1815, and had accounts in London that year with a bookseller, a jeweller and a gunsmith. James France of Bostock had a subscription with W. H. Smith of 192 The Strand for the *Spectator* in the

1840s (LRO, DDHE 77/4; JRUL Eng. MS 1132, f. 20). George Legh made three trips to London in 1849, and one to Amsterdam. Landowners also continued their connections with local towns; the Reform Act 1832 made little difference to the Grosvenor political position in Chester. James France made regular shopping expeditions to Liverpool and Chester from Bostock Hall, and subscribed to two Liverpool journals, including the *Mercury*. Landowners played some part in urban intellectual activity, but only in fields already of interest to them. The earls of Ellesmere and of Sefton were president and a vice-president, respectively, of the Historic Society of Lancashire and Cheshire, founded in Liverpool in 1848, but seem to have played no part in its early proceedings; another ten major landowners subscribed in the first two years of the society (*Proceedings and Papers*, vols I and II). Lord Ellesmere chaired a committee of the Royal Manchester Institution to mount an art exhibition in 1856 (Darcy 1976: 151). Coal-owners were members of the Manchester Geological Society in 1860, but the Manchester Statistical Society held out no interest to landowners (Report, in *Trans. Manchester Stat. Soc.*, for 1858–59; Ashton 1934: 4–12; Report for 1841, in *Trans. Manchester Geol. Soc.*, I, 1859, and see II: 106–10). Regular visits to assizes at Lancaster or Chester figure in the diaries or accounts of James France, Sir Thomas Hesketh and George Legh. Neither these urban connections, nor their involvement as landowners in the new urbanization, nor investment in new transport systems necessarily led landowners to embrace the new industrialized society.

Thus George Legh's 1849 diary records four days' hunting and five days' shooting in Cheshire, while late August, September and part of October were spent walking, grouse shooting, stalking and fishing in Scotland. Men at the Grosvenors' Eaton Hall followed the same pastimes, and race horse trials were an added passion; ladies went walking or driving, or worked on embroidery. In the evening billiards, cards and games, including charades, entertained the house parties. George Legh in 1849 records visits to at least five of his neighbours' houses, while the Grosvenors regularly entertained or were entertained by the Earl of Derby, the Egertons, and Lord and Lady Delamere; the Grosvenors' friendship with the Delameres was, however, spoilt by the politics of the 1832 election (Huxley 1965: 33–5, 43–4, 105). In 1815 Sir Thomas Hesketh went on holiday to the Lake District with the Hulton family (at a cost of £51 10s. 0d. plus £1 5s. 0d. for a guide book). He also went racing at Doncaster, Knutsford and Preston in that year. The May Chester cup was in the Legh engagement diary, while as well as races, there were at least three balls at Knutsford in 1849. The thirteenth Earl of Derby enjoyed a more unusual interest: with a national reputation as a zoologist, he was president in turn of the Linnaean and Zoological societies (Bagley 1985: 159–64).

Conspicuous consumption also continued in time-honoured ways; the grand tour was often an occasion to buy fine pictures and books. Sir John

Leicester of Tabley was a great art patron and collector, while his architectural work at Tabley enhanced *c.* 1830 the existing buildings. Like the Grosvenors, Tabley kept much of his collection in London. Between 1806 and 1821 Grosvenor paid an annual retainer of £100 to have his paintings catalogued, and altered his house to display them (Huxley 1965: 58–9; Jackson-Stopes 1986: 586, 380–1, 580; Pevsner and Hubbard 1971: 349). In Cheshire Doddington Hall reveals the architect Samuel Wyatt at his best, where the intention of the Delves-Broughton family to impress is demonstrated by the lavish treatment of the entrance hall and saloon. The modest sized Poole Hall of 1817 has a sumptuous Regency interior. Architectural historicism in medieval (Peckforton castle for the Tollemache family cost £60,000 between 1844 and 1850), Elizabethan (Walton Hall for Sir Gilbert Greenall), and Gothic (Scarisbrick Hall, Lancashire) helped to empty landowners' pockets (Pevsner 1979b: 218–23; Pevsner and Hubbard 1971: 199, 238, 289, 300–1). The Grosvenors built, rebuilt or extended Eaton Hall between 1803–12, 1823–5, and 1845–54: building expenditure in their Cheshire accounts for March 1806 alone exceeded £2,000 (Pevsner and Hubbard 1971: 208; Scard 1981: 21–2). Lord Crewe had warm air heating installed in 1837, but in the 1820s Lady Grosvenor had found Eaton Hall cold (Scard 1981: 23; Huxley 1965: 34)!

These great houses and their grounds required large numbers of servants. At Bostock Hall wages for ten, sometimes eleven servants in the 1840s cost about £270 a year (JRUL, English MS 1132). The 1861 census tells us that Oulton Hall had twelve domestic servants, a gamekeeper, two gardeners, two grooms and a gatekeeper. The Egertons were not in residence, but at Wennington Hall in north Lancashire a governess, housekeeper, lady's maid, cook, nurse, housemaid, footman, and errand boy looked after William Saunders, his wife, five children and mother-in-law.

An obvious change in landed society by the end of our period is the replacement of the status terms yeoman and husbandman by farmer (cf. p. 70), though a few people still entered such archaic terms in the 1861 census or in their wills (Table 3.9). Farmers were both freeholders and estate tenants; in nineteenth-century Lancashire the great majority of farm land was rented (Mutch 1980: 92–3). A few advertised a second occupation in 1861, keeping pubs (James Cowap of Little Leigh), milling, or even shoemaking or tailoring. The farming families of the 1861 census included newcomers as well as those like the Cowaps who had been there for decades. Looking back from 1871 over his lifetime Richard Lindop of Church Coppenhall remembered all but one of the eleven freeholds in his township passing to other families (Chaloner 1940: 119–21). Among Grosvenor, Delamere and Clifton tenant families there was a mixture of continuity and change (G. Rogers 1981: 336; Scard 1981: 50, 51). The size of farms varied, in five sample townships (Little Budworth, Little Leigh and Marbury – all Cheshire – Lytham and Wennington – both Lancashire) men with holdings of between 4

Table 3.9 Samples of farmers' probate valuations 1850

Lancashire			Cheshire		
Deanery	ave (£)	median (£)	Deanery	ave (£)	median (£)
Amounderness	664	300	Chester	390	300
Blackburn	238	200	Frodsham	571	*
Kendal	no entries		Macclesfield	336	250
Leyland	300	*	Malpas	633	*
Lonsdale	325	*	Middlewich	842	375
Manchester	400	300	Nantwich	1333	525
Warrington	1,810	375	Wirral	333	*

Note: The sample was constructed to contain entries in proportion to the acreage of Lancashire and Cheshire, and within Lancashire roughly in proportion to the acreages north (excluding Furness) and south of the Ribble.
* Medians cannot be calculated.

Source: LRO, probate records, act books WC/35, WR/8, 25, 29. Within these constraints the first 125 relevant entries for 1850 were used.

and 242 acres described themselves as farmer (though little reliance can be put on their estimates of acreage).

The personal wealth of farmers also ranged widely. A sample (Table 3.9) of the personal estates of 125 farmers in 1850 indicates a range from less than £50 to less than £25,000. They averaged £763 over the region. But there were marked differences between the average deanery values, with Amounderness, Warrington, Middlewich and Nantwich deaneries containing the wealthiest men. Probate valuations reflect the life cycle, and neglect gifts made before death, and the ownership of real estate, so that too much weight should not be put on this evidence. Nevertheless, it seems reasonable to conclude that the term 'farmer' encompassed men of greatly differing wealth, and therefore working capital. In general, as the years covered in this chapter advanced, the region's agriculture became more prosperous (see p. 160), which latterly began to show in new housing and farm buildings. But in the early nineteenth century rural housing was poor. It was said to be at its worst in Cheshire on the Wirral, though there were brick houses in the county as early as the 1770s (C. S. Davies 1960: 97, 167–76). Houses were also small, and these conditions persisted: a farm on the Delamere estate in the late 1850s had only one bedroom (Scard 1981: 50). In north-east Lancashire at Leagram in the 1820s the better houses were low, one-storey thatched buildings dating from the later seventeenth century (Weld 1913: 91–2). One farmhouse on the Bolesworth estate may date from this decade, but on the Grosvenor estates, at Aldford and Poulton, the work of the 1850s is cottages rather than farms, which were to come later (Pevsner and Hubbard 1971: 58, 235, 318). In 1871 Presland Hall farm house on the Wilbraham estate in Wettenhall, Cheshire (building *a* on Plate 3.2) was demolished. It had been

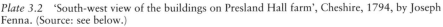

Plate 3.2 'South-west view of the buildings on Presland Hall farm', Cheshire, 1794, by Joseph Fenna. (Source: see below.)

described in 1794 as 'composed of all kinds of materials, successive repairs having substituted brick and slate, in the place of timber and thatch' and 'old but kept in decent repair' (CRO, DTW 2477/B34, 33–4). Nevertheless, there was some modest comfort in farm houses: when James Hooton of Scarisbrick in Lancashire died in 1854 his estate was sworn not to exceed £1,500, and his will empowered his wife to take what furniture she wanted to set up home. At auction the residue was sold for some £32 and Hooton's farm goods made £544, which implies that the investments referred to in his will, plus the household goods, totalled about £900 (LRO, WCW pr. 1854; LRO, DP/438, auction book).

Whereas in much of southern England the live-in farm servant had all but disappeared by 1851, in the north (including Lancashire and Cheshire) he or she appeared in many farm houses (Mingay 1989: 864). Thus in 1861 Richard Taylor of Little Budworth, who claimed to farm eighty-three acres, had a resident dairymaid, a cowman, a carter and a groom plus two other, evidently domestic, servants. The labour requirements of dairy and stock farming encouraged farmers to keep labour to hand, and of course real wages increased to levels which reflected payments by the surrounding industrialists competing for workers; around towns skilled labour was scarce and rates higher in Lancashire by the 1830s and in Cheshire in the 1840s. Nevertheless, at Speke in 1851 labourers already outnumbered farm servants, and the 1861 census shows that Middlewich housed significant numbers of agricultural day labourers, which if common in other towns in rural areas, is further evidence of change in the pattern of labour supply (Marshall 1961; C. S. Davies 1960: 81, 86, 87; Mutch 1980: 172). Some live-in farm servants in fact resided at cottages on the estate, even with a few acres, were presumably married, and yet ate in the farm house (C. S. Davies 1960: 82). The townships in the sample (see p. 150) all contained numbers of labourers living in their own houses. Little Budworth had the fewest, and appears to have been a closed village on the Oulton Park estate. In Little Leigh John Horton had three Irish farm labourers resident, but such migrants had not penetrated Little Budworth, and they were almost absent from Lytham and Wennington. Over twenty heads of agricultural labourers' households in Middlewich had been born in Ireland, and there were another twenty-three labourers who were not head of a household. By contrast eighteen heads of labouring households had been born in England, plus six labourers who were not head of a household.

The difference in living standards between the day labourer, with a cottage and a garden or some land, and the smallest of farmers cannot have been very noticeable. Only above twenty acres might farmers be better off, as such farms were still small enough to work on family labour thereby reducing outgoings (C. S. Davies 1960: 91, 92). In Marbury in 1861 there were no small farms (if everyone correctly filled in their census forms) but thirty-two labourers to work on thirteen farms. While wages reached eight or ten shillings a week for farm labourers in the 1840s, it is easy to anticipate in Marbury the general conclusion that farm labourers lost out on the prosperity of English farming in the mid-nineteenth century (Mingay 1989: 866). Labourers' housing was poor at the start of the period covered in this chapter with wattle-and-daub cottages in Leagram, while David Candland's two bay cottage at Bunbury in 1773 was made of mud walls only six feet high; the nearby Fisher's tenement (Plate 3.3) was perhaps better because by 1795 the timber was nogged with bricks (CRO, DTW 2477/B27, 13–14). Poor quality cottages remained on the Rufford estate in the mid-nineteenth century. In comparison, the estate cottages on the Bolesworth estate at Harthill of 1844 seem like palaces, as do the Wilbraham estate cottages at Rode, or the late 1850s cottages which replaced single-storey thatched buildings in the Grosvenor village of Dodleston, and probably Aldford and Poulton too (C. S. Davies 1960: 173; Mutch 1980: 176; Communication from D. Nuttall 1990; Pevsner and Hubbard 1971; 58, 235, 322 and cf. 200; Weld 1913: 91). Such estate cottages reinforced the social control of landowners (G. Rogers 1981: 350). For the fortunate labourer on the big estates, the end of the period covered by this chapter may have seen some improvement in his house, but there were those whose housing was still poor. As with the farmers, the labouring class was far from homogeneous: the estate of John Barnham of Over Alderley, labourer, was put at under £200 on 19 February 1850, but labourers' probate estates that year were sworn as high as under £450 (see sources for Table 3.9). There were opportunities for labourers to take farms

Plate 3.3 'N.E. view of Fisher's cottage', Bunbury, Cheshire, 1795, by Joseph Fenna. (Source: see p. 153.)

and rise up the social scale, though, as at Aughton between 1851 and 1871, labourers' sons who took farms usually held only small ones (Mutch 1980: 154)!

Rural society still felt a 'taint of serfdom', to quote J. T. Danson in 1855 in a meeting at Chester, complaining about the terms of leases (quoted in Scard 1981: 49). The power of estates and agents over their tenants was formidable, and men whose social behaviour fell out of favour with their lord might find their tenancy gone (Mutch 1980: 97ff). Tenants with a vote were expected to use it as their lord directed, as when in 1844 Lord Sefton gave instructions on whom to vote for (Mutch 1980: 116). In return, tenants and labourers in their different circumstances might benefit not only from improved housing but also from clothing clubs, schooling for children, estate dinners and functions and gifts to the poor (G. Rogers 1981: 341; Scard

1981: 24–7). No doubt such gestures not only bolstered deference but also played some part in keeping the rural areas of the two counties politically docile through much of this period.

Most rural townships contained men providing agricultural services such as blacksmiths, wheelwrights and carriers or carters. They might be estate tenants or freeholders, but many of them were also likely to benefit from work on the estate beyond that handled by the estate's own workers. Shoemakers seem to have been widespread, and all five sample townships had some sort of a shop though perhaps the victualler in Little Budworth kept licensed premises. Clerics and school teachers provided for basic spiritual and educational needs. Little Leigh had a National school from the 1840s on, to which, a plaque tells us, the lord of the manor made substantial contribution as was the case in other villages (eg JRUL, Eng. MS 1132 (Darnhall and Davenham); Scard 1981: 25–6). The impact of new transport systems, and new policing, on the availability of work in rural villages is apparent in the occupations of Little Leigh and Marbury. By 1860 such townships offered a range of services as good or even better than that available in the smallest market towns.

The fortunes of the market towns discussed in Chapters 1 and 2 varied under the onset of industrialization. So far as their role as distribution, manufacturing and service centres was concerned, by 1828 trade directories suggest a three-tier hierarchy, though it would be misleading to expect an exact taxonomy of something so varied as a country town. Directories did not include all the shopkeepers, artisans and professionals in a community, even by the middle of the nineteenth century, and may give prominence to untypical businesses, but there are problems also with using evidence of occupational structure from parish registers, and even from the census returns. Five of the Cheshire and four of the Lancashire market towns have been examined in detail, and Table 3.10 outlines the levels of the three-tier hierarchy. At the top in 1828 all offered a wide range of services, such as schools, surgeons, lawyers, chemists, auctioneers, insurance offices, agents, and the more mundane blacksmith, cooper, wheelwright, and pubs, inns or hotels. Altrincham and Ormskirk alone offered the services of hairdressers, and only Nantwich had a bank listed in the directory. Although all the towns, for example Altrincham, had a range of small-scale manufactures, Colne (cotton textiles), Nantwich (shoes) and Ormskirk (rope and thread making) maintained specialist industries, whereas Altrincham did not; we can judge that Colne was already losing its country-market town status, as manufacturing grew. By 1860 banks had appeared in all these towns; veterinary surgeons had become more widespread, as had hairdressers and specialist greengrocers. Altrincham and its mother parish of Bowdon had begun to house affluent men who worked in Manchester. Such a dormitory function, enabled first by the Bridgewater Canal's flyboats, then by the railway, might have helped to fuel population growth in the town. Of the towns in the middle of

Table 3.10   Examples of the small town hierarchy 1820s and 1860s

Rank by range of function		Rough population levels (source: as Table 3.2)		No. of farmers c. 1860 directory
		1831	*1861*	
Top tier	Altrincham	2,708	6,628	5
	Colne[a]	8,080	7,906	37
	Nantwich	4,886	6,225	—
	Ormskirk	4,251	6,426	—
Middle tier	Garstang	929	714	2
	Sandbach	3,710	4,989	28
	Tarporley	995	1,212	9
Bottom tier	Hornby	383	317	8
	Malpas	1,004	1,037	26

Sources: James Pigot & Co., *New Commercial Directory of Lancashire and Cheshire* (1828); Francis White & Co., *History, Gazetteer, and Directory of Cheshire* (1860); P. Mannex & Co., *Directory of North and East Lancashire* (1868); P. Mannex & Co., *History, Topography and Directory of Mid-Lancashire* (1854).
Note: [a] cf. p. 173.

the hierarchy, the range of shops and services available in Tarporley was clearly expanding, while Sandbach, which in 1828 had a shorter range of business was in 1860 perhaps best distinguished from the top tier only by its lack, in the directory, of some of the more specialist shops, such as china and glass dealers, or a greengrocer. Both these towns witnessed population growth. But more residents were not always necessary to sustain a range of functions, as the case of Garstang shows. In the bottom tier, Hornby's population fell significantly, but in 1828 it had offered at least licensed premises, and the services of a blacksmith and a shoemaker; additionally by *c.* 1860 a school, tailor and a grocer were available everywhere.

A comparison of the range of occupations in the bottom tier towns, with those in the five sample townships (see p. 150), reveals the extent to which these market towns had declined relative to other settlements. Only the market separated Malpas out, and even that was not very significant in 1828 and was 'obsolete' in 1860; the presence then of two vets stressed the connections of Malpas with agriculture. Hornby's market had become a cattle fair by 1828. Malpas enjoyed no carrier services in 1828, though Hornby still had scheduled connections with Lancaster and Kirkby Lonsdale. By 1860 the railway had reached Hornby, though it does not seem to have had much impact, while Malpas was still dependent on horse-drawn omnibuses to Chester and Wrexham. The canal, not mentioned in the 1860 directory, and the railway, two miles away at Beeston, may have contributed to Tarporley's resurgence by 1860, but there were also horse-drawn services to Chester for passengers and goods. Garstang was said to have benefited greatly from its place on the road north to Scotland. Whatever the range of businesses operating in them *c.* 1860, there were no doubt farmers in all of them, thus stressing the rural, agricultural connections of these towns.

Agriculture

At the end of the eighteenth century and in the war years, farming in our region seems to have prospered, and to have been much less depressed in the decades between Waterloo and the Great Exhibition (1815–51) than was the case in other parts of England. However, while historians (eg Armstrong 1988: 62) are right to emphasize diversity of performance over the whole of the country between differing agrarian types and regions, so too within our region there was diversity, and perhaps Lancashire prospered more than Cheshire. Both counties seem to have shared in the growing agricultural prosperity of the 1850s, the start of the years of 'High farming'.

The old, virtually freehold customary tenures persisted in the very north of Lancashire. Further south, a trend towards shorter leases was already established (see p. 78), and one-year tenancies became much more widespread, as for example in the 1820s on the estates of the Stanley of Alderley family (G. Rogers 1981: 155; Scard 1981: 49). On the Earl of Derby's estates there were some nine different types of rent (excluding minerals); in 1835 fines on leases totalled £5,017, 8 per cent of the total rents of £63,094 (LRO, DDK/1806/107). The earl allowed some long-established tenants to remain, while others were put off because of incompetence or old age; on the Cholmondeley estates widows usually kept farms if their sons could take over. Established families of tenantry were preferred by most landlords. Good tenants on occasion successfully maintained their position in a dispute with the lord or his agent, like Mr Done, one of Lord Cholmondeley's tenants in the 1820s. In general, landlords' agents had great influence over the choice and removal of tenants, and though a lord could always direct his agent, it might not be too wide of the mark to see the lord as appellate between tenant and agent. The agent managed the day-to-day affairs of an estate, on terms set out in leases, which could be restrictive: frequency of ploughing, application of manures, and the growing of vegetables were routinely specified. In the nineteenth century some of the more progressive estates in south Lancashire directed farmers' activities at a minute level. On many estates, however, tenant farmers were given considerable freedom of action (Mutch 1980: 97, 98; G. Rogers 1981: 161–3, 334; Scard 1981: 38–53).

Tenant and lord usually shared the cost of minor reorganizations of holdings, such as amalgamating fields by removing hedges or filling in old marl pits. Such operations might be undertaken on a tenant's initiative, as might drainage work. In the wet Cheshire lands as late as the 1840s raised butts, between reins to carry the water away, were the common but not very effective means of drainage. Drainage by tiles, later clay pipes, involved more than one farm and perhaps more than one lord. Large sums of money were spent throughout the region under the Drainage Acts of the 1840s, and privately by estates. Sometimes, as on the Derby estates, the agent carried out the work and the tenants' rents were raised over a period of time towards the cost. Other lords provided the materials, which were often carted by the tenants who might also do the work. Freeholders lacked this framework of support. On the Derby estates 6,000 acres were drained at a cost of £30,000, and by 1849 there were tileries on twenty-two estates scattered over the Lancashire plain. On the Wirral the successful cheese farmer John Byrom drained his estate in 1850–4, at about the time the Manchester and Liverpool Agricultural Society was using a competition to promote improved drainage (Fletcher 1962: 113–16; Mutch 1980: 132–3; G. Rogers 1981: 170; Scard 1981: 56, 83–4). The landlords were responsible for some of the costs of enclosing waste and marsh. Edward Dawson of Aldcliffe took in 166 acres of marsh near Lancaster, and others drained areas of mossland (Fletcher 1962: 104–6). But where enclosure was by Act of Parliament, costs were shared proportionately to the size of holding between the proprietors. In all, some 45 Acts initiated the enclosure of over 25,000 acres of Cheshire, six Acts covered 3,500 acres of High Peak, and in Lancashire about 45,000 acres were enclosed by fifty-one Acts; enclosure by private agreement still continued, and some 300 acres in five places were so enclosed in Lancashire (Tate 1946; M. E. Turner 1978: 78–80, 92–6, 149–52). In Lancashire the most extensive enclosures were in the north of the county, though smaller enclosures of, typically, a couple of hundred acres are to be found south of the Ribble; the 1,076 acres enclosed at Great Crosby by an 1812 Act, and the 3,398 enclosed in Trawden and Colne of 1817 stand out as exceptions. In Cheshire both large and small enclosures were well scattered: in the centre 600 acres on the Bickerton Hills and 8,750 acres of Delamere Forest stand out, and around the periphery 6,000 acres of lowland on Dodleston moor in the Dee valley, and 1,000 acres at Frodsham and Helsby, with 600 and 700 acres on higher ground at Congleton, and at Macclesfield, respectively. The enclosure at Delamere Forest in Cheshire was completed in 1819, twenty-three years after it was first mooted, a time-span which spells out how complex were the interests of both high and low in society when grazing, pannage, and timber rights were affected (Scard 1981: 11–13). Despite these changes, and although much of Lancashire and Cheshire are characterized by ancient enclosure, after 1860 there was still plenty of waste in both counties.

At the close of the eighteenth century the Lancashire plain was mainly arable, producing wheat and or oats. The potato was grown in areas in easy reach of the towns. Small mixed farms concentrating on stock cattle and sheep were still to be found in the east (Fletcher 1962: 100). Three-quarters of Cheshire was pasture, the remaining quarter was ploughed, but mainly to produce animal feedstuffs. Again, there were differences in the east, and in areas such as Frodsham where green crops for the urban market were well established (Fussell 1954: 65). More of Lancashire went over to grass as the years passed, perhaps three-quarters by the 1860s; the proportion of pasture in Cheshire was estimated at only half in 1847 (Mutch 1980: 23, 45, 57–8; Fussell 1954: 72). Lancashire farmers on the plain could produce fodder for urban horses, and green crops for the townspeople. Demand was such that early potatoes fetched a premium price, or farmers could rely on the later main crop; those with the capital to store their product rather than sell immediately could play the market and wait for prices to appreciate as the year advanced. The small farmers in the eastern textile areas aimed to sell milk and meat (Fletcher 1962: 119; Mutch 1980: 44, 60). Cheese making was widespread if less specialist than in Cheshire; helped no doubt by a new fashion for quick-maturing cheeses (Porter 1976: 142; 1861 census, eg for Wennington, Clifton). In Cheshire as early as 1825 the Bank of England's agreement to fund a mortgage on the Mere estate (near Knutsford) was in part based on proximity to the Manchester market, and access to urban markets via the Weaver and the Trent and Mersey Canal (JRUL, Brook of Mere MSS, 3/902/D). By the 1840s dairies close to the towns in the north of the county, on the Wirral, and adjacent to the salt towns of the middle, were switching from cheese to liquid milk sales, a trend which accelerated as the railway network developed (Porter 1976: 144, 145). The impact of these changes should not be exaggerated: the Fylde was still a granary area in the 1860s, while Cheshire cheese continued to be made on the best cheese farms over the whole county, although it was beginning to become concentrated in the south of the county. Dairy farmers sent surplus calves to the urban meat markets, and winter fattening of killing flocks of sheep, more noticeable towards 1860 in Cheshire, also provided meat. In the 1800s sheep soon proved more reliable than salt-prone arable on the Lancashire coastal lands reclaimed from the sea (Fletcher 1962: 94; Mutch 1980: 45; Porter 1976: 146). Other varieties of agriculture in the form of market gardens, especially around Liverpool and south of Manchester, raised food for the townsmen, while the region's nurseries and seedsmen enjoyed a much wider, international trade (Harvey 1976).

Farmers found guano or crushed bone to be new and effective dressings; lime, where new transport facilities made it cheaper, was used more extensively. Marling, the time-honoured way of improving Cheshire, faded out in the 1840s, both as it became expensive and as the newer fertilizers became available (Scard 1981: 85). The drainage schemes already noted (see p. 158) were at least as important as the new dressings in improving output throughout the region. The turnip, scarcely used *c.* 1800, was more favoured as a cattle fodder as the nineteenth century passed. Crop rotations remained varied, and in the mid-nineteenth century there were still Cheshire farmers who would virtually exhaust soil before putting it down to grass (Scard 1981: 82, 83). A steam thresher was in use near Crewe in the 1840s (Chaloner 1950a: 12). In *c.* 1860 sale notices for south-west Lancashire farms suggest that fewer than 2 per cent of farms had some sort of reaper or mower, and fewer than 9 per cent of farms any other type of powered machine. By its nature such evidence will underestimate the ownership of machinery, but it was only in 1853 that the Earl of Sefton undertook the first trial in the area of a reaper, followed in 1854 by some unsuccessful trials at the Warrington show of the Manchester and Liverpool Agricultural Society (Mutch 1980: 78, 377). Machines were intended to save labour costs, and in this respect they made more impact later in the century, though transport systems had already made a saving on farmers' time and effort in getting produce to market.

The rise of formal retail markets in new towns like Crewe, or Hyde, or Birkenhead may have involved farmers in direct contact with retail marketing, but may indicate the existence of a network of middlemen. Cattle auctions did not become widespread until the railways made an impact, later than the close of this chapter (Porter 1976). Close to the towns retail milk sales were made by small farmers, though milk dealers were evident in the 1861 census (eg Barton on Irwell). Old forms of trade, through cheese factors for example, persisted alongside these adaptations by which farmers responded to urban demand for their produce.

There were farmers who went bust. Those who, like John Byrom of Overpool, sold both arable and pastoral products, could benefit most from urban markets and were thus probably the most secure, though not all Cheshire estates would permit the sale of fodder or root crops (Scard 1981: 48, 57). The depression after the Napoleonic wars did not have much effect on Lancashire arable men, but in Cheshire arrears were considerable in the 1820s and 1830s, for example on the Brook of Mere estates in 1832 the rental was £10,093, but arrears totalled £3,893 (JRUL, Brook of Mere MSS, 4/3/902/D). Landlords had to give reductions in rent to support their tenants. The steam packet between Dublin and Liverpool brought in Irish meat and cheese to compete, while Dutch cheese began to attack the London market for Cheshire cheese. But farmers' profits were maintained for rents continued to rise until about 1830 in Cheshire, when they levelled off. In south Lancashire the rise seems to have continued (Fussell 1954: 69–71; Fletcher 1962: 121; G. Rogers 1981: 8, 16; Scard 1981: 46; cf. C. S. Davies 1961: 47). Agricultural societies were propaganda vehicles for new ideas, and introduced competition in farming. Some of the innovative estates, especially the tenants of the Watts family at Speke, were repeatedly successful in winning agricultural society prizes in the 1850s (Mutch 1980: 98). Looking back from 1860, there were contemporary commentators, who have their recent supporters (Freeman, Rodgers and Kinvig 1966: 64), who too readily applied criteria more relevant to the arable south and east of England to criticize the north-west. Yet in 1860, perhaps more so in Cheshire than in Lancashire, the land was worked in ways very similar to those of the eighteenth century.

Transport

Agriculture and the rural communities in most of the region were linked together, and to a wider world, especially to the industrial areas which increasingly became their market, by road, rail and canal by 1860. Road and canal were poor servants of the Wirral, the Fylde, the Forest of Bowland and much of Rossendale, a disadvantage at least partially repaired by the railways. Turnpike development in the region continued until the coming of the railways in the 1830s (Freeman et al. 1966: 84). Not only was the network of roads virtually complete, renewal Acts had softened gradients, surfaces had improved, pack-horses had given way to wagons and by the 1820s mail coaches could complete the London–Manchester run in one day. Toll houses dotted the roads and the posting and coaching inns served the needs of travellers and horses. But the Snake road from Glossop to Sheffield, built in the 1820s, marked the end of the era. In 1833 it had the largest debt relative to toll receipts of any turnpike and by 1839 the two dukes, Devonshire and Norfolk, had invested £30,000 in it and were sureties with the Earl of Surrey for a further £34,500 (Albert 1972: 105, 109–10).

Liverpool's growth, despite its relatively poor road communications, was sustained by a variety of waterways. Manchester was the focus of a web of water routes, which when canal building too came to an end in the 1830s, wanted only a link to the cotton towns in the north-east of the county across Rossendale. The canals had required such engineering triumphs as the Lune aqueduct on the Lancaster canal, the seventy-four locks of the Huddersfield canal, the highest summit level in England, and the 1,640-yard Foulridge tunnel of the Leeds and Liverpool canal. They also changed the character of villages and districts. At Runcorn, St Helens and Ellesmere Port, they were the basis for 'new towns'; at Whaley Bridge the Peak Forest canal linked with the Cromford and High Peak railway to produce an early canal–rail interchange and at Castlefield in Manchester the Bridgewater changed a suburban retreat into a bustling commercial and industrial centre.

The growth in coal carriage that underpinned canal development also fostered the use of tramways for moving coal from pithead to canal, an early example in the region being Sir Thomas Gerard's two-mile line of 1766 joining Pewfall colliery at Garswood to a wharf on the Sankey canal (Ashmore 1969: 113). Stone was also moved in this way, notably on the Peak Forest Tramway which linked the Doveholes quarries in Derbyshire to the

Peak Forest canal and its Derbyshire and Cheshire lime kilns at the beginning of the nineteenth century. These early tramroads were ancillary to canals and roads but the symbiotic growth of Liverpool and Manchester brought the railway to centre stage. In 1810 110 million pounds of cotton passed from Liverpool to Manchester; by 1824 this had risen to over 160 million pounds and complaints of high rates and frequent delays on the Mersey–Irwell Navigation and the Bridgewater Canal, though perhaps not entirely justified, brought a search for alternatives (Hadfield and Biddle 1970: 107–9). A railway was seen as the solution as early as 1821 and the Act for the railway was passed in May 1826 but it was not until Stephenson's famous success at the Rainhill Trials in 1829 that it was decided to use steam locomotives rather than stationary engines. By this time the Bolton and Leigh railway, authorized in 1825, had opened for goods traffic, terminating at the Bridgewater Canal at Leigh.

The building of the Liverpool–Manchester railway was a great feat of engineering (Plate 3.4) and its importance was signalled by the grand opening in September 1830, sadly marred by the fatal accident to William Huskisson at Parkside. The potential of the line was demonstrated on 1 December 1830 when the first freight train carried 135 bales of American cotton, 200 barrels of flour, 63 sacks of oatmeal and 34 sacks of malt to Manchester in its 18 wagons. In the first year of operation it was the 445,000 passengers who took precedence, the first class travelling in closed carriages and the second class in open carriages as they did until 1844 when the third class was created. By 1835, however, when 473,000 people were carried, merchandise traffic had grown from 43,000 to 230,000 tons and coal from 11,000 to 116,000 tons (Carlson 1969: 239–45; G. O. Holt 1978: 22, 25–6).

The railway was promoted and financed largely by Liverpudlians, who went on to promote the Grand Junction railway of 1837 and to play a major role in development in other parts of the country. But, as in the case of the roads and canals, there was no master plan: towns and districts engaged in fierce rivalry for railways and the economic development they would bring. In the north-west the vital links between the cotton towns and the Liverpool–Manchester connection were completed in the 1840s. The railway was a great stimulus to the textile industry of Rossendale where the canals had not penetrated and, by courtesy of the Duke of Norfolk, saved the cotton industry in Glossop, which also lacked canal access. As early as 1845 rail made it possible for orders and yarn to leave Manchester for out-of-town manufacture and to be returned as cloth within 24 hours (Kellett 1969: 172–3).

The railways were, of course, great arteries for coal and opened the

---

Plate 3.4 The Sankey viaduct. The Liverpool–Manchester railway inaugurated a period of great railway viaducts. Here the railway met the Sankey Navigation with its boats and cranes and men hauling tubs presumably for the coal trade. (Source: Baines 1836, III: 682.)

north-west to the Yorkshire coalfield; they also carried in Baltic iron, timber, grain and other imports through Hull with cotton warps and waste as return freight for the Yorkshire textile industry. On Merseyside they were vital to the growth of the chemical industry at Widnes and St Helens and the Lancashire coast saw the railway's golden link bring growth to Blackpool and Lytham from 1846, Morecambe from 1848 and Southport in the 1850s. Earlestown thrived on railway engineering in the 1850s and Crewe was created in 1842 when four lines converged there and the Grand Junction moved in its engine sheds and repair shops.

The railway also brought suburban growth (see Table 3.11). At Liverpool it was at Kirkdale and Everton in the 1830s, at Toxteth and West Derby around 1850. Manchester's middle class, driven out of Ardwick and Deansgate in the early 1800s, moved out to Broughton and in much larger numbers south to Hulme, Victoria Park and Didsbury before the railway pulled them even further south to Bowdon, Knutsford, Wilmslow and Alderley Edge by 1860.

Table 3.11   Liverpool and Manchester principal inner suburbs 1842

			Annual Value	
	Population	*Acreage*	*Land*	*Houses*
Manchester	163,856	1,646	933	790,774
Ardwick	9,906	509	462	44,182
Cheetham	6,082	919	2,410	39,808
Chorlton on M.	28,336	646	434	140,605
Hulme	26,982	477	144	120,808
Liverpool	223,303	1,858	11,228	1,095,265
Everton	9,221	693	1,984	69,837
Toxteth Park	40,235	2,375	6,457	164,353
West Derby	9,760	675	20,549	83,291

Sources: Population from the 1841 Census. Annual values from the *Return of Annual Value of Real Property in England and Wales 1842* (published 1846).

Though there was some urban tunnelling (see Figure 3.1, p. 168), the lines that gave these commuters access to the town centres cut great swathes through poor districts displacing thousands of slum dwellers. Early examples are Exchange Station in Liverpool, which entailed the demolition of 500 properties in multiple occupation, and the Victoria Station approach in Manchester, which removed 250 shops, cottages and cellar dwellings (Kellett 1969: 7–8, 13). These urban railways also proved very profitable to landowners. In Liverpool the Earl of Derby, the Earl of Sefton and the Corporation were major beneficiaries and in Manchester a ring of substantial landowners around the inner district, notably the Earls of Derby and Ducie, Lord Francis Egerton and Sir Thomas de Trafford were able to command high prices. There is perhaps a symbolic element in the sale of Ancoats Hall, rebuilt in 1828, by the Mosleys to the Midland Railway for offices and a goods yard in the late 1860s (Kellett 1969: 155).

The railway did not end the long dissatisfaction with the costs of movement of goods between Liverpool and Manchester. It has been argued that before the railway there was competition between the waterways and carriers but the railway did bring their charges down. Cheaper carriage only focused attention on Liverpool, as illustrated by a broadsheet published in Manchester in 1841, 'Every morsel of bread put into the mouth of the working man in Manchester has, before he saw it, been subject to the tax of Liverpool town and dock dues' (quoted in Hadfield and Biddle 1970: 120). Those dues had risen from £2,781 in 1756 to £221,000 in 1836 and it was alleged that half came from merchandise brought to Manchester. Moreover the railway itself appeared to fall victim to the taint of monopoly in Liverpool, where the London North Western's Lime Street Station which dominated access to the inner areas was accused of high charges and poor facilities in the early 1850s. Manchester in contrast had nine companies with their own or shared stations and in the late 1850s competition became open warfare between some of their staffs (Kellett 1969: 160–70). Manchester and Liverpool were different and the railway was not the last word in their transport relationship.

The continued impact of turnpike roads, of rivers and canals, and then of the railways all served to facilitate Liverpool's role as the chief port of the region. On the Dee, the customs posts at Parkgate were shut down in the 1830s, proclaiming the final exit of the port of Chester. Further north, Lancaster was the fourth port in the country in 1787. Like Liverpool, it built new docks (at Glasson) and benefited from up-to-date transport links through the Lancaster canal, just as the creeks at Preston thrived on the Douglas navigation, and the Leeds–Liverpool canal cut of 1805 (Ashmore 1982: 24). Well into the nineteenth century Fleetwood (1840), Morecambe and Widnes (both 1853) were developed as railway ports (Ashmore 1982: 24–5). Liverpool, which quickly absorbed its intended rival port, Birkenhead, continued to trade west with the Americas, but also developed Indian and Pacific commerce in this period, when its merchants and shippers showed the same penchant for organizing business and attracting capital as they had previously done. The end of English slaving in 1808 does not seem to have had much impact on the port (Hyde 1971: 34). However, competitors were not idle, and perhaps most noticeably in shipbuilding, Liverpool firms found their livelihood threatened, and it is on Liverpool that we now concentrate.

The main Liverpool commodity imports were constant through this period – cocoa, coffee, dyewood, sugar, rum, cotton. But these were now shipped from more than one source, so that the old reliance on the Americas declined. Salt and coal continued as principal commodity exports; by mid-century 452,000 tons of rock and white salt were sent overseas per annum, and a further 166,000 tons to Ireland. Liverpool's manufacturing hinterland extended for a radius of some 100 miles around the port, ensuring a wide range and a growing volume of exports. The rise of a trade in chemical exports to America is but one example of the new developments in the nineteenth century on the old foundations of the region (Hyde 1971: 34–5, 40; see also p. 263). It is, however, on the growth of entrepreneurship and of support services for trade at Liverpool on which we should focus here, rather than on lists of commodities and destinations.

First of all, in the late eighteenth century ships built in Liverpool increased substantially in number. But the yards did not build bigger ships, and this was one reason why English east coast yards, and Canadian yards, were able to offer more competitive prices. By 1835 half the ships used by Liverpool merchants had been constructed elsewhere in England or in Canada (Hyde 1971: 38). Nevertheless, there was some innovation in the port with the development at Laird's yard in Birkenhead of iron ships in the 1820s and 1830s (Hyde 1971: 52).

Liverpool always needed, or anticipated the need for, more docks, and its massive achievements were a tribute to the foresight of the port (see Plate 3.5 and Figure 3.1). Improvements were spread over the period, some like the specialized Duke's Dock, which handled Bridgewater Canal traffic, were extended (in the 1840s with Bridgewater money); most new capacity just provided general quay space (Little 1984: 59). In 1821 the new Prince's Dock cost £650,000. One man, the engineer Jesse Hartley, built between 1824 and 1860 140 acres of wet dock and 10 miles or so of quay space. Much of this was funded through the Corporation-dominated dock trustees, who also received income from dock ratepayers, and from the port dues. By the end of Hartley's reign in 1860 bonded debt on dock construction stood at £4,784,000. Dock administration was always controversial: corporation interests were too cautious for the shippers, while for inland importers and exporters, especially those in Manchester, dues were too expensive and, it was felt, misapplied to subsidize Liverpool rates. Difficulties over a proposed extension of Duke's Dock in the 1780s typify the strained relations between Manchester and Liverpool, which eventually were to lead to the port of Manchester (see p. 241; Hyde 1971: 75–83, 88–9; Little 1984: 55).

The mercantile trading associations of the port contributed to full docks by successfully pressing for the removal of trading restrictions and privileges in 1787 and 1813 and, most notably, the removal of the East India Company's monopoly in 1833. The full benefit of such relaxations came only with steam ships, and on the transatlantic run the entrepreneurial skills of Samuel Cunard, particularly in putting capital together in partnerships, stand out, while the engineering and entrepreneurial skills of Alfred Holt in the 1850s improved steam ship engines and made long-distance steam voyages a reality. Although trade cycles remained a threat, after the early decades of the nine-

---

Plate 3.5   The new Customs House, Liverpool. (Source: Baines 1836, IV: 174–5.)

teenth century the financial liquidity and elasticity of the port avoided col-
lapses as dramatic as those of 1793, 1797 and 1813. In 1793 in particular,
fluctuations in world trade coupled with speculation and over-confidence in
Liverpool contributed to a slump which restricted credit by three-quarters of
a million pounds sterling. Many bankruptcies followed, including that of the
largest house in the city, and they were stemmed only by an Act of Parliament
that permitted the corporation to issue promissory notes (Hyde 1971: 36–8,
41, 54, 55).

Industry

In 1777 the first Arkwright mills were built in Lancashire and a great wave of
mill-building followed the expiry of his patent in 1785. These structures were
large and could be architecturally imposing and though the mule-spinning
mills were not, in their early days, as large or pretentious, they too were
substantial. Wyatt's mill at New Mills, advertised for sale in 1802, was
twenty-five by ten yards, four storeys high and contained fifteen mules with
3,240 spindles (Symonds 1983: 28). By 1787 out of 143 cotton mills in Great
Britain forty-one were in Lancashire, twenty-two in Derbyshire and eight in
Cheshire (E. Baines 1835: 19).

The earliest cotton mills were water-powered and the search for sites
with good catchments and a fall of water took the mill-builders into remote
valleys and townships where both transport and labour could be a problem.
It was these mills using Arkwright's machinery that depended largely upon
the labour of children and though Arkwright himself was never directly
involved, it was his inventions that gave birth to the system of pauper apprentices. It is far from clear how many children were apprenticed but from the
1770s until well into the nineteenth century several thousand children grew
up in apprentice houses, their lives governed by the demands of the mill and
the goodwill or otherwise of their masters and overseers. The mills at Mellor
and Styal, which never had more than 100 apprentices at any one time, have
left reasonably good reputations but even there a working day that ran from
6 am until 7 pm was clearly excessive. Legislation, first attempted in 1802,
failed to protect these children and those who lived at home, and it was not

Figure 3.1 Liverpool in 1836. The dark bands which follow streets are ward boundaries. The
development of the river front docks is clearly visible, while the railway tunnels into the centre of
the city are indicated by dark bands which cross the street pattern; the beginning of the word
'tunnel' is marked, top right. The left of the map shows the expansion of Liverpool into rural
areas. (Source: E. Baines 1836, IV: 54.)

until the Factory Act 1833 that the appointment of factory inspectors began a steady improvement in the employment of children in the mills (Hutchins and Harrison 1911: 2–42).

During the 1780s steam power began to be used to raise water for water wheels and later for directly driving machinery. Water and steam power existed side by side and were sometimes used in tandem into the mid-nineteenth century but many of the valleys where the mills had flourished in the late eighteenth and early nineteenth centuries ran down into dereliction in the late nineteenth century. Like others in the Pennines the Cheesden and Naden valleys between Ramsbottom and Heywood which were crowded with mills, bleach crofts and print works in 1848 were picturesque ruins by the early twentieth century (Ashmore 1969: 40–3). Mill communities such as those developed in the early nineteenth century by millowners like the Gregs at Styal, the Garnetts at Low Moor, near Clitheroe, the Ashtons at Hyde or Hugh Mason at Ashton-under-Lyne succeeded the pauper apprentice houses but they too represented a degree of control over the lives of the workers. In 1844 an astute French visitor could offer the following comment on Ashton's community at Hyde

> The houses inhabited by the workpeople form large and long streets. Mr. Ashton has built 300 of them which he lets at 3s or 3/6d per week. Each house contains upon the ground floor, a sitting room a kitchen and a backyard, and above are two or three bedrooms. The proprietor furnishes at his own charge water to the houses, keeps them in good repair and pays the local rates. Mr. Ashton has built a large and handsome schoolhouse which serves at the same time as a chapel and where 700 children are gathered together on a Sunday.
>
> (Faucher 1844: 106–7)

Where the millowner did not build there was no shortage of speculators to build the houses and shops the workers needed. As the mills grew, terraces of cottages spread around them linking the old farms, nooks and folds of the seventeenth and eighteenth centuries into new urban centres.

The Select Committee Report of 1818 shows the dominance that Manchester had, by then, asserted over the country districts (see Table 3.12). Since Crompton's mule census of 1811 claimed that there were upwards of 650 cotton mills within 60 miles of Bolton, and Wood suggests a figure of 114,000 mill operatives in Great Britain in 1815, most of whom would be in the north-west, it seems likely that this list is very incomplete. It may, however, indicate the relative significance of mills in the various towns. Virtually all were spinning mills for in 1818 there were only fourteen mills in the region which were using power-looms.

The distribution of the mills reflects a number of local factors. Rochdale and Bury were still heavily occupied with the woollen cloth trade. Wigan and

Table 3.12   Location of cotton manufacturing 1818

	Mills	Employees
Manchester, Salford and Eccles	80	19,923
Ashton-under-Lyne	34	4,470
Oldham	19	1,643
Bolton	19	3,262
Preston	15	1,898
Chorley and Blackburn	9	1,219
Bury	7	1,111
Rochdale	7	796
Wigan	8	616
Warrington	5	648
Stockport	30	4,823
Macclesfield, Wilmslow, Congleton	10	1,461
Derbyshire	7	4,073

Source: Kenny 1975: 63.

Warrington had metal and coal to compete with cotton for capital and labour. Macclesfield and Congleton had their well-established silk interests, though that in Stockport gave way to cotton, while in Manchester it continued alongside cotton. Garstang, Lancaster and Ormskirk maintained the linen and sailcloth trade. The Blackburn area, long dominated by cotton and physically as attractive to mill-builders as its Pennine neighbours, had apparently fallen behind as a consequence of strong local resistance to machinery though the weaving trade was strong and buoyant. It was above all Manchester and its immediate environs with its strong finishing and marketing tradition that drew capital and labour to the Irk and Irwell valleys where vast ranges of spinning blocks grew along the canals and reached close to the ancient centre of the parish.

As spinning moved into the mills it was the mule, operated by men, that increasingly took the major role. Between 1779 and the 1830s the number of spindles per mule grew from 48 to over 600, reaching 800 by 1870 (Fowler and Wyke 1987: 2–5). The introduction of the self-acting mule in 1824 reduced the degree of skill needed but the mule spinners were the best-paid mill workers and the leaders in trade union organization and the defence of their wages until the decline of the industry.

While the factory system in spinning was concentrating labour the consequent flow of yarn diffused weaving across the region. Technical change was much slower in weaving and it remained largely a domestic trade until the 1830s though with some concentrations of specialized weavers. In general across the region there was a shift from wool and linen to cotton, from mixed fabrics such as fustians and checks to all-cotton cloths and from heavier cotton cloths such as the old Blackburn greys through calicoes to muslins, both plain and figured. Fustians continued to be made widely in a range of weights and weaves and new cloths of all kinds were introduced. By the

1820s there were few parishes with any textile tradition that were not also weaving cotton.

The new cotton cloths clearly brought prosperity for many weavers. William Radcliffe's account of Mellor in Derbyshire is well known. There, he claimed, families could earn 40 to 120 shillings a week and were able to make dramatic increases in their living standards (Radcliffe 1828). John Higson makes similar observations on Droylsden where weavers could earn 20 to 23 shillings for three days' intensive work (Higson 1859: 92–7). The evidence for Oldknow's weavers at Mellor in Derbyshire suggests lower levels but in general the years between 1780 and 1815 seem to have been the most prosperous for the hand-loom weavers. After the end of the French wars the generality of hand-loom weavers suffered a progressive fall in wages though their numbers continued to increase until the 1830s (see Table 3.13).

Table 3.13   Numbers and wages in the cotton industry in Great Britain

| | Hand-loom weavers | | Operatives in factories | |
Year	No. (000s)	Weekly wage (d.)	No. (000s)	Weekly wage (d.)
1806	184	240	90	121
1810	200	171	100	126
1815	220	162	114	126
1820	240	99	126	124
1825	240	75	173	118
1830	240	75	185	115
1835	188	75	220	116
1840	123	75	262	112
1845	60	75	262	119
1850	43	75	331	110
1855	27	75	371	120
1860	10	75	427	139

Note: The mill wages are an average of all age groups and skills in the mills, those for hand-loom weavers take no account of varieties of cloth or of individual output and are very notional after 1825. Both sets are best taken as indications of general trends.

Source: Summarized from G. H. Wood 1910: 127–8.

The first power loom was invented by Edmund Cartwright in 1786 but it was a clumsy and inefficient device, unsuccessful in its first employment at Doncaster from 1787 to 1793. The first power looms to work in the north-west were at Grimshaw's factory in Manchester in 1790 but his twenty-four Cartwright looms were destroyed when the mill was burnt down by hand-loom weavers. Power looms were being advertised in Manchester in 1806 and, according to Radcliffe, there were some small power loom weaving sheds working in the Manchester area by 1808. Thomas Ashton of Hyde claimed in 1824 that he had been the first person to introduce power looms to any extent, presumably in 1812 when he installed them at his Flowery Field mills (Fourth Report of the Select Committee on Artisans and Machinery, 1824). A note to the Census report for Newton in 1821 offers some support, attributing an increased population there to an increase of steam loom weaving (*VCH. Cheshire*, II: 241). Across the region there were few working before the mid-1820s when the balance tilted irrevocably from hand to power. (See Figure 3.2 for weavers' houses in Preston in 1841.)

The key to the spread of the power loom was clearly efficiency and that could be attained only by its mechanical development. The early pioneers in this improvement were largely in the Stockport area. William Radcliffe, fearful of cheap exported yarn, devised better methods of taking up cloth and warp dressing in 1802 and 1804, William Horrocks, also of Stockport, used the taking up device for improvement in 1803 and in 1822 and 1828 there were further developments by Sharp, Roberts in Manchester and William Dickinson at Blackburn respectively (Kenny 1975: 90). By the mid-1820s a boy or girl of fifteen working two power looms could weave three and a half times as much as the best hand weaver (E. Baines 1835: 239).

After a slow start power looms rapidly grew in numbers. In 1821 Manchester had over 5,000 power looms and in 1824 Baines singled out Hyde, Stockport and Stalybridge where there were 2,470 as leading centres with Middleton and Rawtenstall also strongly developing. By 1833 W. R. Greg could add Bolton and Bury to this list and smaller centres were growing across the region (Table 3.14). As the power looms spread they became concentrated in Lancashire, as Table 3.15 shows. Until about the middle of the nineteenth century most of the power looms were installed by spinners who developed great combined spinning and weaving mills but later the weaving partnership began to produce specialist weavers especially in northeast Lancashire. The rise of the power loom resulted in the decline of the hand loom until in 1860 there were few left, principally worked by specialist weavers in Bolton and north-east Lancashire, though tiny handfuls could be found in towns and villages all over the east of the region.

The passing of the hand-loom weaver was a social as well as an economic phenomenon. The parochial chapelry of Colne, which was wider than the township, offers a good example of a weaving community. Its population may have been about 3,000 in the mid-seventeenth century rising to 9,448 at the 1801 census (C. D. Rogers 1975a: 29). In 1775 a Piece Hall was built for the sale of woollen cloth but by 1824 calico was the staple, some 12,600 pieces being woven each week for the Manchester market. From 1790 to 1812 there were 3,900 burials in the chapel-yard; out of 754 people, predominantly men, for whom occupations were given no fewer than 450 were employed in textiles, 409 of them weavers, and all other occupations were agricultural or country service trades (summarized from Spencer 1968). It was claimed that in the chapelry the whole population of 17,000 lived by the loom. It was in communities like this that William Hewitt found in 1838 large families and forlorn and filthy dwellings, where

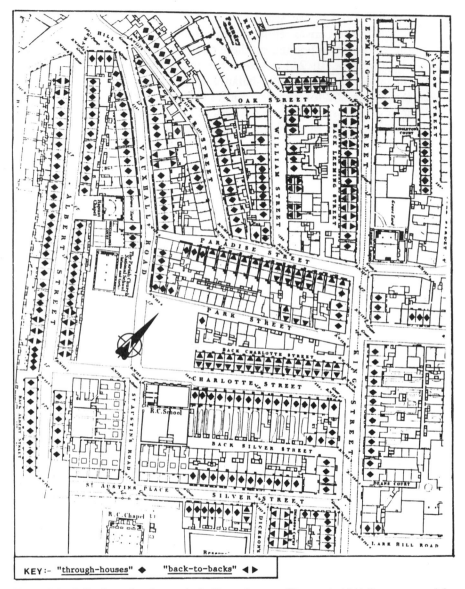

Figure 3.2 Cellar-loomshop houses in the Horrocks area of Preston in 1841. Recent research by Nigel Morgan has reconstructed the weavers' communities of these long-demolished streets. In Albert Street, for example, 68 of the 90 houses were inhabited by hand-loom weavers, in Charlotte Street and Back Charlotte Street, 39 out of 48 and in Silver Street, Back Silver Street and Dickson's Court 28 out of 44. (Source: N. Morgan 1990.)

Table 3.14   Power looms in 1835

	Cotton weaving mills	Looms
Whalley parish	32	4,737
(of which Blackburn)		3,200·
Burnley	10	1,165
Ashton-under-Lyne		4,000
Stockport		4,000
Bury parish		9,000
Manchester parish		15,000
Bolton		under 1,500

Source: adapted from Bythell 1969: 92.

Table 3.15   Estimated number of power looms

	1833	1850	% increase
Lancashire	61,176	176,847	189.2
Cheshire	22,491	29,066	29.2
Yorkshire	4,039	8,102	100.6
Derbyshire	2,403	7,266	202.4

Source: Kenny 1975: 91.

> Any man who has once been through this district might again
> recognise the very locality if he were taken thither blindfold by the
> very smell of oatcake which floats about the village and the sound of
> the shuttles with their eternal 'latitat latitat'.
>
> (Aspin 1969: 53)

As they were plunged into poverty the weavers found no remedy but the poor law.

The spinners had fought a different battle. Their union had its roots in local organizations like the Stockport Friendly Association of Cotton Spinners of 1792 and by 1810 there was a northern network that could keep spinners at Preston and Stalybridge out on strike for three months. Within twenty years of being drawn into the mills they were also seeking to reduce hours. A failed petition to Parliament for a ten-hour day in 1818 was followed by the Ten Hours campaign of the 1820s and 1830s and hopes that the restriction of hours for women and children would also benefit the men. In practice the Factory Acts of 1844 and 1847, which gave women and children the ten-hour day, failed to help the men but in 1853 masters were prevented from working protected persons in relays and all the mill workers won the shorter week. The ten-hour day and, even more, the Saturday half day which resulted transformed the workers' lives and opened up the prospect of Saturday sport, family outings to the market or the country, to relatives or later the local park.

The power loom weavers, many of them young women, were slower to organize than the spinners but they too followed the same path, organizing local price lists in defence of wages by the 1840s and in 1858 forming the first amalgamated society in the region. They fought bitter strikes in 1829, 1830, 1842, 1848 and 1853 often accompanied by disorder, vicious attacks on strikebreakers, known as knobsticks, and in 1831, the murder of a Hyde millowner, which may have had some union complicity.

The bleaching industry was also transformed between 1780 and 1860 as bleaching moved indoors and the old open bleach crofts became a thing of the past. The keys to this change were the use of chlorine as a bleach, the introduction of soda ash in the earlier stage of bucking and the application of steam power to washing and moving the cloth. Before 1800 the bleachers had established their industry where there was plentiful water but with the coming of steam they also needed access to coal. Bolton was a major centre with another concentration in north Cheshire around Stockport but there were also bleach works in most of the east Lancashire parishes. The movement of bleaching indoors had a number of consequences. It made the trade dependent upon the emerging chemical industry and it increased the necessity for capital investment, but it also speeded the processes, made it possible to work all the year round and ended the long fear of thieves (Musson and Robinson 1969: 251–7). In 1781 the Bolton and Manchester masters had set up a society for the prosecution of felons, as a result of which James Holland was executed on Bolton Moor in 1786 for the theft of thirty yards of cloth valued at two shillings a yard from a croft (Sykes 1925: 22). The indoor trade had no need for such savage protection. Bleaching was, on the whole, a healthy trade but it kept its tradition of overwork long after the old seasonal reasons for it had gone. In 1854 H. S. Tremenheere's commission reported that in Lancashire and the west of Scotland women and children were sometimes working up to sixteen hours a day for months at a stretch, a state of affairs not remedied until the Factory Act of 1860 (Hutchins and Harrison 1911: 133–9).

Calico print workers found their lives changed after Bell's invention of the cylinder printing machine in 1783, which paralleled improvements in spinning. Initially the machines, first introduced in Lancashire by Livesey Hargreaves near Preston in 1785, could print only simple patterns but their scope continually increased, though some block printing remained until the end of the nineteenth century. The machines were quick and effective, outproducing block tables in a ratio of 500 to 6, and Lancashire's speed in introducing them drew most of the strength from Scotland, the only other printing region in Britain, by the mid-nineteenth century. Thus the north-west took an increasing share of the national output of printed calico which grew from 1 million pieces of thirty yards in 1796 to 20 million in 1851. Within the region Blackburn had a strong local industry in the early nineteenth century because of the local supply of grey cloth but as power loom weaving developed further south there was a shift to Stockport and Disley and the parish of Glossop. In Lancashire itself the movement was from Blackburn where 500 early block printers had disappeared by the 1840s, to Accrington and Clitheroe from where it spread to Bolton, Bury and Radcliffe, then to Rochdale and Chorley (Turnbull 1951: 81, 106). Many early works had been operated by or in close conjunction with combined spinning and manufacturing firms, like those of the Peels at Bury and the Ashtons at Hyde, but the specialized weaving concerns that followed the introduction of the power loom did not usually print or finish their cloth. Later print works therefore usually printed cloth woven by other firms, as did that of Edmund Potter at Dinting Vale in Glossop, which in 1873 produced 1 million pieces and was probably, as Potter had claimed in 1864, the largest in the world (J. G. Hurst 1948: 67, 71–2).

Speed of operation and a quick turnover of work was vital for the master printers, pressed as they were by merchants and eager to get their full run of any pattern on the market quickly so as to reduce the risk of copying. Overwork was endemic and the children who filled the colour trays for block printers or assisted on the machines worked very long hours beside the adult printers. The Print Works Commission of 1843 (Table 3.16) found the age

Table 3.16 Labour in calico printing, 1843

	Male	Female
Adults 21+	8,620	484
Young persons 13–18	4,147	995
Children under 13	3,616	2,030

Source: Hutchins and Harrison 1911: 123–131.

distribution in the three counties. Out of 565 children taken at random two-thirds had started work under the age of nine, twenty-seven under the age of seven; in the machine shops they were working an average of ten and a half hours a day, and twelve or fourteen hours in the block shops, where sometimes they were in the shop day and night working on rush orders. Legislation quickly followed; in 1845 the Calico Print Works Act prohibited the employment of children under eight, stopped women and children from working nights and laid down that children should attend school for thirty days in each half year.

The great attraction of printing was its relatively high level of wages. In 1849 for a week of 60 hours the Lancashire averages were 35 shillings for machine printers, 28 shillings for block printers, 30 shillings for colour mixers and 25 shillings for block cutters. The engravers who cut the patterns on the rollers commanded 40 shillings a week and even the labourers a respectable 15 shillings. Ten years earlier wages had been higher but machine printing was bringing them down. As in spinning and weaving there had been attempts to stop the introduction of machinery. The first journeymen in Lancashire had come from London and they brought their organization with them; by the end of the eighteenth century the northern journeymen had their own union which persisted in the teeth of the Combination Acts. In the opening years of the nineteenth century the union fought a classic battle for traditional objectives – control of apprenticeship, prohibition of machinery, the hiring of union men only, restricted hours and higher wages, culminating in a strike in 1815 which the men lost. In 1814 the masters had formed their own federation and in 1817, when union delegates from various districts were arrested and imprisoned for three months, the resistance of the block printers was at an end and mechanization could proceed without hindrance. It was then the turn of the machine printers to organize and by the 1840s they had established the Machine Printers' Society with branches in most of the printing districts (see Turnbull 1951: ch. 3).

In contrast to other textile industries, technical change had little impact on felt-hat-making between 1780 and 1860; it was remodelled rather by commercial organisation and changing fashions. Lancashire and Cheshire feltmakers were drawn into a well-developed national network of production and marketing. London set the fashion and the great hatting firms, such as Bowlers and Christys, had their headquarters and retail shops there but carried on much of their manufacturing in the provinces (see Figure 3.3), avoiding the high rents, fuel costs and overheads of the city but, more importantly, also escaping from the grip of the London-based and very militant Fair Trade Union. It was the north-west that benefited most from this movement of the trade (see Table 3.17). By 1851 the trade employed 4,423 men and 1,183 women in the region, tiny compared with the legions of the cotton trade, but offering an alternative to the mill where it was well established.

It was an industry of small units; the largest in the region, Christys of Stockport, employed only 270 people in 1859, though nationally their total workforce was 1,500. Small masters, engaged in bodymaking, might have only three to six people working at their kettles and planks, often drawn from their immediate family and occasionally including women. Like the weavers, many maintained a country way of life with a small plot of land and perhaps a horse or a cow.

Disputes and strikes were endemic with serious turn-outs in 1785, 1807 to 1809, 1810, 1818, 1819, 1821, 1831 and 1834 after which, with felt hatting in decline, the militant mantle passed to the silk hatters. Like other

---

Figure 3.3 The spread of felt hatting, 1550–1800. The figure shows the distribution of felt hatters based on probate records. It illustrates the slow spread of the trade across Cheshire and Lancashire before it began to concentrate in the greater Manchester area in the eighteenth century. (Source: J. H. Smith 1980.)

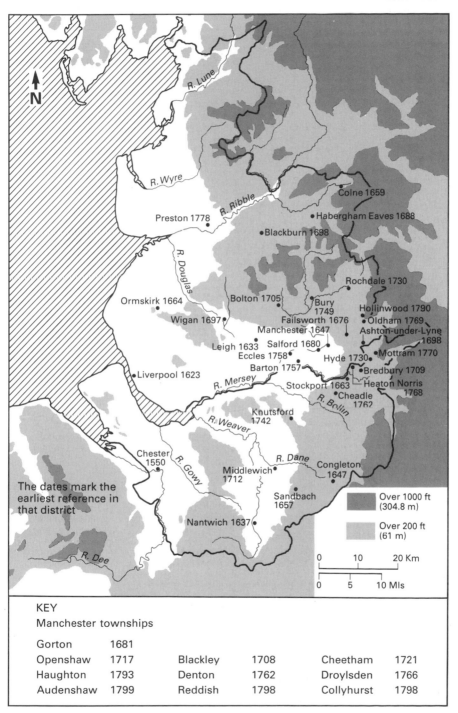

N

R. Lune

R. Wyre

R. Ribble

Preston 1778

Colne 1659

Habergham Eaves 1688

• Blackburn 1698

R. Douglas

Rochdale 1730

Ormskirk 1664

Bolton 1705

Bury
1749

Hollinwood 1790

Wigan 1697•

Failsworth 1676

•Oldham 1769

Manchester 1647

Ashton-under-Lyne
1698

Leigh 1633

Salford 1680

Eccles 1758•

Mottram 1770

•Liverpool 1623

Barton 1757

Hyde 1730

Bredbury 1709

R. Mersey

Stockport 1663

Heaton Norris
1768

Cheadle
1762

R. Bollin

Knutsford
1742

R. Weaver

Chester
1550

R. Gowy

R. Dane

Congleton
1647

Middlewich
1712

Over 1000 ft
(304.8 m)

The dates mark the
earliest reference in
that district

Sandbach
1657

Over 200 ft
(61 m)

Nantwich 1637•

0   10   20 Km

0   5   10 Mls

R. Dee

KEY					
Manchester townships					
Gorton	1681				
Openshaw	1717	Blackley	1708	Cheetham	1721
Haughton	1793	Denton	1762	Droylsden	1766
Audenshaw	1799	Reddish	1798	Collyhurst	1798

Table 3.17 Hatting firms in the north-west

District	1816	1821	1824	1841	1858	1864
Manchester	22	49	58	40	47	15
Stockport	21	20	37	12	15	53
Denton	11	27	26	30	30	127
Ashton	3	—	18	7	—	66
Oldham	1	23	22	—	13	12
Bury	—	—	10	—	10	16
Hyde	—	—	3	5	—	53
Bolton	—	—	8	—	—	—
Rochdale	—	—	10	—	—	—

Sources: Directories and the *Hatters Gazette*. See J. H. Smith 1980.

disputes the hatters' strikes of the early nineteenth century were bitter and violent affairs. Bodymakers who worked through a strike were often visited by the mob, 'the old Bitch and her whelps', who threatened them in their homes, broke their kettles and planks and on occasion beat them. Finishers, who worked on their masters' premises, were sometimes replaced by knob-sticks and in the 1834 turn-out at Stockport these incomers and their families were abused and assaulted in their own homes.

In 1860 the unions had little to show for their years of struggle. Apprenticeship had been greatly widened, there was still no single hatters' union and, during the years of decline in the 1840s and 1850s, wages had gone down though those men still in work could earn more than their cotton mill contemporaries. The hatters' unions had long used the tramping system where union men out of work could tour the hatting districts seeking work at the 'turn houses', inns where the union representative could meet them and take them round the hat shops to look for work but this tradition was of little use when the whole trade suffered from the decline of felt hatting.

It was the fashion for silk hats that damaged the felt hat trade. Silk hats, which were assembled from woven silk, had been known in the late eighteenth century but the rise of the silk topper in the 1840s greatly expanded production. For about twenty years felt hatting was at a very low ebb and many felt hatters endured privation since the silk trade did not require their skills and could be taught to newcomers to hatting.

Getting coal remained pick-and-shovel work over the years of the industrial revolution, though there were technical changes in winding, pumping, in colliery working patterns, and in safety precautions. In March 1854 Joseph Dickinson, Inspector of Mines, read a paper to the Manchester Literary and Philosophical Society which described the collieries of the Lancashire, Cheshire and North Wales coalfield (Figure 3.4). Lancashire then had 334 collieries with 679 pits and Cheshire 28 collieries with 50 pits. On average the Cheshire pits were deeper at 123 yards than those of Lancashire at 118 yards but the deepest shafts of all were two at Pendleton Colliery in Lancashire at

520 yards. In 1852 the two counties produced just under 9 million tons of coal, all but 1 million of which were consumed within the region in addition to coal brought in from south Wales and Yorkshire. Liverpool exported 105,952 tons along the coast and 277,645 to foreign ports and there were also shipments from Preston. Some 50,000 tons were also sent to London by rail. The coal was produced by 27,670 workers underground and 5,870 on the surface with a daily 'get' averaging four tons for hewers.

Dickinson's paper offers the first survey of collieries in the coalfield (Table 3.18, Figure 3.4). He also recorded the ownership of the mines. At

Table 3.18 Collieries in the north-west in 1854

Lancashire	Ashton-under-Lyne	7
	Blackburn	21
	Bolton	43
	Burnley	14
	Bury	11
	Chorley	7
	Leigh	15
	Manchester	15
	Oldham	28
	Rainford	10
	Rochdale, Bacup, Rossendale	84
	St Helens	25
	Wigan	54
Cheshire		28
Derbyshire	(four towns with mines)	4
	Total	366

Source: Dickinson 1855: 71.

Worsley the owners were still the Bridgewater Trustees, the Earl of Crawford and Balcarres held Holland Colliery at Upholland and Haigh at Wigan and Lord Vernon ran his Poynton Colliery in Cheshire. Most collieries were owned singly but there were some companies or partnerships in each district owning up to eight collieries, rarely owning in more than one district (Dickinson 1855). Mineownership could bring great wealth, especially when it was combined with ownership of the land. The Bridgewater collieries at Worsley showed consistently high gross profits, ranging from £1,700 to £5,600 in the 1790s and rising after 1800 when the Duke could increase his Manchester prices to between £6,000 and £24,000 in the first decade of the century (Malet 1977: 91–2). At Haigh near Wigan the Earl of Crawford could write to his son in 1822, 'The basis of our fortune is coal and cannel mines. Colliers we are and colliers we must ever remain' (quoted in Flinn 1984: 37).

The collieries varied greatly in size but the average number underground was 76.4 and, if surface workers are included, 92.5 in Lancashire and

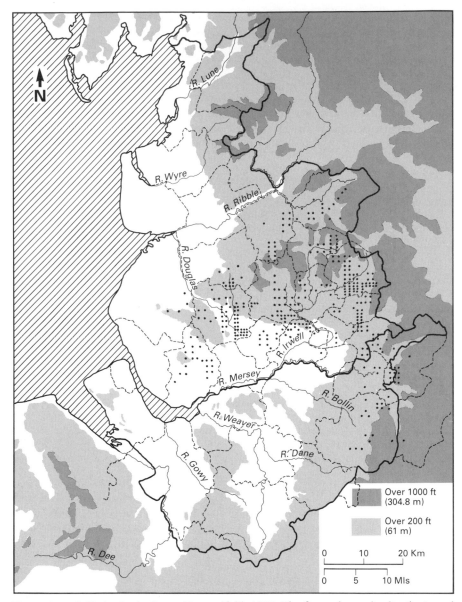

Figure 3.4 Collieries in the Lancashire coalfield, 1854. The figure shows the distribution of collieries as given by Dickinson in 1854. Each dot represents a colliery but not the number of pits within that colliery. The districts used are those of Poor Law Unions and Registration Districts (see Figure 3.5) and the positioning of collieries within them is approximate but is based on the names given by Dickinson (1855) and an examination of early-nineteenth-century maps.

96.4 in Cheshire. For pits these numbers fall to 37.5 underground and 45.5 in all in Lancashire and 42.8 undergound and 54 in all in Cheshire. Clearly the increase in the scale of mining had produced not only deeper shafts but also much more extensive workings, with some larger collieries employing 1,000 to 1,500 men in the 1850s (Challinor 1972: 50). The labour force had grown both by natural increase and immigration, some 1,000 men being estimated to have entered the field from outside between 1780 and 1800 alone (Flinn 1984: 346). The family system described in Chapter 2 was severely weakened.

The technology of the coalfield followed the national pattern with the safety lamp, steam winding and pumping, guide rails in shafts and the use of flat, and later wire, ropes. Trams hauled along rails replaced the dragging of corves underground and on the surface. Pillar and stall working continued alongside longwall but Lancashire stall working, known as straitwork, was carried on in very narrow roads leading a colliery manager in the late nineteenth century to observe

> I have known men constitutionally old and finished at 34 years of age in consequence of working in straitwork . . . So confined is it that the men not only breathe again the same air, but inhale a great amount of coal dust so that their discharges are as black as coal itself. There is a good deal of hard labour in straitwork.
>
> (Quoted in D. Anderson 1975: 58–9)

There is considerable evidence that during the first forty years of the nineteenth century life underground was particularly dangerous, dirty and unpleasant. Deeper shafts and dirtier coal marked the exploitation of more difficult seams and the new technology could not cope with the problems it posed. In the years 1851 to 1853 there were on average 215 deaths in the coalfield each year, an annual loss of 5 per 1,000 employed (Dickinson 1855: 76).

Like its neighbour cotton, coal was disfigured to modern eyes by its use of child labour, including girls, from the late eighteenth century. Once hardened to the haulage of tubs many girls stayed on, even after marriage, to face a life's work there. Opinions about this practice varied. In 1825 when Matthias Dunn, a viewer from the north-east where women were not employed, visited Lancashire he wrote home

> The first pit that I went down was 85 fathoms and I was not a little amused to find the Onsetter sported a pair of golden Earrings, being a fine figuring wench of 24 in the following costume – shift of flannel, a

pair of huge white flannel Trousers, short bedgown and overall, a Smock sark of flannel – her head was bound by a cotton round Cap, underneath which peeped as handsome a set of Curls as need be sported.

(Quoted in Flinn 1984: 333–4)

Others, less inured to life below ground, were not amused and the reports of the Commissioner for Factories in 1833 and the 1842 Report on the Employment of Children paint a horrifying picture of the privations of women and children in the region's pits. Mary Glover, who was 38 in 1842 and worked as a drawer at Ringleybridge, had a robust attitude to her work and its moral dangers

I wear a shift and a pair of trousers when at work, and I will always have a good pair of trousers. I have had many a twopence given me by the boatmen on the canal to show my breeches. I never saw a woman work naked, but I have seen many men work without breeches in the neighbourhood of Bolton. I remember seeing a man who worked stark naked: we used to throw coals at him.

(Aspin 1969: 90)

Society at large took a different view and the Mines Act 1842 prohibited women and children under the age of ten from working underground, but it was several years before the practice died out as women continued to work underground 'on the sly' in defiance of the Act (Challinor 1972: 253). The Act did not affect surface working and left women riddling coal on the surface, the 'pit-brow lasses' who were so attractive to the London barrister A. J. Munby in 1860 (Hudson 1972: 170, 206–7, 274).

Although mines were growing in size and employing more labour the miners of the north-west were less isolated from neighbours in other occupations than those of the Midlands. Mineowners built rows of terraced cottages for them close to the pits as at Hindley and Abram and some communities such as Poynton in Cheshire and Hart Common at Westhoughton, Gin Pit Village at Tyldesley and Parr near Wigan in Lancashire were relatively isolated colliery villages (Ashmore 1969: 119–20; 1982: 9). Family traditions also endured with sons following their fathers into the pit and comparatively few miners' wives working outside the home. Most miners however lived in districts which had an admixture of mining and manufacture. Proximity to neighbours employed in domestic and factory textiles, watch-part, file or nail making, engineering and other trades does not appear to have weakened their militancy in their own affairs but occasionally it involved them in the disputes of their non-mining families and neighbours.

Early trade unionism is difficult to detect. Wigan had ten friendly societies before 1800 and eleven new ones were added before 1824, during the period of the Combination Laws. No doubt other districts could show similar figures. Wigan miners were certainly on strike in 1792 when a mob of 500 threatened to destroy the pit if they did not get higher wages and had to be overawed by the military drawn from Manchester (Flinn 1984: 399–405). The repeal of the Combination Laws seems to have brought the colliers' unions into the open; a Wigan union fought a strike in 1831 and there was another union operating at Bolton at about the same time (D. Anderson 1975: 130; Challinor 1972: 26). There was another strike in the Bolton–Oldham area in 1831 for the right to join the union and for an advance in wages with, once again, the military brought in and the men defeated (Challinor 1972: 26–8). Like the cotton workers the miners found their wages under pressure in the early 1840s and fought a series of violent strikes in their defence, notably at St Helens in 1844, where the military had to restore order. In 1853, for the first time, the tactics of coal and cotton workers diverged. The cotton strike at Preston was peaceful and orderly, the coal strike at Wigan, where 5,000 turned out, showed the traditional features of rioting and mob control of the town and, again, military intervention (Challinor 1972: 46–8).

Evidence for wages is relatively slight. By 1839 average miners' wages across Lancashire were twenty-five shillings per week for fifty hours, falling back to £1 in 1849 and slowly climbing back to twenty-five shillings by 1859 (K. Wood 1984: 54). Despite the fluctuations in miners' wages, in 1827 the colliery owner William Hulton could claim that it was 'almost incredible' to see the contrast between the comfort of the miners in Hulton and the misery of the hand-loom weavers in neighbouring Westhoughton (Aspin 1969: 51).

In 1797 a Manchester directory used the word 'engineer' for the first time as a way of describing the machine and engine makers and founders who had grown in number in the directories from nine in 1788 to fifty-two in 1797 (Musson and Robinson 1969: 432). This new trade brought together a host of skills that had been quietly developing for centuries and harnessed them to the mechanical demands of the early mills – power and production. The origins of machinery for the generation of power, by wind and water and later by steam, lay outside the north-west but the machine-making that equipped the mills was a native growth.

Early mill engineers like James Brindley worked on both motive power and machine making but later developments separated these two branches. In the early mills teams of brickmakers, masons, builders and joiners were brought together with millwrights, turners, smiths and clock-makers who made the machines. When the mill was complete most moved on leaving only a small number to maintain and run it. The region was well stocked with the requisite skills of wood turning, metal founding, wire drawing, watch and clock manufacture and the making of files and tools. At Prescot watch parts and tools, made in local domestic workshops, were collected and sold locally and to watchmakers in London and Coventry. By the 1840s, with the trade exporting through Liverpool, watchpart makers could sometimes earn £3 per week and their respectable lives were contrasted with the rough, drunken and profligate nail makers of the same district (T. C. Barker and Harris 1954: 287).

By the 1790s motive power engineering was becoming dominated by steam, at first, as at Arkwright and Simpson's first Manchester factory in the 1780s for pumping for the water wheel, later for turning the machinery. Water technology was also improving; Thomas Hewes, who settled in Manchester in 1792, invented the suspension water wheel used at Styal and Belper. In steam the early engine makers built Savery and Newcomen engines but the firm of Bateman and Sherratt pirated Boulton and Watt's air pump and condenser until they were taken to law in 1796, when they reverted to atmospheric engines until the expiry of Watt's patent in 1800. They were large ironfounders at Salford and Dukinfield and by 1800 had built at least forty-six engines in Lancashire compared with the fifty-five of Boulton and Watt (Musson and Robinson 1969: 408–23). Although Bateman's was the most important regional foundry in the late eighteenth century many others were being set up. Hewes was replacing timber by cast and wrought iron in mill construction, water wheels and bridges, Peel, Williams and Co. of Phoenix Foundry and later the Soho Foundry at Ancoats made mill gearing, weighing machines and spinning rollers and, by 1825, there were dozens of engineering firms in Manchester and Salford with a great concentration along the Ashton and Rochdale canals. Outside Manchester the pace was equally rapid with firms such as Samuel Lees at Park Bridge, Ashton-under-Lyne, Asa Lees, and Hibbert and Platt at Oldham, Fawcetts at Liverpool, Dobson and Barlow, and Hick, Hargreaves and Co. at Bolton (Plate 3.6) and the Haigh ironworks at Wigan (Ashmore 1969: 73–96).

While the motive power engineers were shifting to steam the machine makers were fusing into a specialized trade, sometimes in small workshops making machines to order. The demands of the textile trade drew in craftsmen from outside the region, especially from Scotland. The Scottish firm of Cannan and Smith at Chowbent provided apprenticeships in the late eighteenth century for four Galloway men who went on to found the firms of McConnel and Kennedy, and Adam and George Murray, both of them textile engineers and leading Manchester spinners.

By the second decade of the nineteenth century machine making had

---

Plate 3.6 Hick, Rothwell, Bolton 1829. The Bolton firm of Hick, Rothwell, later Hick, Hargreaves, pioneered many innovations in steam engineering including a rotary engine. Their works of 1829 is very different from the later production lines of Whitworth or Beyer Peacock.

crystallized out as a separate trade, though progressive spinners and printers kept an interest in the development of improved machinery. The Manchester engineers of this period were however mainly the product of London engineering and, in particular, the training of Henry Maudsley. Richard Roberts, who arrived in 1816, was followed by James Nasmyth and Joseph Whitworth; they brought and developed the machine tool industry and precision engineering. Nasmyth invented the steam hammer and pioneered assembly line production; Whitworth greatly advanced standardization and accurate measurement. William Fairbairn established his firm in 1820 and by the 1840s it was the biggest in Manchester. Fairbairn specialized in cast iron construction for mills such as Orrell's at Stockport, and in iron shipbuilding, and is famous for the Menai and Conway wrought iron tubular bridges designed with Robert Stephenson. Fairbairn also became a large locomotive builder; other general engineers such as Sharp, Roberts at Manchester, Hick, Hargreaves at Bolton and Nasmyth at Patricroft also built locomotives. Other firms came into existence specifically to meet this need, notably the 1830 Vulcan Works of Stephenson and Tayleur at Newton le Willows and that of Beyer, Peacock of Gorton, founded in 1854 on a site close to the Manchester, Sheffield and Lincolnshire Railway (Musson and Robinson 1969: 473–507).

The early growth of textile engineering in and around Manchester has already been described. Between the 1820s and the 1880s Blackburn became the centre for innovation and invention in power looms while Oldham developed spinning technology through the massive firm of Hibbert and Platt, which employed 3,500 people in 1859 (Farnie 1979: 159). By 1841, according to the Select Committee on the Export of Machinery, there were 115 engineering firms in the Manchester area employing 1,811 horsepower and 17,382 hands (Musson and Robinson 1969: 479).

The men who worked in these trades were very different from the country millwrights and watchmakers of early days. The millwrights had strong trade clubs in the early nineteenth century but craftsmen organized themselves into much narrower local societies by the 1820s and 1830s (S. Webb and B. Webb 1913: 187). The masters progressively reduced the skills and time necessary for engineering tasks and sought new labour for their new methods. Nasmyth had to fight a serious strike at Patricroft when he began to train local labour in 1836, for his skilled men clung to apprenticeship and wanted reduced hours and standard rates of pay (Musson and Robinson 1969: 505–7). Opposition to the masters found its focus in the Journeymen Steam Engine and Machine Makers and Millwrights' Friendly Society which had grown out of a Manchester society founded in 1826. By 1848, after amalgamation with other trade societies, it had 7,000 members in the UK. The drawing together of this and other clubs gave birth to the Amalgamated Society of Engineers in 1851, the model for trade unionism until the birth of the general unions in the 1880s.

The New Society

The changes in transport and industry described above had profound effects on the character of the region. While some agricultural villages showed little growth, in many of the coal and textile towns and townships and those associated with transport innovations, population grew on a scale that overwhelmed them. Table 3.3 (p. 136) shows the increasing urban population, and Table 3.19 gives some examples of suburban growth. Both Manchester

Table 3.19 Suburban growth: Manchester and Liverpool

| | Population | | *1861–:–1801* | *Density/acre* |
	1801	*1861*	*Ratio of growth*	*1861*
Liverpool	77,653	269,742	3.47	145.2
excluding				
Toxteth Park	2,069	66,686	32.23	28.1
Parts of Walton parish:				
Everton	499	54,848	109.91	79.1
Kirkdale	393	16,135	41.05	17.5
West Derby	2,636	36,527	13.85	54.1
Manchester town	76,788	357,979	4.66	56.2
including				
Cheetham	752	17,446	23.19	18.9
Chorlton on M.	675	44,795	66.36	69.3
Hulme	1,677	68,433	40.80	143.5

Source: VCH. Lancs., II: 348–9.

and Liverpool had grown substantially in the eighteenth century and between 1801 and 1861 their growth spilled over into neighbouring townships, giving some remarkable increases. Outside these suburban districts growth was slower but the textile townships of Oldham, Blackburn and Preston in Lancashire all returned growth ratios of over six while in Cheshire the small townships of Staley and Newton recorded six (or near six) and Hyde and Dukinfield grew by ratios of over twelve and seventeen respectively.

Textiles played a major part in this expansion. Calculations suggest that some 28 per cent of the region's people were employed in textiles in 1800, 29 per cent in the mid-1820s and 14 per cent in 1860. Hand-loom weavers probably peaked in the 1820s at an estimated 200,000 to 250,000 in all fibres, with a further 150,000 people working in the mills: by 1860 virtually all the cotton workers were in the mills though handloom weaving was still common in woollen and silk manufacture. (Calculations and estimates based on G. H. Wood 1910: 127–8; Bythell 1969: 53–7.)

The growing towns were not entirely dependent on textiles. By 1861

Burnley had the highest percentage of cotton workers with 46 per cent, at Bolton and Oldham cotton was combined with coal-mining and engineering, at Rochdale with woollen manufacture, at Stockport with silk and hatting and at Wigan with coal. But, Wigan apart, the cotton mills were the most significant feature of the urban areas and the smoke, smells, noise and unruly crowds they generated progressively drove out the local gentry and even the millowners themselves. At Bolton, for example, the seventeenth-century Darcy Lever Old Hall was a farm house by 1833, Lostock Hall of 1563 was demolished between 1816 and 1824 and Hall i' th' Wood, already in tenements in the eighteenth century, became the home of tenant farmers (J. S. F. Walker and Tindall 1985: 92–6). Some millowners restored houses on the edge of the towns as did Joseph Kay, a Preston cotton spinner, at Turton Tower in the late 1830s, or they built anew like Peter Marsland, whose house, Woodbank, at Stockport was designed by Thomas Harrison in 1812 (Pevsner 1979b: 250; N. Pevsner and E. Hubbard 1971: 29–30). The growing professional and middle classes could afford elegant terraces in the late eighteenth century: Rodney Street, Percy Street and Abercrombie Square are Liverpool examples with St John Street offering a Manchester parallel. Later it was the villa that predominated for these classes, often built in landscaped parks within carriage distance of the commercial and industrial centres. Prince's Park at Liverpool, designed by Paxton in 1842, was a model for his Birkenhead Park of 1843–7; in Manchester Victoria Park (Plate 3.7), begun in 1836, offered the security of gated streets as well as solid comfort. Later the railway drew the most prosperous out into the clean air of the countryside (Pevsner 1979b: 143, 297, 233, 325).

The growing middle class of entrepreneurs, manufacturers, merchants and professional men who lived in these elegant districts were the major beneficiaries of the new industrial society. To Hyppolite Taine they were merchant princes and to Frederick Engels the complacent and uncaring bourgeoisie, but they asserted themselves in every sphere of the region's life. Their horizons progressively grew beyond the parochial offices and village society that their yeoman, clothier or parish gentry fathers or grandfathers had known. The modern education exemplified at Warrington Academy bore fruit in the Manchester Literary and Philosophical Society which produced early papers on demography, the health of working people and cooperation, the latter given by Robert Owen (Frangopulo 1977: 89–90). It also made

---

Plate 3.7 A middle-class house in Victoria Park. This was one of the first houses built in Victoria Park, by one of the founders of the Park Company, the architect Richard Lane, who lived in it until 1842. Called successively Park Villa, Victoria Villa, Oxford Villa, and finally Oxford Lodge, it was demolished in 1963. Lane sold it in 1850 to the Manchester merchant Ernest Reuss, who occupied it at the 1861 census with his wife and five children, plus seven female servants. Five servants came from Cheshire, one from Montgomeryshire, and one from Nottinghamshire. (Title deeds and Plate, Manchester University archives; 1861 census, enumerator's book.)

Manchester a centre for scientific study and, through the Statistical Society of 1833, of social investigation, building on the work of Percival and Ferriar in the late eighteenth century. By 1844, when Engels bitterly criticized the Manchester middle class for their wilful ignorance of real working-class conditions, there had been a succession of papers on working-class housing, health, education and incomes, many of them heard by visiting MPs. The papers were based on first-hand research, presented solid factual information and expressed opinions freely. Perhaps the most influential of the early reports was that of 1834 on education in Manchester, described by the Central Society for Education as the first scientific study of the topic. It reflected concerns that made Manchester a leading centre of agitation for public education in the 1860s (Ashton 1934). Nor was remedial work neglected. In Manchester the Provident Society of 1833 and the Sanitary Association of 1852 both sought to reform working-class behaviour (M. E. Rose 1985: 105–6).

Culturally the pace was set by Liverpool, which mounted the first provincial exhibition of pictures in 1773, but the Manchester Art Treasures Exhibition of 1857 was on an unprecedented scale. Over 1.3 million people viewed the 16,000 works and listened to the Gentlemen's Concert Orchestra conducted by Charles Hallé in the glass and iron palace at Old Trafford. The Duke of Devonshire had been offensive when asked for support: 'What in the world do you want with art in Manchester. Why can't you stick to your cotton spinning?' The supporting cotton spinners like the Ashtons and engineers such as Fairbairn had the satisfaction of knowing that their exhibition paved the way for the National Gallery (Finke 1985: 109–12).

For the working classes it was a different story. The shift from wool to cotton had already changed the form of the weavers' houses, for wool was normally woven in upper storeys, cotton in basements; the demise of the hand loom brought much greater changes. As the spinning mills, and later the weaving sheds, were built they were surrounded by the rented, terraced cottages that replaced the old weavers' houses. They were observed in Cheshire before 1795 when John Holt wrote of cottages

> near large factories, being frequently built in long ranges adjoining together, and near the works, and sometimes accommodated with small gardens. Many of these kinds of dwellings have been erected by building speculators, as they generally (if the rents are paid) are calculated to yield an interest of £.10 per cent to £.20 per cent.
>
> (J. Holt 1795: 18–19)

Holt described them as built of brick and slate, unlike the old cottages which were of unhewn stone or post and plaster with clay floors and thatched roofs. The cottages Holt described were probably provided with accommodation for looms but after the 1820s the mill cottages were for residence only.

Perhaps those who lived in these new cottages, however modest their construction, were fortunate.

A brief account of developments in Manchester can be taken to rep-
resent what was happening over the urbanizing areas, though that town's
earlier growth had already prompted attempts to tackle its problems. In the
early 1790s before the factory system had begun to make its effects felt, Dr
Ferrier's Report to the Manchester Police Commissioners painted a sad
picture. It described damp cellar dwellings, some with four or five beds, open
privy vaults, dunghills, blind alleys, fixed windows and overcrowded, fever-
ridden lodging houses where the foetid beds were never cold (Aiken 1795:
193–6). Ferriar's was only the first of many such reports. The Kay Report of
1831 found in Parliament Street with 380 persons and Parliament Passage
with thirty houses only one privy (Engels 1845: 94–5). From 1833 the
Manchester Statistical Society looked for national comparisons. In 1834–6
they found some 11.75 per cent of Manchester people living in cellars, 15 per
cent in Liverpool but only 3.75 per cent in Bury and 1.25 per cent in Ashton-
under-Lyne. In 1839 their comparison of Lancashire town housing with that
in Hull and in three Rutland parishes found Lancashire houses poorer and
overcrowded and with higher rents. In 1841 they noted the movement of the
'comfortable classes' out of Manchester and Salford and expressed anxiety
that the eight central townships would soon be inhabited only by 300,000
operatives (Ashton 1934). Poor housing was compounded by lack of water
and sewerage, inadequate lighting and scavenging, few public facilities and a
plethora of public houses and drinking dens.

The years after 1790 justified Ferriar's fears. In 1832 the cholera epi-
demic that entered the region through Hull killed 1,523 in Liverpool, 706 in
Manchester, 216 in Salford and engendered popular hostility to doctors and
hospitals. In 1839 1,343 died of typhus in Lancashire, in 1847 9,076 in
Lancashire and Cheshire. Between 1837 and 1840 smallpox killed 7,105 in
Lancashire, in 1849 it was cholera again with 8,184 deaths, 5,308 in Liver-
pool alone (Midwinter 1969a: 70–2). These were only the dramatic peaks.
Between 1841 and 1851 the average annual death rate in Manchester was 33
per 1,000, in Liverpool it was 36; between 1851 and 1860 it fell to 31 for
Manchester, 30.4 for Liverpool. In 1839 the national death rate was 21,
Lancashire's 29.4; in 1861 it had fallen only to 25.4 (Midwinter 1969a: 116).
In 1843 ten of the fifty towns with death rates over 2 per cent that were
investigated by the Buccleugh Commission were in Lancashire and Liverpool
was the most unhealthy town in England (Midwinter 1969a: 72–9). In 1842
the Report of the Poor Law Commissioners had stated that 'of all who are
born to the labouring classes in Manchester more than 57% die before they
attain five years', a figure comparable with that of fifty years before (D. Simon
1938: 164–6).

But there was improvement, steady if unspectacular. The Police Act
1844 laid down that every house, both existing and new, should have a privy

and ashpit, thus effectively ending the building of back to back houses in the borough. Nevertheless there were still 10,000 back to backs in the borough in 1885 and cellar dwellings, attacked under the New Streets Act of 1853, were not all closed until 1874 (D. Simon 1938: 284–92). Angus Reach, who visited Manchester in 1849 for the *Morning Chronicle*, condemned the back to backs of Ancoats and the cellar dwellings of the older parts of town. He was impressed by Hulme where he found new, broad, airy streets, most of them drained, four-roomed houses with entrances above street level and fitted with foot scrapers, shutters on ground-floor windows and lobbies dividing the parlour from the street. Each house had a back door and a walled yard with a privy/ashpit accessible by a back passage for the removal of refuse (Reach 1972: 6–8).

Industry and transport changes also produced not merely new suburbs but new towns. Southport and Birkenhead were both planned for residential elegance but shipbuilding and engineering transformed the latter into a busy working town. Crewe was a creation of the railways in 1843 and by 1848 some 520 company and 300 private houses had been built as well as shops. The company also provided a church, schooling, sanitation and a water supply though the latter was said to be execrable by 1856, both in quality and quantity (Chaloner 1950a: 46–50, 53).

Pure water was, of course, essential to life and the lack of it was one of the major causes of disease in the growing urban areas. There was little real attempt to make proper provision until the mid-nineteenth century but when the towns did move they planned on a grand scale. Blackburn and Bolton were among the earliest to take action, the former with the Heddlesdon and Pickup Bank reservoirs in 1844, the latter by the Waterworks Company's Belmont reservoir of 1843. These were dwarfed by the massive Manchester Corporation scheme at Longdendale which was started in 1848 and the Liverpool Corporation reservoirs at Rivington of 1852–7. In Manchester, Reach found in 1849 that over 22,000 houses out of 46,000 had no water supply in either house or street but Longdendale water began to enter the town in the early 1850s (Midwinter 1969a: 98–104).

Local Government

In 1906 the Webbs wrote

> At no period did the Rulers of the County enjoy so large a measure of local autonomy as between the accession of the House of Hanover and the close of the Napoleonic wars.
>
> (S. Webb and B. Webb 1906: 556)

These rulers, the JPs, were constrained by the slow processes of presentment and by their preoccupation with social stability and public order. In many townships and manors the officers were faced with more people, many of them incomers, with new forms of wealth and income not based on land and with the turbulence of country people responding to the unfamiliar environment of a more urban life and the discipline of the mills. The Church of England clergy, inheriting the huge parishes of earlier days, could offer little spiritual or educational support to the local gentry or squirearchy and were confronted by strong Catholicism in some parts of the region, deep rooted Nonconformity in others and increasing secular radicalism in the industrializing districts.

In the mid-eighteenth century the private Act of Parliament became an effective device for making improvements in urban areas and Manchester and Liverpool which had obtained such early Acts continued to use them for specific schemes. At Liverpool by 1835 most of the functions of local administration – poor law, the watch, scavenging, lighting, paving and sewering – were the responsibility of commissioners or boards whose finances were controlled by the vestry, the whole body of ratepayers, and not by the corporation (Vigier 1970: 71, 177–9). In Manchester and Salford the Police Act 1792 set up a new body alongside the court leet with its legal concerns and market jurisdiction and the vestry which was responsible for the relief of the poor, highways and the financing of the Church. This new body could levy a rate and make improvements by regulation and, despite later scandals and inefficiencies, the commissioners improved many services, widened the central streets and built the first Town Hall. In 1817 they established the gas works which, profitable from the start, helped to pay for the great Longdendale reservoir scheme from 1848 to 1862. After 1800 other urbanizing townships and boroughs obtained Police Acts, the earliest Blackburn in 1803, Warrington in 1813 and Preston in 1815. They were also obtaining Acts for the establishment of small debt courts, for the provision of water and for the supply of gas. The commissioners set up under Police Acts had to operate within their local administrative networks. In Salford they shared responsibility with an elected borough reeve and constables, poor law overseers, churchwardens and vestry with town meetings as final arbiters of policy. Rochdale also had town meetings that were called for general matters but it was the township meetings that took responsibility for the poor law while the parish meeting appointed churchwardens, who, unusually, had no poor law duties but levied the church rate. Bolton had courts leet for Great and Little Bolton, trustees for the two townships under the Improvement Acts, private gas and water companies, highways surveyors and overseers of the poor nominated by township meetings but appointed by the county magistrates (Garrard 1983: 164–79, 208–12).

The first national encroachment on the old administration was the Poor Law Amendment Act 1834, which gave Lancashire 30 unions in place of the 446 authorities, 202 of them vestries, of the old order. In Cheshire there were then nine unions and in north Derbyshire three. The implementation of the Act in the industrial districts was met by working-class resistance coming on the heels of what they saw as betrayal in the Reform Act 1832 and interpreted as it was by radical journalists as a Malthusian plot to confine the poor in bastilles with the aid of the new Peelite police. The formation of the poor law unions took from 1837 to 1869, the vast majority being completed by 1841 (Figure 3.5), and though there was some violence in Oldham, Rochdale and Colne, the most serious disturbances were just over the Yorkshire border at Fielden's Todmorden (Midwinter 1969a: 23–5). Tories as well as radicals opposed the new poor law, objecting to its impersonal central control and Joseph Raynor Stephens of Stalybridge who fused hatred of the factories, the new poor law and the police in a violent insurrectionism, combined in himself features of both Tory and radical opposition.

In fact poor law expenditure in Lancashire had been the lowest in England before the reform (see Appendix 3.1, p. 213). Outdoor relief was mainly confined to hand-loom weavers and the scope for economies was small (see Midwinter 1969a: 58–9). Alfred Power wrote to Edwin Chadwick in October 1837

> The high rate of wages and superior spirit of independence have preserved the mass from all contact with pauperism during the ordinary circumstances of trade ... in my present district (more especially in Lancashire) the proportion of well governed townships is far greater than would be found in other parts of England previous to the formation of unions.
>
> (Quoted in Midwinter 1969a: 14)

In the event the new poor law was not so very different from the old in the region, outdoor relief continued, new, cleaner and more disciplined work-houses were built and, though expenditure went down less than in other counties, Lancashire's remained the least costly. After the turmoil of the 1830s the anti poor law agitation died away and even the Cotton Famine produced only faint echoes of disorder, mainly at Stalybridge.

The old boroughs had been no more effective than the county magistrates in regulating their towns; the Municipal Corporations Act 1835 revised the charters and regularized the franchise of Liverpool, Preston, Wigan, Clitheroe and Lancaster in Lancashire, Chester, Stockport, Congleton and Macclesfield in Cheshire. It also provided for the granting of new charters to those unincorporated towns struggling with their problems of growth with a

Figure 3.5 Poor Law Unions and Registration Districts in 1871. Comparison with Figures 2.3 and 2.4 shows how the Poor Law Amendment Act 1834 had reduced the number of Poor Law authorities by the amalgamation of parishes and townships. A part of Yorkshire and Derbyshire is included as data collection sometimes reached over county boundaries. (Source: 1871 Parliamentary Census.)

plethora of competing local authorities. Manchester and Bolton, the region's two largest unincorporated towns, were the first to petition, in 1838, stimulated not only by local inefficiency but also by the desire of the Manchester-centred anti Corn Law Liberals to join Birmingham in testing the Act (Garrard 1983: 187). In both towns there were legal disputes with the old authorities who maintained competing police forces, refused to hand over lists of ratepayers or electors or to pay corporation rates but in 1842 the new councils were justified at law. They could then begin to govern their towns though at Bolton they did not have full power until 1850 (Garrard 1983: 164–94). Their success paved the way for other aspiring towns: Salford, Warrington, Ashton-under-Lyne and Oldham in the 1840s, Blackburn, Rochdale and Stalybridge in the 1850s. Outside the boroughs local boards of health under the Public Health Act 1848 were short lived and achieved little. However the new workhouses were built with provision for the sick and in the late 1850s Dr Roberton of the Manchester Statistical Society was actively advocating Florence Nightingale's pavilion hospitals. The first of these in the region was built at Blackburn and the second, which became a national model for its architecture and organization, by Chorlton Guardians at Withington in 1864 (Pickstone 1985: 111–12, 123–5).

Industrialization and the growth of population quickly began to pose problems of law and order. In 1795 John Holt, viewing Lancashire agriculture, wrote bitterly 'who will work for 1s6d a day at a ditch, when he can get 3s6d or 5s a day in a cotton work, and be drunk four days out of seven?' (J. Holt 1795: 212). In Cheshire Thomas Wedge observed that manufactures had increased the demand for luxuries among agricultural labourers, had had a bad effect on their morals and had raised the poor rate (Wedge 1794: 26–7). J. T. Stanley contributed an even stronger note to Holland's *Survey of Cheshire Agriculture* in 1808 claiming that every township was a scene of warfare between the poor and the occupiers of land (Holland 1808: 106–7).

In 1839 the Constabulary Forces Commissioners published their evidence. They believed that crimes of violence had gone down but damage and theft had grown in the countryside, the canals were thoroughfares of looting and the roads dangerous in the neighbourhood of large towns because of footpads and robbers. At Blackstone Edge the 'lower classes were barbarous to an unusual degree', the Wirral was noted for wreck plunderers, Bolton had suffered two recent murders with no arrest and in Manchester the Irish of Little Ireland paid no rates or rent, fought the excise men, resisted warrants and roamed the streets drunk, fighting each other every Saturday night. Liverpool, which had new police under its 1835 charter, had 2,071 houses and premises where thieves resorted, 520 brothels and 625 'houses of ill fame'. Additionally the massive political and industrial disturbances in the industrial districts were far beyond the control of local constables (First Report of the Commissioners . . . 1839). Cheshire had set up a paid county force in 1829 but this was an 'honourable failure' although it survived until

1857 (James 1957). Lancashire established a county force under the permissive Police Act 1839, responding not to Chartism but to a general desire for improved law and order. By 1856 there were twelve police forces in the county and, as the turbulence of the industrial districts eased, they stemmed the tide of crime but failed to turn it back (Midwinter 1969a: 172).

Politics and Religion

The political and industrial disturbances that swept the north-west in the early nineteenth century were a consequence of industrial development and change exacerbated by the disruptive effects of the French wars and by new views on society flowing from the American and French revolutions. The society that Holt and Stanley saw under threat was one in which working people were politically passive except when dearth or high prices drove them to protest by petition or riot in defence of their traditional standards. Industrialization raised the expectations of working people but the war and post-war dislocation, redundancy of old skills caused by new machinery and irregularity of trade often led to disappointment, sometimes despair to which the government, withdrawing from interference in trade matters, would not respond. Working people were therefore forced to act on their own behalf and it was their untutored movements that dominated attention in the first half of the nineteenth century. Less visibly until the Anti Corn Law League the growing manufacturing and mercantile middle classes were conducting their own, more sophisticated campaign. By 1860 they had done what they set out do but for the working classes there was still much to be won.

The change from old to new in working-class politics in the north-west is often dated to the Exchange riot in Manchester in 1812. Food riots and meetings of protest had failed to push the authorities into reducing high prices and the announcement of a meeting of support for the government at the Exchange drew a mob which graduated from horseplay to destruction. This was followed by a food riot at Shudehill and Luddite outbreaks at Middleton and Westhoughton (Prentice 1851: 48–58). Perhaps more significantly, in June 1812, thirty-eight weavers who met in Manchester to petition the House of Commons in favour of peace and parliamentary reform were arrested for combining for a seditious purpose, though they were later found not guilty (Prentice 1851: 76–82). This was the start of the political agitation which combined with traditional mob action and a more vigorous trade unionism to make the north-west the centre of working-class unrest in the first half of the nineteenth century.

The radical reformers of the region formed Hampden clubs in response to the writings of William Cobbett, founded a newspaper, the *Manchester Political Register*, and organized great meetings. On 10 March 1817 they met 12,000 strong on St Peter's Field with blankets on their shoulders to carry their reform petition to London but were stopped by the military, only one reaching Lord Sidmouth, their target. In 1819 a series of large meetings with banners, flags and bands leading the marchers, even at Stockport the hoisting of the Cap of Liberty, and, in early August, reports of secret drilling filled the Manchester magistrates with foreboding. On Monday 16 August their fears spilled over into a clumsy attempt to pluck Orator Hunt from a crowd on St Peter's Field variously estimated at from 60,000 to 150,000 men, women and children. The Manchester Yeomanry, half trained and half drunk, who escorted Nadin the constable became embroiled, the Riot Act was read but hardly heard and the Hussars were ordered in to clear the ground (Plate 3.8). Within ten minutes the field was left to the dead and injured, there were forty-one arrests, eleven dead, one a special constable, and at least four hundred injured. On 21 August the Prince Regent congratulated the magistrates and the *Manchester Observer* coined the word 'Peterloo'. The economic basis of the movement was perhaps indicated by a bathetic postscript; on 16 August 1820 an anniversary meeting on the bloody ground drew only about 1,000 people (see *The Manchester Region History Review*, III, 1989, for new research on Peterloo).

Economic improvement and the repression that followed the Six Acts of 1819 weakened the reform movement and destroyed most of the political clubs. Working people turned back to their trade unions and friendly societies, building a head of steam that was released into industrial action and strikes after the repeal of the Combination Laws in 1824. The middle-class radicals were strengthened by the repeal of the Test and Corporation Acts in 1828 and by the Reform Act 1832. Before that Act the region had twenty-four seats in Parliament, after it thirty-eight, twenty of them for industrial towns, as shown in Table 3.20.

The Reform Act, which the middle-class radical Prentice remembered as 'Symptoms of the Dawn', did nothing for working people who were already turning to John Doherty's failed attempts at national trade unionism in 1829. From 1833 to 1836 they trod the same unsuccessful path with Robert Owen and also failed in their attempts to reduce working hours through the Short-Time Committees of 1832 despite a determined and violent strike at Oldham in April 1834. The national reforms of the 1830s – Parliament, Poor Law, Municipal Reform, County Constabulary – seemed to working people to be designed to throw them into the uncaring hands of their industrial masters whose utilitarian and free trade aspirations were seen as self-serving.

Plate 3.8   Peterloo. The image of Peterloo was a potent symbol for generations of working-class radicals and the passing of time has served rather to fuel than to damp down the controversy that has raged over the events of that day.

Table 3.20 Parliamentary representation in Lancashire and Cheshire

	Before 1832	1832
Clitheroe	2	1
Lancaster	2	2
Preston	2	2
Wigan	2	2
Liverpool	2	2
Chester	2	2
Newton-in-Makerfield	2	—
Manchester	—	2
Blackburn	—	2
Bolton	—	2
Oldham	—	2
Macclesfield	—	2
Stockport	—	2
Salford	—	1
Ashton-under-Lyne	—	1
Bury	—	1
Rochdale	—	1
Warrington	—	1
County seats	10	10

Source: F. W. S. Craig 1971.

In 1838 the gulf between the classes was virtually institutionalized when the middle-class radicals banded together into the Manchester-based Anti Corn Law League and the working-class radicals fell in behind the Charter. The methods and the fate of the two movements were very different. Chartism was a political response to economic and social distress, the 'knife and fork question' of Joseph Raynor Stephens. Initially the Chartists hoped that demonstrations and petitions would achieve their ends. The Kersal Moor meeting of 24 September 1838, for example, brought together between 30,000 and 50,000 people to elect delegates to the Chartist Convention, some marching in under their old Peterloo banners. By the spring of 1839 impatience produced torchlight meetings with inflammatory banners, as at Hyde where firearms were discharged and a violent speech by Stephens earned him eighteen months in Knutsford Gaol (Irving 1890: 49). But behind the bluster, as Sir Charles Napier the military commander detected, there was no popular support for violent insurrection and the failure of the 1839 petition brought only the collapse of the movement. Its revival under Feargus O'Connor in 1841 was no more successful, the petition of 1842 was again rejected and the Plug Riots of that year were industrial rather than political in their nature.

Chartism ebbed and flowed with economic tides but the Anti Corn Law League, founded in March 1839, had one single, clear aim and the resources and organization to pursue it. It set out to persuade every section of society that the Corn Laws, like all obstacles to free trade, were not only the cause of dear food, destructive both to trade and agriculture and a brake on economic progress, but also immoral and anti-Christian. The merchants and manufacturers at the centre (Plate 3.9) of it included those most active in the Manchester Statistical Society, mainly Nonconformists such as R. H. Greg of Styal, Edmund Ashworth of Egerton and Turton, Thomas Ashton of Hyde and Thomas Potter of Manchester, as well as Cobden and, later, John Bright. They were men of large ideas, modern in outlook and well used to the command of large resources. In 1839 the first Manchester subscription raised £6,000 in one month and the annual appeals grew; by 1845 it was possible to raise £60,000 at one meeting in the Free Trade Hall. The Leaguers, like the Chartists, mounted great assemblies, petitioned and kept a semi-permanent delegation in London. They also built their first hall in 1839 and rebuilt it in 1843, distributed thousands of pamphlets through the penny post and sent out their paid lecturers on the railways. By 1841 even the most extreme Chartists had resolved that they would not oppose repeal of the Corn Laws and the war of ideas had been won (Prentice 1853).

The occasion for the repeal of the Corn Laws in May 1846 was the Irish potato blight but Peel acknowledged the great work of Cobden and, by implication, that of the League. Lancashire rejoiced, the League honoured its leaders and then dissolved itself, its work done. The success of the League through the conversion of a Prime Minister of Lancashire manufacturing stock represented not only victory for an ideal but also the new dominance of the manufacturing interest and its Lancashire heartland. It was perhaps the high point of Manchester's influence on national affairs and it was based on economic performance as much as the strength of an idea, as Table 3.21 illustrates.

Table 3.21 Returns of A.V. of real property assessed for property tax

	England & Wales (£)	Lancashire (£)	Lancs. as % of E. & W. (%)
1815	51,790,879	3,087,774	6.0
1843	85,802,735	7,756,228	9.0
1860	112,802,749	11,289,375	10.0

Radical working men remained preoccupied with the franchise. Chartism revived in the trade depression of 1846 and 1847 but to little effect. There was an outbreak of plug rioting in 1848, mainly by boys and youths, the sad murder of a police constable at Ashton-under-Lyne and the dismal failure of the third national petition (H. Davies 1974: 16–28). Working people in general, though still distressed when trade failed, were turning to more immediate and practical issues – to their trade unions, to the Ten Hours movement and to their own affairs.

After 1850, as turbulence declined, the working classes of the region

Mr. COBDEN addressing the League Council.

(From the Painting by J. R. Herbert, R.A. Reproduced by permission of Messrs. T. Agnew & Sons.)

were increasingly perceived as hard working and respectable as opposed to the dangerous mob of earlier years. Perhaps it was the circumstances rather than the people that had changed. The industrial workers had a poor reputation for thrift and were slow to use savings banks but even so by 1853 Manchester and Liverpool were the third and fourth largest in the country respectively, Manchester with just under £1 million deposited (Horne 1947: 144). The hand-loom weavers and others had clubbed together in the late eighteenth century to build terraces of cottages; the terminating building society was a common feature of working-class communities in the first half of the nineteenth. More workers however probably saw their trade union contributions as a form of insurance and the industrial districts were those in which there were the most friendly and burial societies and the highest membership (see Appendix 3.1, p. 213, for 1803). It was Lancashire too which combined cooperative principles and hard-headed thrift into the consumer cooperative movement which replaced Owen's utopian but unsuccessful schemes for cooperative communities. The twenty-eight men who founded the Rochdale store at Toad Lane in December 1844 paid only lip-service to a 'home colony of united interests'; it was the honest, unadulterated food, the interest paid on capital and the dividend on purchases that attracted shareholders. Even before it had really proved itself the principles it espoused produced, in 1847–8, similar societies at Bacup, Todmorden, Leigh, Salford, Padiham and Middleton. By 1851 there were 130 such stores in Great Britain and by 1860 societies at Leeds and Rochdale had set up their own corn mills on a commercial basis (Potter 1891).

There were also growing alternatives to drink as a leisure pursuit. The wakes and rushbearings (Plate 3.10) had become rowdy, secular affairs but Belle Vue at Manchester and the Zoological Gardens at Liverpool, which had grown out of recreation gardens, offered a wide range of entertainments by the 1850s – bands, archery, cricket, boating and dancing and, of course, exotic animals – outings for the family that were made more accessible by the railway. And the new town councils, emulating Birkenhead, were opening public parks, Manchester's Queen's Park and Philips Park, for example, being taken over from the subscribers in 1845. At Salford the council opened the first civic public library in 1850, an example rapidly followed by Manchester and Liverpool (Greenall 1974: 51).

There was perhaps a greater change taking place. Observers of the region in the early nineteenth century were struck by the lack of both religion and education but by 1860 they had been brought together by the Sunday School movement. The religious history of the region in the late eighteenth

---

Plate 3.9 The Anti Corn Law League. Reproductions of this painting took pride of place in town halls across the region so that local people could see the great men who had beaten the landlords and ushered in the reign of plenty. Certainly the Council brought together an array of entrepreneurial power greater than Manchester would ever know again. (Source: Watkin 1891.)

Plate 3.10 Rushbearing in Manchester. Here in Long Millgate are typical features of the secular township rushbearings of the early nineteenth century. The rush cart is decorated with pewter and, perhaps, silver, but it is ridden by drunken, vomiting men. The morris men dance outside the inn, bright flags and banners fly but squealing animals and drunken brawlers crowd the scene. Respectable opinion much preferred the quiet order of Whit walks and gradually whittled away the bucolic traditions of the Wakes, the fair and the rushbearing. (Source: Chetham's Library.)

and early nineteenth centuries is obscure but the Census of Religious Worship of 1851 throws light on the situation as it then was (Table 3.22).

Thus Lancashire recorded lower church attendances than Cheshire, was less Anglican and Wesleyan but returned twice the percentage of Catholics. In general, religious observance was lowest in industrial south-east Lancashire, north-east Cheshire and in Liverpool, highest in west Lancashire and east Lancashire north of Rochdale (see Appendix 3.2, p. 219, for details of borough and country attendances).

The Church of England had, aided by parliamentary grant, built 103 churches in the region after 1800 (see Plate 5.10, p. 364), and even more were built by benefactors; Appendix 3.2 (p. 219) shows that other denominations had been equally active. All had also been quick to follow the example of Robert Raikes in Gloucester. Within two years of his first Sunday School in 1789 Luke Fildes, a Methodist, opened one in a Manchester cellar; by 1843 Edward Baines could claim that there were 218,412 Sunday scholars or one to every five and two-thirds of the people of the manufacturing districts in Lancashire, 30,591 in the Cheshire and Derbyshire districts or one to every

Table 3.22   Religious attendance 1851. See Figures 3.6, 3.7, 3.8 and 3.9

	Lancashire
	(95 out of 1,627 churches did not return attendances)

Population   2,031,236 × 85.0% = 1,726,550
  Total attendances   894,736 × 66.6% =   595,894 = 35%
C of E   „   381,550 = 14.7% ⎤ *see below*
Wesleyan „   188,763 = 7.2% ⎬   *for*
RC   „   146,288 = 5.6% ⎦ *calculation*

	Cheshire
	(39 out of 833 churches did not return attendances)

Population   455,725 × 85.0% =   387,366
  Total attendances   238,358 × 66.6% =   158,746 = 40.9%
C of E   „   110,736 = 19.0% ⎤ *see below*
Wesleyan „   76,967 = 13.25% ⎬   *for*
RC   „   13,623 = 2.3% ⎦ *calculation*

Note: The above calculation assumes 85% of the total population available to go to worship. Attendances are reduced by one-third to take account of people attending more than once.

Source: Census of Religious Worship, 1851, cxcviii, ccix, Tables.

four and a half of the population as well as a total of 30,000 teachers (E. Baines 1843: Returns). Some of these schools, like Stockport and Maccles-field, were huge, and most had adult groups, excursions and a wide range of social activities that reached into most of the working-class homes of the region; after the turn of the century the annual Whit walks became a high point for families as well as scholars. The schools provided not only basic literacy and moral instruction but also established relationships across class barriers that linked the churches with family and work in influential and supportive networks.

Full-time education for working children was slow to develop. The Grammar Schools had become largely exclusive and traditional, and factory schools, introduced under the Factory Act 1833, were very variable but often inadequate. The half-time system introduced for mill children between the ages of eight and thirteen under the Factory Act 1844 ensured that they did receive some education, the only children in the country for whom it was compulsory, but it was hard for them to combine work and school. As in the rest of England the British and National schools spread after 1809 and 1811 so that Baines could defend provision in the industrial districts in 1843 as equal to that in the country at large. Table 3.23 gives his totals.

Table 3.23   Sunday and day schools in the manufacturing districts

	Sunday Schools	*Scholars*	*Day Schools*	*Scholars*
Lancashire	768	218,412	2,195	121,455
Cheshire	73	27,420	169	8,770
N. Derbyshire	16	3,171	19	1,249

Source: E. Baines 1843, returns.

Many children, however, never attended a day school as the Manchester Statistical Society's reports showed, and with the Corn Law battle won in the late 1840s, some of the region's reforming middle class turned to the promotion of national secular education; J. P. Kay-Shuttleworth, the campaign's leader, moved on from sanitation and the poor law to become the founder of popular education. The denominations, who wanted to keep control of their schools, strongly opposed anything that would weaken them (Ashton 1934: 63–5). One minor secular triumph could be welcomed. In 1845 a Manchester merchant, John Owens, left almost £100,000 for the founding of a secular college for the young men of the town and region. Owens College opened in Cobden's former house in Quay Street in 1851, more like a dissenting academy than the old universities, but in its early years its future looked far from secure.

By 1860 the troubled years of class warfare were giving way to the tacit, if often unenthusiastic, cooperation of the working classes in making goods and money and in improving the health and environment of the shock towns of industry. They were also building their trade unions or serving their churches and chapels or friendly society lodges and coming to terms with the new leisure of the ten-hour day. Given a growing common acceptance of the market in economic affairs, cool rationality of the Benthamite stamp in social and political affairs and international peace from the golden touch of free trade there seemed to be no reason why the triumphant Manchester Liberals should not hold the whole region in their grasp. Indeed elections after 1832 seemed to demonstrate just that (see Table 3.24, p. 213).

But there were other currents below the surface. In 1853 the Manchester clergyman Robert Lamb described that town as politically Liberal but he also found strong and widespread Conservative sentiments among working people. He wrote

Paradoxical as it may seem, it is by no means an impossible supposition, that if universal suffrage and vote by ballot were parts of our Constitution, Manchester might return two Conservative members.

(Lamb 1866: 114)

Figures 3.6–3.9 The four maps which follow show the relative strengths of the denominations in 1851, which reflect the rise of Non-conformity in the seventeenth century, the eighteenth-century advent of Methodism and substantial immigration of Irish Roman Catholics from the 1790s. The maps are derived from Appendix 3.2B. They do not take account of borough attendance within the districts which are almost invariably lower. It should be noted that some districts were under-recorded, especially for Anglican worship and that the collection of data occasionally reached over county boundaries, hence the inclusion of part of Yorkshire which falls under Clitheroe and Hayfield and Chapel-en-le-Frith in Derbyshire.

Figure 3.6 Census of religious worship in 1851: Anglican attendances.

Figure 3.7 Census of religious worship in 1851: Roman Catholic attendances.

N

LANCASTER

GARSTANG

CLITHEROE

FYLDE

PRESTON

BURNLEY

BLACKBURN

HASLINGDEN

CHORLEY

ROCHDALE

ORMSKIRK

BOLTON

BURY

WIGAN

OLDHAM

MANCHESTER

LEIGH

SALFORD

ASHTON-UNDER-LYNE

BARTON

CHORLTON

WEST
DERBY

HAYFIELD

BIRKENHEAD

PRESCOT

WARRINGTON

STOCKPORT

WIRRAL

RUNCORN

ALTRINCHAM

CHAPEL-
EN-LE-
FRITH

MACCLESFIELD

CHESTER
(GREAT
BOUGHTON)

NORTHWICH

CONGLETON

NANTWICH

0   10   20 Km

0   5   10 Mls

KEY   1–5%   11–20%

6–10%   21–24%

Figure 3.8 Census of religious worship in 1851: non-Calvinistic Methodist attendances.

211

Figure 3.9 Census of religious worship in 1851: other Nonconformist attendances.

Table 3.24 Parliamentary elections 1832–59 Lancashire, Cheshire and North Derbyshire

Election	Conservative	Liberal
1832	8	30
1835	14	24
1837	16	22
1841	18	20
1847	12	26
1852	13	25
1857	13	25
1859	16	22

Source: F. W. S. Craig 1977.

Appendices

Appendix 3.1
Parliamentary Reports on the Poor Law 1803

	Number of parishes or places			Population 1801
	1776	1785	1803	
Cheshire	480	486	491	191,751
Lancashire	434	435	452	672,731
(*including north of sands*)				

	1803 Persons relieved excl. non-parishioners	Percentage of resident population relieved
Cheshire	22,152	12
Lancashire	46,200	7

	Friendly Societies (FS) percentage belonging	number of FS enrolled
Cheshire	8	109
Lancashire	16	957

	Per head of population total raised by rates	Expenditure on poor
Cheshire	8s. 10¼d.	7s. 3¼d.
Lancashire	6s. 10¼d.	4s. 9¼d.

Average Rate per Hundred 1803

Cheshire

Broxton Higher Division	2s. 4¾d.
Broxton Lower Division	2s. 2¾d.
Bucklow	3s. 11d.
Eddisbury First Div.	3s. 6½d.
Eddisbury Second Div.	3s. 9d.
Macclesfield	4s. 0¼d.
Nantwich	4s. 2d.
Northwich	5s. 5¼d.
Wirral Higher Div.	1s. 8¼d.
Wirral Lower Div.	1s. 6¼d.
Chester City	3s. 7¼d.

Lancashire

Amounderness	4s. 8¼d.
Blackburn Upper	6s. 10¼d.
Blackburn Lower	4s. 4½d.
Leyland	5s. 11¾d.
Lonsdale	3s. 4½d.
Salford	3s. 2¾d.
West Derby	3s. 11¼d.
Liverpool	NA
Wigan	5s. 0d.

High rate parishes and places
ie 5s. and over in the £ spent on the poor.

d. in £

Cheshire

Broxton Higher Hundred	47 places	
nil		
Broxton Lower Hundred	36 places	
Christleton Ch. & Parva		64.44
Bucklow Hundred	71 places	
Ashton on Mersey		83.42
Aston by Budworth		74.12
Baguley		89.76
Great Budworth		64.89
Little Leigh		61.12
Marston		71.48
Sale		69.31
Walton Inferior		76.20

Eddisbury First Div.	23 places	
Calveley		61.31
Rushton		74.67
Spurstow		65.90
Weever		67.96
Eddisbury Second Div.	37 places	
Mouldsworth		67.68
Weaverham Lordsh.		173.67
Weaverham Townsh.		154.56
Macclesfield Hundred	72 places	
Bollington		70.08
Bollin Fee		66.74
Dukinfield		62.73
Hattersley		131.04
Hyde		104.16
Macclesfield Townsh.		61.56
Matley		68.40
Mottram in Long. Townsh.		61.59
Somerford Booths		135.24
Nantwich Hundred	61 places	
Acton		82.72
Bartherton		67.00
Faddiley		63.22
Haslington		135.73*
Nantwich Townsh.		96.86*
Norbury		94.80
Sound		78.20
Worleston		122.40
Northwich Hundred	63 places	
Minshull Vernon		160.92
Northwich		115.08*
Occlestone		245.71
Shurlach		78.00
Smallwood		73.16
Swettenham		104.14
Wharton		64.68
Wirral Higher Div.	35 places	
nil		

215

Wirral Lower Div.	37 places	
Caldey		73.26
Chester City	10 places	
nil		

Lancashire

Amounderness Hundred	63 places	
Claughton		62.08*
Freckleton		69.54
Garstang		84.00
Holleth		60.03
Hethersal		65.40
Kirkland		76.44
Lytham		69.30
Blackburn Upper Div.	45 places	
Barley with Whitley		74.67
Briercliffe		102.06
Burnley		77.00
Cliviger		127.92
Colne		60.30
Cowpe, Lench etc.		68.06
Habergham Eaves		117.00
Hallows Reedley		81.12
Great and Little Marsden		98.80
Padiham		82.08
Simonstone		67.00
Worsthorne with Hurstwood		120.06
Blackburn Lower Div.	37 places but 20 do not record rates.	
Clayton le Dale		70.40
Wilton		65.52
Leyland Hundred	40 places	
Heapey		75.64
Hoghton		68.40
Wheelton		68.04
Withnell		69.96
Wrightington		61.88
Lonsdale North and South	71 places	
Roberindale		86.24
Lower Tatham		65.00*

Salford Hundred	98 places	
Barton upon Irwell		96.48
Bircle cum Bamford		91.64
Blackley		114.31
Chaderton		132.44
Chorlton cum Hardy		67.00
Clifton		225.78
Denton		72.00
Droylsden		65.34
Farnworth		99.75
Flixton		132.00*
Gorton		61.56
Harpurhey		62.56
Hopwood		180.09
Haughton		74.42
Little Hulton		83.70
Middle Hulton		153.76
Levenshulme		124.80
Darcy Lever		115.20
Little Lever		96.12
Manchester		69.12
Moston		71.00
Newton (Manchester)		126.72
Oldham		100.80
Openshaw		72.24
Pendlebury		110.50
Pendleton		87.60
Pilkington		88.32
Pilsworth		288.00
Rusholme		68.16
Thornham		151.20
Tonge (Prestwich Parish)		62.04
Urmston		70.80
Wardleworth		81.00
Westhoughton		103.50
Wuerdle and Wardale		85.32
West Derby	92 places	
Atherton		81.27
Houghton		81.60
Ince in Makerfield		88.92
Prescot		69.16
Tildesley		66.88

Derbyshire
  Part of High Peak   10 places, none over 60d.

* These places have workhouses which may attract income from other places or parishes. The full rate may not therefore be applicable to them.

Appendix 3.2
A   Churches and Chapels 1801–51

(from the *Census of Religious Worship* 1851, Table D)

	Churches and chapels existing before 1801	in 1851
Cheshire		
C of E	130	252
Presbyterian	—	5
Independent/Cong.	13	66
All Baptists	5	12
Soc. of Friends	6	10
Unitarians	10	14
Moravians	1	3
All Wesleyans	32	402
Calvinistic Meths.	1	12
Brethren	—	5
Isolated congrgs.	2	7
RC	2	17
Latter Day Saints	3	9
Lancashire		
C of E	218	529
Presbyterian	5	22
Irish Presb.	—	1
Independent/Cong.	31	170
All Baptists	23	100
Soc. of Friends	14	27
Unitarians	26	35
Moravians	1	2
All Wesleyans	45	521
Calvinistic Meths.	3	19
Sandemanians	—	1
New Church	1	21

Brethren	1	5
Isolated Congrgs.	4	36
RC	38	114
Greek Church	—	1
Cath. & Apostolic	—	1
Latter Day Saints	1	15
Jews	2	7

B   Rank order and percentage attendances at worship 1851

(from the *Census of Religious Worship* 1851)

A = Total attendances and percentage
B = C of E
C = Non-Calvinist Methodist
D = Roman Catholic
E = Other major Protestant denominations
(All percentages are calculated on the total population available to attend (85 per cent) and attendances (66.6 per cent) and are the best estimates of the percentage of the district's population attending in total and in each denomination.)

Boroughs

	A		B		C		D		E	
	RO	%	RO	%	RO	%	RO	%	RO	%
Warrington	1	46	1	25	2	12	6	3.8	11	2.4
Chester	2	45	2	24	6	9	11	1.9	2	10.9
Wigan	3	40	3	19	14	4	11	1.7	8	4.7
Rochdale	4	40	14	8*	1	15	13	1.8	1	11.8
Ashton-u-Lyne	5	36	5	14	3	11	9	3.5	3	7.2
Bury	6	35	7	13*	7	8	14	1.6	4	6.7
Macclesfield	7	35	4	16	5	10	7	3.7	12	2.2
Liverpool	8	35	6	14	15	3	1	11.5		—
Stockport	9	34	11	12	4	11	5	4.3	7	4.8
Salford	10	30	9	12*	11	5	4	4.4	14	2.0
Blackburn	11	30	8	13*	12	5	10	3.1	5	5.8
Bolton	12	29	10	12	8	7	8	3.7	10	3.3
Manchester	13	28	12	9	10	5	3	6.3	9	4.0
Oldham	14	25	13	9*	9	6	15	1.1	6	5.0
Preston	15	20	15	4†	13	5	2	7.1*	13	2.0

(The * or † indicates failure to make returns. In Salford 10% of Anglican churches failed, in Manchester and Oldham 20% and in Rochdale and Bury 30%. In Preston 70% of the Anglican churches made no return and 30% of RC churches also failed. The rank orders and percentages for these places are therefore to be treated as understatements.)

Poor Law Unions and Registration Districts

	A		B		C		D		E	
	RO	%	RO	%	RO	%	RO	%	RO	%
Clitheroe	1	62	3	26	10	14	4	10.0	8	6
Haslingden	2	61	13	19	1	24*	32	0.8	1	13
Garstang	3	57	1	27	22	7	1	14.0	—	
Runcorn	4	49	8	21	8	17	23	1.9	13	5
Nantwich	5	47	10	21	4	21	35	0.6	28	2
Hayfield	6	47	31	12	2	22	15	3.3	4	8
Congleton	7	46	11	20*	5	20	30	0.9	27	2
Warrington	8	46	5	25	21	7	11	6.9	19	4
Burnley	9	46	24	14*	7	18*	25	1.6	3	8
Ormskirk	10	45	2	27	30	5	10	7.3	25	3
Northwich	11	44	14	19	6	19*	28	1.2	26	2
Fylde	12	44	7	24*	27	6	12	6.0†	9	6
G. Boughton	13	43	6	24	15	10	31	0.9	18	4
Altrincham	14	42	19	16*	11	14	27	1.3	7	6
Lancaster	15	42	4	25	29	5	14	3.9	—	
West Derby	16	40	12	20	26	6	5	9.7	24	3
Ch.e.l.Frith	17	40	20	16*	3	22	—		—	
Rochdale	18	40	33	11*	9	15*	33	0.7	2	8
Macclesfield	19	38	16	18	13	12	18	2.9	33	1
Wirral	20	38	9	21	32	5	13	5.3	23	3
Chorley	21	37	27	12*	23	7	2	12.8	29	2
Blackburn	22	37	21	15	18	8*	17	3.0	5	7
Leigh	23	37	17	17*	16	10	19	2.6	11	5
Stockport	24	37	26	12	14	12	21	2.3	6	7
Bury	25	36	22	15*	17	9	26	1.3	14	5
Prescot	26	36	15	19*	34	4	7	8.5	31	1
Wigan	27	35	18	16	35	3	8	8.0	20	4
Barton-Irwell	28	34	28	12*	12	13	29	1.2	17	4
Ashton-u-Lyne	29	33	25	13*	19	8	24	1.7	10	5
Bolton	30	33	23	14*	20	8	22	2.0	15	5
Liverpool	31	33	32	11	36	2	3	12.0	22	3
Chorlton	32	29	29	12	25	6	20	2.3	16	4
Manchester	33	28	36	9*	31	5	9	7.4	30	2
Preston	34	28	34	11*	33	4	6	8.7	32	1
Salford	35	27	30	12*	28	6	16	3.3	2	3
Oldham	36	26	35	9	24	7	34	0.7	12	5

(Once again many Anglican churches failed to make returns – 10% at Congleton, Burnley, Chapel, Leigh, Bury and Bolton; 20% at Fylde, Rochdale, Prescot, Ashton, Manchester and Salford; 30% at Altrincham, Chorley, Barton and Preston. Methodist under-recording was 10% at Haslingden, Burnley, Northwich, Rochdale and Blackburn. Catholic under-recording was 20% at Preston, 25% at Clitheroe and 40% at Fylde.)

Chapter 4

1860–1920

Between 1860 and 1920 the old traditions of domestic industry and the semi-rural world in which they had flourished gave way to acceptance of the disciplines of working and living in larger units of industrial and urban society. The turbulence of the first half of the century died down as conditions improved both at the workplace and in the maturing industrial towns. The townspeople's needs stimulated agriculture in the region. Urban employers attempted, with some success, to enlist the goodwill of their workpeople by paternalistic leadership, and to gain the support of their townspeople by municipal improvement, using both public funding and private munificence. Working-class radicalism found orderly outlets in the Cooperative and trade union movements, content, until the rebirth of socialism late in the century, to seek political ends through the Conservative or Liberal parties. Religion seems to have regained lost prestige, if not greater observance, but, early disturbances in south-east Lancashire apart, only in Liverpool did it still stir the dangerous emotions of previous years. The economic base seemed almost as strong in 1914 as it had in 1860 with coal and cotton, hatting, glass, chemicals, paper, shipping, and docks flourishing, and engineering branching into exciting innovations. But before 1914 commercial difficulties had begun to weaken faith in free trade; limited liability and company mergers threatened paternalism, and socialism had struck new roots. Nevertheless, it is likely that on the outbreak of war few either expected, or, perhaps, wanted, a very different society from that which, in its best years, had made so much progress.

Population

The pace of population growth in the region slackened, and by the 1921 census Lancashire had lost its position as the fastest growing county in

England and Wales. Table 4.1 shows that from 1861 to 1921 Cheshire's population grew by 103 per cent, Lancashire's by 101 per cent but the adjoining part of north-west Derbyshire by only 59 per cent. The lower proportional growth in Derbyshire stands out, while Lancashire and Cheshire grew at a much faster rate in the 1870s. During the first two decades of the twentieth century the proportional growth of population in Cheshire was almost twice that of Lancashire.

Table 4.1 Population 1871–1921

| | Cheshire | | Lancashire[a] | | Part of Derbyshire | |
	% up on previous		% up on previous		% up on previous	
1861		505,428		2,393,702		39,123
1871	11	561,201	15	2,764,412	2	39,866
1881	25	644,037	22	3,363,501	14	46,365
1891	16[b]	743,869	13[b]	3,811,188	13[c]	52,181
1901	11	827,191	12	4,286,664	10	57,590
1911	15	954,779	9	4,664,496	9	62,692
1921	7	1,025,724	3	4,809,374	−1	62,093

Notes:
[a] The population of Lancashire north of the sands as given in *VCH. Lancs.*, II for 1871–1901, and of the Barrow and Ulverston registration districts in 1911 and 1921, has been deducted from the county totals.
[b] The figures for 1871 and 1881 are for the ancient county, for 1891 and later for the administrative county and county boroughs; the per cent increases ignore these differences.
[c] The Derbyshire figures for 1871 and 1881 are for ecclesiastical areas, for 1891 based on civil parishes, and for 1901 and later for administrative areas; the per cent changes ignore these differences.
Source: Cheshire: *VCH. Cheshire*, II: 202; Lancashire: decennial census returns; Derbyshire: *VCH. Derbys.*, II: 196–8 and decennial census returns.

The region shared in the national shifts which affected population growth after the 1860s. Nationally, fertility began to decline from 1876, and mortality to improve from the 1870s. Lancashire, especially, witnessed a drop in fertility that was above the national figure, whereas reductions in mortality (which were perhaps mainly due to the reduced impact of disease) matched the national average. From the 1860s the size of completed families among textile workers was dropping, and while abortion may have contributed to this, it is possible that working women were exchanging advice on sexual matters that promoted family limitation. Child mortality remained high in the cotton towns, but with puzzling variations which defy general explanation. By and large it appears to have been a combination of poor sanitation and inappropriate diet that caused the high mortality in industrial areas, especially those with a high proportion of working mothers but there were variations within those areas. Why, for example, was infant mortality high in Burnley but low in Nelson, and high on the Fylde coast (Walton 1987: 309–10)?

The census statisticians of 1901 thought that Lancashire was a net gainer from migration between 1891 and 1901, and Cheshire marginally so too. The three censuses of 1871, 1901 and 1921 show that the proportion who had been born outside the region fell from 9.2 per cent to 3.9 per cent, though this is no measure either of how long these migrants stayed, or of the demographic impact of any children they may have had. A substantial proportion of migrants lived in the major urban settlements, especially in Lancashire. People born in Ireland figured prominently among both rural and urban dwelling migrants, and though that prominence declined as time passed, as Table 4.2 shows, the Irish accounted for more than half of those born outside England and Wales (except in Cheshire in 1921). Their numbers may have been affected by the seasonality of agricultural work, a major source of employment, but they also worked in textiles and chemicals and provided an unskilled labour force in many trades.

The Wirral and Liverpool also had significant numbers of Welsh, over 20,000 in Liverpool in 1901; their chapels and churches, like those of the Scots, are enduring monuments to migrant communities. But there were people from further afield active in the region: for example prominent members of the Manchester merchant community were of German origin, while in the 1880s Baltic peoples contributed to the development of the mid-Cheshire chemical industries.

The 1921 Census no doubt reveals parallels with the in-migration of the preceding fifty or so years. Lancashire was not in the top ten counties in the number of Scots-born residents (though Cheshire was ninth) but it had a higher proportion of Irish-born than any other English county with Cheshire second. Bootle now had the highest proportion of Irish-born of any large English town with 656 males per 10,000 and 501 females per 10,000. Liverpool was second, Salford sixth, Manchester seventh and St Helens, with 316 males and 134 females per 10,000, was eighth. The attraction of the two ends of the Mersey for the foreign-born was also clear. Manchester was third of the large towns in its proportion of foreign-born, Salford sixth, Liverpool, with a Chinese community of over 400, eleventh, and Wallasey twenty-first.

Manchester and, to a lesser extent, Liverpool had attracted a high proportion of the Polish and Russian immigrants into England. Manchester recorded 8.5 per cent of Russians and 4 per cent of Poles who had entered England, Liverpool 4.3 per cent and 2.8 per cent. Many of these were Jewish and the pattern of Jewish settlement in the region had swung decisively towards Manchester, now the second Jewish centre in the country. In 1850 they numbered some 2,500 in Liverpool, 2,000 in Manchester. By 1910, swelled by the diaspora from eastern Europe after the Russian May Laws of 1882, the Manchester community had reached 30,000 with Liverpool at under 8,000. The community leaders were merchants, manufacturers and

Table 4.2   Aspects of migration in 1871, 1901 and 1921

| | CHESHIRE | | LANCASHIRE | |
	Whole county	*County boroughs only[a]*	*Whole county*	*County boroughs only[a]*
Pop. 1871	561,201	110,534	2,764,412	1,058,034
CBs % of county		20%		38%
of whom 'migrants'[b]	34,306	8,610	268,011	178,228
% of pop.	6%	8%	10%	17%
CBs % of 'migrants'		25%		67%
of whom Irish	23,942	7,306	200,061	121,578
% of pop.	4%	7%	7%	11%
% of 'migrants'	70%	85%	75%	68%
Pop. 1901	827,191	281,700	4,286,664	2,502,021
CBs % of county		34%		58%
of whom 'migrants'	36,099	20,549	264,694	187,634
% of pop.	4%	7%	6%	7%
CBs % of 'migrants'		57%		71%
of whom Irish	18,268	10,495	145,301	103,312
% of pop.	2%	4%	3%	4%
% of 'migrants'	51%	51%	55%	55%
Pop. 1921	1,025,724	400,497	4,809,374	3,113,902
CBs % of county		39%		65%
of whom 'migrants'	38,329	23,035	191,855	146,636
% of pop.	4%	6%	4%	3%
CBs % of 'migrants'		60%		76%
of whom Irish	15,853	9,762	100,667	74,415
% of pop.	1.5%	2.4%	2%	2.4%
% of 'migrants'	41%	42%	52%	51%

Notes:
[a] County boroughs not created until 1888. In the 1871 census tables the Cheshire towns included were Chester, Macclesfield and Stockport; Lancashire – Bolton, Lancaster, Liverpool, Manchester and Preston. In 1901, though not a CB, Wallasey was included as having a population of over 50,000.
[b] Throughout the table 'migrants' are defined as people born outside England and Wales.
Source: Decennial census returns.

professional men who played an important role in the development of the city and university. There was also a continuing influx of families with only their labour to offer and they produced concentrations of poor people in the needle trades especially in the Cheetham Hill district round the Cathedral in Manchester (B. Williams 1976).

Even before 1860, in-migration had not resulted in a rigid separation of people into exclusive enclaves by country of origin or religious persuasion. There had been strong clustering, notably by the Irish and the Jews, but this was not dissimilar to the drawing together of families from the surrounding countryside identified by Anderson in Preston during the middle years of the century (M. Anderson 1971). Intermarriage was not uncommon. Alice Foley, who was born in Bolton in 1891, had an Irish father who could not settle to the routines of working life in a mill-town but had literary tastes that embraced Dickens, George Eliot and Shakespeare. Her mother, the child of native Bolton hand-loom weavers, could neither read nor write but carried the family through the ups and downs caused by her husband's inability to stay in a job or out of the pub (Foley 1973: 8, 12). Even the small cotton towns could demonstrate this intermingling. Ada Monk was born in Hadfield in north Derbyshire in 1894, the child of a Preston weaver who became an overlooker in Hadfield during a strike, and a Cornish mother who was one of a large group who had moved north to seek work in the mills (J. H. Smith 1975).

Assimilation of this kind could be held back, even prevented, especially where strong religious attitudes prevailed but the barriers were not insuperable. Alice Foley's father was Catholic, her mother indifferent in religion but Protestant by background. Religious difference and events in or connected with troubles in Ireland (Plate 4.1) could provoke Anglo-Irish disturbances in the towns and construction sites and the entry of numbers of poor east European Jews after 1882 sparked off some anti-Semitic journalism and overt harassment in Manchester. In general, however, people were more united by their place in the economic and social hierarchy than divided by place of origin. Even in education, so closely tied to religion in the region, Anglicans, Catholics and Jews were likely to be on the same side in supporting church schools against the non-denominational, Board provision sought by Nonconformists.

Migration was however more complex than simply the arrival of people born outside the region: people moved around within the counties. One obvious effect of this was the growth of suburbs (referred to on p. 282) as people moved from the industrial hearts of the older cities; another was the loss of rural population. Between 1881 and 1891 maps of net migration show central, southern and eastern Cheshire to be losing people and the same is true for north-east Lancashire and parts of the Fylde; between 1901 and 1911 the trend is more widespread in northern and central Lancashire, and still commonplace in Cheshire. The effect of these changes between 1881 and 1911 was to reduce population density in these areas (R. Lawton 1962: 196, 198, 205).

It is not easy to divide the region into urban and rural parts: municipal and county boroughs were certainly urban in character, but counting only

Plate 4.1 Hyde Road gaol, Manchester. It was while in charge of a van carrying two Fenians to this prison that Sergeant Brett was murdered by a rescue party of armed men on 18 September 1867. The execution of three of the rescue party gave the Fenians their 'Manchester martyrs'.

them undoubtedly excludes the urban, or sometimes more accurately suburban, nature of urban sanitary districts and, later, urban district councils, which encompassed much agricultural, rural land. Thus in 1901 only 20 per cent of Cheshire's population, and 5.3 per cent of that of Lancashire (including the parts now in Cumbria) lived in rural districts. Table 4.3 enumerates the populations of places which became a borough or county borough by 1921. Measures of urban growth made using Table 4.3 are distorted by boundary changes. For example, if we compare the figures for Manchester in 1881 and 1891, we have to take account of the three suburbs which were brought into the city during the 1880s; nevertheless we may note a trend of increasing urbanisation. On the other hand, the decline of some of the Lancashire textile centres (Blackburn, Bolton, Burnley, Bury, Oldham and Rochdale) between 1911 and 1921 was real and not the product of boundary changes.

In the second decade of the twentieth century urban growth was no longer greatest in the manufacturing or mining areas, but on the Wirral (a suburb of Liverpool), and in the seaside towns of Blackpool and Southport, all of which shared some of the highest proportional increases in population in the country. Liverpool was throughout this period the second largest city of the land; Manchester was third until between 1911 and 1921 when Birmingham pushed it down to fourth place. Among the English and Welsh towns counted as the most populous in the census reports, the proportion located in our region fell from 23 per cent in 1871 to 17 per cent in 1921.

Landowning Society

Industrialization and urbanization continued to change the face of much of south-west and south-east Lancashire. In Cheshire the impact was chiefly apparent around the salt towns of Northwich and Wharton (Winsford), in the urban explosion of Birkenhead, and in the north-east of the county. But most of central and southern Cheshire, and central and northern Lancashire remained dominated by landed and agricultural interests. Landed families continued to come and go. Table 4.4 shows that in our two sample hundreds of West Derby and Northwich a high proportion of properties was owned in 1923–4 by the same family in 1873, but about one-fifth had changed hands, a proportion which is enlarged if we allow that the evidence for some of the 'don't know' properties in the table is probably deficient as a result of change in ownership. The pace of change of property ownership was greatest in the years between 1873 and the First World War, rather than during the war and

Table 4.3 Urban populations 1871–1921 (Key to typefaces and notes p. 230.)

	1871	1881	1891	1901	1911	1921
CHESHIRE						
Birkenhead[a]	45,418	84,006	99,857	110,915	130,794	145,577
Chester	35,257	36,794	37,105	38,309	39,028	40,802
Congleton	11,344	11,116	10,744	10,707	11,309	11,762
Crewe[b]	17,810	24,385	28,761	42,074	44,960	46,497
Dukinfield	14,085	16,942	17,408	18,929	19,422	19,509
Hyde	14,213	28,630	30,670	32,766	33,437	33,424
Macc'field	35,450	37,514	36,009	34,624	34,797	33,846
St'bridge	21,092	22,785	26,783	27,673	26,513	25,216
Stockport	53,014	59,553	70,263	78,897	108,682	123,309
Wallasey[c]	14,819	—	—	53,579	78,504	90,809
DERBYSHIRE						
Buxton	—	—	—	—	13,760	15,641
Glossop	17,046	19,574	22,416	21,526	21,688	20,531
LANCASHIRE						
Accrington	21,788	31,435	38,603	43,122	45,029	43,595
Ashton-u-L	37,389	37,040	40,463	43,890	45,172	43,335
Bacup	17,199	—	23,498	22,505	22,318	21,263
Blackburn	76,339	104,014	120,064	127,626	133,052	126,643
Blackpool	6,100	14,229	23,846	47,348	58,371	99,639
Bolton	82,853	105,414	115,002	168,215	180,851	178,683
Bootle	16,247	27,374	49,217	58,556	69,876	76,487
Burnley	40,858	58,751	87,016	97,043	106,322	103,157
Bury	32,611	52,213	57,212	58,029	58,648	56,403
Chorley[d]	16,864	19,478	23,087	26,852	30,315	30,581
Clitheroe	8,208	10,176	10,815	11,414	12,500	12,202
Colne	8,633	10,313	14,023	23,000	25,689	24,752
Darwen[e]	21,278	29,744	34,192	38,212	40,332	37,906
Eccles[f]	—	—	29,633	34,369	41,944	44,242
Haslingden[g]	7,698	—	18,225	18,543	18,719	17,486
Heywood	21,248	22,979	23,185	25,458	26,697	26,693
Lancaster	17,245	20,663	31,083	40,329	41,410	40,212
Leigh	—	—	—	40,001	44,103	45,532
Liverpool	493,405	552,508	517,980	684,958	746,421	802,940
Manchester	351,189	341,414	505,368	543,872	714,333	730,307
Middleton[h]	14,587	—	22,162	25,178	27,980	28,290
Morecambe[i]	—	—	—	11,978	12,131	19,178
Mossley	10,578	—	14,162	13,452	13,205	12,703
Nelson	5,580	—	22,700	32,816	39,479	39,841
Oldham	82,629	111,343	131,463	137,246	147,483	144,983
Preston	85,427	96,537	107,573	112,989	117,088	117,406
Rawtenstall	—	—	29,507	31,053	30,516	28,376
Rochdale	44,559	68,866	71,401	83,114	91,428	90,816
St Helens	45,134	75,403	71,288	84,410	96,551	102,460
Salford	124,801	176,235	198,139	220,957	231,357	234,045
Southport	18,086	32,206	41,406	48,083	57,643	76,621
Warrington	32,144	41,452	52,748	64,642	72,166	76,811
Widnes[j]	14,359	24,935	30,011	28,580	31,541	38,860
Wigan	39,110	48,194	55,013	60,764	89,152	89,421

Table 4.3   Urban populations 1871–1921 (*continued*)

Notes:
[a] Under an Improvement Commission in 1871.
[b] 1871 figure for Monks Coppenhall township.
[c] 1901 figure for the Urban District.
[d] Incorporated 1881.
[e] 1881 called Over Darwen.
[f] Not incorporated until 1892.
[g] In 1871 considered a town by the district superintendent registrar.
[h] Local Board District called Middleton and Tonge.
[i] Not incorporated until 1902.
[j] Not incorporated until 1892.

Sources: Township figures from *VCH. Cheshire,* II, and *VCH. Lancs.,* II; other figures from decennial census returns. Township figures in ordinary type, local board districts are <u>underlined</u>, boroughs in *italic*, county boroughs in **bold**.

Table 4.4   Ownership of property in two sample hundreds

	Constant		Changed		Don't know		Total	
	No.	%	No.	%	No.	%	No.	%
1873–1924								
Northwich	33	52	10	16	20	32	63	100
West Derby	38	61	13	21	11	18	62	100
Both	71	57	23	18	31	25	125	100
1873–1906/13								
Northwich	36	57	17	27	10	16	63	100
West Derby	39	63	10	16	13	21	62	100
Both	75	60	27	22	23	18	125	100
1906/13–1923/4								
Northwich	40	63	8	13	15	24	63	100
West Derby	47	76	2	3	13	21	62	100
Both	87	70	10	8	28	22	125	100

Sources: Ormerod 1882; *VCH. Lancs.;* CRO, Local valuation records, NVA/2 (*c.* 1910–14); Kelly 1906; 1913; 1923; 1924.

its aftermath (1914–1923/4). A number of causes, acting distinctly or in combination, brought such changes about.

Landowners' annual incomes had increased: the Earl of Derby's from £163,000 in 1876 to £300,000 in 1900. The rents of the Clifton family of Lytham rose by almost £5,000 between 1870 and 1880, when they amounted to £37,754, but by rather less between 1880 and 1900 when they totalled £42,000. The Hesketh family income increased from £3,900 in 1842 to £12,500 in 1905; by 1905 the Leghs of High Legh enjoyed over £20,763 per year (G. Rogers 1981: 7, 9, 44; JRUL Cornwall-Legh MSS, unlisted). The rate of these increases was not smooth, however. Rents fell or stagnated during the agricultural depression in the 1880s and 1890s, and urban rents and coal-mining ventures, which had regularly boosted agricultural incomes, became less reliable (G. Rogers 1986: 262–4). At the same time, the expensive dynastic reassurance which a large family provided, or the extravagance of individuals, helped to ensure that some families entered the last quarter of the nineteenth century with an accumulation of debt.

After his father's death in 1869, the fifteenth Earl of Derby arranged to set £50,000 a year aside to meet accumulated debts of £420,000, and settlements, legacies and taxes; the total of £680,000 would be paid off in fourteen years (Bagley 1985: 190). When he died in 1882 J. T. Clifton owed £30,000 on personal debts from gaming, foreign cruises and hunting; in 1894, after £20,000 was paid off, debt on Clifton family settlements alone still reached £126,000. A few years later, in 1900, their total debts were £590,000. Proper and sensible expenditure on drainage, on land purchases (though sometimes to enhance their landowner's social control of parish affairs), and speculative urban development, figured in this total. Such levels of indebtedness could not cope with demands from tenants for rent rebates, nor provide improvement capital for agriculture, nor fund further borrowing (Rogers 1981: 62–70). Interest payments alone might consume between £18,000 and £24,000 of the Cliftons' income in 1900, but between 1890 and 1916 the Clifton estate sold about a quarter of their 1883 acreage to reduce the burden of debt (B. R. Mitchell 1988: 678, 681, 683; G. Rogers 1986: 252, 265). A similar tale of personal extravagance by successive heads of the Standish family of Duxbury (near Chorley, Lancs) encouraged the eventual heiresses' relatives, with no patrimonial emotion to hinder them, to sell, at first in parcels from 1878, then the Hall as a 300-acre parkland estate in 1898, leaving some half (about 3,000 acres) of the old estate as an efficient, cost-effective farm in the early 1900s (W. Walker 1990). New levels of taxation in the form of death duties, and the taxes on land values and rights proposed in the 1909 'People's Budget', struck at and alarmed landowners. The earls of Crawford and Balcarres paid death duties of £10,000 in 1880 and £103,000 in 1913 on net estate of £321,000 (Offner 1981: 363–71; Vincent 1984: 7).

Demography had varied results. The Heskeths, owners of the West Derby manor of North Meols, failed in the male line in 1876, and the female inheritance was secured by a change of name. The daughters of Captain Egerton-Warburton of Arley, Cheshire, who was killed in the First World War, married into the peerage and so their name was submerged, though one daughter kept the estate (personal interview). Part of the Northwich hundred estates of the Cheshire branch of the Ackers family, who a century or so before were Manchester merchants, were added by marriage to the already substantial Shakerley holdings; the Shakerley heir, a younger son, appended Ackers to his name for a time (Burke 1949). Part went to the neighbouring Baker-Wilbraham estates.

The effect of these changes was that some families disappeared and new landowners emerged. Examples include the Lathom family, who in 1882 sold their Bradwall (Cheshire) estate to Thomas Barlow, a Manchester merchant (CRO, DDX 132/1), and the company director and baronet, Sir Jabez Johnson-Ferguson, who acquired the Earl of Wilton's estate at Kenyon. This sale had no effect on the Earl's status, but for the Lathoms, Bradwall was the sum of their estate in the 1872–3 survey, and marked their removal from Cheshire landowning society.

Absentees had always featured among owners in the two counties, but the Earl of Crawford and Balcarres' remark on 'the flight of professional people to Southport and of the landowners to more attractive counties further afield', is apposite to West Derby hundred before the First World War where owners lived, for example, in Berkshire, Wiltshire, Oxford and Torquay, but in marked contrast with Northwich hundred. In another form of absenteeism a duke of Westminster, a Marquess of Cholmondeley, the Marquess of Crewe (in any case a collateral descendant), an earl of Crawford and Balcarres, and two earls of Derby were all heavily involved in national politics in these years, though they never neglected their home estates and localities (Bagley 1985; Huxley 1967; Vincent 1984: 1–2; Pope-Hennessey 1955).

Such patterns of social mobility would have been recognizable in previous centuries, and in the same way continental expeditions, the pursuit of game, public schools and Oxbridge (for men), membership of London clubs, horse racing and large households of servants, continued from earlier times, on occasion despite the personal tastes of an individual, such as the fifteenth Earl of Derby's hostility towards shooting (Bagley 1985: 193, cf. 198; Bateman 1883; Huxley 1967). The possession of a town house in London usually marked some prominence in politics, but was also characteristic of the largest landowners (Lee 1963: 18–19, 23). The Crawford and Balcarres family were perhaps pre-eminent as patrons of the arts, and as scholars and scientists among the region's landowners (Vincent 1984: 3, 7). The grand house too remained, and although few were built anew, the Grosvenors reconstructed Eaton Hall (Plate 4.2) again, between 1870 and 1883 (Pevsner 1979a; 1979b; Pevsner and Hubbard 1971: 208, but nb 10). There were new currents in landed society. The Wigan solicitor who bought Duxbury Hall and park was perhaps half gentleman, half professional, and symptomatic of that type of landowner whose 'seats' were large, rural villa-type houses emulating the old gentry, though usually lacking the acreage. Dawpool House at Thurstaston on the Wirral, rebuilt for a Liverpool shipowner, was perhaps the most architecturally pleasing of these (Girouard 1979: 75–7, 403). Properties of this type were built earlier than the last quarter of the century, but the occupants' names come and go in the directories of the period. In parts of northern Lancashire these new men, typified *c.* 1900 by Captain Peter Orm-

---

Plate 4.2   Eaton Hall, *c.* 1909. (Source: Driver 1909.)

rod of Wyresdale Hall, were beginning to submerge the old gentry society, and replace it with a more varied, meritocratic one, including successful business men. This change never entirely submerged the leading families of the old society, especially in Cheshire where in the 1900s landowners seem to have been more prominent in local government than in Lancashire. Four of the nineteen Cheshire county aldermen in 1906 were established gentry, and six of the elected councillors. Between 12 and 15 per cent of magistrates were established gentry families, and here Lancashire, except in the south-east, had more in common with Cheshire. Five mid-Cheshire gentry actively served as trustees of the Weaver Navigation under the Weaver Navigation Act 1895, alongside representatives of the county and district councils (Kelly 1906; G. Rogers 1981: 371; Lee 1963: 56–9; Weaver Trustees' Minutes for 1895 and 1896).

If one chooses to emphasize continuity among landowning families themselves, other aspects of rural society certainly changed. By 1914 some landowners had begun to sell their tenanted farms, agricultural labourers had been on strike, and by 1920 the horizons of rural society had been further broadened by the war.

The larger estates continued to rebuild farm houses, which, with freeholders' own constructions, are a tribute to the prosperity of farming in the first decade covered by this chapter. The Duke of Westminster in Cheshire built or rebuilt some forty-eight farm houses for his tenant farmers (Huxley 1967: 145; Pevsner and Hubbard 1971, *sub* Douglas). If farmers' standards of living improved as a consequence, it is nevertheless clear in Lancashire, less so in Cheshire, that tenant farmers' dormant anxieties about security of tenure, capricious agents and paternalist landlords were vitalized by the adverse price regimes of the 1880s and 1890s. In the eyes of many tenants the owners were unresponsive: rents were kept up, a landowner would not, for example, invest in the new buildings needed to support larger runs of stock on the cheaper foodstuffs becoming available, while older farmers' clubs were owner dominated and unwilling to discuss tenure (Huxley 1967: 146; cf. Mutch 1980: 269–70, 278). The emergence of a variety of new farmers' organizations in Lancashire, and such bodies as the Chester Farmers' Club, though sometimes divided over the interests of owner-occupiers and tenant farmers, combined with rent arrearages and the inability of some owners to find tenants, to produce rent reductions. Owners and agents did not give in easily, and a few tenants were evicted for their outspoken ideas, before rents came down. On an estate the collective pressure of these clubs fractured the traditional relationship between lord and individual tenant (Mutch 1980: 280–311). Ironically, two decades later owners and all types of farmers were united against the demands of labourers.

The large estates had also built or rebuilt labourers' cottages, and again the Grosvenor estate in Cheshire is a notable example where over 300 cottages were constructed (Huxley 1967: 145; Pevsner and Hubbard 1971, *sub* Douglas). Better housed or not, there were overall fewer labourers by 1921 as Table 4.5 shows (unfortunately the 1921 census did not distinguish

Table 4.5   Numbers of agricultural labourers, farm servants and farmers' relatives 1871–1921

	1871			1921	
	Labrs	*Servants*	*Relatives*	*Labrs*	*Relatives*
CHESHIRE	13,768	5,585	5,817	13,531	2,946
LANCASHIRE	21,791	9,630	12,217	19,264	6,225

Note: Males and females have been conflated.

Source: Decennial census returns; includes Lancashire north of the sands.

between live-in servants and non-resident labourers). Counting the 1871 categories of farm servants and farm labourers together, by 1921 the number in Cheshire had fallen by 25 per cent, and in Lancashire by 37 per cent, almost all males in both counties. The drop of resident relatives, the other element of the farm workforce, by almost 50 per cent in both counties was almost entirely of females. Live-in labour especially in dairy farming remained common before the First World War. Machinery in arable and green crop work had by 1913 reduced the need for labour, and this had affected the numbers of casual Irish migrant workers; such changes were partially offset by the increasing number of market garden farms and the demand for dairy products. Dairying needed part-time labour to milk, and some at least of that was done by married labourers' wives (Royal Commission 1919, II: 67, 68; Mutch 1980: 334, 336; Whetham 1978: 59).

Farm wages remained comparatively high in the region compared to elsewhere, but the same industrial competition for labour that kept up wages also taught farmworkers about overtime payments and the value of Saturday afternoons off work. These were the main demands which strikers on south-west Lancashire farms in 1913 achieved. Their success measures a number of changes in rural society. First, in contrast to earlier periods of discontent, a trade union recruited many labourers as members, including Irish migrants who might otherwise have been used as strike breakers. Second, the farm workers received effective support from non-agricultural workers in the rural community: the railways, which we saw in Chapter 3 creating jobs, for example in rural Marbury, brought with them residents who did not depend on agriculture, men who had the ability to cut the Lancashire farmers off from their markets. Liverpool dockers also acted to help the farmworkers but the railwaymen's support was vital. Rural communities were no longer dominated by farm employers. One thing which did not change was the reluctance of great estates to accept a role for 'outside' influences in their community and on their estates. (Mutch 1980: 339ff). Other strikes in north Cheshire and on the market gardening area of the Wirral were also successful (Whetham 1978: 62).

Such issues were still alive in Cheshire after the war. Labourers, it was argued, were no longer willing to work as required, but wanted set hours; the 1913 strike should caution us against too readily explaining such changes in attitude by reference to wartime experience, as some employers' evidence before the 1919 Royal Commission argued. Wartime conditions no doubt helped to push up wages, to as much as 50s. for a 54-hour week plus house and garden and cheap milk, in 1919 in Cheshire, compared to about 20s. a week for a 13-hour day before the war. Live-in labour continued to be used, and more of it was needed, the farmers argued, because wives in the community were unwilling to milk now that their men were better paid (Royal Commission 1919, II: 39, 40, 41, 43, 47–8, 59, 61, 63, 67–8).

Country villages did have more to offer those with leisure time, most obviously in activities in the village hall, and in village sports teams. Oulton Park Cricket Club started on the lawn in front of Oulton Hall in 1865, and with two members of the Grey-Egerton family playing for it before the First World War, it perhaps personified the old order in rural society (*Cheshire Times*, II, no. 7). Those who could travel found a gradually widening circle of entertainment: farmer Alfred Barber from Higher Whitley, Cheshire, went to Belle Vue (Manchester) in August 1884, but in the country, at Ormskirk for example in 1913, the delights of the Picturedrome might be accompanied by a visit to the fried fish dealer (Barber MSS; Kelly 1913)! Of the small country towns studied in Chapter 3 (see p. 155), Colne must be considered urban (see Table 4.3); the others had all increased in population size by 1911. Banks, schools and at least one hospital were available in Nantwich and Ormskirk; Sandbach lacked a hospital but all had at least one fried fish dealer. Each also offered a variety of industries to supplement their connections with the surrounding countryside and large public rooms to host balls and other functions. Even small towns like Garstang, Malpas (both Rural District Councils) and Tarporley (an Urban District Council) could provide public halls seating 400 to 600 people and banking services through agencies or sub-branches. Hornby no longer had much claim to be a town, though it was the place where Lunesdale Rural District Council and the Poor Law Union Board met and its population of only 439 could bank for three-quarters of an hour on a Friday evening in the church school. The web of railways and omnibus services meant an enormous decrease in travelling time between rural places, and from the countryside to the urban centres. The ubiquitous cycle agencies provided the support for another means of country transport (Kelly 1913 and 1914).

Agriculture

The reclamation of waste culminated in the enclosure of Carrington Moss, though farmers had for long nibbled away at its edges; some 1,013 acres of rough shooting were brought into cultivation by 1897 (A. D. M. Phillips 1980). Pipe drainage also continued, though the onset of the agricultural depression, which lasted from 1879 until well into the 1890s, eventually reduced such investment (Perry 1973: 115; G. Rogers 1986: 260).

Tenure changed only slowly after 1870: annual leases became more common, with fewer restrictions on the farmers, though covenants controlling rotations and the ploughing of permanent grass still appeared in Cheshire leases dated 1918 (Barber MSS; Fletcher 1961: 96). In the 1890s Lancashire rents fell by between 7 and 25 per cent, but any gain for farmers had to be offset against declining prices (G. Rogers 1986: 262–3). By 1900, Cheshire rents were probably stagnant at about £2 an acre (Mercer 1963: 7). On the Fylde there was continuity of tenure, if tenants would stay in the adverse conditions which strained relationships between lord and tenants; pressure for increased compensation for improvements and for tenant-right came at a financially awkward time for landlords (G. Rogers 1981: 336, 361, 363). In the first two decades of the twentieth century the sale of tenanted farms in both counties began to reverse the long-established dominance of great estates over agricultural land, and whereas 90 per cent of Cheshire had been occupied by tenants about 1900, a quarter of that land had been sold to owner-occupiers by 1920 (Mercer 1963: 17; Sturmey 1955: 260). Interest on the capital to make such purchases might exceed the rent previously paid, except perhaps where sitting tenants were given very favourable terms, so putting farm costs up. 'Pleasure' farmers who were not primarily interested in profit, and Cooperative Wholesale Societies (who sometimes engrossed holdings) emerged as new types of farm owners (Royal Commission 1919, II: 45, 49). Cheshire was a county of small-size farms, as Table 4.6 shows. Many

Table 4.6 Cheshire: size of holdings 1919

Acreage	No.	%		
1–5	3,139	26		
5–20	3,480	29	}	46%
20–50	2,148	18		
50–100	1,715	14		
100–150	931	8	}	27%
150–300	701	6		
300+	76	0.6		
	12,190			

Source: Royal Commission 1919, III: 56.

dairy farms in eastern Lancashire were small, as were the increasingly numerous market gardens in both counties, though on the outskirts of Liverpool and Southport, small farms fell prey most easily to builders (Mutch 1980: 336). On the Fylde farms were small, though at Lytham there were twenty-four of over fifty acres each by 1892 (G. Rogers 1981: 157). These proportions were close to the national distribution of holdings by size (Whetham 1978: 45). The smallest holdings were often for the accommodation of horses; those below fifty acres might have been managed with family labour alone.

Small Lancashire farms producing pigs, poultry, potatoes, fruit and vegetables flourished where they were well connected to population centres; in Cheshire, Wallasey produced vegetables for Liverpool, and Sale and Altrincham grew them for Manchester. Fletcher termed the east Lancashire dairy farmers mere 'cowkeepers', recognizing the Fylde as the large-scale dairy farming area, and identifying stock farming as important in the north of the county. By 1914 there was more grass than arable in Lancashire as a whole, but in south-west Lancashire green and grain crops for local urban markets increased in acreage after 1900. In that year corn and root crops were most important in north Cheshire, with temporary grass in the rotation. The Wirral (except Wallasey) and mid-Cheshire had less corn and roots and more grass, while south Cheshire was dominated by permanent grass. Here cheese production remained important, chiefly because the farms were ill served for the milk markets (Mercer 1963: 18–19; Fletcher 1961: 78–9; Porter 1976: 144; Mutch 1980: 331; Orwin and Whetham 1964: 284; Rogers 1986: 214; Whetham 1978: 34). The state's extension of grain growing in both counties after 1917 proved only temporary (Mercer 1963: 16; Whetham 1978: 115, 141). There was of course an element of competition between the different areas of the region, notably so when Cheshire began to overproduce milk. In 1879 an Ormskirk dealer listed Cheshire, as well as Cornwall and Jersey, potatoes among his competitors for the Manchester new potato market, and Ormskirk new potatoes ceased to be quoted there after 1880 (Mutch 1980: 264–5).

Everywhere, farming methods and the marketing of produce changed. Machinery, chiefly reapers, binders, threshers and fertilizer spreaders, became more common; Kelly's Directory chose to emphasize those agricultural contractors with threshers (Kelly 1896; Mercer 1963: 16). However, especially in the dairying and market gardening areas of the region, manual labour remained vital; changes leading to higher labour costs were discussed above (p. 235). New types of grassland seed were introduced, in part through the zeal of individuals such as James Hunter of Chester who was in touch with agricultural research outside the region (Mercer 1963: 19). The potato-wart testing station at Ormskirk was an example of new work to combat the growing problem of potato disease in the region (Orwin and Whetham 1964: 355). Potato men were using new machinery and sprays (Mutch 1980: 334;

Royal Commission 1919, III: 40, 54). The Large White pig herd at Worsley was one example of continuing landlord interest in farming, but farmers were becoming more independent of landlord influence as they combined together to argue their own interests. Cheshire was especially vociferous: its Chamber of Agriculture was set up in 1868, and Cheshire evidence was much more prominent than that of Lancashire to the 1919 Royal Commission on agriculture. Tenant farmer organizations sprang up later (see p. 234). Some farmers established their own agent in Manchester to sell milk, thus cutting out middlemen, and the Cheshire, Shropshire and North Wales Farmers' Supply Association was located in Nantwich by 1896. Despite their interest in state guarantees and cooperation, there was emphasis on the individual farmer's managerial skills and responsibilities by witnesses before the 1919 Commission, perhaps prompted by inept state intervention in milk, potato and corn production (Kelly 1896; Royal Commission 1919, II, III *passim*; Mercer 1963: 22, 23; Orwin and Whetham 1964: 365; Whetham 1978: 53, 110, 111, 115).

Cheshire, and to a lesser extent Lancashire, enjoyed a reputation for dairy farming though many farmers sold more than one product. For example, Alfred Barber at Higher Whitley in 1884 sold cheese to Manchester and butter locally; surprisingly there is no evidence of milk sales in his diary. He reared fat calves and cows for the local butchers and sold oats (as far away as Manchester), bought store pigs in Warrington and sold fat pigs in Culcheth. He grew early, main crop and late potatoes from Scottish seed, which were sold to the Manchester Cooperative Society and to merchants in Oldham (Barber MSS). Even after artificial feeds became widely used dairy men used their arable for fodder (Royal Commission 1919, eg II: 59; III: 93, 95). The 1901 Milk and Dairies Order began to pressure farmers to protect the quality of their milk on the farm; it could be further adulterated by the journey to the railway station, by the motion of the trains, and of course it could be soured by heat (Whetham 1978: 25). Water cooling was an obvious precaution that was in use by 1919 (Royal Commission 1919, II: 63). The region combined well to improve standards when Manchester City Council's decision to buy tuberculosis free milk from tested cows stimulated work in Cheshire which culminated in 1921 with the establishment at Tilstone of a tested herd (Mercer 1963: 23–4). Although Lancashire farmers supplied much milk to the towns, Manchester, Liverpool and the Wirral consumed about 80 per cent of Cheshire's milk in 1915 (Porter 1976: 145). Chester and Preston were the main cheese marketing centres; production of a high quality product continued to earn premium prices just as it had in earlier centuries, although now competition at the bottom end of the market was massive (Whetham 1978: 22). Cheese was important, for it could help to absorb overproduction, whether of a seasonal or annual nature. Cheshire was overproducing in the 1890s and depots which could both sell milk as liquid or in other forms were developed; at best they did not lose money. More specialist consumers of milk were factories like that of the Anglo-Swiss Condensed Milk Co. at Middlewich, which could address the very lowest levels of the urban milk market (Kelly 1896; Mercer 1963: 21–2; Whetham 1978: 24). The industry generated a trade in cattle as newly calved cows were bought for milk, and dry animals and calves sold for slaughter; again, railway communications helped locate the cattle auctions (Porter 1976: 146).

Despite problems with disease, with yet more competition from overseas (for example, the Jersey potato), with over-production, and with inept state regulation, farming appears to have been generally successful, though some individuals fared disastrously. Pastoral Cheshire is thought to have suffered the least of all England in the depression of the 1880s and 1890s. Lancashire, with its concentration on dairy, pig and poultry for the local markets has also been pronounced well insulated against a depression to which cereal producers were most vulnerable. However, in both counties, the lack of investment and the prosperity of previous decades contrasted starkly with the 1880s and 1890s, and the rising numbers of bankruptcies among farmers was alarming. Economic adversity may have driven a wedge between lord and tenant (Fletcher 1961; Mutch 1980: 303–4; Perry 1970: 115, 134, 137, 140; Porter 1976: 147; G. Rogers 1986: 250–1, 260). Cheshire men found wartime farming remunerative, but were afraid for the future in 1919 (Royal Commission 1919, II: 39, 61). The number of Cheshire farmers in 1921 was roughly constant compared to 1871 (if the census figures compare like with like) as Table 4.7 shows; there had also been an increase in the number of nurserymen/gardeners. Lancashire (the pre-1974 county) had witnessed a more modest percentage increase in nurserymen, and a noticeable decline in the number of farmers.

Table 4.7 Farmers and nurserymen in 1871 and 1921

	Farmers/graziers			*Nurserymen/gardeners*		
	1871	*1921*	*% ch.*	*1871*	*1921*	*% ch.*
Cheshire	7,878	7,489	−5	2,724	7,179	+164
Lancashire	18,051	14,690	−17	6,275	9,729	+55

Notes: Nurserymen and gardeners are separate categories in 1871 but not in 1921; figures for males and females have been conflated.

Source: Decennial census.

Transport

Food from the local farms, or imported from the other side of the world, raw materials, and finished products were all transported by cart, canal boat, rail wagon, coaster and eventually motor vehicle; people went a few miles to market on the omnibus, or even walked. Yet in the land of King Cotton it is probably sensible to start a survey of transport at Liverpool's waterside. New steamship routes added to the trade of the region, especially with the opening of the Suez Canal; the virtual American monopoly of cotton supply could now easily be shared with the Far East. Cotton, however, declined as a proportion of Liverpool's imports (valued at current prices) from 40 per cent to 30 per cent as grain, rubber, wool, copper, and tin became relatively more important. The old staples of sugar and tobacco met a similar fate. As might be expected, cloth dominated exports, with heavy engineering and especially railway goods, and the port's re-export trade to Europe of raw materials also expanded (Hyde 1971: 95–6, 98–9).

Bigger and better designed ships, accommodated in more and larger docks (some seven miles of river frontage by 1913), more imposing passenger liners (Plate 4.3), the fierce entrepreneurship of such as Alfred Jones, who for a time enjoyed a monopoly of shipping, lighterage, and credit facilities in West Africa, and aggressive competition despite the existence of English and foreign shipping cartels, all combined to reduce freight charges. These were perhaps the great days of the port (Hyde 1971: 101, 106, 126). Yet even the railways could not overcome the fears of south-east Lancashire concerns that freight and shipping companies exploited them. There was a case to answer: in 1881 large road carriers were offering to undercut the railways by 25 per cent for horse-drawn loads with a guaranteed minimum of 1,000 tons per week from Liverpool docks to Manchester warehouses (Kellett 1969: 196). The Liverpool–Manchester rail link which had, by its success, revolutionized inland carriage, had fallen victim to the disease it was meant to cure. Neither a reduction of 10 per cent for leading classes of freight in 1885 nor modified terminal charges at Liverpool could assuage south-east Lancashire's leaders. After the Manchester Ship Canal opened, competition in the port became even more fierce, and from 1905 the decline in Dock Board receipts in comparison with the earnings of shipping companies shows the impact of the port of Manchester (Hyde 1971: 138–9).

Proposals for a sea route to Manchester were made in 1824, 1838 and 1840 when surveys showed that such a canal was feasible (D. Owen 1977: 107). In 1852–3, it was claimed, Liverpool dues amounted to £115,000 clear of expenses of which only £4,770 were spent on the port; high river, canal and railway freight charges were a continual source of complaint. By 1876 it was said to be cheaper to bring goods from Hull by rail than from Liverpool and George Hicks wrote a letter to the *Manchester Guardian* which stimulated a new initiative strengthened by the depression of the 'cotton corners' of 1879 and 1881. This time the proposal found a determined and influential leader, Daniel Adamson of Hyde, who initiated two surveys of which that of Leader Williams for a canal with locks found approval. The Manchester committee then entered 'the most protracted struggle ever known in the

history of Private Bill legislation' and, after two failures, obtained the Act for the canal in August 1885 (Farnie 1980: 157; D. Owen 1977: 113). The optimistic belief that small local subscriptions would raise the £9 million needed for the purchase of the Bridgewater Canal and the construction of the cut proved false. Indeed, even after Baring and Rothschild had taken up £4 million of preference shares, it was still necessary for the Corporation of Manchester to lend £5 million before the canal was completed in 1894 at a total cost of £15.25 million. Some sixteen thousand men and ninety-seven steam excavators had carved a twenty-six foot deep canal for sea-going vessels with locks, swing and high-level bridges and aqueduct for thirty-five and a half miles from Eastham to Salford (Ashmore 1982: 21). The old dream had been realized.

The opposition from Liverpool, the railway companies and the shipping lines that had delayed the Act for the canal did not end with its completion. The effects of this hostility are perhaps over-emphasized in Plate 4.4, but it certainly diminished both cargoes and revenues and prevented Manchester from becoming the major port for incoming cotton and outgoing cloth and yarn and from drawing in the anticipated trade (D. Owen 1977: 119–20; Farnie 1980: 176–81). Nevertheless the canal made Manchester a customs port which embraced the whole canal to Eastham, absorbed the port of Runcorn and took in the rivers Mersey and Irwell and the lower reaches of the Weaver. It reduced rates of carriage, railway and port charges and made Manchester a major centre for imports. In 1898 Manchester Liners gave the port its own fleet of vessels trading with north America and, by 1920, the canal was used extensively for the export of coal, salt, textiles and textile machinery and the import of cotton, grain, fruit, timber and lamp oil. (See Farnie 1980 for a full discussion of the economics of the canal.)

One of the bitterest opponents of the Manchester Ship Canal was Sir Humphrey Francis de Trafford, whose Trafford estate, already bounded to the south by the Bridgewater Canal, was cut off to the north by five miles of Ship Canal from Barton to Old Trafford. The building of a sandstone wall ten feet high did little to reconcile him to his new neighbour: in 1893 and 1894 he engaged in abortive negotiations with Manchester Corporation for the sale of his 1,183 acres of park and farm land. In 1896 the Corporation offered £260,000 but this was refused and the estate was sold for £360,000 to the company promoter E. T. Hooley, who resold it to his newly floated Trafford Estates Ltd for £900,000. Initially it was intended to develop it as a superior residential estate but Marshall Stevens, the general manager of the company, persuaded him to shift to industry and, after Hooley resigned as chairman in 1897, he built the world's first industrial estate. From 1897 roads, tramways,

---

Plate 4.3   Liners in the Mersey, *c.* 1917. Looking over Pier Head, with ferry boats in the midground, and a liner at the landing stage. (Source: Cunard 1917.)

railways, sewers, water, light and power were provided, land was sold cheaply for a model village which had 600 houses by 1903; in 1911 Manchester's first airport was built there. Initially the park attracted the warehousing and timber merchants, contractors and carriers linked to the canal and the grain millers and oil installations that also used it. From 1898 it was the new capital-intensive engineering firms that moved in. In 1899 the British Westinghouse Electric Company bought 130 acres and built the United Kingdom's largest engineering works making steam turbines and turbo generators, employing 6,000 by 1903. In 1910 the Ford Motor Company built an assembly plant; during the First World War the estate was in full swing producing munitions, chemicals and aircraft. It then had over 100 firms operating and vacant land fell from 51 per cent in 1915 to 34 per cent in 1921. As early as 1903 there were 12,000 people working in the park.

Trafford Park can be seen, with the Manchester docks, as a nineteenth-century parallel to the eighteenth-century development of the Castlefield basin of the Bridgewater Canal. Both transformed hitherto rural and residential areas into bustling communications, distributive and industrial districts with associated working-class housing and both reached out to an underdeveloped west. Each in its time became a focus for new and growing industries but where Castlefield saw unplanned and uncontrolled growth the Ship Canal district, Trafford Park in particular, had a planned infrastructure which aimed at harmonizing human and industrial needs. The Canal and the Park drew development in Manchester to the west, stimulating growth in Salford, Eccles and above all in Stretford, which grew more rapidly than any other district in the region at the turn of the century. They also revitalized Manchester itself and went hand in hand with a strong revival of municipal confidence and activity which qualify Beatrice Webb's jaundiced view of the Manchester City Council of the period. The Corporation had also through its close support of the Ship Canal conferred benefits on its neighbours; in 1911 for example two-thirds of the shipments of Dobson and Barlow of Bolton went by way of the Canal. Manchester had asserted itself as the leader in the economic life of south-east Lancashire and had staked a claim to the banks of the Mersey to the edge of Liverpool itself. Cotton had been the *raison d'être* of the Canal but significantly, there were few cotton firms at Trafford Park. In 1920 it was the new and technologically advanced engineering industries that took advantage of the new transport link.

As the Ship Canal was under construction the turnpike age in the north-west ended when in November 1890 the last trust in the region, that for the

---

Plate 4.4 The Manchester Ship Canal above Eastham. This photograph, taken as the canal was being completed, shows a tug and lighters steaming down to the Mersey estuary. Later, ocean-going vessels would dwarf the canal works as they headed east for Manchester. (Source: Hetherington 1894.)

Blackburn–Preston road, was not renewed. By the early twentieth century tolls from road users had given way to rates and minor roads were administered by Town, District and Rural District councils, major ones by the County Councils. In Lancashire, roads leading to towns of 25,000 inhabitants were so classified and maintained. (See S. Webb and B. Webb 1920: 192–237 for the decline of turnpikes and change in financing road maintenance.) It was not until after 1920 with Manchester an important car manufacturing centre that road again became a real competitor with rail. By 1860 there were few areas of the region not served by the railway. Gaps in north Cheshire and north Derbyshire were closed in the 1860s and a not conspicuously successful attempt was made to open up the agricultural and coastal districts of the north Fylde with the 1864 Garstang and Knot End railway. There was more success in the Wirral during the 1870s and 1880s (Figure 4.1) (G. O. Holt 1978: 50–5). The railways had taken freight from both road and canal, though the latter remained useful for heavy, bulky and non-perishable cargoes, most falling under the control of the railway companies. The great railway sidings such as Adswood and Dewsnap, Bamfurlong and Lostock Hall, became sub-worlds of ceaseless activity by day and night.

The legacy of unfettered competition was to be found in lines competing for the same limited traffic and in uncoordinated stations. Oldham had five stations by 1862, Southport three separate railways, each with its own terminus from 1884 to 1897, and travellers in other towns found similar difficulties. Many stations were inadequate and badly sited. The first Wigan station, for example, described as a hovel, was replaced in 1860 by one further west and, finally, in 1896 by an improved one to the east (G. O. Holt 1978: 101). The age of great railway engineering feats was not yet over. In 1869 generations of ferries were replaced by the Runcorn high-level bridge, in 1885 the Mersey railway tunnel was constructed, fouled by smoke until the line was electrified in 1903, and the Midland Railway spent £3 million on the Heysham harbour scheme from which voyages to Belfast began in 1904 (G. O. Holt 1978: 236). Electrification, after the pioneering Mersey tunnel work, was introduced on a number of Manchester and Liverpool local lines before the First World War.

In general the railways did little to encourage working-class residence outside the towns: landowners with railway access to the towns preferred more profitable middle-class development and daily rail travel was too expensive for working people. As late as the 1890s there were few people travelling on cheap daily tickets in Manchester, probably under 10,000, and in Liverpool only one-tenth of that number (Kellett 1969: 383, 94). For them the railway was much more a means of temporary escape. The seaside resorts, New Brighton, Southport, Morecambe and, above all, Blackpool were creatures of the railway until the Second World War. In 1919 the Lancashire–Yorkshire railway is said to have carried what was probably the country's heaviest holiday traffic to and from Blackpool, 1 million passengers from the

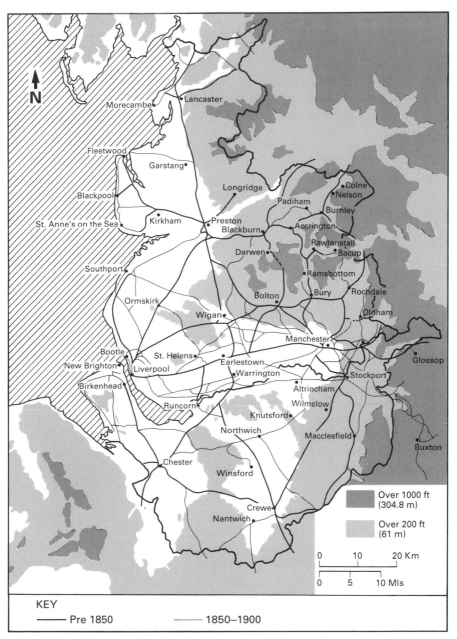

Figure 4.1 The railway network *c.* 1900. In 1900 the internal combustion engine was only just beginning the growth that would eventually eat into the viability of the railways. The map shows the two stages of railway development before and after 1850. It also demonstrates how the railway had filled the gaps left by the earlier phase of canal and turnpike construction. (Sources: Ordnance Survey Lancashire 1904, Ordnance Survey Cheshire 1900 and T. W. Freeman et al. 1966.)

Manchester area, with 130,000 reached on two August weekends (G. O. Holt 1978: 221). But the Wakes was not the only occasion for travel; private or group trips were increasingly popular. Manchester's Belle Vue grew with the railway and did not long outlive its heyday while at Buxton the annual Well Dressing a few days after the railway opened in 1863 brought in 20,000 to 30,000 day trippers by train. What the railway did for regional and national travel the trams did on the local scene. Birkenhead pioneered the use of horse-drawn trams in 1860 but it was at Blackpool that a private company introduced the first electric trams on the promenade in 1885, the system being taken over by the Corporation in 1892 (Ashmore 1982: 19; Walton 1978: 55).

Industry

By 1860 the 369,059 operatives in the cotton mills of the north-west depended principally upon raw cotton from the southern states of the USA, a dependence that brought four years of deprivation when civil war broke out there in 1861 (Return of Cotton Factories 1862, see Farnie 1979: 335–9 for discussion of the returns).

At the end of 1860 and in the first half of 1861 English stocks of both cotton and cloth were high and demand for raw cotton was relatively low. By October 1861, however, partly as a result of a failure of the Confederacy to ship out its cotton before the blockade became effective, some mills were closing and others were going on short time: the Cotton Famine had begun. Faced with mounting unemployment the Boards of Guardians rapidly found themselves in difficulties. Mill workers' wages had been rising in the 1850s but few had been able to save much. Their shares in the cooperative spinning and weaving companies formed since the Companies Act 1856 lost value, some of the companies being forced to wind up. Their accounts at savings banks were quickly withdrawn, reducing deposits in the banks of the cotton towns by over £500,000 between 1861 and 1864. The friendly societies suspended their contributions and Cooperative society sales fell by some £900,000. Their own savings gone, many working people had a choice between destitution and application to the Boards of Guardians. In February 1862 Ashton, Stockport and Preston set up relief committees to succour these people and by the end of 1862 they were established all over the region with a central executive in Manchester (Watts 1866: 132–55).

Even with the assistance of the relief committees, which depended upon voluntary contributions and which, in 1862, spent one and a half times as much as the Boards of Guardians, the latter were forced into huge rate increases. In December 1862 485,434 people were relieved, close to 50 per cent of the people of the cotton districts, and their poverty dragged down many of the shopkeepers and others who depended on their expenditure (Table 4.8). Coal-mining, mill engineering and other service trades also de-

Table 4.8 Numbers relieved by the Guardians and relief committees (November each year)

	1861	1862	1863	1864	1865
Ashton	1,827	56,363	23,568	20,638	1,417
Barton	663	3,910	1,230	1,220	896
Blackburn	4,110	38,104	9,457	10,012	4,083
Bolton	3,200	19,525	8,013	6,543	3,166
Burnley	1,503	17,502	3,016	6,948	1,557
Bury	1,782	20,926	10,048	15,113	2,932
Chorley	1,350	7,527	3,409	2,471	1,155
Chorlton	2,042	15,367	9,984	5,694	3,993
Clitheroe	624	1,379	976	1,138	547
Fylde	633	1,282	1,086	771	699
Garstang	567	1,026	696	807	458
Glossop	221	7,605	6,752	3,263	195
Haslingden	946	17,346	3,340	7,108	1,243
Lancaster	903	1,129	1,025	901	789
Leigh	636	2,722	1,091	901	806
Macclesfield	2,158	5,609	2,775	2,429	2,319
Manchester	4,678	52,477	13,818	9,035	5,046
Oldham	1,622	28,851	8,371	9,164	1,892
Preston	4,805	49,171	17,489	13,226	2,377
Prestwich	601	4,794	11,958	1,078	593
Rochdale	2,060	24,961	8,132	6,243	1,789
Saddleworth	237	2,414	1,287	988	261
Salford	2,507	16,663	5,600	3,600	2,265
Skipton	1,902	2,635	1,856	2,030	1,354
Stockport	1,674	34,612	10,661	8,593	1,189
Todmorden	795	7,590	1,689	2,696	668
Warrington	1,131	1,992	1,416	1,458	1,220
Wigan	2,360	14,959	11,527	5,855	3,538
Total	47,537	458,441	170,268	149,923	48,267

Source: Watts 1866: 451.

clined and many small cotton masters were ruined or forced into retirement. In these circumstances poor rate increases of 1,500 per cent as at Glossop or 1,600 per cent at Ashton were required but could not be collected while the same factors reduced the ability of the relief committees to raise money locally. It was against this background that a 'Lancashire Lad' wrote to *The Times* and to the Lord Mayor of London in April 1862, as a result of which the Mansion House Fund was set up. Between May 1862 and June 1865 it sent £508,806 to the north, channelled mainly through the central executive of the relief committee in Manchester. The Boards of Guardians still needed assistance; in 1862 they were given powers to borrow and seek help from other Unions in their counties. In July 1863 they were allowed to borrow from the Public Works Loans Commissioners for local improvement; some 90 places took out 150 separate loans totalling £1.85 million. All over the region cotton operatives took to pick and shovel in the making of new streets and highways, in laying sewers and the building of waterworks (Watts 1866: 112–31).

During 1863 there was a marked fall in numbers relieved caused first by tighter organization and later by improvements in employment (Table 4.8). American cotton was very expensive but millowners were experimenting with mixtures of Egyptian, Indian and Chinese cotton, often very dirty, fraudulently packed and difficult to spin and weave (Ashmore 1972: 112; Lamb 1866, II: 336–8). These 'Surat' and other eastern cottons did provide work for the operatives though they bitterly cursed the difficulties of working it and the low wages it brought. The arrival of the first loads of American cotton in 1864 and 1865 was greeted with rapturous processions and celebrations in the cotton towns (eg Scott et al. 1973: 77).

The response of the operatives to distress was unlike that of twenty years earlier. Instead of sullen bitterness, hostility and riot they faced hardship with dignity and stoicism apart from some riotous behaviour at Stalybridge and Preston and relatively minor squabbles at Glossop, Stockport and Manchester. A close observer, the Anglican clergyman Robert Lamb, noted in late 1862 that the workers did not blame the government nor did they feel that Britain should intervene between the belligerents (Lamb 1866, I: 280–1). They did resent the labour test and some, later, objected to labouring on public works on the grounds that it would make their hands unfit for working cotton. Perhaps they would have been less patient had they known that many of the larger millowners were able to maintain profitability right through the war. Liverpool merchants too took advantage of the world shortage of cotton by holding substantial stocks, mainly of Surat, and re-exporting it at inflated prices. Had these re-exports been kept down to 1850s levels then from 1862 to 1865 the Lancashire mills would have been supplied at only one-seventh less than in the 1850s (Farnie 1979: 149–50). It was not so much the dearth of cotton but over-production, speculation and uncertainty, combined with a slow adaptation to Surat, that caused distress for working people.

Not all the millowners were speculators or careless of their workers' needs. Many were active in relief works, in setting up schools for reading and writing or sewing and in providing readings, lectures and entertainments. One employer at Hazel Grove gave provisions and coal directly to his workers as well as contributing to relief committees and remitting cottage rents. Two firms at Newton Moor in Hyde also remitted rents to the amount of £4,000 and there were similar examples across the region. Even so the burden of hardship was very unequally shared yet the general deprivation failed to provoke violent protest, reduced trade union activity to very low levels and gave the working mills a relatively docile if unhappy workforce.

For most of the middle class the patchwork of Guardians and charitable relief was enough but Edmund Potter the great calico printer and Radical Liberal proposed that the state should maintain the unemployed so that they would be in good heart and working condition when trade revived. Robert Lamb's view of this was the conventional one

> Mr. Edmund Potter's scheme . . . is one of the many illustrations we have, how a man clever in the details of his own business seems to get bewildered when he steps into the wider area of social politics.
>
> (Lamb 1866, I: 339)

It would have been instructive to hear the comments of the overlooker that Edwin Waugh spoke to in Blackburn in 1862. He had a family of thirteen, with three children under the age of ten and seven of the family working in the mill. Before the Cotton Famine the family income had been 80s. per week but Waugh found them living on 6s. a week from the relief fund (Waugh 1881, *M/C Examiner 1862*: 22–3). Many such left their towns, some left the country, 50,000 in 1862, and others gave up cotton for hatting or some other trade (Farnie 1979: 157–62). Despite slower overall population growth in the 1860s some cotton towns were still growing at a rapid rate. In Oldham the expansion of Hibbert and Platt's textile engineering works from 3,500 in 1859 to 7,000 in 1871, in Blackburn the weaving of new cloths for India on locally improved dobby looms, and in Rochdale the shift to wool that increased employment in that branch in Lancashire from 9,227 in 1861 to 17,180 in 1870, all helped growth (Farnie 1979: 159–60). Blackburn, Bolton, Burnley, Oldham, and Rochdale all grew by proportions equal to or in excess of the whole county.

The Cotton Famine tested other national views about the character of north-western life. Lancashire had a high illegitimacy rate, 7.27 per cent against 6.99 per cent for England and Wales in the 1850s but it increased only slightly in the cotton towns during the bleak years – 5,408 such births in 1861, then for succeeding years 5,706, 5,735 and, in 1864, 5,536. Nor was the high Lancashire rate necessarily a sign of immorality. The nineteenth-century cotton towns had proportionately fewer prostitutes than resorts, ports or agricultural towns and the proportion of women engaged in prostitution fell during the years 1860 to 1863. Crime also decreased, though Lancashire still had a higher proportion of female criminals than the generality of England and Wales (Watts 1866: 348–55).

During the Cotton Famine unemployment and reduced wages pulled standards of living down to very low levels. Operative families in good times spent an average of 2s. 7½d. per head each week on food alone but the Guardians offered only one to two shillings per head per week; in October

1863 the Central Relief Committee's scale ran from 3s. 6d. for a single person to 14s. for a man, wife and six children. Marriages in the cotton districts fell from 19,155 in 1861 to 16,263 in 1862 then rose to 18,233 before falling back to 17,490 in 1864. The birth rate showed little change – 2.57 per 1,000 in 1861, 2.68 in 1862 and 2.66 in 1863 – but the general death rate fell in 1862 and, after an epidemic in 1863, fell again in 1864. The infant death rate was even more significant; in the four years 1861 to 1864 it was recorded at 184, 166, 170 and 163. This progressive improvement, interrupted only by the epidemic year, has been attributed to two major factors: the presence at home of mothers who would normally have been in the mill and the increased sobriety of parents who had little money for tippling (Hewitt 1958: 101–20). It may well be that a fall in child minding coupled with an increase in breast feeding resulted in safer and better nutrition for babies.

After the distress of the Cotton Famine and three depressed years that followed it the cotton industry settled again to a high level of production against a background of fierce competition with cyclical disturbances in 1877–9, 1884–5 and 1891–3. Consumption of cotton rose from 1,075 million pounds in 1870 to 2,178 million in 1913 before the dislocation of the First World War. Cloth exports rose from 3,267 million linear yards in 1870 to a peak of 7,073.5 million in 1913, the value rising from £71.4 million in 1870 to £126.5 million. Cotton was no longer as dominant as it had been in 1830, when it represented 50.7 per cent of all British exports, but it still remained very important at 24.1 per cent (Sandberg 1974: 4).

Table 4.9 Mills by function

| | Combined mill | | Specialist spinning | | Specialist weaving | |
	mills	*employees (ave.)*	*mills*	*employees (ave.)*	*mills*	*employees (ave.)*
1850	436	310	517	108	196	100
1890	357	429	596	165	793	188

Source: Kenny 1975: 141.

The organization of the industry had changed as it developed. In the mid-nineteenth century there were few specialized weavers but by 1890 the balance had shifted (Table 4.9). As can be seen, the combined mills were much larger employers than the specialists and some were giants (Plate 4.5).

Plate 4.5 Butts Mill, Leigh. Butts Mill, designed by E. A. H. Stott of Stott and Sons with machinery by Dobson and Barlow, was built for the Butts Spinning Company in 1907. It used Egyptian cotton and in 1912 had 95,376 twist mule spindles and 36,452 weft spindles with about 400 workers in 1919. It closed in 1959.

Horrocks, Crewdson & Co., for example, was founded by John Horrocks, a spinner from Bolton, at Preston in 1791 as a one horse-power spinning mill but it developed into the largest spinning firm in the world from 1799 to the 1830s and by 1920 employed over 6,000 workers at Preston, Moses Gate at Bolton and the Piccadilly warehouse. The weekly output of cloth was then over 600 miles long (Amalgamated Cotton Mills Trust Limited, intr.; Farnie and Yonekawa 1988: 172). But, as Table 4.9 shows, combined mills were declining in number as specialist spinners and, even more, weaving firms grew.

These changes were accompanied by geographic shifts. Already by the 1880s Manchester was in relative decline as a manufacturing centre, along with north-east Cheshire and north-west Derbyshire. South-east Lancashire had become dominant in spinning: Oldham, specializing in the coarser yarns, was the largest centre with 24 per cent of Lancashire's spindles; Bolton, the fine spinning centre, had 11 per cent. The other major spinning districts were Manchester, Preston, Ashton, Stockport, Rochdale, Blackburn, Leigh and Mossley, where the firm of John Mayall took over from Horrocks, Miller as the world's largest spinner before 1857, a position it kept until the late 1880s (Farnie and Yonekawa 1988: 173). Weaving showed a dramatic increase in the Nelson, Colne and Burnley districts and combined manufacture at Preston, Chorley and Blackburn.

The early mills had been founded and managed by individuals, men of the stamp of Arkwright, Oldknow, Peel, Ashton or Horrocks. From the 1820s to the 1860s the family and the partnership were the normal forms of ownership with successful dynasties rising to rival and sometimes overshadow the local gentry. During the 1850s cooperative associations of producers were set up under the Industrial and Provident Society Act 1852 with the intention of enabling working men both to control their own working lives and to share in the profits of their industry. They quickly lost egalitarian principles and evolved into capitalistic joint-stock companies with small shareholders. Oldham, which had been a comparatively late starter in the factory system with turbulent relations in the early nineteenth century, provided the great exemplar. In 1858 working men there set up a cooperative which in 1862 built the Sun Mill for spinning and weaving. Originally conceived as a producers' association it became a highly successful spinning company with small shareholders drawing good dividends and paying close attention to its management and operations. This use of low denomination shares and democratic voting became the pattern for further flotations which established the 'Oldham Limiteds' as attractive investments for working people. The 1877–9 depression, however, sent them back to more traditional and secure ways of employing their savings (Farnie 1979: 248–66).

The Oldham Limiteds built new mills but other companies were formed to take over existing mills and family concerns took advantage of companies legislation to limit their liability by registering as private companies. Oldham became the centre for joint-stock spinning with Oldham entrepreneurs, architects and contractors active in promoting it not only there but also in other districts (Plate 4.5). Weaving, which required much less capital and could be established in rented premises, had many more individuals or small partnerships splitting away from cooperatives and these were to be found further north, in Blackburn, Burnley, Nelson and Colne. This comparative ease of entry into weaving combined with lower technical requirements made it possible to take advantage of the cheaper labour there, much of it drawn from agriculture (Kenny 1975: 162–3). It also produced much fiercer competition in weaving and the 'cooperative capitalist' became a target for heavy criticism in the *Cotton Factory Times*, for example on 8 August 1890:

> They are driving the trade from the country
> With their shoddy and white china clay
> For the warps the weavers can't weave them
> Though enveloped in steam all the day.
>
> *Cotton Factory Times*, 8 August 1890

Faced with the heavy competition and recurrent slumps of the late nineteenth century, mills and companies began to draw together in trusts and amalgamations during the 1880s and 1890s. J. & P. Coats, English Sewing Cotton and the Fine Cotton Spinners' Association, the latter with over 2.5 million spindles, 2 million more than its nearest rival, were all established during this period. At a lower level, many smaller but thriving concerns were buying or building mills and expanding their businesses. From 1900 a new boom brought new mills and new concerns in many parts of the region but especially north of Manchester. Fortunes could be made in a few years by men with capital even though they lacked real knowledge of or concern for the industry (Bowker 1928: 9–11).

The First World War brought restrictions for the cotton trade but increased its profitability, 1918 bringing the highest profit for any year on record (Bowker 1928: 33). Peace released a flood of pent-up orders and 1919 and 1920 saw spinning and weaving profits rise to extraordinary heights which induced a state of euphoria culminating in a great wave of re-flotations and re-capitalization of mill companies. All involved a greatly increased shareholding based on the belief that the high profits would continue. The cotton trade seemed to have entered a new golden age (Bowker 1928: 37).

The importance of textiles is clear from Tables 4.10 and 4.11. Many of the region's towns and districts were dominated by cotton, as Table 4.11 demonstrates. In all some 11.2 per cent of the population of Lancashire and 6 per cent of that of Cheshire worked in the textile trades, 10.8 per cent across the region with dependence on cotton very great in some of the towns and districts. As in earlier times, between one-quarter and one-third of women in the mills were wives or widows and at any one time some 60,000 to 80,000 children under five probably had mothers who worked in the mills (estimates based on Hewitt 1958: 14–17, 45, 107).

Table 4.10   Employment in textile manufacture 1871 and 1901

1871[1]	Lancashire and Cheshire		
	Male	*Female*	*Total*
Cotton & flax	176,471	252,205	428,676
Wool & worsted	10,393	7,930	18,323
Silk	12,577	22,070	34,647
Mixed	12,836	7,131	19,967
Total	212,277	289,336	501,613
1901[2]	*Lancashire*	*Cheshire*	*Derbyshire*
Cotton spinning	123,525	15,143	3,386
Cotton weaving	275,449	16,991	6,998
Cotton unspecified	37,561	2,738	1,374
Cotton finishing	32,064	3,718	2,465
Woollen & worsted	7,889	200	200
Silk	2,679	7,720	662
Hemp	5,093	451	240
Mixed	7,920	1,847	10,370
Flax/linen	3,655	1,761	62
Total	495,865	50,569	26,352
Regional total		572,786	

Sources:
[1] Decennial Census, 1871, III: 11.
[2] Kenny 1975: Table 8.2.

Organization of the cotton workers in trade unions was hampered by the many different skills they practised, by the virtual male monopoly of mule spinning and by the distribution of the trade across the region. Both spinners and weavers wanted to defend or improve their wages, reduce hours and establish better conditions at work. Both followed the same policy of bringing together local associations into federations; the Spinner's Amalgamation had 84 per cent of the mule spinners by 1884 and 40,000 weavers, 28 per cent of the total, belonged to the weavers' association of that year, the number rising to 75,000 by 1892 (Bullen 1984: 20). The object of the associations was to negotiate price lists for work that would, operate across the region, the 'uniform' lists that dominated wage discussions. Other smaller groups in the mills also set up their own associations and in 1899 the United Textile Factory Workers' Association was established with 120,000 members to provide machinery for cooperation. The weavers' associations included both men and women but the spinners' union was male only; females spinning on

Table 4.11   Textile operatives 1921

Definition: All those occupied in textiles – all fibres including cotton, wool and silk; rope making; all branches including spinning, weaving, bleaching, dyeing, printing and ancillaries such as reed making; all persons so occupied in any capacity.

Only those places with 5 per cent or over occupied in textiles have been listed; and Figure 4.2 shows the geography of textile concentrations.

	Occupied population		Occupied in textiles	
	Male	Female	Male	Female
LANCASHIRE				
County boroughs				
Blackburn	41,736	33,416	11,701	24,999
Bolton	60,699	33,555	13,668	19,807
Burnley	35,154	26,051	11,734	20,217
Bury	19,510	12,367	3,699	7,326
Manchester	237,951	126,001	5,907	15,270
Oldham	50,184	29,595	13,504	20,760
Preston	37,925	26,669	6,523	17,084
Rochdale	31,665	19,521	8,638	13,018
Salford	75,982	38,779	3,167	7,117
Warrington	25,788	9,793	216	1,947
Wigan	29,855	12,607	769	5,444
Municipal boroughs and urban districts				
Accrington	15,362	9,629	2,152	6,803
Ashton in Makerfield	7,710	2,297	38	688
Ashton-u-Lyne	14,731	8,783	2,801	5,109
Bacup	7,500	4,651	2,069	2,899
Chadderton	9,954	5,649	3,864	4,567
Chorley	10,054	6,943	2,233	4,898
Colne	8,675	5,821	3,984	4,617
Darwen	12,858	10,471	4,174	8,601
Eccles	14,867	6,724	708	1,882
Farnworth	9,223	5,634	1,927	4,090
Heywood	8,972	6,355	2,824	4,883
Hindley	8,081	3,013	240	1,732
Ince in Makerfield	7,600	2,703	125	1,499
Lancaster	11,874	5,241	367	1,204
Leigh	15,678	7,186	1,807	4,655
Middleton	9,807	5,712	3,672	3,891
Nelson	14,512	10,046	8,582	8,202
Radcliffe	8,593	5,536	2,394	3,680
Rawtenstall	9,785	6,082	3,020	3,504
Swinton & P.	10,134	5,112	806	2,737
Urban areas under 20,000 population				
Abram	2,477	713	21	276
Adlington	1,470	796	333	538
Aspull	2,628	927	49	525
Atherton	6,831	2,990	803	1,568
Audenshaw	2,615	1,463	211	512

Table 4.11   Textile operatives 1921 (*continued*)

	Occupied population		Occupied in textiles	
	Male	*Female*	*Male*	*Female*
Barrowford	1,945	1,378	1,167	1,143
Blackrod	1,289	538	182	315
Brierfield	2,891	2,103	1,699	1,757
Church	2,327	1,572	569	1,261
Clayton Moor	2,905	2,055	603	1,685
Clitheroe	4,037	2,967	1,368	2,215
Crompton	5,202	3,154	2,803	2,603
Croston	662	378	107	283
Denton	6,003	3,646	311	1,080
Droylsden	4,677	2,417	726	1,185
Failsworth	5,943	3,044	1,461	1,844
Fulwood	2,292	998	98	164
Golborne	2,445	763	46	197
Gt Harwood	4,507	3,851	2,254	3,346
Haslingden	6,185	4,216	2,682	3,473
Horwich	5,608	2,217	374	1,152
Hurst	2,637	1,607	676	1,153
Kearsley	3,237	1,849	572	1,306
Kirkham	1,254	800	342	595
Lees	1,622	965	739	748
Leyland	3,133	1,725	458	806
Littleboro	4,128	2,307	1,809	1,692
Lit. Hulton	2,721	1,348	169	1,018
Lit. Lever	1,703	960	322	711
Longridge	1,429	863	327	586
Milnrow	2,945	1,766	1,052	1,390
Mossley	4,441	2,505	2,165	1,992
Norden	1,425	762	557	479
Orrell	2,304	859	45	381
Oswald/le	5,101	3,674	1,534	3,056
Padiham	4,302	3,289	2,803	2,790
Ramsbottom	5,449	3,557	1,843	2,722
Rishton	2,435	1,825	958	1,494
Royton	5,829	3,510	2,962	2,800
Standish	2,541	951	140	453
Tottington	2,126	1,465	642	927
Trawden	1,002	560	584	507
Turton	4,104	2,110	1,463	1,133
Tyldesley	5,466	2,223	299	1,349
Walton Dale	4,079	2,869	1,437	2,330
Wardle	1,521	870	565	573
Westhoughton	5,422	2,319	404	1,523
Whitefield	2,282	1,340	538	643
Whitworth	3,013	2,099	1,274	1,770
Withnell	1,098	722	363	548
Worsley	4,712	2,458	500	1,328
Rural districts				
Blackburn	3,171	1,921	686	1,123

Table 4.11   Textile operatives 1921 (*continued*)

	Occupied population		Occupied in textiles	
	Male	Female	Male	Female
Burnley	6,770	4,127	2,440	3,323
Bury	3,282	1,827	1,001	1,134
Chorley	7,358	3,914	1,185	2,699
Clitheroe	2,218	998	329	378
Fylde	4,296	1,724	281	609
Leigh	3,498	1,407	249	824
Limehurst	3,302	1,513	637	928
Preston	6,675	3,404	576	1,294
CHESHIRE				
County and municipal boroughs				
Congleton	3,623	2,313	756	1,082
Dukinfield	6,481	3,809	1,514	2,627
Stockport	40,370	23,786	6,415	10,291
Hyde	11,216	7,505	2,113	4,364
Macclesfield	10,410	7,995	2,372	3,682
Stalybridge	8,418	5,600	2,404	4,085
Urban districts				
Bollington	1,716	1,046	651	669
Bredbury/Rom	3,162	1,478	291	398
Buglawton	468	242	91	111
Compstall	308	219	82	157
Hazel Grove	3,254	1,645	258	394
Hollingworth	837	554	351	384
Marple	2,107	1,220	414	611
Mottram in Longdendale	962	648	262	448
Yeardsley/Wh.	586	256	133	117
Disley	1,025	435	226	96
Tintwistle	689	395	158	263
DERBYSHIRE (part of High Peak)				
Municipal boroughs				
Glossop	6,798	4,908	2,046	3,398
Urban and rural districts				
New Mills	2,945	1,249	884	628
Chapel en le Frith	5,635	2,036	405	386
Glossop RD	1,249	758	276	440
Hayfield	1,521	619	349	170

Source: Decennial census 1921, HMSO 1923

the ring frames introduced from the USA in the 1880s joined the card room unions.

The spinners were involved in a losing strike at Bolton in 1877 and were also defeated at Oldham in 1885. In 1878 100,000 weavers, mainly in northeast Lancashire, lost a two-month strike marked by the burning down of an employer's house and the deployment of troops. A further spinners' lock-out at Bolton in 1892 encouraged the employers, who were now collaborating in

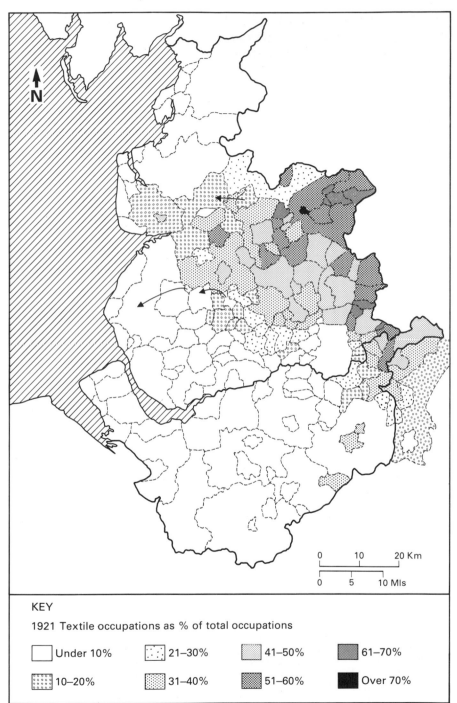

KEY

1921 Textile occupations as % of total occupations

☐ Under 10%	⬚ 21–30%	▨ 41–50%	▨ 61–70%
▨ 10–20%	▨ 31–40%	▨ 51–60%	■ Over 70%

their own associations at Bolton and Oldham, to meet the unions. The result of this was the Brooklands Agreement, which delayed wage claims or reductions, limited their size and set up a joint conciliation committee. The Agreement was much praised but it broke down in 1908 over a wage reduction and was abrogated in 1913 when the union withdrew (Mills 1917: 93–122). The weavers had not been involved. In 1908 they fought a long strike against Ashton Brothers at Hyde over the extended use of American Northrop automatic looms and won an advance of pay but only at the expense of working twenty looms per weaver. This was seen as a clear indication that the union was favouring men against women since the greater productivity would entail job losses and employers were more likely to favour keeping on men than women (Fowler 1986).

By 1860 the bleaching trade had virtually completed its transition to indoor chemical-based operation, the cloth winding quickly through the crofts, drawn by steam power. It remained generally prosperous and, as the century advanced, the bleach-masters, already collaborating in wage negotiations, drew even closer together. In 1900, following the many examples around them, some sixty bleaching and finishing firms amalgamated into the Bleachers' Association. By 1904 it employed 10,780 workers, rising to 14,478 in 1925. Only fourteen of the Association's works lay outside the north-west (Sykes 1925: 36–8).

The calico printing trade remained prosperous until the 1880s, drawing in much new capital under the limited liability legislation which was principally employed in the improvement and mechanization of existing works. Machines increasingly replaced the old block tables and capacity increased to a point where the British printers, overwhelmingly situated in the north-west, could print up to 2,000 million yards a year against a world demand of only 1,200 million. Inefficiency, bribery of colourmen and price cutting combined with large fixed capitals and long credit to produce twenty-five failures between 1889 and 1892 (Turnbull 1951: 121). The solution, as in sewing thread, was amalgamation. Between 1897 and 1899 some 90 per cent of the printing trade grouped itself into three associations: F. Steiner & Co., the United Turkey Red Co., and (the largest) the Calico Printers' Association (CPA). The CPA brought together forty-six printing firms, thirteen in the Glasgow area the rest in the north-west, and thirteen merchant houses in Manchester and Glasgow. Three spinning and weaving concerns with their print works also came in, the association then controlling 277,000 spindles,

---

Figure 4.2 The distribution of textile operatives in 1921. This figure shows the dependence of boroughs and urban and rural districts on the manufacture and processing of textiles in 1921. It includes bleaching, dyeing and printing but excludes the manufacture of textile machinery which made dependence greater especially in Oldham, Blackburn and other eastern towns. (Source: The 1921 Decennial Census. The local government boundaries are those in use before reorganization in 1974, see Figure 5.2.)

6,656 looms and 830 printing machines. In 1902 other textile and engineering firms were drawn on to the committee of management (Turnbull 1951: 436–58).

This period saw improvements in design, particularly of furnishing fabrics springing from the influence of William Morris, though most printers were quick to adopt the new synthetic dyestuffs that Morris rejected. The improvement was not sustained; after 1900 the Art Nouveau movement ended Britain's short period of design leadership.

As the block printers followed the hand-loom weavers into history the machine printers inherited their legacy of long hours, up to seventy-five hours in busy periods, with ancillary workers sometimes working a hundred hours in a week until 1894, when fifty-eight became standard. Wages were good however and the Machine Printers' Union with high benefits and control of apprenticeship never fought a general strike (Turnbull 1951: 210–25). By 1901 the cotton finishing trades employed some 38,000 people, principally in printing (Kenny 1975: Table 8.2).

In 1859 Christys, Britain's most successful hatting company, confounded the domestic bodymakers by introducing American fur and wool forming machines into their Stockport works. They also mechanized the finishing process by the installation of powered lathes. The old felt hatters, already demoralized by the decline of their trade in the previous twenty years, would not work the bodymaking machines and this opened the door not only to men new to the trade but also to women. The felt hatters had already lost their union to the silk hatters, who still worked in small shops and tramped in the old way. They now formed a new union for themselves and a parallel one for the women and, after a long lock-out in the early 1900s, succeeded in unionizing all the north-western works by 1912. By then the trade was changing as the bespoke and specialist hatters of the nineteenth century began to give way to multiple retailers who could exert great influence through their large purchases.

In 1911 there were 12,494 people employed in felt hatting, overwhelmingly in Lancashire and Cheshire. The largest firm, Christys, employed about 1,400 people but the other firms ranged in size from a handful of workers to about 500. Wages were good for the skilled finishers who were all men, less so for the makers, men, women and youths but not lower than in textiles. Both branches were unhealthy, principally from dust in the finishing shops and damp in the plankshops. In 1897 hatters' rates for phthisis were 67 per cent above the average and in 1900 the average age at death of male union members was forty-five years nine months; by 1927 with hours reduced from fifty-five to forty-six this age had risen to sixty-four (J. H. Smith 1980).

Glass and soap making were both established in the region long before 1860 but in the late nineteenth century were entering a period of growth and technical development which made the lower Mersey an attractive site. Glass making had begun its shift towards the north with the use of coal as a fuel in the seventeenth century and by the 1750s there were glasshouses at Warrington, Liverpool and St Helens using local coal and potash imported through Liverpool. Glasshouses were also established at Atherton and Manchester in the mid-eighteenth century (Ashmore 1969: 123–30). The improvement in domestic standards that stimulated the glass industry also influenced the soap trade, which had an additional stimulus in the expansion of textile manufacture with its growing demand for soft soap used in the washing of cloth. Both Manchester and Liverpool shared in the late-eighteenth-century expansion of soap boiling but Liverpool, with its access to Scottish and Irish kelp for alkali and to imported vegetable oils as well as its export advantages, proved to be the most magnetic. By 1820 the Merseyside manufacturers were making twice as much soft soap as London and two-thirds as much hard soap, mainly for export (T. C. Barker and Harris 1954: 223).

Both glass makers and soap boilers needed alkali, the imported sources for which were expensive and unreliable, but in 1822 James Muspratt set up a factory at Liverpool to make soda from common salt under the Leblanc patent. This was the start of a rising demand for salt, a new bed of which had been discovered before 1800. Producers faced English and foreign competition and were prone to over-produce, which led in turn to price-fixing cartels. Cheshire production rose, re-emphasizing the importance of the River Weaver Navigation (Plate 4.6); from 300,000 tons per year in 1823, output reached 1 million in 1850 and 1.75 million in 1876 before starting to decline. Winsford replaced Northwich as the leading producer of salt, accounting for some two-thirds of production in 1888. Middlewich and Sandbach were smaller scale, but active, producers: there were just 69 pans at Sandbach in 1880; a new works was commissioned at Middlewich in 1890. None of the salt producers were large towns compared to the chemical giants of south Lancashire: the populations of Winsford and Northwich stabilized in the early twentieth century at around 20,000. Apart from Boulton and Watt engines for pumps, there was little technological change until the early twentieth century when the new vacuum process of salt manufacture was developed at Winsford; a vacuum plant was built at Runcorn in 1911. From the 1890s both the Brunner, Mond Company at Winnington and Castner-Kellner at Runcorn invested capital in overland pipelines from Northwich to ensure supplies of brine (Ashmore 1982: 11–13, 49, 51, 60, 61; Chaloner 1960: 131–5; 1961: 71, 72).

In the Leblanc process salt and sulphuric acid reacted together, the resulting sodium sulphate being burned with lime and coal to produce crude soda, which was then refined. Muspratt made his own sulphuric acid; water-borne carriage reduced the costs on his other raw materials. His soda being rapidly taken up by the glass makers and soap boilers, he built another works at St Helens with J. C. Gamble before 1830 and was followed by others at St Helens and Widnes, though not all succeeded. Muspratt's initiative gave

Plate 4.6 The British Salt Company, Anderton, 1856. This view from the River Weaver shows both the continuing importance of that navigation and the devastating effects of the salt industry on the local landscape. Paradoxically the old salt spoil heaps now sport orchids in their season.

Merseyside a lead not only in the making of hard soap but also in the heavy chemical industry that developed from his first soda works. The Leblanc works were chiefly set up at Widnes and St Helens and they, with their successors, transformed these quiet communities of farms and cottage industries into busy but grossly polluted industrial concentrations. One of the major drawbacks to the Leblanc process was that it discharged hydrochloric acid into the atmosphere and produced large amounts of alkali waste that had to be dumped. Undesirable apart the chemical reaction when rain brought acid rain and alkali waste together made life almost intolerable. As early as 1827 there were letters in the *Liverpool Mercury* complaining about the blackening of buildings, especially the church of St Martin, on which a correspondent commented

> For my part I don't mind if they [the walls of St Martin's] are as black as Warren's blacking, provided the church is white inside. But I am more concerned for my lungs, and likewise for the minister and congregation.
>
> (Quoted in T. C. Barker and Harris 1954: 226)

A number of cases against alkali manufacturers forced them into the installation of towers for the condensing of hydrochloric gas, invented by William Gossage in 1836, but these were not a complete solution. Brown vegetation and dead trees marked the chemical districts for the rest of the century. Indeed the condensation of hydrochloric acid merely changed the form of pollution for, while some could be used in the manufacture of bleaching powder for the textile trade, much was unused and poured into ditches and drains to find its way to the river. The utilization of waste products faced the industry with a long series of problems and challenges before and after the Alkali Act 1863 (Hardie 1950: 82–112).

At the end of the nineteenth century the Leblanc process gave way to the Solvay process, which used ammoniacal brine and carbon dioxide and was introduced into England by Ludwig Mond in 1872. In 1873 he and Brunner built a works at Winnington, on land bought from an absentee landlord; in 1920 they took over the Castner-Kellner Co. of Runcorn, which made soda by electrolysis, a process allowing developments in aluminium, synthetic ammonia and sodium cyanide. Cheap Solvay soda meant cheaper bleaching powder, which impinged on the Leblanc producers. In 1890 the large Leblanc companies, including three at Widnes, had come together in the United Alkali Company, which in 1900 employed 4,221 people at Widnes (Hardie 1950: 152). The industry had passed from individual entrepreneurs to national combine in little over a hundred years.

As the heavy chemical industry grew and changed, its distribution shifted. Liverpool, which had housed glass, soap and alkali, lost most of its manufacture while vitriol making, widely dispersed in Lancashire – for

example at Wigan, Oldham, Blackburn, Bolton and Manchester in the late eighteenth and early nineteenth centuries – became more concentrated on Merseyside. Warrington had not developed an alkali industry and St Helens (Plate 4.7), the site of early concentration of Leblanc works, became more important in coal-mining and glass manufacture during the later nineteenth century as Widnes, Runcorn and, later, Northwich, became the chemical centres. (See Ashmore 1969, Hardie 1950 and T. C. Barker and Harris 1954 for discussion of these developments.)

In the early nineteenth century soap making was already established at Liverpool, Manchester and Warrington but by mid-century it was Merseyside which had taken the lead with Crosfield's at Warrington among the top 10 per cent of British makers. Later in the century they faced competition from Gossage's Widnes soapworks of 1855 and William Hesketh Lever's Warrington works of 1885. In 1889 Lever moved to his new works at Port Sunlight and despite a long struggle Crosfield's were drawn into that dynamic salesman's empire in 1919. They had pioneered work on the hardening of fats and the refining of vegetable oils which were invaluable to the developing Lever interests. Crosfield's had grown dramatically from 250 employees in the 1850s to 800 in 1896 and 2,500 in 1924 (Musson 1965). By 1920 Lever's controlled 60 per cent of the British soap industry and their only major home competitor was the Cooperative Wholesale Society (CWS) (Plate 4.8; C. Wilson 1954, I: 246–63).

Like soap, glass making was well developed by the mid-nineteenth century with all four types – bottle, plate, crown and flint – being produced in the region. The Ravenhead company dated from the late eighteenth century; a second St Helens crown glass company of 1826, Pilkington's, introduced Belgian workers and new techniques before mid-century. By 1867 William Pilkington could claim, perhaps with some exaggeration, that the town made two-thirds of the country's plate glass and one-tenth of its flint and bottle glass. By 1900 Pilkington's were the chief manufacturers of window glass in Britain and the sole producers of plate glass: glass making rivalled coal-mining as the town's largest employer (Table 4.12; T. C. Barker and Harris 1954: 202–22, 356–66, 447–52).

Widnes had a population of only 2,209 in 1841 and growth was not remarkable until the period 1865–75, when it doubled to some 20,000, almost entirely because of the shift of the alkali industry from St Helens (Hardic 1950: 64). By 1892 there were fourteen Leblanc works in Widnes and four in Runcorn employing 6,093 men to produce the Widnes described in *Pearson's Magazine* in 1896:

Plate 4.7   Kurtz Alkali works, Sutton, near St Helens, *c.* 1890. The coal and chemical towns, newer than the cotton towns, exceeded them in squalor chiefly because of the sprawling nature of the works, the spoil heaps and the corrosive pollution of air, water and land that the industry engendered. (Source: Catalyst: The Museum of the Chemical Industry.)

Plate 4.8 The Soap Trust, 1906. In 1906 William Lever won a great libel action against Associated Newspapers following a campaign that they had mounted against his reducing the weight of tablets of soap during a period of rising raw material prices. This *Daily Mirror* cartoon is typical of the vitriolic nature of the press campaign.

Table 4.12   Industrial employment in St Helens, 1882 and 1901

	1882	*1901*
Coal-mining	3,000	over 6,000
Glass works	3,764	6,255
Chemicals	1,132	1,077
Metal working	900	1,300

Source: T. C. Barker and Harris 1954: 451.

> Widnes is picturesque by the excess of its ugliness. . . . Squalid
> cottages, large areas of muddy waste, with a pigsty here and there, and
> perhaps a gipsy's van in a desert of puddles and mud; black alleys,
> intricate gangways over an intricate network of railways, high
> chimneys on every side, and below these such grotesque shapes of
> towers and bubbling cauldrons and tanks and wheels, as seem the very
> nightmare of industrialism.
>
> (Quoted in Hardie 1950: 108)

The Merseyside towns were created largely by immigration and they were
very different from those of textile Lancashire. The early mill towns could
draw on much local enterprise from the yeomen, clothiers or putters-out just
as they had already a pool of native spinners and weavers. They also grew by
the absorption of the small communities of domestic workers into urban
networks that kept some traditional patterns. The soap entrepreneurs – Gossage, Hudson, Crosfield and Lever – were British as were the glass manufac
turers. In the heavy chemical industry and in dyestuffs, however, the leading
role as the industries developed was taken by men with continental backgrounds. Some were born abroad, like Alfred Mond, who arrived in England
from Germany in 1862, Ivan Levinstein, who set up in Manchester in 1864,
and Charles Dreyfus, who founded Clayton Aniline about 1881. Others, such
as John Tomlinson Brunner, born at Everton in 1839, were of continental
extraction and Henry Roscoe is a leading example of the many British scientists and technologists who had received a scientific education in Germany or
Switzerland. Most of the chemical firms relied heavily on men with continental experience or training. Brunner-Mond, in particular, developed a scientific
community at their Winnington Hall headquarters that brought together
British and continental chemists. These men were of high profile in local
society on Merseyside and in north Cheshire, forming a class remote from
local landed society, which viewed the newcomers with hostility. Around
Widnes, the old gentry, personified by the Gerards, resented the desecration
and ruin of the landscape and the deadly pollution of the alkali trade so that
Tory–Liberal antagonism was intensified by the legal disputes it engendered.
The leading manufacturers also took major roles in local government as the
new towns took on the trappings of municipal authority giving parliamentary

elections a town versus country colour on top of political differences. The entrepreneurs shared an obsessive interest in science that overflowed into philosophy producing a flowering of European intellect under the clouds of hydrochloric smoke. It was a local discussion group that gave birth to the Society of Chemical Industry at Widnes, a successor to the Faraday Club that already existed there (see Hardie 1950).

The men who worked in the chemical plants, glass works and soap works had equally diverse origins. Coal-mining in the area had traditionally enrolled native sons and they provided most of the manpower for its expansion. The other growth industries were small-scale, at least in the early days, not highly organized and very varied in their nature. Of the 6,093 men in the Runcorn and Widnes alkali works in 1892 only 18 per cent were process workers, the rest being bricklayers, coopers, plumbers, joiners, fitters and masons: trades that could be drawn from all over the British Isles. There was immigration from Ireland in the 1840s and from Wales, the chemical industry in particular providing good wages for heavy, dirty or dangerous jobs. In the 1880s Poles and Lithuanians were settling in Widnes, perhaps to 5 per cent of the population; the traditional elements of a common industry and indigenous people so evident in cotton towns of similar size were less manifest on Merseyside (Hardie 1950: 122).

The chemical process workers alternated between ten-hour day and fourteen-hour night shifts, artisans worked a fifty-four hour week and bleach packers, whose work was arduous, unpleasant and dangerous, had a thirty-four hour week. Glass makers, before the flow process, were called out when the tanks were ready and worked until they were empty; the soap makers worked twelve-hour shifts until 1906. Wages were good in all four local trades, with colliers perhaps at the lower end, earning 20s. to 25s. per week in the 1840s. The glass makers and soap boilers kept both craft tradition and high wages to compensate for their long and irregular hours, glass makers earning from 22s. to over 50s., depending on the branch, in the 1840s and maintaining these values into the 1890s. Many Scotsmen were to be found among the highly mobile glass workers but process work in alkali and probably in soap relied heavily on Welsh and Irish immigrants, especially the latter who came into the area in a steady stream from the 1840s. Colliers however tended to remain Lancastrian (T. C. Barker and Harris 1959: 280–8).

In general, industrial relations were relatively peaceful in these industries, though the colliers were drawn into violent regional strikes as well as endemic local disputes. The other trades probably had early trade clubs and were organized in trade unions in the later nineteenth century, but they appear to have had few serious disputes until 1920, when there was a clerical strike at Port Sunlight. Despite the unhealthy conditions of work the evidence suggests that mortality rates, though high, were better in Widnes and St Helens than in Manchester. The birth rate was high as might be expected in an area of high immigration. Perhaps relatively high wages, demonstrated by the large number of friendly societies in mid-nineteenth century St Helens, combined with the tendency for married women to stay at home to mitigate the bleak ugliness and sterility of the workers' surroundings (T. C. Barker and Harris 1954: 453–69).

The alkali trade was not the only branch of chemicals to establish itself in the north-west. Manchester's central role in the finishing and selling of linen and cotton cloth in the eighteenth century drew dyers as well as bleachers to north Manchester; it was in Blackley and Crumpsall that dyers began to dye Turkey Red late in the century. One of the pioneers of this trade was Angel Deloney or Delaunay, recorded in Bancks' *Manchester Directory* of 1800. Most of the dyes of that period were vegetable, insect or lichen dyes and the preparatory processing produced many mills for grinding logwood and other dyewoods all over the eastern part of the region, for example at Oakenshaw in 1846. Even before Perkin made his great discoveries in coal-based aniline dyes in London in 1856 and alizarene in 1869 there were chemical experimenters at work in Lancashire. James Thomson of Clitheroe, who died in 1850, was working on metallic dyestuffs and indigo discharges; by 1832 there were ninety-four indigo mills at Pin Mill, Ardwick. John Mercer, later inventor of a process for giving cloth a lustre by impregnation with caustic soda, developed the use of antimony for yellow and orange at Broad Oak print works in 1817; later, as chemist at Oakenshaw print works, he introduced dyes made from chrome and manganese brown (Floud 1961: 8–14).

It was, however, the coal-based dyes of Perkin that revolutionized the trade; Manchester became an early centre, with Roberts-Dale's Cornbrook Works at Hulme established in the early 1860s to make aniline yellow. A much more important initiative was that of Ivan Levinstein of Berlin, who took a house at Blackley and began making sulphuric acid and naphthalene at Delaunay's old works in 1864, followed twelve years later by Charles Dreyfus from Alsace who started the Clayton Aniline Company not far away. A different chemical use of coal had already begun at Calvert's Carbolic Works in 1857, strategically sited near Bradford gas works. By 1900 there were about a dozen aniline works in the Manchester district but in general the British dyestuffs industry had fallen far behind its German competitors, provoking a dyestuffs crisis during the First World War (Ashmore 1969: 135–6).

As in the case of alkali, the dyestuffs industry in Lancashire owed much to the German combination of technical education and industrial experience for its foundation and, though Levinstein was not the most benevolent of employers, his Swiss and German chemists made a great contribution to British dyestuffs. In 1919 he took his firm into the British Dyestuffs Corporation, Dreyfus meanwhile having been bought out by the Swiss firm CIBA in 1911.

There was another branch of the chemical industry, pharmaceuticals, pioneered by the Henrys of Manchester, whose works operated from 1810 to the 1930s, basing its reputation on the famous Henry's Powders. They also gave Priestley's invention of carbonated water to a grateful world by developing apparatus for the commercial manufacture of soda water at their works in Cupid's Alley off Deansgate in Manchester, beginning perhaps as early as the 1780s (Musson and Robinson 1969: 234–9). A more famous name in pills was that left by Thomas Beecham, born in 1820, who graduated from tending sheep in Oxfordshire in 1828 to making and selling pills in Wigan in 1848, before moving to St Helens in 1858–9. His 'guinea a box' campaign, postal sales and huge advertising produced an output of 9 million pills a day by 1890 (T. C. Barker and Harris 1954: 378). By the turn of the century most of the larger towns of the region had a manufacturing chemist making a range of patent medicines for the relief of the chronic conditions prevalent among the local population.

By 1865 Lancashire had taken the lead in paper production in England; over half the mills built between then and 1920 were in the north-west, over fifty in all (Shorter 1971: 148–51). Limited liability encouraged larger machine mills though the largest, Bridge Hall, employed only 470 people in 1865; total employment in the region was only 3,000 in 1871. The basic raw material changed from refuse cotton and bagging from the mills to imported esparto grass and wood pulp, the latter treated chemically after 1886. As in other industries good access to Liverpool and the presence of clean water, coal and chemicals encouraged the regional growth of the trade. Clean water, however, was a disappearing asset. The chemicals and fibres in use were serious pollutants; the paper makers, like the bleachers, dyers and printers, used the Mersey and its headwaters as open sewers. The offenders were reluctant to make improvements: at Springfield Mill in 1903, for example, there is a reference to 'being continually pestered about our water pollution which is becoming more serious year by year' (Lyddon and Marshall 1975: 172). As their sources of raw material increasingly lay abroad the paper makers entered into international agreements, then into combines like that of Olive and Partington, who developed links through the Kellner-Partington wood pulp company in the 1890s. Local paper supplies complemented Manchester's other transport links and its role as regional capital in making it England's second newspaper publishing centre at the turn of the century.

From 1860 to 1920 engineering grew into the second industry in the region and by 1923 there were 177,000 employed in it in Lancashire alone with a further 26,000 in shipbuilding and marine engineering and 25,000 in the manufacture of non-ferrous metal and iron and steel. The roots of this great industry lay in textiles with its insatiable demand for mules, looms and carding engines, in calico printing with multi-colour machines and in the unceasing demand for steam power for mill and locomotive engines. During the 1860s and 1870s mechanization spread to the hatting, shoemaking and clothing industries, coal-mining required cutting and conveyor machinery, improved ventilation and winding gear and gas-making plants generated their own needs. Later the mills needed humidifiers and sprinkler systems, corn milling and food processing were mechanized and the chemical industry developed its own engineering suppliers. Towards the end of the century the development of electricity and the internal combustion engine found a focus at Trafford Park though they were also established in other parts of the region.

Some of the firms of the early nineteenth century barely outlived their founders. William Fairbairn's great firm of 1820, the biggest in Manchester by the 1840s, died with him in 1874. Peel, Williams and Co. of Ancoats, founded before 1800, lasted for two generations before being wound up on the death of the founder's last surviving son in 1887 (Musson and Robinson 1969: 471, 488). The firm of Whitworth had a different destiny. Joseph himself died in 1887 but his development of cannon and armour plating for warships brought a merger with Armstrongs of Elswick in 1897 (Ashmore 1969: 93).

The individual entrepreneur remained a significant figure in the second half of the nineteenth century but it was no longer the Scots who set the pace. In Manchester Hans Renold, who took over a Salford driving-chain business in 1879, was Swiss. Henry Simon, born in Silesia, brought roller flour milling and coke ovens from the continent in 1879 and 1880 and the Italian engineer Sebastian Ferranti began manufacturing electrical power equipment in 1883, transferring to Hollinwood in 1896. At Trafford Park it was an American, George Westinghouse, who established the firm that became Metropolitan Vickers and later GEC/AEI; Ford were pioneers of mass motor car production there. Not all the enterprise came from abroad. Beyer-Peacock, the great locomotive makers at Gorton, united both home and foreign backgrounds. The Kenyons of Ashton set up a rope works at Dukinfield in 1866 that moved into engineering in 1909, Mather and Platt, already great makers of textile finishing machinery, began to manufacture Edison's dynamo in 1882, first at Salford, later at Newton Heath, and there was a host of makers of internal combustion engines. Crossley Brothers, founded in 1863, made gas engines at Openshaw and, after 1917, motor cars at Stockport; Mirrlees, Bickerton and Day made diesel oil engines at Hazel Grove, the National Gas and Oil Engine Co. was founded in Ashton in 1889 and Frederick Royce made his first cars in Manchester. At Sandbach, Foden's progressed from the making of steam traction engines to diesel lorries. Aircraft manufacture began with Alliott Verdon-Roe in a mill off Great Ancoats Street before he moved to Chadderton (Ashmore 1969: 94–6).

Outside Manchester, engineering boomed in all the mining and manufacturing districts. Oldham was particularly strong in textile machine making with Asa Lees and Co. and the massive Platt Brothers works, world leader in textile machinery in the second half of the nineteenth century, which employed 7,000 hands in 1871 and 9,000 in 1880. Among Bolton's engineering concerns was the equally famous firm of Dobson and Barlow which kept a family connection from its foundation in 1790 by Isaac Dobson from Patterdale into the twentieth century. The firm specialized in preparatory and spinning machinery, growing from 980 men in 1851 to 3,000 in 1890, when it claimed it could equip twelve first-class spinning mills a year. Its chimney stack, known locally as 'Blinkhorn's', may serve as an outstanding example of that once-familiar Lancashire symbol. Built in 1842 it was 376.5 feet high with a circumference of 127.5 feet at the base and 24 feet at the top; 900,000 bricks and 120 tons of stone went into its construction. Preston housed the large printing engineers Foster, founded in 1860, with 1,000 hands in 1890, and in 1900 Dick Kerr and Co. set up their firm equipping trams and trains there. Wigan was the home of Walker Brothers, specialists in air compressors for ventilating collieries, and there were large wagon works dating from the 1860s at Lancaster and Chorley as well as the railway works at Crewe, Gorton, Earlestown and Horwich.

Specialization also fostered local growth. Turner-Atherton at Denton made hat-making machinery but Oldhams in the same town also developed mining machinery then, with increasing familiarity with electricity underground, were early makers of storage batteries. At about the same time Chloride began battery making at Clifton in the Irwell valley. North-east Lancashire made power looms, Bury became a centre for paper-making machinery, St Helens had Robert Daglish, who made machinery for the glass industry; in Liverpool and Birkenhead marine engineering dominated. Iron founders, boiler makers and general engineers abounded in every town, leading examples being the two Adamson firms of Dukinfield and Hyde, and even Chester joined in the expansion with its highly successful Hydraulic Engineering Company of the 1870s (Ashmore 1969: 78–96). At Birkenhead, Laird Brothers (later Cammell Laird's) had been early innovators in making iron ships, and they survived as shipbuilders on the Mersey where other firms failed or turned to ship repairing. Lairds later came to specialize in large warships, both for the United Kingdom and for foreign buyers; they obtained substantial orders under successive Defence Acts from 1889 (Pollard and Robertson 1979: 65–6, 84, 214).

The tendency of firms at the turn of the century was to greater size (illustrated by Lairds), to limited liability and to many more links with other firms in Britain and abroad so as to take advantage of foreign patents. The region was a great powerhouse of engineering but in the developing fields competition was international and, by 1920, Lancashire could no longer claim to lead the way.

Production in the Lancashire and Cheshire coalfield grew during the later nineteenth century, reached a peak in 1907 and began to fall back (Table 4.13). In 1868 there were over 390 collieries working in Lancashire and Cheshire and there were still over 300 in 1914 (T. Baines 1867, II: 316; Ashmore 1969: 97). The Lancashire pits were deep; Rose Bridge at Wigan reached 816 yards in 1869 and Ashton-under-Lyne 896 yards in 1881. They

Table 4.13   Coal production (tons) and employment 1875–1920

	Lancashire		Cheshire	
	Output	*Employees*	*Output*	*Employees*
1875	17,930,051	64,544	688,865	2,744
1900	24,842,208	85,336	699,451	2,640
1907	26,183,274	94,331	381,654	1,197
1920	18,784,699	115,453	236,379	1,133 (1914)

Source: Gibson 1922: 28, 30, 48.

were also dangerous, with twenty-one major disasters in the late nineteenth century; the worst in the history of the field was when 343 of the men and boys in Number 3 Bank Pit at Hulton were killed as was one of the rescue party (Duckham and Duckham 1973: 202–7). These were only peaks in a high annual toll of death and injury. In the Wigan district alone there were ten serious accidents between 1868 and 1871, which left 317 dead and 150 widows with 354 fatherless children (Challinor 1972: 159). Not only colliers were killed. Between 1854 and 1896 every general manager at Blundell's collieries was killed in the pit (Challinor 1972: 51). In 1879 no fewer than 5,000 of the 27,000 men enrolled in the Miners' Permanent Relief Society, founded in 1872, drew benefits.

By the late 1860s some very large coal concerns had emerged. Andrew Knowles and Son employed 3,000 men at their pits at Farnworth and Kearsley but they were dwarfed by the Wigan Coal and Iron Company which was established in 1865 by an amalgamation of the Earl of Crawford's collieries, the ironworks and collieries of the Kirkless Hall Company and two other colliery companies. Capitalized at over £2 million the concern employed over 10,000 hands, had 30 shafts working coal under 12 townships and produced close on 2 million tons of coal per year by the 1880s (Ind of Lancs, Anonymous *c.* 1890: 177). The problems of the field stimulated mining engineering and by the late nineteenth century Wigan could claim to be the 'Coalopolis' of Britain (Plates 4.9 and 4.10). In 1857 the Mining and Mechanical School was established there and, in 1893, *The Science and Art of Mining* began publication. The coal-owners were not only technically progressive, but also in 1908 pioneered the provision of a rescue station for teams to help in pit disasters; in 1913 the first pithead baths in England were opened at Howe Bridge and Gibfield Collieries at Atherton (K. Wood 1984: 108).

The miners, whose wages were subject to frequent fluctuations, were, like the cotton workers, seeking wider and more centralized bargaining. Wigan took the lead in organizing district unions and the period was punctuated by a series of offensive and defensive strikes. These were usually marked by escalating violence as the sacking of union men and the introduction of knobsticks brought fierce reactions from the strikers. In 1864 it was Parr that was affected, in 1867 Farnworth and Kearsley, and in 1868 Wigan,

St Helens and the south Lancashire field. In 1869 at Tyldesley the initiative was running down and the district unions were collapsing. Prosperity revived with the early 1870s and a revived union, more centralized than before, was able to give wages an additional push that took Wigan to the top of the national scale with 6s. 9d. per shift; four other Lancashire districts were in the top twenty in the national wages league (Challinor 1972: 110). Once again however a downturn came, in 1874, and wages fell with owners seeking even greater reductions. The resultant strike which began in January 1881 brought 56,000 men out and culminated on 4 February, in a battle between 10,000 miners and a force of police and Hussars at Howe Bridge between Leigh and Atherton. In the course of the strike the miners had set up the Lancashire and Cheshire Miners' Federation, which fought the next great dispute of 1893 when the owners locked out 300,000 men across the country for resisting a 25 per cent reduction in wages. The men won after sixteen weeks and this encouraged further movement towards central control in an attempt to prevent the sporadic and piecemeal actions which had been such a feature of industrial relations in the coalfield (Challinor 1972: 158–234).

By the 1890s the growth of a regional market of over 4 million people had strengthened the port of Liverpool, which had massive imports of cotton, grain, cattle and sheep, sugar, cheese and edible oils, many with associated processing and packing plants. The Liverpool importers were great innovators. George Reddich, who imported Scotch cattle in the 1860s, brought in the first Canadian cattle in 1874, devised the first shipboard lairages and, in 1875, introduced the first regular cattle service from the USA. Warrington's began importing American cheese in 1868 and were, by the 1890s, the largest cheese factors in the UK, with branches in London, Montreal and Chicago. Grain imports fostered a huge milling industry, Bibby's being a leading example. Edible oils became a major industry and sugar refining grew. With improved transport and the introduction of canning the fish trade had become international. At the end of the century Birrells had a 'gigantic' herring and kipper trade, the fish arriving by rail and coasting vessels. Mussons were oyster merchants with their own beds all round the Irish and English coasts; there was a galaxy of importers of canned salmon and meat as well as meat products, fruit and vegetables (*Century's Progress*, Anonymous 1892: 202–78). In 1905 exports to the value of over £138 million and imports of over £139 million passed through the port, compared with Manchester's exports of £13.5 million and imports of £23 million (Bartholomew 1907: G.26–7).

The Manchester Ship Canal brought cotton, fruit, grain and timber into

---

Plate 4.9 Miners at the coal-face, Wigan. This face is relatively high for the Lancashire coalfield and is being worked longwall. The overman is testing for gas while one collier undercuts the face and another appears to be drilling. Safety lamps and stout props are in evidence but many pits were far more cramped than this.

Plate 4.10   Pit brow lasses, Wigan. The hard work of south Lancashire colliers was matched by that of their wives and daughters. These Wigan pit brow lasses pose for their portrait: a pleasant change from their daily work screening coal, hauling tubs and loading props. Their labour was valued until well after the Second World War.

278

the port of Manchester, encouraging local processing and manufacture and strengthening the city's regional role. By then the Corporation markets were huge wholesale marts: for fish at Smithfield, for fruit and vegetables at Camp-field and for meat at Water Street which, with the Corn and Produce Exchange, made the city one of Britain's largest distributive centres. Corn storage and milling, pioneered by the CWS, which had made Manchester its headquarters, were well established alongside the Ship Canal. Fruit imports made jam making profitable; Duerr's, established at Guide Bridge in 1884, is one example, and the combination of flour and fruit encouraged biscuit production, again pioneered by the CWS. The CWS was also active in intro-ducing margarine and sweet production, using imported edible oils and sugar, but one confectionary firm of the 1890s, Harrisons, could trace a direct descent from Sarah Harrison, who had already been well established at Deansgate in 1800. The finest furniture trade remained Lancaster based where Gillows, founded before 1731, employed 240 hands in the 1890s, but cheap timber carried on the Ship Canal resulted in a growing packing case and box manufacture in the Manchester area (*Century's Progress*, Anony-mous 1892: 66–201).

In retailing, the emergence of the multiple food store and the depart-ment store began to threaten the specialist retailer. In 1831 S. & J. Watts had set up a sale room on Bridge Street in Manchester, which they sold to the new partnership of Kendal, Milne and Faulkner in 1835. Starting with fabrics, this firm expanded into furniture and dress, built a large new shop on Deansgate and, by the 1890s, employed 750 people in furniture making and upholster-ing. They fitted out the newly built Grand Hotel and had a special arrange-ment with Morris and Co. of London for the provision of 'Morris fabrics'. David Lewis established his first store in Liverpool in 1856 and built a second in Manchester in 1879, leaving a name associated not only with shopping but also with the hotel, restaurant and theatre in Liverpool and playing fields and homes for handicapped people set up for the two cities under his will (Mid-winter 1971: 151–8). By the First World War trains and trams made the cities attractive for the region's shoppers and local shops and 'co-ops' had glamorous rivals in the great city stores.

A greater variety of occupations for women and family budgets that allowed for more convenience and occasional luxury produced more wants. Working people could now compare city prices and quality with local shops but most everyday purchases were still made very locally and in small amounts. Local specialities became regionally famous: Bury black puddings (which had mysteriously migrated from Rochdale), Eccles cake, Godley rock and Everton toffee; convenience foods multiplied, for example tinned salmon and sardines, canned and potted meats and extracts, tripe and cowheels, sauces, relishes and pickles, pies and sausages, and above all fish and chips, said to have been first made by Mr Dyson at his tripe shop in Oldham in 1866. Oranges and lemons poured into the Manchester docks from 1894, bananas from 1902 (though that trade was lost to Garston in 1911) and apples and pears from across the world. The rhubarb and gooseberries that had filled the sour tarts of earlier generations were in eclipse.

Social and Cultural Life

The changes that had given local power and national influence to the manufacturing and mercantile middle classes in the 1830s and 1840s reached their full fruition in the years before the First World War. They dominated the councils and commissions of the peace in the manufacturing towns, were prominent in their churches and chapels and formed the pinnacles of local society. In Manchester and Liverpool and to a lesser extent in other towns suburban dispersal diluted this central role but even in Manchester, where Beatrice Potter criticized the councillors of the late nineteenth century as inferior to their predecessors, there was still a core of very substantial and powerful men. The dominance of the middle class found its physical expression in the transformation of the towns. As councillors they initiated great schemes of public works, not only utilitarian as in the provision of water and sanitation or the passing of by-laws governing housing, but also symbolic in their great town halls. Their private munificence was poured into churches, universities, schools and hospitals, libraries and art galleries, parks and baths, not motivated only by political or religious rivalry: the coats of arms of Manchester's national and international trading partners that decorate the ceiling of the great hall in the Town Hall of 1868 reveal a Hanseatic civic pride.

The new or reconstituted boroughs had begun to attack the accumulated evils of their physical environment long before the Torrens Act 1868 and subsequent legislation laid down compulsory national standards. It was easier to legislate against nuisances than to eradicate them. In Manchester, cellar dwellings had been condemned in 1853 but the last did not close until 1874; there were still 10,000 back to backs in 1885, forty years after their prohibition in 1844, 100 surviving until 1913. Nevertheless standards of working-class housing were rising even if the long terraces of cottages (usually brick, but stone in the east of the region) with their tiny yards and narrow back alleys had a bleakly utilitarian appearance. The movement of

Plate 4.11 Rylance Row, off Standishgate, Wigan 1900. The low cottages on the right have a late-eighteenth-century appearance; those on the left are rather higher with doorsteps that stop the filth of the road from seeping in and also a raised pavement. But all the houses are small, must lack all amenity and view only each other across the greasy setts. Port Sunlight is another world.

industry into the factories had freed homes from the dust and congestion of domestic industry releasing space for greater domestic comfort and cleanliness. Municipal planning which set working-class housing in pleasant environs had to wait for the building of estates after the turn of the century but the region provided one private enterprise model for emulation. In 1888 William Hesketh Lever bought fifty-six acres of land for his factory and workers' houses at Bromborough Pool and laid out the village of Port Sunlight. By 1900 there were 400 houses of three and four bedrooms with bathrooms and outside WCs. The houses, 'not of the mechanical joyless kind of Bromborough Pool Village' built by Price the candle manufacturer thirty years before, were gabled and varied in design (Plate 4.12), set in groups among trees and gardens and provided with allotments and recreation grounds and, after 1922, with an art gallery (Pevsner and Hubbard 1971: 41, 304; Rubinstein 1974: 262). Landowners such as Lord Crewe and the Duke of Westminster built good farm houses and cottages round their estates and, like others, the millowner Hugh Mason built solid houses with good arrangements for his Ashton workpeople, but Lever brought together industrial work, the amenities of the country and improved housing.

The Port Sunlight combination of internal amenity and external space, light and a garden environment was one answer to the problem of urban squalor. A second was the apartment block as pioneered at Birkenhead in 1845. Liverpool Corporation built flats at Vauxhall Road in 1868–9 and the thirteen blocks of five-storey tenements known as Victoria Square Dwellings in 1885, the 271 tenements of the latter being considered model dwellings by the architect T. L. Worthington. In Manchester a cotton mill in Jersey Street was converted into 149 dwellings by a limited company; the Lancashire–Yorkshire Railway Company built flats in Salford and, in 1889, Manchester Corporation built its own Victoria Square flats in Ancoats (Worthington 1893: 81, 154–6). By 1905 the corporation was building three-bedroom houses with baths at Blackley and from 1906 there were private garden suburb developments at Hollins Green at Oldham and at Burnage in Manchester (Pevsner 1979a: 124, 305). The full development of the municipal garden suburb had to wait until after 1920.

Between 1860 and 1920 the affluent middle class began to move out of the desirable inner suburbs such as Victoria Park in Manchester to the country areas beyond and they sought architects of distinction. Thomas Worthington's The Towers at Didsbury, built for John Edward Taylor of the *Manchester Guardian* in 1865, was a mansion but the very substantial middle-class house was much more typical of the period, an early example being The Firs at Fallowfield, designed by Walters for Sir Joseph Whitworth in 1851. By the end of the century the most modern houses were being built in suburbs beyond the city. Edgar Wood, for example, was active at Hale, Bramhall and Middleton. We have already remarked on the penetration of the countryside by wealthy urbanites (see p. 232) and in the country town of

Plate 4.12 Houses at Port Sunlight. William Lever's estate set new standards for workers' houses and the environment in which they should be set. These houses, Kenyon Peel Cottages, were a close copy of Kenyon Peel Hall.

Knutsford there were houses by Voysey, Percy, Thomas and Hubert Worthington and Baillie Scott (Pevsner 1979a; Pevsner and Hubbard 1971; Bott and Williams 1975).

Above all this was the age of the great town halls. They were usually Gothic, as at Manchester, Rochdale and Chester, but Bolton and Stockport favoured English Baroque Classicism and Preston in 1906 neo-Georgian (Pevsner 1979a; Pevsner and Hubbard 1971). There was a major growth of other large public buildings; schools such as Nicholl's Hospital at Ardwick in Manchester and the Stonyhurst School extensions, prisons at Preston, Walton and Strangeways, where the Gothic Assize courts were also built, massive hospitals, both voluntary and Poor Law Infirmaries, the new University buildings in Liverpool and Manchester and the Municipal College of Technology there; the peak of library building in the region, the John Rylands Library on Deansgate, Manchester, was built between 1890 and 1899. Church building slackened towards the end of the century as population growth slowed but restoration went on apace and Liverpool planned an Anglican cathedral that was intended to be the greatest in England. Work on

283

Sir Giles Gilbert Scott's massive design began in 1906 but progress was slow and 1920 marked only an early stage in its building. Of the new churches of the period one was outstanding: 'the only Lancashire church that would be indispensable in a survey of the development of twentieth century church design in England', according to Pevsner (1979a: 48). This was Edgar Wood's First Church of Christ Scientist at Victoria Park in Manchester, built in 1903 and now externally restored after some years of neglect.

Mill building changed with the emergence of the limited companies. Sir William Houldsworth's massive mills of 1865 at Reddish were intended to form the hub of a model estate but later mills lacked this community dimension. The spinning mills of the turn of the century built by or under the influence of the 'Oldham Limiteds' were of a common type, comparatively compact and functional with water towers and detached engine houses, but not without distinction. The new textile companies also built massive head offices and warehouses no less grand and often following the styles of the early nineteenth century but they now had to share the Manchester streets with other commercial giants. Railway stations had become large and imposing, Manchester Central's huge shed being exceeded in size only by St Pancras. Liverpool's Lime Street Station of 1868–71 also had a wide-spanned iron shed and a five-storey hotel. Banks and department stores had grown in size and the insurance companies made an enormous mark. The Waterhouse Prudential buildings at Manchester in 1881 and Liverpool in 1885–6 were matched by Paul Waterhouse's Refuge Assurance building of 1891 in Manchester but Liverpool also had the Royal Liver Building of 1908–10, not only impressive but also an early exercise in the use of reinforced concrete (Pevsner 1979a: 39, 47).

By the latter years of the nineteenth century new housing was expected to conform to national standards. Public and commercial building reflected the tastes and aspirations of some part of the middle class. Even buildings that had to cater for a mass market shared, if they sometimes exaggerated, the features of their neighbours. Thus shops and the larger public houses were not grossly different in style from banks or offices and in the seaside towns the Winter Gardens and Empress Ballroom at Blackpool and the People's Palace at Morecambe aimed at a certain level of dignity. The piers had grown new recreational functions: the Tower at New Brighton and the Tower and Wheel at Blackpool were less traditional and less dignified, but where Paris showed the way who could complain. Belle Vue was perhaps more unashamedly vulgar but it shared with the seaside towns and the travelling fairs that

---

Plate 4.13 Blackpool before the First World War. This postcard was sent to a Rochdale girl holidaying in Blackpool in 1913. The message reads 'Dear Miss, I hope you are going up and down with the boys. Your sweetheart is going about with girls. I hope you are enjoying yourself there the weather is lovely here. He has 4 girls every night. From your boy's niece Sarah.'

Weaving Shed,
Lancashire Cotton Mill.

"Th'll be owding beams on
Monday, eh!

I am holding my own at Blackpool

agglomeration of steam-driven rides and brassy music that were the stuff of wakes and holidays.

The success of the middle classes in asserting political and religious influence and in reshaping the urban landscape was less apparent in cultural life. The Manchester Art Treasures Exhibition of 1857 had demonstrated the wealth both of Old Masters and modern works possessed by local industrialists and others, but hopes that it would elevate the taste of the people were not fulfilled. The Exhibition did not produce a transformation of art and design in the region though the foundation of the Manchester Academy of Fine Arts in 1859 owed something to the opportunities it presented (MacDonald 1985: 42–3). It had, however, given Charles Hallé an audience for his specially assembled orchestra and the Hallé Orchestra prospered on the patronage of the Manchester middle class, especially in its earlier years on the support of the German community. Liverpool too had its Philharmonic Orchestra to meet the musical needs of the Merseyside middle class. Working-class musical taste ranged from the rapidly vanishing folk music and street ballads to music hall songs and brass bands, with religious music, especially the oratorios, for the more serious minded. In general working-class interest in other forms of music seems to have been slow to develop though the light operas of Gilbert and Sullivan and grand opera by touring companies such as Moody-Manners or Carl Rosa were drawing big audiences in the larger towns by the turn of the century. Transport developments helped. The railway brought in the middle-class Hallé patrons from Alderley Edge and Wilmslow; later the tram performed the same service for the working people of the city and its suburbs. The Socialism of Morris and Blatchford was opening new cultural as well as political horizons for adventurous young workers and many responded with eager curiosity (Foley 1973: 66).

The theatre too benefited from the new stirrings at the end of the century. The classical repertoire of the middle class and the polished comedies and dramas of high society were well established; the increasingly respectable music halls, equestrian dramas and melodramas no doubt crossed many social boundaries, though principally working class in their audiences. The attempt, in 1891, to bring London standards of music hall provision to Manchester through the Palace of Varieties on Oxford Road failed in face of temperance opposition (Waters 1986). What was new, and did succeed, was the drama of social issues, often with a regional background and provenance, that Miss Horniman brought to the Gaiety Theatre in Manchester from 1908 to 1921. Here, in the pit or gallery, the enquiring mill girl or mechanic was drawn into the problems posed by Shaw or Galsworthy or the familiar situations brought to dramatic life by Allan Monkhouse or Harold Brighouse (Foley 1973: 75). No doubt the middle-class stalls and the democratic gallery had different views on what passed on the stage but they both shared a common experience.

The common participation, however partial and separate, that grew in music and theatre did not extend so much to art. The private patronage of the enlightened middle class kept pace with current developments in art and design, supporting the Pre-Raphaelites, encouraging the Century Guild of the 1880s and the Arts and Crafts movement. The Ford Madox Brown murals of 1881 to 1893 in Manchester Town Hall brought together many Manchester men and motives in that act of public patronage (Evans 1985: 250–68). The social purpose that Ruskin and Morris saw as a major function of art proved elusive. From 1886 to 1918, when the City Council took it over, T. C. Horsfall's foundation, the Manchester Art Museum, housed a collection of pictures and sculptures, some of it in a schools loans collection at Ancoats Hall, from 1895 in conjunction with the University Settlement there. It also provided concerts and lectures, drawing large numbers of attenders, but art and design, whether private and domestic or public and environmental, failed to strike chords in the breasts of most of the regional community. The Manchester City Art Gallery of 1882, formerly the Royal Manchester Institution, and the Whitworth Art Gallery of 1890, though open to all, set art aside in a hushed reverence far from the daily living contact and participation that Ruskin and Morris, Horsfall and Charles Rowley had hoped would transform both physical environment and relations between people (Rowley n.d.: 195–206; M. Harrison 1985: 120–40). In Liverpool the modernism of the Pre-Raphaelites had split the Academy, founded in 1810, during the late 1850s and from 1867 it was Liverpool Corporation's Autumn exhibitions that provided the stimulus for discussion and emulation. The building of the Walker Art Gallery in 1877 encouraged the foundation of the now famous permanent collection. Artistic affairs in the city were complicated in the early 1900s by a secession of young artists at University College which gave birth to the Sandon Studios Society but the period also saw a great opportunity missed. In 1907 W. H. Lever proposed that five new chairs in the arts should be established at the university, one to be endowed by himself and all to be offered to eminent practitioners; the university failed to seek further endowments and the offer was withdrawn (Ingram 1990: 10–17).

The locally printed word swelled to a flood. Manchester was increasingly the home for northern editions of national newspapers and Liverpool had a strong local press, but the *Manchester Guardian* was the voice of that Liberalism which Manchester had so long promulgated. Its national influence reached a peak under the editorship of C. P. Scott whose brilliant journalists made their marks in academic and theatrical fields as well as in the columns of the newspaper. There were other, less permanent, publications. Between 1860 and 1900 over 200 journals and magazines were launched in Manchester, varying from halfpenny weeklies to 1s. 6d. quarterlies, a very varied list (Beetham 1985: 171). The people of the region mainly read London publications but, in contrast to the first half of the century, and perhaps a reflection of increasing literacy, there was a flood of local dialect writing. The most successful of these was *Ben Brierley's Journal*, established in 1869 as a twopenny monthly but in 1874 reduced to a penny and printed weekly. It achieved a circulation of 10,000 and closed in 1891 only when Brierley was too ill to continue (Beetham 1985: 180–2). The dialect writers owed much to Robert Burns, both in their sentiments and choice of subjects, while they derived their dialect and wry humour from John Collier without emulating his polemics or country crudeness. At their best they could strike deep emotional chords or offer shrewdly humorous comments: at their worst, late in the nineteenth century, they could sink into banal and bathetic philosophizing. When writing about their own times they were on occasion critical, even bitter, about the circumstances of working-class life but more often they viewed it with wry humour: they cast many backward glances at a simpler life measured by the click of the shuttle in country folds and nooks. Brierley and Edwin Waugh achieved regional status and both were among Madox Brown's circle of friends when he was living in Manchester, others found middle-class patronage while a few were themselves members of that class. In general however dialect writing appears to have been directed at the working people of the region, while the substantial novels with Lancashire themes of middle-class writers such as Mrs Linnaeus Banks and Mrs Humphrey Ward were aimed at a national and predominantly middle-class readership. Dialect writing maintained some vigour up to the end of the century and beyond but the emergence of a mass circulation press skilfully aimed at the same readership coupled with a loss of vitality in the writing itself reduced it to a very minor level. It is perhaps significant that Ammon Wrigley, born in 1862 and the most successful of that generation of regional working-class writers, published largely in standard English.

The second half of the nineteenth century was a period of great change in outdoor activities. Hunting, shooting and fishing, once within reach even of the hand-loom weavers, were progressively restricted to the shrinking countryside and to those who controlled limpid waters and the battue shoots of the grouse moors. Parallel with this change the grosser forms of animal or human combat had either been made illegal, like bull and bear baiting, or had become identified with the coarsest sections of society. The low public houses adjoining the slums of Manchester and Liverpool housed bare-knuckle fighting, badger drawing, dog fights and rat-killing contests when these had ceased to be normal features of public holidays. But the Ten Hours legislation of the 1850s had given the mill workers a Saturday half-holiday, secular and free from the religious feelings that inhibited the free use of Sunday. It was, above all, team sport that came to occupy this space.

The team games, cricket and football, of the early nineteenth century had tended to roughness and violence, lack of organization and uncertainty about rules. Cricket had been the first to organize. In 1781 a team from Haughton near Denton played the men of Bredbury and in 1807 a group of Liverpool gentlemen formed the 'original and unrivalled Mosslake Fields cricket society' (Brooke and Goodyear 1991: 10). Rochdale Cricket Club was founded in 1824, Glossop in 1833 and Oldham and Middleton in 1852; there was a strong regional network when Lancashire Cricket Club was established at the Manchester club's ground at Old Trafford in 1864. Francis Thompson recalled early years there

> And a ghostly batsman plays to the bowling of a ghost,
> And I look through my tears at a soundless clapping host
> As the run-stealers flicker to and fro,
> O my Hornby and my Barlow long ago.
> (Quoted in Frangopulo 1977: 68–70)

Lancashire, captained by the amateur Hornby, had a good run with three county championships between 1880 and 1910. The players were a mix of largely local professionals and gentlemen amateurs, many from the public schools. Marlborough provided fifteen who made their début in these years, Harrow and Rossall fourteen each and Rugby ten with Uppingham, Eton and Cheltenham also well represented (Brooke and Goodyear 1991). The same blend of gentlemen and local amateurs with professional stiffening brought large attendances to the local leagues which were well established by 1900.

Football had been much more an occasional eruption, often associated with Shrove Tuesday, but schools had brought it under some control and the more regulated version spread from them into the general community. The Football Association was formed in 1863 and the Rugby Union in 1870, both then amateur, but it was the Association game that engaged a mass following in the region. The earliest football clubs were offshoots of other organizations. Bolton in 1874 and Everton in 1878 were formed by Sunday Schools, Burnley by the YMCA in 1882, Blackburn by the old boys of the Grammar School in 1874. Cricket clubs also established football teams such as Crewe, which met at the Alexandra Hotel in 1877, and Preston in 1881. Manchester United grew out of the Lancashire and Yorkshire railwaymen's Newton Heath of 1880; Liverpool was founded at Anfield Road when Everton were evicted after a disagreement with the club's founder in 1892. The first north-western club in the FA Cup Final, established in 1871, was Blackburn Rovers in 1882; in the following year Blackburn Olympic won it. That team included three weavers, a spinner, a cotton operative and a foundry worker. Working men like these could not afford to subsidize their hobby. In 1883 players were allowed rail fares for semi-final or final Cup games but Lancashire, which had started importing Scottish players, had to threaten a breakaway before the Football Association legalized payments and regulated the playing season in 1885. In 1888, when the Football League was set up, half of its twelve clubs were from the north-west: Accrington Stanley, Blackburn Rovers, Bolton Wanderers, Burnley, Everton and Preston North End. Before the First World

War Lancashire men had taken the game to Moscow, where they founded the club that became Dynamo, to Poland and Romania and, through Jimmy Hogan, to the Netherlands and Austria. Numbers of spectators grew rapidly from the 1880s. In 1893 the Cup Final at Fallowfield drew 45,000; in 1913 there were 120,000 at the Crystal Palace final (Walvin 1975: 57–83, 97–107). The region still retains two records and one notable first. In 1887 Hyde United were beaten 26-nil by Preston in the English Cup and in 1899–1900 tiny Glossop had one season in the First Division of the League. Local millowner Samuel Hill Wood spent £10,000 over seventeen years to achieve this feat (Middleton 1932: 551; Scott et al. 1973: 92–3). The pioneering event was the first floodlit match, which was played between Blackburn Rovers and Accrington Stanley at Blackburn in November 1878, when the ground was lit by electric arc lamps (Aspin 1969: 143–4).

The demand for broken-time payment that made soccer professional split the handling code in 1895, when the Rugby League (originally the Northern Union) was formed in a breakaway from the amateur Union. The Gentlemen of Manchester had played the Gentlemen of Liverpool as early as 1857 at Edge Hill and gentlemen dominated the game in the region until the split in 1895. The split was a disaster for the Union game. Lancashire won the national championship in 1891 but did not win it again until 1935. Rugby League grew rapidly to reach ninety-eight clubs by 1898 but it failed to take root in other parts of the country where working men played rugby (G. Williams 1989). Within the north-west it was weaker than soccer in the cities and cotton towns and found its greatest strength in the mining districts of south-west Lancashire, though it reached out to Swinton and Salford, Oldham and the old woollen town of Rochdale, which linked it with the Yorkshire woollen and mining districts where it was strong.

The Union game remained largely the province of those who could afford amateur status, thus joining golf as a mainly middle-class recreation. It was in Manchester that golf had first been introduced to England by Scottish exiles in 1818; the Royal Liverpool club at Hoylake, founded in the 1860s, was the second in England and inaugurated the amateur championship in 1885 (Lowerson 1989). Tennis had grown from the sphairistike played at Buxton in the late nineteenth century and with its centre at Didsbury became a major middle-class social game, as bowls had become for the working class. After the turn of the century municipal provision began to extend more facilities to working people to participate rather than merely spectate. Under the Unemployed Workmen's Act 1905 Manchester, for example, provided forty-six tennis courts, two bowling greens, thirteen football pitches and nine cricket pitches on its ninety-acre Platt Fields (H. Walker 1989).

The region, Chester apart, was hardly a rowing centre, given its heavily polluted waters. It did however become noted for one other, rather surprising sport. The pollution of rivers and the filthy atmosphere had encouraged local authorities to provide baths and wash-houses; swimming baths, sometimes built with aid from private benefactors, were often included. Competitive swimming and water polo rapidly took root. At Hyde the opening of the baths in 1895 stimulated four young men to form the Hyde Seal Swimming Club and to start playing water polo. Between 1903 and 1921 the club won the Northern Cup every year, the English Cup eight times and the World Championship three times. The little cotton town dominated the game in Europe (Middleton 1932: 553–4).

Whether amateur or professional, working-class sport, like much else in society, depended heavily on the patronage of the middle classes. They provided the funding for the basic facilities, usually privately, and guaranteed payments of expenses or wages or offered jobs to tempt sportsmen to their towns. Their paternalism may not have been entirely altruistic but in general they shared that local pride which united all classes on the day of the match and willed their town to be victorious.

The combination of middle-class leadership and local patriotism was not confined to sport. In 1901 the Manchester Statistical Society learned to its dismay that of 11,000 local men who had volunteered for service in the South African war, 8,000 were rejected as unfit and only 1,200 of the remainder were of the standard that a soldier ought to be (Ashton 1934: 117). The Haldane Reforms that followed the Boer War replaced the old Militia and Volunteers by territorial regiments recruited on an even more local basis than the county regiments of the regular army. They also instituted regular training at local drill halls with summer camps for the young men who volunteered. In 1914, when the new system was put to the test, twenty-three battalions of 1,000 men each were with the British Expeditionary Force (BEF) in France and by 1915 there were a further twenty-six. Another local recruiting device, the Pals battalions, was strongly supported in the north-west, with Manchester holding the record with fifteen battalions and Accrington recruiting its men in ten days with help from Burnley, Chorley and Blackburn. One further innovation was the Bantam division for men between five feet and five feet three inches, to accommodate the colliers and industrial workers who could not meet normal standards. The fact that Lord Derby became Director-General of Recruiting in October 1915 gave an added fillip to the 30th Division, which consisted of two Manchester brigades and one from Liverpool.

The strength of these battalions lay in a social cohesion that carried over from peacetime, with neighbours and workmates serving under officers who were members of local landed, millowning and merchant families. They shared common points of reference and enough understanding of each other to work together in war as they had in peace. But their strength was also their weakness. The landing at Gallipoli where the Lancashire Fusiliers suffered heavily brought sorrow to the region but other battles brought greater concentrations of casualties. On the first day in the battle of the Somme, 1 July 1916, the region sent twenty-seven battalions into action; Lancashire suffered over 6,000 casualties and some battalions were almost annihilated. The word that got back to Accrington was that only seven men had survived from their battalion and townspeople besieged the mayor's house seeking news. They were not very far wrong. Out of 700 men who went into action, 585 were casualties and the town went into mourning (Middlebrook 1971: 1–25, 260, 318).

Much has been written about the destruction of the flower of British youth during the war and about the disillusion of those who came back. Perhaps another casualty of those sad years was the stability and continuity of life in the countryside and the cotton and coal towns of the north-west. Since the middle of the nineteenth century there had been a growth of confidence in the ability of the region and its leaders to provide improving standards of life and a softening of social tensions. That confidence was shaken by the horrors of the war; the depleted ranks of the middle and working classes were left to consider (Plate 4.14) the merits of the hierarchical system that had done so much for the amelioration of life before the war but had not prevented the slaughter of the trenches.

Politics and Society

During the first half of the nineteenth century many observers noted the irreligious radicalism of the region's working class. In 1844, for example, Engels was in no doubt that the traditional forces in English life were in decay. The working man, he claimed,

> does not understand religious questions, does not trouble himself about them, knows nothing of the fanaticism that holds the bourgeoisie bound; and if he chances to have any religion, he has it only in name, not even in theory. . . . All the writers are unanimous on this point, that the workers are not religious and do not attend church.
> (Engels 1969: 155)

Yet, some forty years later, Beatrice Potter could record a very different impression:

Plate 4.14 Belle Vue, 1919. A feature of Belle Vue entertainments was the presentation of mock battles on an island in the lake. These involved dozens of extras acting as soldiers and firework simulation of gun and artillery fire. To reproduce Ypres in 1919 seems grossly insensitive but the crowded paddle steamer passing the set indicates that many did not take that view. (Source: Chetham's Library.)

> In living among mill hands of East Lancashire, I was impressed with
> the depth and realism of their religious faith. It seemed to absorb the
> entire nature, to claim as its own all the energy unused in the actual
> struggle for existence. . . . Even the social intercourse was based on
> religious sympathy and common religious effort.
>
> (B. Webb 1926: 187)

Perhaps both were to some degree right. Except among the Irish Catholics,
and to a lesser extent the Methodists, many urban working men seem not to
have been regular attenders at church or chapel. They had, however, been
largely educated at Sunday Schools and church or chapel day schools to
which they sent their own children; the most significant events in their own
and their families' lives were marked by the religious ceremonies of their
denomination. For the family too had survived the threat perceived by Dis-
raeli and Engels in the 1840s. Family and denomination were linked together
intimately and made up two of the interlocking circles in which most working
people lived out their lives before the First World War. They were complemented by the economic circles of the workplace and the trade union, the co-
op and the friendly society. It was within these circles that most made their
childhood friendships and found their marriage partners, sharing not only
religious views but also common social attitudes to such matters as drink or
gambling, Sunday observance, dancing or the theatre. The family was the
foundation of the denominations.

Thomas Shaw of Ashton-under-Lyne, a mill worker born in 1823, was
superintendent of St Peter's Sunday School there at the age of twenty and his
two sons both became National School teachers; Mrs Stevens of Glossop,
born in 1899, 'went to Shrewsbury Street Methodist as my mother was
brought up there as her father was one of the founders there' and Alice Foley
at Bolton was 'freed from compulsory attendance at Mass and Confession'
only by the death of her Irish father, her mother not being a Catholic (T.
Shaw 1902; J. H. Smith 1975; Foley 1973: 67). Continuity was important
and became easier as the people of the industrial districts became more settled
in their workplaces and homes, establishing patterns of residence close to
kinfolk as in Preston in 1851 (M. Anderson 1971: 56–9).

The coming of the railways had however begun to disperse the middle
class, first from Manchester and Liverpool, then from other industrial towns,
leaving many Old Dissenting chapels with reduced congregations. The Methodists with their wide range of foundations faced a less serious problem; both
Catholics and Anglicans made great efforts to build churches and schools and
to hold their working-class adherents. No doubt there were many families,
especially in the larger towns, that remained largely untouched by any
religious influence and they became the particular mission of the Salvation
Army and the Church Army late in the century. For most of the people of the
region however it was the religious calendar that ruled the year. Mrs Doris

Hurst, born in the Longdendale industrial village of Tintwistle in 1897, recalled her childhood as a sequence of Church festivals – Easter Sunday with three services and Sunday School, Whitsuntide and the Walks at Stalybridge, Sunday School Sermons and procession in June, the Sunday School Treat in July with refreshments at the local millowner's home, the Harvest Festival in the autumn, Prize Giving in October and on to Christmas and the Sunday School feast. Only Wakes week had lost its religious character, with day trips or longer holidays at Blackpool, Southport or New Brighton (D. Hurst 1978). And into that calendar also had to be fitted choir performances and bell ringing, men's and women's societies, bazaars and tea parties, even sports clubs and, for the less austere denominations, dancing and amateur dramatics. The sacred and the secular were intermingled, holidays from work kept a religious connotation and the social life of the church or chapel offered to men a cheap, safe and largely democratic alternative to pubs and music halls, low life and gambling and to women and children virtually the only respectable recreation outside the home. Church and chapel had come to terms with working people and gained in popularity as they adapted.

The third circle of working-class life, work, had, especially but not only in the cotton towns, become interlocked with those of the family and the Church. Outwork greatly declined as mechanization reached the hatting, shoemaking and tailoring trades after mid-century and most people worked in mills, factories or workshops from leaving school. The firms themselves were largely based on families or small partnerships until late in the century; owners and managers sought to develop strong family ties, with generations following each other into the same employment. Many of the larger firms had further developed the strong paternalistic roles already evident before 1860, extending their activities in housing and, as they gave up the provision of food or fuel because of the Truck Acts, shifting into recreational or token pension advantages. Educational activities such as those at Lee's Sunnyside Institute at Daubhill, Bolton, were not highly successful but the funding of brass bands, treats and railway excursions by employers was matched by demonstrations of loyalty by employees. The coming of age of sons of the millowners was always a great occasion: at Hurst in 1860 1,000 sat down to dinner to celebrate the majority of John Whittaker of the local cotton dynasty and in Ashton the streets and mills were decorated when leading millowner Hugh Mason's son reached twenty-one. Funerals brought the same manifestations. At Bolton in 1898 30,000 turned out when Alfred Dobson was buried; in 1880 the bearers of one of the Heskeths of Astley Bridge included an overlooker, a head mechanic and a warper (see Joyce 1980: ch. 5 for a full discussion).

Nor did the fourth circle of working-class life differ very greatly. Both trade unions and co-ops were largely non-political in party terms until very close to the start of the First World War. Life in the mills and works was not without tensions; indeed they grew as the competition became more severe, but the disputes and strikes were fought out within the system as it existed rather than against it. For their part the co-ops emulated the educational and charitable work of the churches, providing scholarships and soup kitchens for the poor, and followed the millowners in running cheap trips to places of interest such as the seaside, Edinburgh, London or even Paris (eg B. Smith 1969). The Cooperative Women's Guilds were perhaps the most forward looking of the cooperators and, with the emergence of women trade unionists in the cotton and hatting trades, they helped to provide the seed bed for the women's suffrage movement which grew strongly in the region before the First World War.

The interrelationships that integrated religion, family and work extended into education and politics. In 1867 the Manchester Statistical Society again visited St Michael's and New Cross as they had in 1834. They found that of 733 children of school age, 258 (35 per cent) had never been to school and that of the adults only 53 per cent could read and 35 per cent write (Ashton 1934: 66). Over half a century of voluntary schooling had failed to reach a great mass of working people. The Manchester reformers and, with them, the national government, were being pushed reluctantly into compulsion, already extended from children in textile mills to those working in all manufactures and workshops in 1867. They were also moving to an increased role for the state and local authorities. But the voluntary principle remained dominant in Lancashire despite Forster's Education Act 1870. In that year the county had just over 1,000 schools enjoying grant aid totalling about £100,000 and with some 200,000 children in average attendance. Of these schools 545 were Anglican, 125 Catholic, 88 were foundations of the British and Foreign Schools Society and 87 were Wesleyan. There were perhaps 70,000 children in non-aided schools and some 100,000 with no schooling at all. Liverpool and Ashton-under-Lyne had poor provision; Lancaster, Preston, Salford and parts of Manchester were much better (Midwinter 1969b: 187). Cheshire was, perhaps, better provided with elementary schools. Bramhall, with a population of 2,000 and no school, and Macclesfield, where there was accommodation only for one-third of the potential scholars, were black spots but they were the worst. Chester with about 6,000 places and Congleton with 2,250 were matched by the eastern industrial towns of Stockport, Stalybridge and Hyde for good provision, though municipal expenditure in Stockport and Stalybridge was very low (*VCH. Cheshire*, III: 210).

School boards were not much favoured in either county. In Lancashire there were fifty boards by 1902 covering 2.5 million of the county's 4 million inhabitants, the rest being served by school attendance committees. The board schools were a small minority, only 257 of the county's 1,814 schools, against 815 Anglican, 305 Catholic and 437 other denominational or miscellaneous schools. The boards provided only one in seven of the county's schools against one-third to one-half in the country as a whole (Midwinter

1969b: 187ff). In Cheshire too opposition from the religious bodies and the ratepayers resulted in the establishment of relatively few boards and at Stockport where one was set up it was disbanded in 1879. At Birkenhead obstruction by ratepayers prevented a board being set up though as late as 1890 there was still a deficiency of 2,500 places. In the late 1870s expenditure on education was low in the county. Dukinfield spent only 0.75d. per head of the child population, while Congleton, Macclesfield, Stalybridge and Stockport spent under 1d. against the 3.4d. spent in the comparable industrial town of Rochdale in Lancashire. It is hardly surprising that Cheshire fell well below the national average in the pass rate in the three Rs, Congleton returning the lowest rate (*VCH. Cheshire*, III: 210–12).

It was not only low expenditure that hampered the children's education. Both employers and parents resisted compulsory attendance, farmers and country labourers proving as obdurate as the town millowners and operatives. As late as June 1891 the *Cotton Factory Times*, influential among working people in the region, ran as a leader an attack on the raising of the starting age for half-timers from ten to twelve.

> If, as is the case, the children are willing and even anxious to go to work, and the parents are agreeable, whilst employers accept them, what has anyone else to do with it?
>
> *Cotton Factory Times* 5 June 1891

The Trades Union Congress (TUC), which had supported the proposal, was dismissed – 'luckily, no one at present pays any attention to their views' (*Cotton Factory Times* 5 June 1891). In February 1892 the same paper promised that employers and operatives would be 'formidable enemies' to Mr Mundella's attempt to end the half-time system and not allow children to start work until aged thirteen (*Cotton Factory Times* 5 February 1892). The practical consequences of this are clear from school log-books. At Whitfield in Glossop the master recorded in 1866, 'The class of children we generally get as half-timers are the scum of the town'. No doubt they were drawn from the poorer families where there was least regard for school (Whitfield School Logbook). It was not until the ending of half-time working in 1918 that this long struggle ended in favour of the schools and of the children who had suffered not only educational deprivation but social humiliation. By then the Education Act 1902 had extended secondary and technical education, though many of the new Education Committees still provided only elementary education.

While the slow movement towards compulsion and effective supervision in elementary education was taking place the voluntary spirit was transforming further and higher education. Colleges for ministerial and teacher training spread across the region and successors to the Mechanics' Institutes were established from the 1880s. In Manchester the Technical

School, opened in 1882, benefited from the will of Joseph Whitworth, a source that also gave the university its art gallery. By 1895 the Technical School had developed into the Municipal College of Technology. Owens College, which had opened with high hopes in 1851, fell into serious decline in the late 1850s but revived with the arrival of Professor Henry Roscoe, whose advocacy of research gave it new life. In 1860–1 the college amalgamated with the Working Men's College of 1858, bringing in more evening students, and by 1867 it was looking for extended premises. The committee established in that year under the leadership of Thomas Ashton raised double its target of £100,000 and in 1870 the new Gothic college designed by Waterhouse began to take shape on Oxford Road. In 1872 it was united with the Royal Manchester School of Medicine of 1822, in 1873 the Museum was opened and in 1877 a Women's College was opened on Brunswick Street. In 1883 the Women's College was absorbed into Owens, the Brunswick Street building becoming a day training college for teachers in 1889. By 1894 Owens, its building extended in 1892, had 1,000 day and 400 evening students, several imposing halls of residence and aspirations far beyond the regional scope of 1851. The greatest advance however was the granting of the charter in 1880 which established Victoria University with power to award degrees. In 1883 medical degrees were added and in 1885 and 1888 respectively University College, Liverpool, and Yorkshire College, Leeds, became colleges of the University. University College, Liverpool, had been first proposed in 1878 by the Revd Charles Beard but progress was slow until 1880, when William Rathbone injected new life into the campaign to raise funds. The college obtained its charter in 1881 and started life in a disused lunatic asylum on a site close to the Royal Infirmary and the Medical School, founded in 1834. When the college joined Victoria University in 1884 it amalgamated with the Medical School and its new School of Tropical Medicine was established. In 1903 the federal university came to an end and in 1904 Manchester and Liverpool received their separate charters. Liverpool, which had set up the first school of architecture and applied arts in England grew from 581 students in 1901 to over 1,000 in 1907 (*VCH. Lancs.*, IV: 54). Manchester, which had introduced the first chairs in education and in economic history in England and had opened all courses to women in 1900, had almost 1,800 students in 1911, 206 of them in the Faculty of Technology at the Municipal College (Charlton 1951).

In politics the Liberals who had fought and won the battle against the Corn Law and had set in train the improvement of the industrial districts might have anticipated a long domination of their north-western stonghold but, with Free Trade accepted, their hold on the region declined towards the end of the century. Traditional loyalty to the crown, at a low ebb before 1850, was manifest at Queen Victoria's visits to Manchester in 1851 and 1857, when the streets were crowded. Nationalist and Protestant feelings were strengthened by the continuing Irish immigration and the erection of the two Catholic dioceses of Liverpool in 1850 and Salford in 1855. The domination of politics by religion was most marked in Liverpool, claimed to be the centre of Catholicism in England, in Wigan where Tory Protestantism rather than Chartism had been the popular cause of the 1830s, and in Preston, which was like Liverpool a centre of Irish immigration (T. Burke 1910: 1; Joyce 1980: 251). In these towns there was consistent Orange strength of feeling which maintained Toryism. Further east, where the Irish were fewer in number, Manchester excepted, anti-Catholic feeling had been evident in the early part of the century and could burst into violence as it did along the Pennine edge at Ashton, Stalybridge, Rochdale, Oldham and Bacup in the Murphy riots of 1867–9 (Joyce 1980: 257–61; see Bowman 1960: 234–5 for the riots in Ashton-under-Lyne). These mill town outbursts reflected strong feelings but they were not the sole political concerns of the people.

The major struggle was between an evangelical Anglicanism that accepted both industry and free trade but looked back to an almost aggressive Englishness of empire and military pomp and colour, of horse and hound, of ale and bucolic pastimes, and a range of Nonconformist denominations that preached and tried to practise rational economy and international harmony based on trade, improving recreation, tea parties and teetotalism, thrift and respectability. *Laissez-faire* opposition to factory legislation and trade unions tainted the Liberals more than the Conservatives, the Nonconformist desire for non-denominational education could be seen as an attack on the established Church and initiatives in Ireland, from the disestablishment of the Irish Church to Gladstone's Home Rule proposals threatened the integrity of Church and kingdom alike. As always people cast their votes from a mixture of motives but that deep conservatism detected by Lamb in mid-century had roots in religion and an idea of Englishness that was easier to feel than to define.

It was late in the century before working people again began to assert separate political aims. After the confrontations of the 1830s and 1840s they had largely merged their interests in those of their employers or the middle-class leaders of the parties they supported so that both Conservatism and Liberalism ran through society in vertical strata (Table 4.14). By 1900 the working class was seeking a distinctive voice both within the existing parties through the adoption of working-class candidates like James Mawdsley, the Spinners' secretary, who fought Oldham as a Conservative in 1899 and through the new collectivist parties that were being established. During the 1880s H. M. Hyndman began a Social Democratic Federation campaign mainly centred on Burnley and by 1893 there were twenty-two branches in the Lancashire District Council. In 1891 John Trevor left his pulpit at Upper Brook Street Unitarian church in Manchester to found the first Labour Church, which had particularly strong successors at Ashton, Bolton, Hyde and Stockport. The Independent Labour Party was introduced from the east and by 1893 the region had 32 out of the nation's 120 branches, by 1895 73

Table 4.14   Parliamentary elections 1859–1910

| | Lancashire, Cheshire and North Derbyshire / High Peak[a] | | | |
	Conservative/Tory	Liberal	Irish Nat.	Electorate[b]
1859	16	22		112,248
1865	17	21		125,291
1868	32	16		305,862
1874	35	13		362,608
1880	19	29		406,387
1885	46	24	1	
1886	59	11	1	
1892	45	25	1	
1895	60	10	1	
1900	56	14	1	
1906	16	54	1	
1910 Jan.	23	47	1	
1910 Dec.	32	38	1	

Notes:
[a] 1832–1867 38 MPs; 1868–1885 48 MPs; 1885–1914 71 MPs
[b] Between 1885 and 1910 the English electorate increased from 4,094,674 to 5,774,897 (F. W. S. Craig 1976).
Source: 1859–80 F. W. S. Craig 1977; 1885–1910 Clarke 1971.

out of 305 (Clarke 1971: 40–1). Branches of the Fabian movement were mainly short lived but their books and pamphlets were to be found in co-op and other libraries and Robert Blatchford's Clarion Movement found a home in the Labour Churches and had an immediate appeal through its combination of politics with cycling, sporting and recreational activities. Alice Foley, then a Bolton mill girl, later remembered family readings of the *Clarion* and *Merry England* and recalled joining the Bolton Labour Church:

> The service opened with a hymn usually set to a martial air; we seemed forever to be marching somewhere, even if we often failed to reach the destination. An appropriate reading was given by the Chairman, who was known locally as the 'Jolly Spinner'; then followed a recital of the Socialist Ten Commandments. In those days we were inordinately proud of our positive affirmations of faith as compared with the orthodox religious negatives.
>
> (Foley 1973: 68)

All this was heady stuff and, as the Conservatives became more clearly the party of possessors with the entry of former Liberal and Nonconformist families in the 1890s, it was the Liberals, whose progressive policies took fifty-four seats in the region in 1906, that were the beneficiaries. But in

February 1903 the textile workers had balloted on affiliation to the Labour Representation Committee and had voted in favour by 84,154 votes to 19,856 (Clarke 1971: 92). The north-west was moving towards a new political alignment and the war and its aftermath speeded that move as the old settled structures of the region's life broke down beyond repair.

Chapter 5

1920–1974

The End of Localism

Between 1920 and the late 1970s a combination of economic forces, growth and change in communications and the mass media, and political developments drew all England into one net. In the north-west the decline of cotton, coal and, later, heavy engineering diluted the common vocabularies and shared experiences that had united the most populous parts of the region. In the retail trade the pioneering regional chain stores of the late nineteenth century grew into huge national concerns that catered for everyday needs and submerged the corner shops and specialist retailers in a tide of standardized supermarkets. The cooperative societies that had led the way in many of these developments reached a peak in commanding mass markets in the region in the decades before and after the Second World War but declined under the onslaught of the more style- and fashion-conscious supermarket chains of the 1960s. Local breweries were absorbed by national companies as lighter standard beers came into favour.

Physical movement became cheaper and easier as car ownership grew, slowly in the inter-war years then with increasing speed after the Second World War. Cheaper air travel offered another dimension and working people whose fathers had looked no further than Blackpool or Morecambe took their holidays in Majorca, Greece and further afield. The spread of literacy and the popular press in the late nineteenth century had already produced a national medium for the formation of views and attitudes and this was strengthened by radio from the 1920s and television from the 1950s. The cinema provided throughout not only a means of escape but also a window on to other worlds, not all of them fictional, but most of them new and exotic. Political changes brought coal, gas, electricity, the railways, much of road haulage, steel, education, health services and hospitals, welfare provision and town and country planning under direct central control or very powerful central influence. The prevailing current was towards the centre and most of the countervailing eddies were either archaic, as in the revival of folk songs or local traditions, or commercial as in television series such as *Z Cars*, set in Skelmersdale, or *Coronation Street*, which idealized the street communities that were already passing.

Control from the centre was mediated by the growth of regional administration but here the north-west posed problems. The growth of the eighteenth and nineteenth centuries had produced a plethora of boroughs and urban districts which had swamped the ancient primacy of Chester and Lancaster. Two of these modern creations, Manchester and Liverpool, had outgrown their neighbours and competed with each other for dominance. By the 1920s each had all the trappings of a regional capital: city status, cathedrals, universities with medical schools and teaching hospitals, orchestras and important cultural facilities, daily newspapers of reputation and financial, commercial and insurance concentrations of national importance. Their economic roles were, in many ways, complementary but their regional ambitions were not. Their strengths increasingly split the region between east and west.

Population

In 1971 for the first time a decennial census recorded a fall in the population of Lancashire while Cheshire showed a greater increase than ever before. After the Second World War Cheshire's population had grown more rapidly than that of its sister county and the rate of difference between them widened in each of the three post-war Censuses, as Table 5.1 shows. Lancashire's

Table 5.1   County populations 1921–71[a]

	Year	Number		% change
Lancashire[b]	1921	4,815,654[c]		
	1931	4,935,030		+2.5
	1951	5,009,627		+1.5
	1961	5,023,923		+0.3
	1971	5,010,857		−0.3
Total Increase 1921–71			+4.1	
Cheshire	1921	1,020,097[c]		
	1931	1,087,558		+6.6
	1951	1,258,507		+15.7
	1961	1,368,741		+8.8
	1971	1,546,387		+13.0
Total Increase 1921–71			+51.6	

Notes: [a] Decennial totals follow later inter-census adjustments.
[b] Figures for north of the sands deducted from county totals.
[c] Note [a] explains difference from Table 4.2.

Sources: Decennial census returns.

declining population was caused by a number of factors but they all stemmed from its previous industrial development and success. Almost all the towns showing a reduction in population in Table 5.2 were in Lancashire and most of them had been heavily involved in the cotton industry. Bacup lost 29 per cent of its population, Blackburn, Burnley, Oldham, Colne and Darwen lost over 20 per cent, Bolton, Accrington and Preston over 10 per cent with Dukinfield and Stalybridge in Cheshire also over 10 per cent. All had lost many jobs in cotton manufacturing and had been unable to replace them until the short recovery after 1945. That expansion however failed to tempt back enough former cotton workers or their children, for the depression of the 1920s and 1930s had reduced local populations of an age to work in the mills and had deterred those that remained from taking up mill employment.

As in the early nineteenth century immigration into the region helped to staff the mills and to supply labour for the lower paid or less desirable jobs that the native Lancastrians and Cestrians were unwilling to fill. From 1945 the mills were hiring displaced persons from Eastern Europe: during the 1950s and 1960s it was the Indian sub-continent that provided labour for the new night shifts as competition forced three-shift working. It was therefore in the cotton towns that the Asian immigrants mainly settled, though Manchester proved magnetic, Liverpool rather less so. Those from the Caribbean concentrated most in Liverpool and Manchester, where Lascar seamen had begun to form local communities since 1869, when Joseph Salter found eighteen Lascars in Liverpool and fourteen in Manchester (Fryer 1984: 262). By early 1919 there were between 2,000 and 5,000 Black people in Liverpool and there was rioting there later in the year sparked off by fights between Scandinavians and West Indians (Fryer 1984: 300–1). Up to the 1940s most of the New Commonwealth immigrant communities were African or Caribbean brought in by merchant shipping or wartime service in the armed forces. The great influx after that decade changed the ports themselves but it also introduced new communities into towns that lacked the cosmopolitan experience of Liverpool and Manchester. They had kept a far more local and traditional character but changed rapidly.

In 1971, as Table 5.3 shows, over 9 per cent of Rochdale's people had been born abroad, a similar proportion to that in Manchester, in Blackburn, Oldham and Bolton it was over 7 per cent, in Bury and Salford over 5 per cent. In Blackburn and Rochdale the Asian-born accounted for over 4 per cent, in Bolton and Preston over 3 per cent, in Burnley, Bury and Manchester between 1 and 2 per cent. Manchester provided, as always, a variety of occupations but in the other towns the mills that many of the immigrants came to work in were closing down one by one in the 1950s, 1960s and 1970s. Immigration had been a significant factor in slowing the population decline of the cotton towns and in maintaining a workforce in the mills but as the industry continued to shrink the new Lancastrians were faced with the prospect of unemployment. They were also locked into the terraced streets

Table 5.2 Borough and selected rural district populations[a]

	1921[b]	1931	1951	1961	1971	I or D
Lancashire						
County Boroughs						
Blackburn	126,950	122,791	111,218	106,242	101,816	−20%
Blackpool	102,014	106,095	147,332	153,185	151,860	+48%
Bolton	178,683	177,250	167,167	160,789	154,199	−14%
Bootle	76,487	76,800	75,123	82,920	74,294	−3%
Burnley	103,186	98,258	84,987	80,559	76,513	−26%
Bury	58,672	58,345	58,838	60,149	67,849	+16%
Liverpool	805,412	856,072	790,838	745,750	610,133	−24%
Manchester	735,665	766,311	703,082	661,791	543,650	−26%
Oldham	144,983	140,314	123,218	115,346	105,913	−27%
Preston	117,957	119,665	121,367	113,341	98,088	−17%
Rochdale	95,844	95,527	88,429	85,787	91,454	−5%
St Helens	103,098	107,452	112,521	108,674	104,341	+1%
Salford	234,045	223,438	178,194	155,090	130,976	−44%
Southport	76,621	78,928	84,039	82,004	84,574	+10%
Warrington	78,648	81,561	80,735	75,964	68,317	−13%
Wigan	89,421	85,357	84,560	78,690	81,147	−9%
Municipal Boroughs and larger Urban Districts						
Accrington	44,975	42,991	40,685	39,018	36,894	−18%
Ashton-u-L	52,041	52,175	52,089	50,154	48,952	−6%
Bacup	21,263	20,590	18,374	17,308	15,118	−29%
Chadderton	28,721	27,450	31,124	32,568	32,435	+12%
Chorley	30,706	30,951	32,640	31,315	31,659	+3%
Colne	24,871	23,918	20,670	19,430	18,940	−24%
Crosby	44,468	50,569	58,478	59,166	57,497	+29%
Darwen	37,906	36,012	30,827	29,475	28,926	−24%
Denton	17,620	17,384	25,603	31,089	38,154	+17%
Eccles	44,629	44,838	43,926	43,173	38,505	−14%
Farnworth	27,894	28,717	28,616	27,502	26,862	−4%
Fleetwood	19,438	23,001	27,537	27,686	28,590	+47%
Formby	6,318	7,965	10,436	11,734	23,520	+272%
Haslingden	17,486	16,639	14,513	14,360	14,924	−15%
Heywood	27,495	26,727	25,201	24,090	30,440	+11%
Huyton	5,172	5,199	55,796	63,089	66,775	+1191%
Lancaster	40,417	43,649	51,679	48,253	49,584	+23%
Leigh	45,532	45,317	48,728	46,174	46,181	+1%
Litherland	16,384	15,959	23,628	24,871	23,717	+44%
Lytham/St A.	25,877	25,764	30,343	36,189	40,299	+56%
Middleton	28,256	29,183	32,607	56,668	53,512	+89%
Morecambe/H	24,205	24,542	37,006	40,228	41,908	+73%
Nelson	39,815	38,277	34,384	32,292	31,249	−22%
Prestwich	18,750	23,881	34,466	34,209	32,911	+76%
Radcliffe	27,710	27,317	27,556	26,726	29,278	+6%
Rawtenstall	28,376	28,587	25,437	23,890	21,432	−24%
Skelmersdale	6,684	6,177	12,639	13,841	30,582	+358%
Stretford	46,572	56,817	61,874	60,364	54,297	+17%
Swinton & P.	33,448	35,545	41,309	40,470	40,167	+20%

Table 5.2 Borough and selected rural district populations[a] (*continued*)

	1921[b]	1931	1951	1961	1971	I or D
Thornton Cl.	6,248	10,292	15,443	20,648	26,837	+330%
Urmston	8,297	9,284	39,237	43,068	44,578	+437%
Whitefield	6,902	9,107	12,914	14,372	21,873	+216%
Widnes	38,860	40,619	48,785	52,186	56,949	+47%
Rural Districts showing the greatest increases						
Blackburn	9,849	11,230	13,239	15,053	20,379	+106%
Chorley	21,837	22,043	27,198	28,567	37,900	+73%
Fylde	12,582	15,750	16,243	17,370	20,265	+61%
Preston	23,007	29,758	37,989	43,592	52,733	+319%
Warrington	12,129	16,035	36,745	30,732	50,420	+315%
West Lancs	19,386	22,088	39,993	55,565	71,412	+268%
Whiston	19,523	22,873	35,488	43,786	85,637	+338%

Cheshire

County Boroughs

	1921[b]	1931	1951	1961	1971	I or D
Birkenhead	149,820	151,513	142,501	141,813	137,852	−8%
Chester	43,343	45,747	56,952	59,268	62,911	+45%
Stockport	123,994	126,362	141,801	142,543	139,644	+13%
Wallasey	95,119	98,361	101,369	103,209	97,215	+2%
Municipal Boroughs and Urban Districts						
Altrincham	25,513	29,353	39,789	41,122	40,787	+60%
Bebington	22,253	31,877	47,844	52,814	61,582	+177%
Bredb/Rom.	10,059	11,690	17,667	21,621	28,529	+184%
Cheadle/Gat.	11,050	18,535	31,511	45,621	60,799	+450%
Congleton	13,461	14,666	15,502	16,823	20,341	+51%
Crewe	47,760	48,321	52,423	53,195	51,421	+7%
Dukinfield	19,558	19,385	18,451	17,316	17,315	−11%
Ellesmere P.	16,432	23,057	32,698	44,717	61,637	+275%
Hazel G & B.	9,830	13,178	19,674	29,917	39,619	+303%
Hoylake	18,889	19,745	30,936	32,273	32,277	+71%
Hyde	33,651	32,313	31,494	31,741	37,095	+10%
Knutsford	5,610	6,173	6,617	9,389	13,776	+146%
Macclesfield	34,483	35,552	36,052	37,644	44,401	+29%
Marple	10,197	11,088	13,073	16,300	23,665	+132%
Midd/wich	5,589	5,857	6,736	6,863	7,848	+40%
Nantwich	8,763	8,639	8,843	10,438	11,683	+33%
Northwich	20,969	20,827	20,160	19,542	18,136	−13%
Runcorn	21,391	22,587	26,245	28,436	35,999	+68%
Sale	24,102	28,071	43,168	51,336	55,769	+131%
Stalybridge	25,347	24,978	22,541	21,947	22,805	−10%
Wilmslow	10,337	11,956	19,536	21,389	29,040	+181%
Winsford	11,179	11,346	12,738	12,760	24,932	+123%
Wirral	5,915	9,599	17,362	21,894	26,885	+355%
Rural Districts except Disley and Tintwistle						
Bucklow	9,927	10,094	11,185	17,299	20,191	+103%
Chester	13,160	14,518	25,495	28,288	34,671	+163%
Congleton	10,970	10,876	13,145	13,992	19,175	+74%

Table 5.2 Borough and selected rural district populations[a] (*continued*)

	1921[b]	1931	1951	1961	1971	I or D
Macclesfield	15,569	17,675	19,878	23,351	28,210	+81%
Nantwich	23,381	23,869	27,505	27,662	34,093	+45%·
Northwich	23,739	26,180	35,038	39,498	43,169	+81%
Runcorn	25,240	27,580	33,259	37,560	44,930	+78%
Tarvin	14,851	14,388	14,606	14,497	18,123	+22%
Derbyshire Municipal Boroughs						
Buxton	16,863	16,884	19,568	19,155	20,324	+20%
Glossop	21,048	20,001	18,004	17,500	24,272	+15%

Notes: [a] Decennial totals follow later inter-census adjustments.
[b] See note [a] for differences between these figures and Table 4.3.
Source: Decennial census returns.

close to the mills and other places of employment where they had first settled, repeating the pattern established by the Irish in the early nineteenth century and the Manchester Jews a little later.

Industrial decline was not the only cause of urban population fall. All over the region movement out of the smoke and noise of the towns into suburbia became possible for more and more people both through private purchase and the building of council estates on the edges of the towns. Manchester and Liverpool were, of course, the greatest losers of population through these means; even the assimilation of the vast Wythenshawe estate left the city of Manchester with a fall of 26 per cent by 1971, with Liverpool close behind at 24 per cent. Salford lost even more (44 per cent) as it intensively redeveloped its tightly packed streets.

The towns showing increases were the obverse of the above. Those with new or buoyant industries, mainly in the west or south of the region, grew remarkably. Ellesmere Port grew by 275 per cent with its port activities, oil and car manufacturing, Winsford by 123 per cent through chemicals and new town development. Macclesfield grew by 29 per cent with a developing pharmaceutical industry and as a satellite suburb of Manchester. Some of the older industrial towns also expanded, Runcorn, with its new town status, by 68 per cent, Widnes by 47 per cent, Bury by 16 per cent. Lancaster and Chester too were still growing by 23 and 45 per cent respectively while the Cheshire towns of Congleton, Middlewich and Nantwich showed similar increases.

The fastest growing areas however were not those based on industry or trade but the residential suburbs and the seaside retirement areas. Around Manchester, Cheadle and Gatley with 450 per cent and Hazel Grove and Bramhall with 303 per cent growth headed a ring of suburbs that took in Altrincham, Bredbury and Romiley, Marple, Prestwich, Sale and Wilmslow with rates of 60 to 181 per cent. Even old industrial towns such as Middleton, Hyde and Glossop, where there was room for Manchester overspill schemes,

Table 5.3   Immigration in the north-west 1971

	% of Total population All Imm.	Old C/W[a]	New C/W[a]	Ir.Rep.[b]	Other
		Residents not born in the UK Number			
Lancashire	4.13	7,190	71,715	77,815	55,133
Blackburn	7.72	135	5,220	1,205	1,305
Blackpool	2.69	325	695	1,585	1,495
Bolton	7.29	230	7,065	1,770	2,190
Bootle	2.26	70	215	1,040	355
Burnley	3.45	85	1,005	905	645
Bury	5.06	80	1,030	920	1,405
Liverpool	3.26	765	5,435	8,470	5,270
Manchester	9.36	805	17,290	23,040	9,760
Oldham	7.21	130	3,960	1,320	2,230
Preston	8.09	105	4,640	1,835	1,365
Rochdale	9.50	120	4,435	1,990	2,145
St. Helens	1.49	90	245	815	415
Salford	5.76	155	1,325	3,975	2,095
Southport	3.55	240	520	1,085	1,160
Warrington	2.84	60	385	935	565
Wigan	1.28	65	215	505	260

Lancs. MBs and UDs showing substantial immigration

Stretford	12.9	85	2,590	3,155	1,215
Cheshire	2.97	3,225	8,625	17,340	16,805
Birkenhead	2.98	195	660	2,085	1,180
Chester	4.25	160	535	1,110	875
Stockport	3.35	275	835	2,165	1,415
Wallasey	3.04	255	510	1,365	835
Sale	4.12	100	375	1,135	690

	New Commonwealth Immigration	
	of which America (mainly W. Indies)	Asia (mainly India & Pakistan)
Lancashire	13,225	46,675
Blackburn	55	4,535
Bolton	435	5,000
Burnley	35	860
Bury	100	850
Liverpool	1,115	2,915
Manchester	7,120	7,710
Oldham	555	3,085
Preston	740	3,235
Rochdale	110	3,965
Salford	180	750
Cheshire	1,005	5,550
Birkenhead	55	475
Stockport	130	555
Wallasey	35	345

Notes: [a] C/W = Commonwealth
   [b] Irish Republic

Source: Decennial Census 1971.

shared in this suburban growth. Liverpool had a similar satellite ring. Skelmersdale, a council initiative matching Wythenshawe, grew by 358 per cent, closely matched by private development in the Wirral at 355 per cent. Hoylake, Crosby and Bebington with the slower growing Southport completed the Liverpool growth areas. The seaside in general was not growing as rapidly as the suburbs with Thornton-Clevelys at 330 per cent far above the 47 to 73 per cent of Blackpool, Fleetwood, Lytham St Annes and Morecambe.

Agriculture, Landowning and Rural Society

Agriculture remained the most important food-producing industry, though Fleetwood, employing about 1,300 people and with catches worth £4 million a year *c.* 1967, was, as the third most important fishing port in England and Wales, another regional source of food (D. M. Smith 1969: 41). As Table 5.6 (p. 213) shows, there were significant and changing numbers of market gardeners and nurserymen in the region in the twentieth century. Space precludes an examination of them, and forces the omission of forestry. In a modern industrial society, it is easy to treat agricultural areas as vast leisure parks, to undervalue agriculture as an industry. Yet Cheshire has continued over the centuries to be synonymous with cheese, and remains so, even if only a small proportion of Cheshire cheese is now made in the county. And, in terms of acreage, and despite the loss of agricultural land in this period, much of northern and western Lancashire, and of southern and central Cheshire was predominantly agricultural. Land loss between 1945 and 1962 amounted to some 3.4 per cent of agricultural land, chiefly to housing in Cheshire, especially on the Wirral, and to housing, extractive industries, and tipping in Lancashire. Improvements in output more than made up for this attrition (W. J. Thomas and Perkins 1962: 158).

The regional pattern of farming remained essentially constant between 1920 and 1974, but within each region and each type of farming there was considerable change. In Cheshire, the amount of arable declined by about one-third between the wars. As in the First World War, grassland was ploughed up during the Second World War, but the acreage of arable soon fell back, though farmers became less attached to permanent grass. Surviving areas of marshland and mossland were cultivated under wartime pressure. In the largely permanent grass (75 per cent of acreage) region of south Cheshire, milk production, with pig farming, dominated. On the higher ground of eastern and north-eastern Cheshire, and eastern Lancashire as far north as the Ribble valley, sheep and poultry were reared, together with an upland form of dairying which depended on milk sales for the urban areas so closely intertwined with the usually small farms. The dairy business was regarded as profitable, and increased in extent. Such farming extended into north-west Derbyshire, but sheep and grouse moors were important there. North-east Lancashire remained a sheep and mixed livestock region, with large acreages (on average three and a half times that of farms on the Fylde in 1962) necessary to offset the adverse climate and poor soils where one-third of the land was but rough grazing. In the west of Lancashire, the Fylde was dominated by dairying and mixed farming with dense populations of pigs and poultry. South of the Ribble arable dominated, with grains and vegetables occupying nearly equal acreages. Vegetable production was important on the Wirral and in much of northern Cheshire; in the central northern parts of the county dairying too was of significance. Indeed, W. B. Mercer argued that the cash income from, and routine of, potato growing, on perhaps a mere 10 per cent of the acreage, dominated farming in this region (W. J. Thomas and Perkins 1962: 162; Mercer 1963: 28, 33, 62, 69–72, 81–2, 170, 197; Coppock 1976: 115, 117, 136–51, 168, 189, 195; Whetham 1978: 304, 306–7; MAFF 1972; 1982).

Few new crops figured in this farming: peas began to be grown in north Cheshire in the late 1950s for canning and freezing, and as a time-honoured fodder crop; fifty-nine farms in the region produced peas in 1981 (MAFF 1982: this figure is unlikely to be affected by the boundary changes of 1974). If we call silage a new crop, it is very difficult to chart its spread in the twentieth century (Coppock 1976: 117). Its use on Taylor's Fold Farm, Matley, in north-east Cheshire, in the 1920s and 1930s was remarkable, and in Cheshire it spread widely in the last years of our period (Mercer 1963: 156). Rape was sown as much for farm subsidies as for its utility. Oats has declined over this period, certainly after the Second World War, while new varieties of barley have stimulated a marked increase in its acreage. Some of these changes, plus the continuing competition for labour between agriculture and manufacturing, and the resentment of the long hours involved in dairy farming, led to changes in work patterns. By the end of the period our region had over twenty tractors per 1,000 acres, mainly those of lower horsepower (Coppock 1976: 64). Machine milking could not entirely replace people but did reduce the demand on labour and improve the quality of milk. Arable producers began to use expensive harvesters and driers. Silage in conjunction with frequent ploughing and re-seeding of grassland (leys) attacked acreages of permanent grass; silage making is the attribute for which later-twentieth-century farming contractors have become valued. Chemical fertilizers and pest controls, and after the Second World War, antibiotics and artificial insemination had an impact on the quality of produce and animals, but improvements in animal quality had a longer history. After the First World War many Cheshire farmers had re-stocked to get rid of herds infected with tuberculosis (TB), and the experiments begun before the war continued. Accreditation of TB-free herds was introduced in 1935, and tuberculin testing was completed in Cheshire by 1960.

The region probably secured a more stable price regime after the Milk Marketing Board was introduced in 1933; in contrast to south and east England, the price paid to producers went up. The Potato Marketing Board had an equally important effect on farm incomes (Whetham 1978: 246–55). Business management also improved, and government paper work during the Second World War is said to have forced some Cheshire farmers to have become more cost conscious. Output may have increased by 25 per cent in the war, and rising yields have more than offset the loss of agricultural land since the war. Capital intensive machinery both performed best on larger farms, and permitted individual farmers to work larger acreages (W. J. Thomas and Perkins 1962: 159; Mercer 1963: 35). However, such improvements leading to increased prosperity for farmers were accompanied by a 43 per cent fall in the numbers of farms, as Table 5.4 shows. The losses were greatest

Table 5.4   Size of farms 1920–71

	<5 acres	*5–50 acres*	*50–300 acres*	*300+ acres*	*Totals*
CHESHIRE					
1920	2,721	5,467	3,364	68	11,620
1951	2,303	4,267	3,263	62	9,895
1971	644	2,549	2,741	108	6,042[a]
LANCASHIRE (pre-1974)					
1920	2,528	10,596	5,106	75	18,305
1951	4,735	8,101	4,661	52	17,549
1971	1,976	4,617	3,914	126	10,633[b]

Notes: [a] Omits 125 holdings with no crops or grass
   [b] Omits 255 holdings with no crops or grass

Source: MAFF Annual Statistics

between 1951 and 1971; by 1962 amalgamations were most numerous among the prospering farms in the arable region of south-west Lancashire. In east Lancashire and north-east Cheshire where the optimum economic size of a farm was about 100 acres, the extent of the problem was evident by the fact that such an acreage might comprise three existing farms. Why did the number of small farms in Lancashire increase between 1920 and 1951? The number of very large farms doubled after the Second World War, but there were still over 2,600 holdings under five acres in the two counties in 1971, and over 7,200 of between five and fifty acres. Of course different types of agricultural regime were typified by different sizes of farm: in 1962 (excluding those under five acres) the average size of farms in the five farming sub-regions varied from 47 to 171 acres.

Some new manufacturing industry located in these predominantly agricultural areas: in Sandbach for example, where Foden/ERF lorries were made, there were 831 males and 28 female workers in metals and engineering

311

in 1951. The 1951 census of occupations for Poulton-le-Fylde and for Knutsford (as examples of the small market towns whose fortunes we have followed in previous chapters) reveals numbers of metal and engineering workers, some no doubt manufacturing, though many of them serviced agricultural plant and cars. Service occupations dominated, alongside shops, building trades and professions – together over one-third in Poulton and nearly half in Knutsford. How many of the administrative, managerial and clerical residents travelled elsewhere to work? In the last years of our period the construction of motorways increased the number of rural dwellers who commuted long distances to urban employment. There was work not directly tied to the land, and for both men and women, as Table 5.5 shows. Alongside

Table 5.5   Occupations in Poulton-le-Fylde and Knutsford in 1951

	Poulton-le-Fylde			Knutsford		
Numbers in census	*Male*	*Female*	*Total*	*Male*	*Female*	*Total*
	2,807	980	3,787	2,343	910	3,253
% following each occupation	%	%	%	%	%	%
Agriculture	12	4	9	8	1	6
Manufacturing	10	11	10	15	5	12
Building	10	—	7	14	—	10
Food, drink, cafés and entertainment	5	31	5	5	44	16
Shop keepers and shop assistants	6	17	12	6	17	9
Transport	7	2	6	8	2	6
Administrative, managerial, clerical	11	22	14	10	19	12
Professions	6	8	6	7	10	7
Unskilled	4	1	3	5	0.5	4
Other	9	4	7	8	2	6
Retired	22	—	16	15	—	11

Source: Occupational tables, 1951 decennial census.

the provision of work outside agriculture, the reduction in the number of holdings, and the impact of labour-saving devices, reduced the numbers of employers and employees in agriculture. Again, as Table 5.6 shows, the reduction was most marked between 1951 and 1971. The processing, packaging and marketing of farm produce off the farm involved as many as 80,000 jobs scattered through the region in the late 1960s (D. M. Smith 1969: 41).

The nature of rural communities had changed in other ways. By 1970, not counting farms which were part owned and part rented, more farms were owned than rented in contrast with the dominance of the great estates at the start of the twentieth century; owner-occupied farms covered a mere 89,764 acres in 1911, but that area had nearly quadrupled to 353,200 (MAFF 1911; 1972). Others were tenants of the county councils under the small-holding

Table 5.6 Views of the workforce on the land, 1921–71

	1921		1951		1971	
	Male	*Female*	*Male*	*Female*	*Male*	*Female*
CHESHIRE						
Farmers[1]	6,449	640	6,896	555	5,420*	761*
Farmers[2]					6,007	
Gardeners &						
nurserymen[1]	6,858	321	5,812	281	4,065	51
Labourers[1]	16,061	1,605	11,284	2,213	4,065*	1,522*
Labourers[2]			15,128	2,191	5,797	1,617
LANCASHIRE						
Farmers[1]	13,562	1,128	13,892	814	9,685*	1,288*
Farmers[2]					9,802	
Gardeners &						
nurserymen[1]	4,399	330	5,889	274	9,047	92
Labourers[1]	23,821	1,836	15,850	2,639	5,636*	2,945*
Labourers[2]			20,397	2,801	8,019	3,068

Note: Census returns give an individual's estimate of his or her own status, while MAFF returns collect data on a different basis.

Sources:
[1] Calculated from decennial census returns; *for 1971 extrapolated from the 10% sample of occupations.
[2] Figures from MAFF censuses, which count farmers, directors and partners, whole time and part time, as farmers; and also casual workers who may not have recorded themselves as farm workers in a decennial census.
Cf D. M. Smith 1969: 41; for Cheshire see Mercer 1963: 37.

Acts which created farms for soldiers after the First World War. With controlled rents and guaranteed rights of family inheritance for tenant farmers, large estates found it less attractive to lease farms; some home farms were developed as a consequence, while others sold up. Nevertheless, the owners of both small and large holdings continued to find tenants despite the fact that average rents per acre in Cheshire were among the highest in Britain: in 1976 in excess of £7 per acre, compared with between £4 and £5 in Lancashire; prime Cheshire land sold for about £2,000 per acre in that decade (Coppock 1976: 58). Large estates continued in existence, though there were fewer than in 1872: figures collected for Cheshire for *c.* 1951 show nineteen owners of 3,000-plus acres totalling 27 per cent of the acreage of agricultural land (51 per cent held by estates of 3,000-plus acres in 1872), and 127 owners of estates totalling between 300 and 3,000 acres, or 21 per cent (21 per cent in 1872 also). It is not clear whether the proportion of agricultural land owned by public companies, local authorities and charities increased, but in 1951 they had 13 per cent of the Cheshire acreage (Mercer 1963: 191).

The fortunes of landed estates varied, as they had done in previous centuries: the breakup of estates apparent before the First World War continued. In the sample hundred of Northwich, Brereton Hall became a school, as did Bostock Hall – the heart of the nineteenth-century France Hayhurst estate – the half-timbered Little Moreton Hall was given to the National Trust in 1938, and Somerford Hall was pulled down. In West Derby hundred Rufford Old Hall was passed, with an endowment, to the National Trust in 1936 by Lord Hesketh (Fedden and Joekes 1973: 103). The Scarisbricks broke up their family trust in 1925 and the estate was split into three lots; Scarisbrick Hall was sold and pulled down soon after, but one of the lots remained with the family name until 1978 (Liddle 1982: 164, 166).

No doubt at least some such disposals were the legacy of previously contracted debt (see p. 231), but some estates were well managed and viable. Attitudes to estate ownership changed, industrial pollution threatened old family homes (for example, Norton Priory and Marbury Hall in Cheshire were reportedly pulled down because of it), big houses could not prudently be maintained, and the state became more invasive. The Hesketh estate was showing, at £8,000 per year, its highest profit since 1899 when it was sold up in 1927 for personal reasons (Liddle 1982: 164). Lord Egerton gave Tatton Hall to the National Trust, but over 2,000 more acres went first to the Treasury in lieu of death duties before being transferred to the Trust in 1960 (Fedden and Joekes 1973: 14).

Among all the change there was also a continuity – in the deployment of family professional and entrepreneurial skills, and in the accidents of inheritance – which would not have been strange to a seventeenth-century landowner. Captain Egerton-Warburton of Arley, Cheshire, had an estate of about 7,500 acres in 1914. He was killed in the First World War, shortly after his own father's death, leaving two infant daughters; Arley passed to one of these, who later married Viscount Ashbrook. The peripheral but patrimonial property of Warburton was sold after the First World War to pay off, as Viscountess Ashbrook remembers, two lots of death duties. It also provided portions for the Captain's brother and sisters; some 250 more acres at Stockton Heath were sold by 1940. About 1,000 acres went as a wartime airfield at Appleton Thorn in the Second World War. The Great Budworth estate, in need of expensive renovation, but generating only controlled rent, was sold after the Second World War. Viscountess Ashbrook characterizes declining landowning families between the two world wars as those without an income besides that from their rents, and capital from land sales; professional practice helped to provide that supplement at Arley. In the 1950s and 1960s the home farm was developed as an alternative to letting farms. The impact of these changes left a viable estate of some 4,500 acres in 1963. Thus after the First World War the family could continue to spend the season in London and live from May to September at Arley, bringing with them a household of twelve or thirteen servants, in addition to the resident estate staff. There were only three resident servants in the late 1960s and a large part of the house had to be demolished in 1968, though the family still live in part (Interview, cf

F. M. L. Thompson 1963: 327–335; C. Foster, private communication to CBP, 1991; Mercer 1963: 171; Pevsner and Hubbard 1971: 62).

By 1970 the resident gentry and aristocracy had been reduced to very small proportions, if Burke's volumes of the landed gentry and peerage and baronetage, published between 1965 and 1972, give an accurate snapshot of the regional situation. Many of the other old families of the region no longer valued the territorial connection, and lived elsewhere in the British Isles or abroad. Among those families resident, one of the landed gentry was a nineteenth-century arrival and one dated from the twentieth century while in the peerage and baronetage there were more recent creations. Five of these families had been ennobled in the twentieth century and four in the nineteenth century though most were landed gentry before their titles were created. A few individuals from established landowning families had continued to play a role in local government, and as Justices of the Peace (eg Kelly 1939; Lee 1963: 179, 188, 189; Marshall 1977: 9). On Lancashire County Council those members who called themselves 'gentry or landowners' (perhaps, therefore, including families without large acreages of land) declined from a quarter in 1928 to 7 per cent in 1971 (Marshall 1977: 220, 221; for Cheshire see Lee et al. 1974: 190). The greatest families of early times had kept their regional presence. The Stanleys remained at Knowsley and Wildboarclough in Cheshire, the Cavendishes flourished at Chatsworth, the Grosvenors at Eaton (who again demolished Eaton Hall beginning in 1961 and built a new house – Pevsner and Hubbard 1971: 207), the Molyneux at Croxteth Hall, the Cholmondeleys at Cholmondeley, and the Grey Earls of Stamford at Dunham Massey. Other families and estates that had survived the vicissitudes of time were the Bromley-Davenports at Capesthorne and the Blundells at Crosby. At the end of the period only twenty-one landed gentry families acknowledged residence in the region. The twenty families of the peerage and baronetage for whom Burke recorded addresses in the region were not necessarily landowners.

Employment and Industry

The fifty years after 1920 saw the greatest change in the economy of the north-west since the late eighteenth century. Manufacturing and extractive industry had fallen and were now outstripped by the service industries. The region appeared to have recovered well from the collapse of its two major industries but between the boom year of 1920 and the low unemployment of 1971 there was a much sadder story (Table 5.7).

Between 1923 and 1931 unemployment in the industrial areas rose to

Table 5.7 Industrial and service employment 1921–71

Occupational group	Total employees	
	1921	1971
Textiles	600,000	152,000
Coal-mining	111,500	15,000
Engineering (excl. shipbldg and marine)	244,000	486,000
Chemicals (incl. soap)	49,000	84,000
Glass making	15,000	22,000
Clothing & footwear	108,000	80,000
Food, drink & tobacco	87,000	119,000
Building & contracting	87,000	191,000
Gas, water & electricity	24,000	44,000
Distributive trades	230,000	397,000
Transport	184,000	202,000
Personal services	200,000	259,000
inc. domestic servants	97,000	16,500
Central & local govt & defence	144,857	145,180
	(incl. postal workers & teachers)	(excl. postal workers & teachers)
Professional & technical	56,000	338,000

Sources: Decennial Census 1921; industrial tables for pre-1974 Lancs. & parts of Cheshire & Derbys; Decennial Census 1971, 10% sample.

almost half a million; even after five years of partial recovery there were still 250,000 out of work in 1936, two-thirds of them male and 'roughly one in five or six of those prepared to work' (Economic Research Section 1936: 3). Failure to gain government help as a Special Area in the early 1930s was mitigated by a share in the award of re-armament contracts in 1936 and subsequent years, the region again becoming a great arsenal during the war years. The high level of employment thus generated continued after the war and was maintained into the 1970s.

The crisis of the 1920s and 1930s directed the eyes of the region's governors and entrepreneurs to its urban and industrial structure. The flight from the towns expanded opportunities in suburban building and services but there was a sharp distinction between the coal and cotton districts, which had few expanding industries and little to offer them, and the city and suburbs of Manchester, the Fylde and parts of the Mersey–Irwell axis which had a better spread of employment. In the coal and cotton area, the mining centres of St Helens, Wigan, Leigh, Westhoughton and Hindley lost 40,000 emigrants (11 per cent of their 1921 population) by 1931. The weaving district round Blackburn, Burnley and Rossendale, with a population of 500,000, still had an unemployment rate of 26 per cent in 1935. The spinning centres fared rather better, especially Bolton and Preston, while Rochdale fell into that fortunate group of industrial towns with a broader base which also included Lancaster and Stockport, where unemployment was under 10 per cent in

1936 (Lancashire Ind. Devt. Assoc. 1949: 17). Liverpool and Merseyside were less fortunate, with unemployment at 27 per cent from 1933 to 1935 and still at the high level of almost 19 per cent in 1939 despite the corporation acquiring special powers to build industrial estates in 1936 (Economic Research Section 1936).

The end of the war in 1945 brought a boom in cotton manufacture, especially for export, and a massive demand for coal, neither of which were very long sustained. It also brought government intervention through the Distribution of Industry Acts of 1945 and 1958, the Local Employment Act 1960 and the Industrial Development Act 1966. The major regional consequence of this legislation was the scheduling of Merseyside as a Development Area, a status that it maintained throughout the period from 1949. Loans, grants and employment premiums did much to attract new industries into Merseyside but a less helpful government initiative, Industrial Development Certificates, necessary for establishing large new factories, tended to direct enterprise away from rather than towards the rest of the region (D. M. Smith 1969: 115–20). A shorter period of development status for north-east Lancashire from 1945 to 1960 brought new industry there in light electric and electronic engineering, gas appliances and an extension to the Michelin rubber factory. South-central Lancashire also held development status from 1946 to 1961 and this brought forty-five new factories employing 8,000 people in food processing, asbestos and box manufacture.

D. M. Smith, in his 1969 survey of the region, identified sub-regions which can be broadly summarized in the following way. Greater Manchester with its 2.5 million people kept a very broad economic base though engineering was the major industry with machine tools in the south, aero-engines and electrical engineering prominent. The roll call of engineering in all its branches was impressive: Ferranti with six factories and 10,000 employees, AEI with 16,000 at Trafford Park, Simon Engineering and Mirlees International at Stockport with 3,500 and 2,500 employees respectively and a host of others only a little smaller. Textiles were far less important than formerly but finishing was still substantial and the clothing trade employed 30,000 in Manchester and Salford. Dyestuffs remained a Manchester trade with 17,000 and food, drink and tobacco not only kept their Manchester base with 11,000, with a further 10,000 at Stretford and Stockport, but also had spread east to Hyde where there were 2,500 in the well-established food industry and 1,300 in tobacco in a converted cotton mill. Further east, mills in Glossop were in use for pickle manufacture and food canning. The sub-region had kept other traditional industries, notably paper, printing and publishing and rubber manufacture. At its heart the city of Manchester with its financial, insurance, commercial and leisure services and its growing government, health and educational provision was making good the loss of the Exchange and the decline of cotton warehousing with a wide range of occupations.

On Merseyside with its 1.5 million people, Liverpool still looked to the port and the docks as a major source of employment. The Dock Labour Act 1947 and the further decasualization of labour in 1967 were intended to foster continuous employment, better relations and greater efficiency. Petroleum apart, however, the port's share in both export and import traffic fell in the post-war period; a combination of low investment and dockers' resistance to change did not encourage confidence in a revival (R. Lawton and Cunningham 1970: 235–57). The new container terminal of 1971 did little to slow the decline. The dock area had been progressively losing manufacturing since the 1930s, first to new sites at Aintree, Speke and Kirkby, then later to Winsford, Runcorn and Skelmersdale with the development of the new towns. The traditional food industries had grown and prospered – Bibby, Tate and Lyle, Huntley and Palmer, Kraft, Cadbury, Bird's Eye, and Van den Bergh. There was ship building at Birkenhead (Plate 5.1) and chemicals at Bebington-Bromborough, Runcorn and Widnes. Development status had brought Plessey and English-Electric to Liverpool; the giant BICC plant at Prescot carried on that area's ancient metal tradition but it was vehicles that now set the pace. Investment had been huge and by the late 1960s there were impressive achievements: Ford at Halewood with 14,000 jobs, Vauxhall at Ellesmere Port with 11,500, and Standard-Triumph, Joseph Lucas, Girling, AC-Delco and Champion Plugs also in the sub-region. D. M. Smith (1969: 165) was bullish: 'as a location for the motor industry Merseyside now looks very good'. The high wages of that industry offered great hopes of strong growth in the consumer service trades.

Merseyside was also benefiting from the shift in the paper industry which, while still strong in the Pennines, was investing heavily in Warrington, Wigan and, above all, in Ellesmere Port in its search for cheaper transport costs. Even textiles was introduced with the opening of a Courtauld factory at the old mining village of Skelmersdale, now a new town of over 16,000 people. The chemical industry, with oil and petro-chemicals, was transforming the estuary at Tranmere, Stanlow and Ellesmere Port, with Runcorn housing the great Mond division of ICI. Finally, power generation produced the large conventional generating set at Fiddler's Ferry, the atomic plant at Capenhurst and the headquarters of three atomic groups at Risley as well as the Nuclear Physics Laboratory at Daresbury. There were, however, clouds over this great growth of sunrise industries. The car plants had tended to draw their labour not from the unemployed but from those already in steady employment with other firms, leaving them searching for skilled labour. More seriously Kirkby had disappointed many firms who had problems 'with

---

Plate 5.1 The launch of HMS *Ark Royal*, 3 May 1950. Camell Laird's yard built passenger liners, other merchant, and naval ships, including in the 1960s and 1970s nuclear submarines. The construction and fitting out of *Ark Royal* dominated the skyline for years. One of the authors, a small boy in the crowd, vividly remembers standing alongside the towering hull of the aircraft carrier.

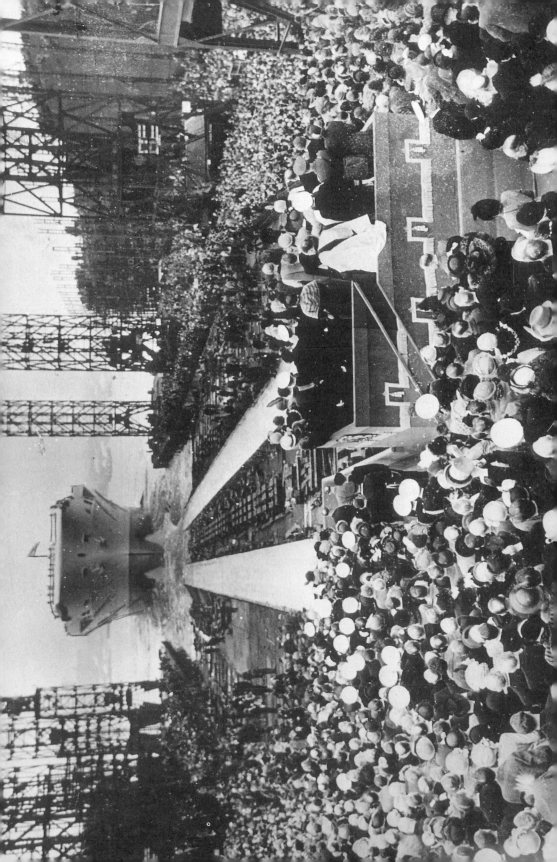

local militancy and a casual attitude to employment which had its roots in the old organisation of labour in the docks' (D. M. Smith 1969: 133–4).

With most of the major new industrial development taking place along the Mersey corridor the rest of Lancashire found difficulty in attracting enough new industry to replace its losses in cotton and coal. In Central Lancashire the southern coalfield based on St Helens, Wigan, Warrington and Leigh had lost jobs in cotton and coal and in railway engineering at Horwich and Newton-le-Willows. The legacy of coal and chemicals remained in spoil heaps and flashes of water, in poor housing and a degraded environment. The north of this sub-region, with Preston as its largest town, had more success in changing its industrial base with vehicles at Leyland, aircraft, electric loco-motives, ordnance and the atomic energy plant at Selwick. Textiles still employed one-quarter of industrial workers in 1969 but it now took second place to vehicle manufacture. Some 900,000 people lived in Central Lanca-shire and, for them, the transition from cotton and coal was as yet incom-plete.

North-east Lancashire suffered greatly in the depression of the 1930s and the draining away of textile jobs continued in the post-war period. Between 1914 and 1967 the population of the Calder–Darwen valleys, the great weaving belt, fell from 520,000 to some 420,000. New industries were introduced at Blackburn and Burnley in the 1930s and, under Development Area status in the 1950s, at Burnley, Padiham and Nelson and Colne but they did little to stem the tide. Rossendale to the south had lost almost one-fifth of its 1930s population by the late 1960s when the cotton mills and the slipper industry, both in decline, employed four-fifths of its manufacturing popu-lation. In 1969 this was the most economically deprived sub-region of the north-west.

North and west Lancashire, with their agricultural base and the seaside towns of Southport, Blackpool and Morecambe, had escaped both the derel-iction and declining employment of the industrial areas though seasonal unemployment was a perennial problem for the resorts. Lancaster with its sub-regional marketing and administrative roles had a usefully diversified economy; Blackpool, after wartime involvement in aircraft manufacture, developed a range of light industries; Heysham shared in the westward move of the fuel and power industry with a Shell refinery and, in 1969, the siting of the nuclear power station.

In Cheshire and the High Peak of Derbyshire the old textile towns had varying fortunes. Stockport and Hyde had long had a broader base than cotton and they replaced many of their textile, hatting and clothing jobs by metal and engineering in Stockport, tobacco and chemicals in Hyde. Glossop developed food processing and Chapel-en-le-Frith shared in the expansion of the vehicle trade through the Ferodo brake-lining works while Buxton, still an important quarrying centre, sought a new role for its spa facilities. Mac-clesfield's silk industry, like that of Congleton, was in long decline but pharmaceuticals with Glaxo and ICI was growing, that industry also taking root in suburban Wilmslow and rural Cheshire. At Crewe losses in railway engineering were compensated by growth at Rolls-Royce. The major signs of growth in Cheshire were at Sandbach, where Fodens and ERF were expanding their production of lorries, in the Chester area, where the massive Shotton steelworks and Hawker Siddeley increased employment, and above all at Winsford, where computers and cables were fuelling a great population rise in the 1960s.

Back in the spring of 1920 the Lancashire cotton industry promised hopes of even higher profitability for the millowners and full employment and high wages for the operatives but by the end of the year the bubble had burst. The unsatisfied demand of the war years had been met and the Eastern markets, largely for cheaper goods, which had taken over 67 per cent of exports in 1913 began to look to cheaper local suppliers and to Japan (Allen 1951: 197–8). At first it was the coarse spinners of the Oldham area and the large combined mills producing the cheaper grey cloth that felt the force of this competition while the fine spinners of Bolton and the specialist weavers of more expensive cloths remained relatively prosperous. By 1939 however as foreign producers raised their sights, only the very highest quality of Lancashire cloth was unaffected by international competition and the fine Egyptian sector was facing problems similar to those of the coarser American. The home market remained almost entirely British but year by year exporting became more difficult, not helped by Indian tariffs and Gandhi's Indian boycott of British goods. In 1912 the British cotton industry had produced 1,963 million pounds of yarn and 8,050 million square yards of cloth; by 1938 this had fallen to 1,070 million pounds of yarn and 3,126 million square yards of cloth. During the same period employment in manufacturing fell from 622,000 in over 2,000 mills in 1912 to 349,000 in under 1,200 mills in 1938 (Allen 1951: 196).

The combines of the late nineteenth century could do little to mitigate the unregulated competitiveness of the trade and, though there was a growth of combines in 1919 and 1920, there were still large numbers of firms in both spinning and weaving fighting for orders. By 1923 two new combines – Crosses and Winkworth Consolidated Mills of Bolton and the Amalgamated Cotton Mills Trust with its headquarters at Preston – had been formed, standing second and third behind the Fine Spinners' Association in the world ranking of spinners. The Amalgamated Cotton Mills Trust, formed in 1918, took in Horrocks-Crewdson of Preston and Bolton, Eckersleys of Wigan, Hyde-Buckley at Mossley, Stalybridge and Chorley, Acme Spinning of Pendlebury, Ashworths of Astley Bridge and ten other companies. After the amalgamation the combine owned nearly sixty spinning mills and weaving sheds with 2.5 million spindles, 1,800 looms and 17,800 employees (ACMF 1920). Alongside this and similar giants were weaving firms employing a handful of operatives on under 100 looms.

Raw cotton was bought by the spinners from Liverpool import merchants through brokers, the spun yarn then passing through agents to the manufacturers except in the combined mills where spinning and weaving were in the hands of one firm. Most of the specialist weavers worked to the orders of Manchester merchant converters who bought cloth for finishing and sale. The trade was marked by great specialization with only minimal internal regulation. Competition and free trade were regarded as its life blood.

Given this background the trade was slow to see the full implications of the 1921 downturn. At first the merchants, spinners and manufacturers pinned their hopes on a fall in the price of raw cotton and on attempts to reduce the high wages they had conceded in 1920. Raw cotton prices did indeed fall and, by 1929, real wages were back at the level of 1914 but trade did not improve (Fowler and Wyke 1987: 166). Manufacturers looked to the spread of automatic looms and spinners installed more ring frames but they failed to turn the tide. Slowly both masters and operatives began to realize that there would never again be work for all the mills and machines of Lancashire. At the start of the depression both owners and unions had responded traditionally with short-time working which distributed the available work and earnings and kept the labour force intact ready for the next upturn. This proved to be an ineffective way of cutting production because many mills, over-capitalized in the 1920 boom and now largely controlled by banks, maintained full production, selling at low or non-existent margins. Attempts within the industry in 1927 and 1928 to collaborate on the regulation of output and maintenance of prices also collapsed because of underselling. Reluctantly the industry began to look to central reorganization.

In 1920 the region had 59 million spindles and 792,000 looms, more than in 1912, and they were competing suicidally for the available work. In 1929 the Lancashire Cotton Corporation was established to encourage the amalgamation of firms and to acquire and scrap 10 million spindles and 30,000 looms (Plate 5.2). Its efforts and the attrition of competition reduced the number of spindles to 44 million by the end of 1934. However, orders had fallen still further and there remained 13.5 million more spindles than work for them to do. Unable to cope with its problems the once arrogant and independent cotton trade then became the object of legislation with Acts of Parliament for scrapping spindles in 1936 and for compulsory minimum prices in 1939 (Allen 1951: 212–14).

During the First World War the government had established a Control Board to regulate the mills using American cotton; during the Second World War, cotton, like other industries, was concentrated, with 40 per cent of capacity closed, so as to make the best use of resources. The end of the war again brought a great boom in demand especially since Japan, Lancashire's leading rival, was virtually incapacitated, not recovering until the end of the 1940s. The period from 1945 to 1950 was therefore the most prosperous for

Plate 5.2 A weaver, 1936. Thousands of young women in the region started their adult lives as weavers and despite long hours, hard work and unhealthy conditions they valued the independence it gave them. 'Ah con allus get four looms' was the housewife's standard response to an over-complaining husband. (Source: Manchester Guardian 1936.)

Lancashire since 1919–20, with high export demand and the home market limited only by rationing. During these years production increased over 50 per cent and labour, which had fallen to some 209,000 in 1945, rose to 300,000 in 1951 (Allen 1951: 202; D. M. Smith 1969: 141). Once again however the boom ended in slump as foreign rivals recovered and, for the first time, began to make inroads into the home market. By 1958 for the first time in almost two hundred years cotton imports outstripped cotton exports and Lancashire begged successive governments for protection against Third World producers.

Even during the war years the British government had been closely studying American industry to see how low productivity could be improved after the war. The Platt Report, which dealt with cotton, was highly critical of Lancashire and its findings were the basis of recommendations by a government working party at the end of the war. There were to be great changes in organization and marketing, re-equipment with ring spindles and, less certainly, automatic looms; the Cotton Board was reconstituted to speed the process of change. The scrapping of redundant mule spindles by legislative action was carried out by Acts of Parliament in 1948 and 1959, the latter offering subsidies to firms leaving the industry and, for the first time, obliging firms to make redundancy payments to operatives forced to leave their jobs. Plans proposed by the unions in 1957 focused on raw cotton purchasing, greater capital investment including state subsidies, amalgamations, bulk orders, merchanting and multi-shift working. Up to 1947 the cotton unions had clung to single-shift working and their acceptance of two shifts in that year was followed by continued resistance at local level until the end of the 1950s when two and, in some mills, three-shift working began to become common. The night shift was very often worked by immigrants, women ring spinners on the 2 to 10 pm shift handing over their frames at 10 pm to Asian men (Bullen 1984: 64–8; Fowler and Wyke 1987: 200–12).

Decline continued. By 1967 there were only about 44,000 weavers and 40,000 spinners, overwhelmingly now women on ring frames, in a total labour force of 120,000 workers in cotton and man-made fibres. The industry was dominated by a handful of big groups – Courtaulds, Viyella International, English Calico, Carrington & Dewhurst, and Coates-Paton. Many of the new plants they built were outside the traditional area, at Skelmersdale for example, and, more worrying for Lancashire, in Cumberland and County Durham. The late 1970s and early 1980s, surprisingly, saw the industry, though even more reduced in size, prospering on the basis of very high quality cloth rapidly produced in short runs for the fashion trade and by the manufacture of highly specialized fabrics of man-made fibres for a range of new technological uses. By this time, however, textiles was a very minor feature of economic life in the north-west; tens of thousands of people whose parents and grandparents had worked in the mill had to visit museums to see the cards and ring frames, mules and looms that they had heard so much about. Even the language of Lancashire had been redolent of cotton and the mill and expressions such as 'at t' far end', 'stopped for bobbins' or 'jinny bant' died with the trade that had given birth to them.

As the industry declined there was an anguished search for the causes of its downfall. American comparisons showed its low productivity and this was ascribed both to conservative operatives – mule spinners clinging to obsolete machines and male hegemony, weavers resisting automatic looms, and resistance to multi-shift working – and to employers who were technically backward, greedy and complacent. There was criticism also of Lancashire's openness to rivals, of technical colleges with ranks of eager Indian and Japanese students learning Lancashire's secrets and of engineers and machine makers exporting the tools which would destroy Lancashire's trade. The over-capitalization of 1920 merited reproof because of the capital burdens it laid on many firms and the failure of governments to protect the trade provoked bitterness. Perhaps none of these made much difference in the long run. Lancashire could not maintain its cotton industry without a combination of the high technology and productivity of the best American practices and the low wages of the Third World. For both owners and operatives this was to ask for changes out of tune with the century of struggle that had produced a *modus vivendi* that served them well until the world turned upside down. Their past success was a handicap they could not overcome (see Sandberg 1974 for discussion of costings).

The 1920s and 1930s were a trough of deep depression in the cotton and coal districts. Unemployment there was between 140,000 and 180,000 from 1923 to 1929, then rose to 490,000 in 1931, fell to 250,000 in 1936, then more rapidly as re-armament got under way. The severity of the depression varied with industrial geography. In 1911 some 25 per cent of the population of the textile area had been employed in cotton manufacture or finishing or in textile engineering, the percentage rising to 58 per cent in Blackburn and 60 per cent in Burnley (Economic Research Section 1936: 3–12). Ten years later, in Haslingden over 42 per cent of the total population over the age of twelve was employed in textiles, in Glossop, Heywood, Chadderton, Middleton, Mossley, Stalybridge and Radcliffe, one-third or more, in Bolton, Bury, Oldham, Rochdale, Bacup, Dukinfield, Hyde, Rawtenstall and Farnworth a quarter and in Ashton-under-Lyne and Macclesfield close to a quarter (W. H. Barker 1927: 53–4).

By the late 1960s the textile area had contracted largely to the districts north of Manchester though there were still outposts in other parts of the region. Between 1953 and 1967, for example, Glossop had lost 1,500 textile jobs, Middleton 3,500, Burnley 8,000 and Oldham 15,000. Nevertheless the demand for labour in other industries kept unemployment below 4 per cent during the 1960s and it was not until the late 1970s that it again rose to levels that caused concern.

As the industry declined the unions found themselves fighting a long and increasingly hopeless rearguard campaign against wage reductions, double-shift working, increased looms and the transfer of spinning from mules to ring frames. Not called out in the General Strike in 1926 many mills faced difficulties caused by lack of fuel or transport. In 1929 there was a lock-out affecting 388,000 employees; in 1932 the industry's last great dispute, after bringing the whole of the Burnley district to a standstill, spread to most of the north-east and parts of south-east Lancashire. In both disputes the unions succeeded only in moderating the wage reductions required by the employers (Fowler and Wyke 1987: 169–76).

Improving trade after 1936, the Second World War and the post-war boom briefly revived the industry, hours continued to fall, from forty-eight in 1919 to forty-five in 1946 with Saturdays off, paid holidays were introduced in 1941 and there was increased concern for health in the workplace, especially in relation to spinners' cancer. But step by step the unions were forced to give up positions they had fought to hold for decades. In spinning women piecers became common during the war and, in 1945, piecers were abolished, replaced by assistants paid by the employers. Weavers, desperate for work, sometimes put part of their wages back into the firm and accepted six and eight loom working as well as automatic looms in the firms that re-equipped. All the employees had to accept closer measurement of workloads; in 1957 the decisive move was made to two- and, in some mills, three-shift working. During the 1920s and 1930s rayon and artificial silk had been introduced; after the war, nylon and other man-made fibres were also extensively used, often in mixed fabrics reminiscent of the early days of the Lancashire textile trade (Bullen 1984: 57, 64–8).

The spinners had had a long tradition of organizing pressure on the government of the day in the interests of factory reform, first through the Factory Reform Association and later in the United Textile Factory Workers' Association (UTFWA). In the changed conditions after 1920 the UTFWA looked to the government for more fundamental intervention, twice proposing nationalization of the industry but with little support from the members. In 1953 the UTFWA asked Harold Wilson to prepare a memorandum on the future of the industry but its publication in 1957 was of little real effect.

The membership of the unions fell in unison with the trade. The Weavers reached a peak of 211,000 in 1920, falling to 25,000 in 1975. Over the same period the Spinners declined from 54,886 to 508, closing down in 1976. In 1925 the industry had supported eight major unions, exclusive of the calico printers, as well as a number of smaller ones, each with its own traditions and preoccupations. In 1974 they all came together in one body, the Amalgamated Textile Workers' Union.

Despite the flight of people from the region it was still felt by observers that the people of Lancashire were not mobile enough and this was attributed to peculiarly regional circumstances. The first was the traditional role of women in the cotton trade. In the north-west in 1935 46 per cent of the women unemployed were married but many of them hoped to recover mill jobs and were reluctant to lose that chance by leaving the region. By 1924 women in cotton had slipped from their 1906 position of third in the national league table of hourly earnings for women but they were still only thirteenth out of ninety-six industries. Where married women were working, their wages were, of course, an inducement to unemployed husbands to stay in the region rather than risk all by moving.

A second factor making for immobility was the piecing system in mule spinning. A mule spinner usually needed five or six little piecers and four or five big piecers in his working life, of whom only one would normally expect to become a spinner. The surplus piecers left the mill in adolescence and their early twenties to find other jobs, engineering commonly at Oldham, for example (Fowler and Wyke 1987: 125). In the late nineteenth century the fortunate big piecers who became spinners seem to have got their mules at about twenty-four and then moved on to good wages but the slump of the 1920s trapped the piecers in a hopeless situation. There were few jobs outside the industry and moving out meant giving up their many years of piecing, which was a kind of apprenticeship. Contraction within the trade however prolonged their piecing life, perhaps even to the point of extinguishing all hope of full men's wages. By 1934 the majority of big piecers was over twenty-four years old, 16 per cent were over thirty-one, 30 per cent were married and 12 per cent had children: their wages ranged between 26s. 11d. and 35s. 6d. per week when the Unemployment Assistance scale was 28s. for a man and wife with one child (Jewkes and Gray 1935).

There was one less tangible factor. The departure of the great mill- and mineowners who had dominated the industrial districts, the demise of their mills and mines, the fading of the Sunday Schools with their religious influence and that of the church and chapel-based societies, all progressively eroded the foundations of community life. For many only the family remained to offer help as it had done since the mill towns began to settle down in the mid-nineteenth century. These family networks of the terraced streets where grandparents, parents, children and siblings lived within walking distance of each other had a strong hold. But they too were under attack from slum clearance, from the new municipal housing estates of the 1920s and 1930s and the massive clearances and redevelopment of the 1960s. Mobility was no longer entirely voluntary.

The decline of the cotton industry as it was eroded by foreign competition faced the Lancashire coalfield with a fall in regional demand and pressure on prices at a time when its own internal problems made it difficult to respond. During the years of expansion in the eighteenth and nineteenth centuries the shallower, more easily worked seams of good quality coal had been mined to exhaustion and by the 1920s coal-owners were forced to work either inferior coal or deeper seams. Poorer coal meant lower prices but the good coal in deeper seams was costly both in capital and in the demands it made on the colliers. By 1930 coal was being won at depths of 4,500 feet and the heat and dust of these workings produced probably the worst working conditions in the country. Men in the deeper parts of the mines of Central Lancashire could lose up to 12 pounds body weight in an eight-hour shift and salt tablets had to be issued (Lane and Anderson undated: intr.). As difficulties increased profits fell and the capitalization that followed the long-looked-for nationalization of 1947 was nullified by a national and regional fall in demand in the late 1950s and 1960s. Much of the Lancashire coal was intermixed with shale or rock and even skilful washing and screening could not make it competitive with better coal from other coalfields or stave off the growing use of oil. By 1968, a sign of the times, half of the output of the coalfield went into the generation of electricity, with Agecroft and Bold Collieries feeding directly into power stations (D. M. Smith 1969: 154). The increasing emphasis on smokeless zones that characterized the 1960s and 1970s reduced the demand for raw coal for domestic fires and North Sea gas dealt it a further blow (Table 5.8).

Table 5.8   Lancashire mines and output

Year	Tonnage	Number of mines
1920	18,784,699	240
1930	14,905,273	189
1940	13,617,300	150
1950	12,271,927	80
1960	10,978,671	48
1970	5,572,249	12
1975	4,245,607	9

Source: Lane and Anderson, undated: intr.

As the industry declined it became concentrated into a smaller number of larger units principally situated on the east–west line of the southern edge of the field from Pendlebury west to St Helens. Small pits like those in Rossendale and the Rochdale–Ashton-under-Lyne areas were increasingly uneconomic. Deane Colliery at Bolton is an example: in 1935 it had only 133 colliers and 23 surface workers hand-getting 1,000 tons of coal each week for the Bolton market, which it served by road (Saxelby 1953: 86). It closed in 1968. These small pits were not the only casualties. Between 1953 and 1965, as the industry lost 27,000 jobs, substantial pits like Ashton Moss were closed and by 1970 the great Bradford pit in Manchester had ended its life. Two new pits were opened – Agecroft at Pendlebury in 1960 and Parkside at Newton-le-Willows in 1964, employing 3,500 men. In the same period Mosley Common and Astley Green each employed between 2,000 and 3,000 men (D. M. Smith 1969: 153–5; Freeman et al. 1966: 130). In 1968 Mosley Common closed as did Worsley some 200 years after its waterborne coal had offered cheap warmth to the poor of Manchester. By the 1970s only Hapton Valley and two other pits north of Accrington lay outside the coal corridor of the southern field.

The collapse of coal markets in late 1920 affected all the British mining areas and the north-western miners were strong supporters of their national leaders' campaigns to resist increases in hours or reductions of wages. In 1921 they turned out in the national strike that lasted from April until July but had to give way on a national sliding scale. It solved nothing and by 1925 owners and men were further apart than ever. The owners' proposals for wage reductions, district scales of pay and increased hours were staved off by government subsidy but its expiry at the end of April 1926 and the entrenched position of owners and miners led into a further strike. This time the TUC threw its forces into support and the nine days of the General Strike were the consequence. The supporting unions called off their action on 12 May but the miners stayed out for six months, driven back on the owners' terms by the exhaustion of their funds. In the early days of the strike the Lancashire and Cheshire Miners' Federation had paid 15s. per head to strikers but in mid-June this was considerably reduced and the men were progressively forced on to the Poor Law (T. Davies 1976: 13). The owners' victory was no solution for over-production; it did nothing to halt the decline of the region's pits.

Between 1920 and 1950 employment fell from 116,000 to 50,000 then to 38,000 in the early 1960s and 20,000 at the end of that decade. Where there were no local alternatives the prospects for redundant miners were poor indeed. George Orwell's account of Wigan revealed the human consequences of this long decline. In 1936 the town had 10,000 insured workers unemployed, which suggested that some 30,000 out of Wigan's 87,000 people were living on the dole. Between 4,000 and 5,000 miners had been continually unemployed for the past seven years and a typical budget that Orwell recorded suggests the narrowness of their lives (Table 5.9).

The rent of 9s. 0½d. suggests a two-up two-down house but Wigan had many smaller and poorer houses: 200 families were housed in shanty dwellings – old buses, gypsy caravans and wagons where they paid rents of 5s. per week (Orwell 1937: 61–2, 76, 92).

In the late 1930s trade began to revive and during the war and the immediate post-war years coal was wanted at any price. Mining rapidly became a reserved occupation and 'Bevin boys' were recruited into the pits as an alternative to national service in the armed forces. The nationalization of the industry in 1947 was seen not only as a solution to the pre-war difficulties of industrial relations and a step towards socialism but also as a means of securing the country's greatest natural asset. The government aimed at a national total of 730,000 mineworkers by the end of 1947 but as demand fell numbers began to fall again and in the late 1950s the National Coal Board (NCB) agreed to pay lump sums, originally £200, to miners on compulsory

Table 5.9   Budget for an unemployed miner with a wife and two children: allowance 32s. per week

	s.	d.		s.	d.
Rent	9	0½	Flour (2 stone)	3	4
Clothing club	3	0	Yeast		4
Coal	2	0	Potatoes	1	0
Gas	1	3	Dripping		10
Milk		10½	Margarine		10
Union fees		3	Bacon	1	2
Insurance		2	Sugar	1	9
Meat	2	6	Tea	1	0
Jam		7½	Peas & cabbage		6
Carrots & onions		4	Quaker oats		4½
Soap, etc.		10			

Total expenditure 32s. per week

retirement at the age of sixty-five. During the 1960s this natural depletion of manpower was not enough and uneconomic as well as exhausted pits were listed for closure. The reaction of Lancashire miners to these closures varied considerably. Joe Gormley, who was secretary of the Lancashire area at that time, recalled how Mosley Common and two or three pits around it were closed in 1968 despite vast reserves and unequalled facilities. In his view the miners there made closure inevitable because of a long record of poor industrial relations. At another small pit in Accrington the miners refused to fight to keep it open despite union advice, preferring to claim their redundancy pay (Gormley 1982: 52–8). In the mid-1980s, while there were only five pits left in the Lancashire coalfield, open cast working was also being carried on.

The 1920s and 1930s were decades of decline in the hatting trade. In 1921 the industry employed 8,574 in felt hatting and perhaps another 300 in silk, but by 1951 only 4,647 remained in felt and fewer than 80 in silk. Both the home market and exports were in serious decline with foreign competition making inroads both at home and abroad. At home a growing informality of dress and the spread of motor cars and buses reduced the number of hats that men bought, and the chain retailers who were replacing the old specialist hatters proved to be ruthless buyers. Abroad, political boycotts in Ireland and India, quotas and tariffs in many countries and cheap exports from Italy and Eastern Europe robbed Denton and Stockport of traditional markets. Women remained more faithful to their hats until after the Second World War but there the north-west faced competition from Luton where a more flexible, cheaper system of production based on non-union labour developed after 1920. As early as 1922 the English hatmakers had the capacity to make over 2 million dozen hats but could sell only 790,000 dozen; this over-capacity grew more serious year by year. Faced with this problem the master hatters joined together in advertising campaigns which brought little reward but they were slow to move towards amalgamation or rational-

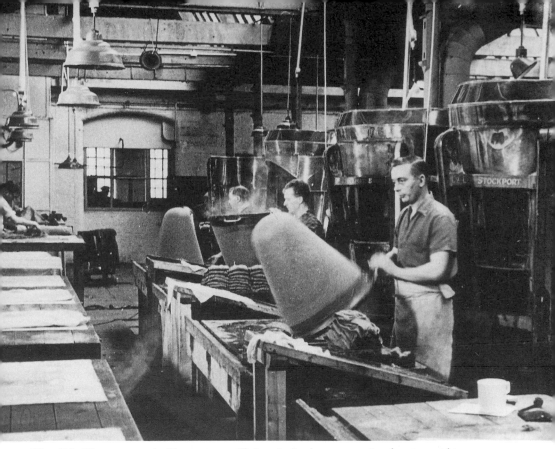

Plate 5.3 Hatters at work. These men, at Christys in Stockport, are using forming machines which blow fur on to perforated cones in the first stage of hat making. The machines they are using are derived from those brought in 1860 from the USA, which first mechanized felt hatting.

ization. Firms such as Wilsons and Moores at Denton, Battersbys, Christys and Lincoln Bennett at Stockport could trace their histories back for 100 or 150 years, many had strong family involvement and all valued their independence. Even in 1939 when some smaller firms had gone out of business there were still almost 100 felt hat manufacturers in Great Britain as well as several hundred small firms engaged in finishing and trimming ladies' hats.

The Second World War dislocated production and markets and in 1942 Board of Trade pressure brought concentration of the Stockport and Denton firms into groups sharing factories, production and profits. The arrangements proved profitable but the end of the war revived independence and competition. By 1958 there were only nineteen firms, the largest with some 600 employees (Plate 5.3); in 1966 the two major fur felt hatters of Denton and those of Stockport amalgamated as Associated British Hat Manufacturers Ltd (ABHM) with 1,100 employees and a 40 per cent stake in the fur felt market. Later, as shrinkage continued, the Christy name was revived at Stockport where ABHM had concentrated its working. By 1972 Stockport, Denton, Failsworth and Bury each had one hat firm with a total of just over

1,000 employees. The north-western membership of the men's and women's unions, which had been 3,644 in 1939, had fallen to 842 by 1970. It might have been expected that the industry would totally disappear in the 1970s and 1980s but Christys and Failsworth Hats outlived most of their European and American competitors, kept the modest home market and were exporting widely in the early 1980s (J. H. Smith 1980).

In 1921 the collapse of the pulp and paper market ended the age of the great pulp merchants and in 1926 the General Strike hampered paper production. The number of mills declined but units became larger and there were specialized developments such as a cigarette paper mill in the 1920s, high-speed newsprint mills like Mersey mills at Ellesmere Port in 1930, board mills at Warrington and soft tissue mills at Oakenclough and Ramsbottom. Despite these innovations, the 1920s were depressed. Wartime brought concentration, as in so many industries, then the post-war boom faded in 1951 to give way to heavy closures in the 1960s. Nevertheless in 1969 the paper and board industry in the region employed 50,000 people, mainly in the Pennine fringes of the textile area but also at Liverpool, Warrington and Ellesmere Port. At Darwen almost one-quarter of the industrial workers were employed in paper, at Radcliffe, Saddleworth and New Mills almost one in five, with other large groups at Manchester, Blackburn, Bury and Hyde (D. M. Smith 1969: 58–9). At Little Lever, Cream Mill, first let by Oliver Heywood to James Crompton in 1677, had been bought by the *Liverpool Daily Post and Echo* in the 1960s and was united with two other local mills as Trinity Mills Ltd in 1968 (Lyddon and Marshall 1975: 128). Many of the other old mills had closed as the Lancashire–Derbyshire Pennine edges were losing their locational advantages. By the 1970s there was a marked shift to locations on estuaries and navigable waters, exemplified by Bowater's Mersey Mill on the Manchester Ship Canal. The north-west still ranked with Kent as the country's major producer of paper, employing one-fifth of the people in the national trade.

The region was also important in the printing trade with 40,000 employees in printing and publishing in the late 1960s. Manchester was England's second largest newspaper publishing centre, second only to London, with a string of national dailies and Sundays producing their northern editions there. It was a sad day when the *Manchester Guardian* became merely the *Guardian* and moved its editorial office to London.

The Infrastructure

The shift to regionalism under strong national direction that had emerged in the nineteenth century most obviously in the poor law, public health and education extended more widely after 1920. Local government itself became increasingly subject to standards set by central government.

In the mid-1930s George Orwell, commenting on the industrial landscape, felt that the smoke and filth must go on for ever, but he saw only the surface (Orwell 1937: 18). The Manchester University team who studied the region in the early 1930s looked more deeply. In their view industrial Lancashire was reasonably provided with basic services but, like Orwell, they felt that it needed an immense spring clean to get rid of derelict mills, slagheaps and flashes from mining subsidence. They found that local authorities were ready with slum clearance schemes but were confronted with thousands of small and inadequate houses, poor buildings and badly planned streets. It was not encouraging to find that most town councils placed a new town hall close to the top of their list of priorities. Progress had, of course, been made before 1920 in meeting the most basic needs of the people of the region by the provision of pure water, by the regulation of housebuilding and the provision of sanitary facilities but there was still much to be done. Indeed rising standards had outpaced the improvements of the past so that the 'by-law' streets built after 1868, the Manchester and Liverpool flats of the 1890s and the houses reconditioned or built before the First World War which shared water taps or lacked baths had themselves become cases for improvement or demolition (E. D. Simon and Inman 1935: 11–19). The infrastructure itself was outdated.

If the physical appearance of the region was unlikely to attract new industry then there were positive disincentives in the state of the roads. Many were paved with granite setts, essential to horse-drawn carts in the hilly towns; in the most urban areas they were bisected by tram lines, for Lancashire had probably the most highly developed tramway system in the country. There was also the problem of the bridges; no fewer than 250 in the industrial districts were deemed to be unsafe for heavy vehicles (Economic Research Section 1936: 107–15). The region needed to shift from horse and rail, coal and steam to electricity and road transport and to remedy, in its years of poverty, what it had allowed to develop or failed to correct in its years of prosperity.

It was not until the 1930s that the road system was significantly improved, most notably by the East Lancashire road which linked Manchester and Liverpool, avoiding the intervening towns in the interests of speedy communication between the two cities. It did little for the old cotton towns but greatly accelerated the development of north-east Liverpool, especially Kirkby where the new industries looked to road transport (Freeman et al. 1966: 188–9). The most important post-war development was the building of the first motorway in Britain, the eight and a half mile Preston bypass of the M6 in 1958, which by the mid-1960s linked with the M1 in the south and was open as far north as Carnforth. By the 1980s the motorway network was easily accessible to all the major and most of the minor towns of the region and the Manchester motorway ring was close to completion but access to the east was limited to one road, the M62, and to the south the M6 was congested. Perhaps the most spectacular feature of the new roads was the high bridge over the Ship Canal on the M6, though it soared above an increasingly empty waterway.

Manchester took an early interest in flying, stimulated by Alcock and Brown's transatlantic crossing. In 1930 Barton aerodrome (Plate 5.4) was opened but it was quickly felt that the site was inadequate; in 1938 the new municipal airport was opened at Ringway on the edge of the Wythenshawe estate. Initially it comprised four grass landing strips and a combined terminal building and hangar, but during the war concrete runways were built and new buildings were added. By 1964 the airport, still under municipal control, and now graced by a new terminal building and extended runways of 1962, was handling over 1 million passengers a year, making it the third busiest in Great Britain (Central Office of Information 1966: 388). It is perhaps significant that the last scheduled sailing from Liverpool to New York, fittingly by Cunard, took place in 1966 (G. O. Holt 1978: 27).

As road and air transport grew the railways declined; rapidly after 1945. Nationalization in 1948, responding to the needs of the system rather than the *amour propre* of the two great cities, placed Manchester in the Eastern Region and the rest of the north-west in the London–Midland region. Nationalization alone was no cure for the railway's problems and in 1963 the Beeching Report recommended an extensive reduction of the region's network. Some 131 passenger stations and halts were scheduled for closure; thirty-three passenger services were withdrawn and fourteen modified as well as changes and concentration in freight services (British Railways Board 1963). Passenger closures were unpopular and gave rise to mass petitions and to pressure on politicians so that the closure programme, subject to ministerial decision, dragged on into the 1970s (Gourvish 1986). Although some villages, such as Hayfield in Derbyshire, lost their stations and services, the effects across the region were not as severe as had been anticipated. In Greater Manchester, for example, very few suburban services were withdrawn and though Exchange and Central stations were closed, Victoria, Oxford Road and the rebuilt and modernized Piccadilly stations could take most of the diverted services. Manchester's two main rail termini remained separated as they had always been. Electric and diesel trains had replaced steam by 1968 and car–bus–rail interchanges were planned, the first being at Altrincham in 1976 (H. P. White 1980). The canals had long preceded the railways in decline but as late as 1948 the Lancashire canals and inland waterways still carried over 812,000 tons of coal (Griffin 1977: 139). The

---

Plate 5.4 Barton aerodrome, 1936. When this photograph was taken in 1936 the new airport at Ringway, later Manchester airport, was already under construction. The aeroplane on the left was used for passengers, the other for training. (Source: Manchester Guardian 1936.)

progressive reduction in these and other bulk cargoes left the canals with no function, though by the 1970s there was a growing perception of their value for recreational purposes.

Up to the Second World War cotton remained the most valuable import and export cargo carried along the Ship Canal but machinery replaced it in exports during the war, becoming displaced by petroleum products in 1951, with oil becoming the most valuable import in 1952. Two factors lay behind these changes. First was the long-term decline of the cotton industry and the failure of engineering in Manchester to maintain the lead it had established before the First World War. Second was the rapid rise of the internal combustion engine and the petro-chemicals industries which increasingly replaced coal. These changes intensified the movement towards the west that had begun with Trafford Park and Barton, then on to Irlam and Partington. Decline in the Manchester docks and growth at the western end of the canal then had the unforeseen consequence of promoting the growth of Merseyside rather than that of Manchester.

Oil had been imported along the canal from its opening, first lamp-oil in casks brought into the docks, then, for security, when tankers began to use the canal in 1897, discharged into tanks at Mode Wheel and, after 1902, at the oil berth at Barton. By 1899 Manchester was the second port for oil imports after London, providing oil for the West Riding and the Midlands by way of canal barges and railway tankers. From 1920 to 1938 Barton was developed as a refinery centre but the construction of the company's oil dock at Stanlow near Ellesmere Port, opened in 1922, brought Shell-Mex, while the deepening of the canal from Eastham to Stanlow increased its potential as the major oil centre. After the Second World War the increasing size of tankers made it necessary to move docking facilities further west, to Eastham in 1954, Tranmere in 1960 and, finally, to Amlwch in Anglesey between 1973 and 1977. By this date however Stanlow was the largest refinery site in Britain with pipelines to Amlwch and to Bromborough, Avonmouth and eastern England. The latter were a legacy of the Second World War when Stanlow not only had provided the airfields of eastern England with aviation fuel but also had supplied the Allied armies in Normandy with fuel through PLUTO (pipe line under the ocean), itself manufactured at Trafford Park. The eastern section of the canal drew some benefit from the oil boom. At Eccles the Lankro Chemical plant, founded in 1937, was acquired by Shell in 1968 following that company's acquisition of a chemical refinery at Partington in 1957 and in 1970 the company built a new chemical plant costing £120 million at Carrington. To the west however expansion was on a greater scale. Runcorn grew rapidly during and after the 1960s, becoming the shopping and administrative centre of the new borough of Halton in 1974. Ellesmere Port's growth was even more remarkable. It passed Runcorn in population in the 1920s, acquired a new link road to north Wales and south Lancashire in 1934 and had the Bowater paper mill of 1929 and the Vauxhall factory of 1958 and assembly plant of 1961 as well as its huge Stanlow oil and petrol base. In 1976 Ellesmere Port's exports were greater than those of Manchester and the decay of the Manchester docks and decline of Trafford Park were in stark contrast to the boom conditions at the other end of the canal. Manchester's discomfiture could only be increased by the growth of the car industry in Merseyside when Manchester's pioneering efforts through Ford, Rolls-Royce and Crossleys had come to naught. Not only oil but also wider manufacture was shifting from east to west, much of it influenced, like the paper industry, by the canal which Manchester Corporation had made possible. (For the Manchester Ship Canal see Farnie 1980: 141–69.)

At the Liverpool end of the Ship Canal, capital had continued to be invested in the docks, some £2 million between the wars, but the rate of growth of tonnage fell. This was mostly the effect of fluctuations in the basic industries which traded through the port. Growth was slow again from 1945 until 1955, despite reconstruction and improvement of the docks. After 1955 it began to accelerate, but by the late 1960s decline was apparent. Dock labour costs had increased significantly as reflected in shipping charges for the port and it had an adverse reputation for strike action. Capital was still invested in the port facilities, for example the Gladstone container port, but structural change was also taking place. Passengers were moving to air; ominous change in transatlantic trade to a more European orientation meant that Liverpool was no longer an obvious port of call, let alone destination; as the Liverpool shipping lines became merged in consortia whose headquarters were in London, so a rationale for trading through Liverpool disappeared. Although construction of a container port had begun before 1970, in that year one of the consortia announced that the Far East container trade would move to Southampton (Hyde 1971: 166, 193, 205, 207, 208, 210).

At the Manchester end of the Ship Canal, Trafford Park continued to expand almost until the end of our period. Ford moved to Dagenham in 1931 but by 1933 the park housed over 200 firms; unleased land declined to 15 per cent in 1945 and 8 per cent in 1958. The Westinghouse Company, Metropolitan Vickers since 1919, was at the heart of this expansion, growing to a peak employment of 30,000 in 1943–4 when the park was an arsenal of war with 75,000 employees. The horrific air raids of December 1940 destroyed Trafford Hall and devastated much of the park but at the end of the war it remained busy and prosperous, with motorway links and rail Freightliners developed from 1967 to 1970. By 1967 60,000 people were employed there but the next ten years were a story of great decline. By 1976 the park had work for only 15,000 and there was no sign of improvement. After the First World War the industrial estate had become a popular device for attracting industry, at Slough in Berkshire for example; during the 1960s government aid and local authority assistance encouraged wide provision for industrial location and relocation. Even Trafford Estates acquired land for development in other parts of England in the 1960s and 1970s. As the park's industries ran down there were no incomers to replace them. It was not until the mid-1980s that both docks and park began a process of renewal designed to bring in housing, industry, distributive and service trades in the hope of pumping new life into Salford and Stretford. Entrepreneurs could hardly hope for the mass employment of skilled labour that had formerly existed (Farnie 1980: 118–40).

As industrial growth moved westwards along the Mersey and the Liverpool docks declined, Manchester, Liverpool and the old cotton towns had to cope with the environmental legacy of their own past industrial and population growth. Although the region was not overcrowded by the standards of some others, the most urban districts could rival any in filth and squalor. One example must stand for many. A housing survey by the Manchester and Salford Better Housing Council in the 1930s reported that in Angel Meadow 21 per cent of families visited were overcrowded, in Chorlton on Medlock 23 per cent, in Ancoats 31 per cent, in Hulme 44 per cent. At a house in Chorlton the tap and sink were in the yard and unusable in frosty weather; the dark and miserable house contained a man, wife and seven children ranging in age from one to fifteen 'and a large, if varying, number of rats' (E. D. Simon and Inman 1935: 60–2). The city's population was still growing and a deficiency of houses of 9,000 in 1921 had grown to 13,500 in 1931 without taking account of the 80,000 houses 'in the slum belt' of which 30,000 had been condemned by the Medical Officer of Health. Municipal targets of 3,000 new houses per year had proved impossible to achieve and private builders were more interested in the suburbs than the city though they had built 12,000 houses between 1923 and 1933, just over half as many as the Corporation.

Manchester's solution to its housing problem was the acquisition of the Wythenshawe estate south of the city and its development as a satellite intended to house 100,000 people. It began in 1926 when Sir Ernest and Lady Simon presented Wythenshawe Hall and Park with 250 acres to the Corporation, which then purchased the neighbouring Tatton estate of 2,500 acres. Additional land was bought later, the estate was incorporated into the city in 1930 and the garden suburb was laid out by Barry Parker in 1931. It was notable for its wide parkways, low density of building and retention of open spaces and patches of woodland (E. D. Simon and Inman 1935: 43). By 1939 over 8,000 houses had been built and by 1945 there were over 37,000 people living there (Nicholas 1945: 147). There was provision for light industry, shops, churches, schools, a library and a hospital and other normal services but Pevsner in 1969 commented on the slowness with which a centre that would focus shopping and communal facilities had been provided (Pevsner 1979b: 341). Not conceived as an independent new town, the estate depended upon the city to provide most of the work and recreation for its people but the standards of housing and environment were an advance on pre-war council housing at Blackley and elsewhere.

The device of extending boundaries to house satellite estates was not adopted after the Second World War, when Manchester, Salford and Liverpool, all declining in population, made a massive onslaught on the sub-standard housing that still persisted. None had land within its boundaries for the rehousing that was needed. The region as a whole had an enormous burden of bad housing, that is, one-fifth of the nation's slums: 400,000 houses in 1969 with a need for 550,000 new dwellings by 1981 (D. M. Smith 1969: 214). By 1974 the estimate for new housing had dropped to 300,000 but there were now 814,000 of the region's 2,392,000 dwellings either unfit or in need of treatment. Salford topped the list of those authorities with unfit housing at 15.2 per cent with Manchester, Oldham and Blackburn not far behind at over 14 per cent (SPNW 1974: 106–11).

There was also a need to revive old industrial or mining areas. Planning for redevelopment had begun during the war, in Manchester for example in 1943; by 1965 the fruits of those studies could be seen in a vast diaspora intended to clear the sub-standard areas of Manchester, Liverpool and Salford. In 1945 the Manchester City Surveyor, R. Nicholas, had rejected city flats in favour of overspill or satellite towns and twenty years later there were completed overspill schemes at Huyton, Penwortham, Cheadle and Gatley, Hazel Grove and Bramhall, Knutsford and Marple. Estates were under construction at Netherton, Kirkby, Eccleston, Halewood, Irlam, Sale, Partington, Wilmslow, Bredbury and Romiley, Glossop, Hattersley, Denton, Whitefield, Middleton and Heywood. Estates were also proposed at Crompton and Padgate (Dept of Economic Affairs 1965: 82). Some of these developments were very substantial: the population of Kirkby grew from 3,210 in 1951 to 52,139 by 1961, in effect a new town but without many of a town's facilities. Kirkby also had both tower block and low-rise flats, thus combining what Nicholas had rejected for the city with distance from all the social and recreational amenities that Liverpool had to offer. Good internal facilities in the flats could not compensate for the shortcomings of the external environment. The estate was not the only overspill device. At Skelmersdale a new town was rising on a decayed mining village, a second new town had been agreed at Runcorn and there were two further proposals, at Warrington and in the Leyland–Chorley area, to be designated Central Lancashire New Town. Other towns were designated expanding towns and construction was proceeding at Worsley, Ellesmere Port, Winsford and Macclesfield and agreed at Westhoughton (Dept of Economic Affairs 1965: 82). By 1969 Crewe was also scheduled to take overspill from Manchester and Wilmslow was being considered for a major scheme, Liverpool was expected to send 40,000 people to Widnes and Ellesmere Port and it was proposed that Burnley, alone among the major cotton towns, should take 16,000 to 18,000 people from the north-west and Greater London (D. M. Smith 1969: 222).

Planners were thinking even greater thoughts. By 1969 the Manchester City Planning Officer was suggesting a 'giant dispersed city extending from the Pennines to the sea through Manchester and Liverpool with thousands of acres of new housing set in man-made forests on either side of the M6 and huge industrial plants along the new motorways and the Ship Canal'. Other possibilities were 'Weaver City' based on Northwich, Winsford and Crewe, 140,000 more people in a linked Macclesfield–Congleton and a new Liverpool overspill on the Welsh side of the Dee. Estuary barrages at Morecambe Bay, the Ribble and the Dee would also extend possibilities for development in those areas (D. M. Smith 1969: 226–7). In 1973 the Strategic Planning Team for the North-West also expressed preference for development in the Mersey belt though not in such ambitious terms, their Mersey Belt including the old cotton towns north and east of Manchester as well as the Mersey corridor itself. They also supported growth in Central Lancashire New Town (SPNW 1974: 219–43). The team also offered a note of caution. 'Opposition', they said, 'to slum clearance has grown in recent years', going on to cite discontent with the rents, locations, amenities and environment of new council housing (Plate 5.5). They concluded 'The disruption of long established communities relying on strong family ties and friendship patterns is feared' (SPNW 1974: 111). Few of the communities they described had escaped the planners; *Coronation Street* had replaced the real world. The 1974 planners, however, while welcoming the opportunities for 'renewal on a large scale', were also now advocating conservation in the old Pennine industrial towns where many stone-built houses were worthy of retention (SPNW 1974: 43).

The infrastructure of the mid-1970s showed distinct improvements over pre-war days. Between 1965 and 1974 at least 175 miles of new motorway were built, electrification of the railways, fast inter-city rail and the growth of Manchester Airport, third in the country in aircraft movements and fourth in passengers handled, were giving the region good communications. Indeed these road and rail links made the region the leading growth sector for mail order business in the 1970s (D. M. Smith 1969: 136). But the past still hung like the Ancient Mariner's albatross. The region was the worst in Great Britain for air and river pollution and derelict land, though rather better than average for overcrowding. Manchester had been the first local authority to impose smoke control orders in 1952; during the 1960s the frequency of fogs in the city centre fell by 40 per cent while winter sunshine increased by 55 per cent over that in the period from 1948 to 1957. However, some parts of the region were slow to change and the proximity of urban areas meant that the poor performance of Wigan, St Helens, Blackburn or Hyndburn could reduce the effectiveness of more active neighbours such as Burnley, Warrington, Knowsley or Pendle.

Plate 5.5 Council housing, Woodchurch, Birkenhead. This recent photograph shows the varied layout and spaciousness of the estate which was begun in 1946.

The rivers were even more depressing. Pollution began high on the Pennine headwaters of the Mersey and its tributaries, which gathered industrial and domestic waste on their way to the Mersey tidal section, where crude sewage from Widnes, Runcorn and the Mersey conurbation gave a final blessing before the tired waters entered the sea (Table 5.10). Man-

Table 5.10   River pollution

| | The north-west | | England & Wales | |
Class	miles	%	miles	%
1 Unpolluted	739	40.9	17,682	74.1
2 Doubtful	465	25.7	3,709	15.4
3 Poor quality	274	15.2	1,372	5.7
4 Gross	330	18.3	1,161	4.8

Source: SPNW 1974: 80.

chester's sewage sludge was carried down the Ship Canal for dumping in the Irish Sea, the repository for the region's waterborne waste. The creation of River Authorities and, from April 1974, the Regional Water Authorities could effect no miraculous cure. For almost two hundred years the rivers had been convenient drains and the region lacked both the will and the means to remedy that long neglect. Where canal and river flowed side by side anglers fished the canal waters without a glance at the barren rivers.

The land matched the water. In 1974 the region had 15,000 acres of derelict land, the highest proportion of any region in England and Wales. It was made up of 33 per cent spoil heaps, 20 per cent excavations, 12 per cent service land and buildings and 35 per cent other, including abandoned railways. Some 45 per cent of it lay in Greater Manchester but it blighted many parts of the region; the shabbiness of old industrial and commercial areas not technically derelict added to the depressing character of those districts. In 1972–3 Operation Eyesore began with 6,000 schemes costing £17 million and the region began the biggest change of face it had made since the building of the mills.

The decline of cotton left the region with a huge legacy of mills built between the 1780s and the 1920s: their fate was problematical. Between 1951 and 1962 some 477 mills were converted to other uses as opposed to only 145 not reoccupied, but many of the reoccupants were themselves transient (D. M. Smith 1969: 127–30). A recent study of the Oldham district shows what happened in that great slice of the industry which embraces Oldham itself, Royton, Failsworth, Chadderton, Shaw and Lees as well as the Saddleworth villages which worked both cotton and wool. Some 470 mills have been traced, the earliest built in the late eighteenth century for wool and converted to cotton, the latest built in 1926, Elk Mill at Royton, the last to be built in Lancashire for mule spinning. During the nineteenth century some sixty-four were demolished but demolitions were far outstripped by new building. During the first twenty years of the twentieth century sixty-five new mills were built and many others extended against twenty-six demolished but after 1920 there were few new mills (Table 5.11). The 1920s and 1930s with

Table 5.11 Mills demolished in Oldham Metropolitan Borough

1920s	20
1930s	60
1940s	9
1950s	19
1960s	36
1970s	49
1980–5	23

Source: Gurr and Hunt 1985: *passim.*

their high level of demolition gave way to the building shortages and heavy re-use of the war and immediate post-war period. Since the 1960s the pace of demolition has again quickened and the forest of chimneys has been thinned. By 1985 over 310 of the mills had gone, 123 were still standing, in whole or in part, converted to other uses; only 32 were used for textile manufacture or related trades. A townscape of mills and terraced cottages had given way to the urban bypass and relief roads, supermarkets and garages, vacant sites and inner city low-rise industrial development that now typify the cotton towns. Some of the mills had strange destinies. German Mill in Failsworth, renamed Louvain in the First World War, was used as a boxing stadium; the site of Holt's Mill in Oldham, founded in 1779, ended a varied life as part of a golf course; part of Victoria at Uppermill survives as a museum as does the engine house of Dee Mill at Shaw and part of Brookside Mill at Grotton became, in 1935, the changing rooms for the old mill reservoir which had become a 'Lido'. Most were demolished to make room for road improvements, houses, schools, car parks, superstores and churches, their former glories sometimes marked by a passing reference to the mill name in the new development. Those that found new occupiers housed mail order stores, engineers, plastic manufacture and storage; often a number of small firms settled uneasily in corners of vast spinning rooms haunted by a lost clatter of clogs and whirring of spindles (Gurr and Hunt 1985).

The new industrial buildings were unlike the old. Conventional power generation brought cooling towers (as at Fiddler's Ferry and Ince), atomic energy brought the massive buildings of Heysham and Capenhurst, while the familiar gasometers fell under the onslaught of North Sea gas. The single-floor factory of Heinz at Kitt Green, Wigan, was a model of what the modern manufacturer sought; the Geigy Pharmaceutical Building at Hurdsfield, Macclesfield, represents the light chemical expansion into Cheshire and the CIS Building in Manchester the high-rise demands of new office building. Few towns got their new town halls but Manchester did achieve its Town Hall Extension and the new Central Library, while the universities and polytechnics of Manchester, Liverpool, Salford and Preston expanded in a variety of building styles; the new university at Lancaster was able to plan afresh. Perhaps the most significant urban developments of the 1960s and early 1970s were the town centre shopping developments, culminating in Manchester's gigantic Arndale Centre, and the extensive clearances again seen at their most extreme in the same city. There in 1969 Pevsner found 350 acres under clearance: 'the largest development area of Manchester, many say of England, and some of Europe' (Pevsner 1979b: 332). Pevsner was troubled by the prevalence of the tower block for municipal housing, posing the question 'Will they not be the slums of fifty years hence', but as he wrote councils were already turning away from that solution back to low-rise flats and the short terrace, though it was not so easy to restore the lost communality of the past (Pevsner 1979b: 272).

The hospitals and health care of the 1920s had developed over almost two centuries from three uncoordinated forms of initiative. Voluntary hospitals, starting at Liverpool in 1745 and Manchester in 1752 and established later in most of the major boroughs of the region, kept their primacy. Many were now specialized, some in Manchester and Liverpool were teaching hospitals and, in general, they dealt with acute surgical and medical cases and pioneered new developments in diagnosis and treatment. The Poor Law authorities had built infirmaries after 1834, some of them, such as Withington, innovative in their construction and many of them vast, but in general, repositories for the chronic sick. The local authorities had been prodded into the provision of isolation hospitals for the fevers and infectious diseases of the nineteenth century and for tuberculosis around the turn of the century. There were also cottage hospitals in the smaller, rural towns of the region, especially in Cheshire.

The economic decline that began in 1921 faced the voluntary hospitals with financial problems during the 1920s. During the late 1930s the decline of middle-class patronage was, to some extent, matched by a growth of contributions from patients and large numbers of working people but expansion and improvement was very difficult. Provision was unequal: in 1938 there were nationally 1.4 voluntary beds per 1,000 people but both Preston and Lancaster had 2.3, while Blackburn, Burnley and Salford were below at 1.2 to 1.3 and Stockport had only 0.6. In 1929 the Poor Law hospitals were transferred to the municipal authorities and only Bury of the region's county boroughs failed to inherit a Poor Law Infirmary. At Manchester the Corporation took over 4,790 beds, over twice as many as were provided by the voluntary hospitals. The municipalities were also active during this period in the provision of maternity homes, many of them like Bank Hall at Burnley or Aspland at Hyde, the homes of the departing gentry or industrialists. The hospitals of the two great cities drew their patients from all over the region, but both voluntary and municipal hospitals in the larger boroughs provided services for their hinterlands.

Just before the Second World War there were national discussions on the regionalization of hospital services; in 1942 and 1943 these were extended to cover the whole pattern and funding of provision in the post-war world. It had originally been thought that the north-west would be one region but, with Liverpool making the pace, it quickly became apparent that the two great cities with their universities and teaching hospitals needed separate treatment. Thus, when the hospitals passed under the control of the National Health Service in July 1948, two Regional Boards were established in Liverpool and Manchester. This division was maintained in the Hospital Plan of 1962 and in the change to Regional Health Authorities in 1974. The Mersey authority then covered west Lancashire and parts of Cheshire from Chester to Crewe and including Macclesfield. Manchester embraced the rest of Lancashire south of the sands as far west as Wigan, the extreme north-east of Cheshire and a sliver of the High Peak. By then the former distinctiveness of the region manifest in high infant mortality, the heaviest incidence of chest diseases such as bronchitis and *cor pulmonale* (the heart disease that it caused), rickets and tuberculosis was disappearing. Improved conditions of life and work and the advance of medicine were producing a healthier population than the region had seen for two hundred years. (See Pickstone 1985 for hospital provision in the Manchester region to 1945.)

In 1921 the school-leaving age rose to fourteen under the Education Act 1918 and ended that long bane of north-western childhood, half-time working. This paved the way for the development of secondary education which, until the Second World War, was based on selection at the age of eleven for either grammar schools or the public elementary schools, themselves either 'modern' schools or the senior classes of all-age schools. Within education, however, there had been a long debate about the desirability of selection and the bi-partite system which was under increasing attack after 1945, not only within the profession but also by influential groups in society. The Education Act 1944 raised the school-leaving age to fifteen, though this was not implemented until 1947, and recommended a further increase to sixteen, which was accomplished in 1970–1. The selective system was now increasingly perceived as inequitable, socially divisive and wasteful of ability when unskilled labour was in decline with the rise of technological occupations that demanded more developed skills and adaptability. The alternative advocated was the comprehensive school, which would take in all children at eleven, absorbing the grammar schools which, in any case, were unable to accommodate all the children attempting to enter them. Those of conservative views rallied to the defence of the grammar schools and, with government taking progressively more power over education, the debate became a political struggle.

The industrial areas of the region were quick to adopt the new educational philosophy. Oldham proposed a comprehensive system as early as 1945, though inability to build the schools prevented their achieving it; Bolton had similar early plans. During the 1950s, Manchester, Liverpool and Derbyshire were at odds with unsympathetic government in their comprehensive strategies though Kirkby, as a new town, was able to establish schools of this type. During the late 1960s as political power swung towards them, the authorities in favour of change were able to implement their plans. Manchester, Liverpool, Preston, Rochdale, Blackburn, St Helens, Bolton, Wigan and Oldham among the county boroughs went comprehensive, and Lancashire and Derbyshire took the same path. In July 1965 the Department of Education and Science gave all authorities one year to submit plans to end selection and eliminate separatism in secondary education. Cheshire and the more conservative boroughs were obliged to fall in line.

Separatism had rested on two foundations: a belief in innate intelligence which could be assessed at eleven and was thereafter unchanging and the view that the most able children need the stimulation of highly academic schools. The first foundation crumbled with new psychological approaches after the 1950s but the latter remained firm. Eric James, High Master of Manchester Grammar School, stated this case in 1947 and others inside and outside the profession were strong supporters (Rubinstein and Simon 1969). As the state system became comprehensive, those, both teachers and parents, who took a different view threw their weight behind the direct-grant schools. These could operate outside the state system and became increasingly attractive on social as well as educational grounds. The local authority comprehensives were often amalgamations of grammar, technical and secondary schools with problems of dispersed sites, teachers from different traditions, and inadequate administrative and disciplinary structures for their great size. Private and direct-grant schools and, above all, the public schools could offer a degree of social distinction and continuity as well as high educational standards. Religious bodies, especially the Roman Catholics, also faced problems where their children were widely dispersed or where they had great regard for well-established Catholic grammar schools. In the north-west, as elsewhere, the comprehensive school was only one of many forms of secondary school; many middle-class children were educated outside the state system and bright children of the working class were still creamed off into direct-grant schools like Manchester Grammar School. The major problem for the region was the low regard in which education was held in many of the old industrial boroughs which had fewer children staying on at school after sixteen and poorer results in public examinations than the average for the country.

The end of the First World War released a flood of students for the universities. Owens College was originally conceived as a college for Manchester and its vicinity, but had reached out to become a national university well before 1900 and as Manchester University was to grow as an international academic centre during the twentieth century. Both Manchester and

Liverpool universities had been founded and had grown on the basis of private initiatives; in the 1913–14 session there were 1,178 students at Liverpool, 290 of them part-time. The expansion following the war produced 2,605 students, 415 of them part-time, in 1919–20. Table 5.12 shows how

Table 5.12   University of Manchester: student numbers

	Male	Female	Total
1921–2	1,120	558	1,678
1945–6	1,354	934	2,288
1955–6	4,078	1,176	5,254
1965–6	7,357	2,369	9,726
1975–6	10,259	4,595	14,854

numbers at Manchester grew, and the trend at Liverpool was parallel. The combination of expansion in demand and decline in the regional economy forced them into dependence on government funding; a Liverpool University appeal for development and renovation funds, launched in 1920, raised only £350,000 of its £1 million target. The income of Manchester University grew from £183,282 in 1922 to £28,580,707 in 1976, the proportion attributable to Treasury grant rising from £56,000 (or 30.5 per cent) in 1922 to £21,338,188 (or 74.65 per cent) in 1976.

In the early 1960s overseas students began to be specifically recorded as their numbers grew. At Manchester in 1963–4 they totalled 951 and steadily increased to 2,316 in 1975–6. The university also drew students from all over the United Kingdom, and had to increase the number of student residences. In 1945 some 500 students were living in halls of residence, some 21 per cent of the student population. By 1975 4,760 were living in halls, 6,867 in 'digs' or privately rented flats or houses and 3,057 at home.

The growth in student numbers had to be accommodated. Liverpool combined old and new buildings centred on Abercrombie Square: in 1973 there were 111 professors, about 1,200 other lecturers and 7,250 students in the precinct of over eighty-five acres. Students' halls were some distance away, and there were off-campus residences at Manchester too. There, faculty buildings expanded the campus as did the university theatre of 1965; the precinct centre of 1971 included Cornbrook House student residence and Manchester Business School. The merger of the University Library and John Rylands Library brought together a collection of over 2 million books and manuscripts and off campus the nuclear reactor at Risley and Jodrell Bank's radio telescopes added to Manchester's international reputation. Expansion took a different form in Lancaster, where the university was founded in 1964 to be one of the new institutions of the Robbins era. Regionally it is also important as a recognition of the needs of the neglected north of the region against the hegemony of the south. It soon moved from a converted furniture factory in the town to its hillside site at Bailrigg, where from 1966 it developed its collegiate university buildings. Its planning and architecture were modern in style and its programme of studies took a modern form of tapering down from three subjects in the first year to two in the last two years. Innovation was also signalled in research with the establishment of a Department of Higher Education by 1968. (For Lancaster see Beloff 1968: 122–39; Stewart 1989: 104, 106; for Liverpool see Liverpool University 1981: 13–16; for Manchester see Manchester University, *Annual Reports of Council to Court.*)

Another tradition of university education in the region came from early-nineteenth-century working-class education. In 1902 Manchester opened the Municipal School of Technology, the finest building for advanced technical education in Britain and a long stride from its origins as a humble Mechanics' Institution in 1824. In 1904, though still controlled and largely financed by the city council, it became the Faculty of Technology in the University of Manchester. In 1956 it passed out of the hands of the city to achieve independence though still intimately linked with the University, becoming the University of Manchester Institute of Science and Technology in 1966. Massive extensions in the period after the Second World War produced a campus of twenty-eight acres with 3,505 full-time students in 1974. It had developed teaching and research in the application of science to industry, commerce and management to serve the regional community but the regional decline and international growth of the 'classic' industries made it international in its scope. In 1967, for example, almost half the graduating class of engineers and half the PhDs emigrated to the USA while their places were taken by undergraduates and graduates from the developing countries (Cardwell 1974). Salford University's origins were similar, as it is the indirect descendant of the Mechanics' Institute of the 1830s transmuted through municipal Institute status in 1896, College in 1921, College of Advanced Technology in 1956 to University in 1967. Its role throughout has been to provide a high level of scientific and technical education and research which relates to the economic and social needs of the surrounding community. This regional role has not precluded international links but has encouraged great flexibility in research and course provision. It also posed problems as the great basic industries of the nineteenth century declined and the college had to adapt to new needs. Its site, on a bend of the River Irwell and embracing the former Manchester racecourse, accommodated some 3,500 full-time students and 450 academic staff in the early 1970s (Gordon 1975).

Britain's ceaseless search for a structure of technical education that would restore lost industrial prowess produced the polytechnic movement of the early 1970s. Typically, both Manchester and Liverpool were the seats of new institutions in 1970, Manchester by the union of three existing institutions, Liverpool with four. Additionally, however, the needs of the north of the region were considered and in 1973 Preston (later to become Lancashire)

Polytechnic was set up by uniting three institutions. The early leader, not only in the region but also in the provinces, was Manchester with six faculties as well as extra-faculty units embracing a wide spread of disciplines from catering and art and design through the humanities and social sciences to management and technology.

The uncoordinated growth of the nineteenth and early twentieth centuries left the region with a rich assortment of colleges, especially for teacher training. The James Committee of 1971 examined teacher training against a background of demographic downturn and the 1972 White Paper that resulted, reduced places in colleges of education nationally from 114,000 to between 60,000 and 70,000. Some of the colleges sought salvation under an umbrella of university validation, and others in polytechnic mergers, as in Manchester; some colleges, like Crewe and Alsager in Cheshire, amalgamated and widened their curriculum. But in 1974 many faced a bleak future (Stewart 1989: 184, 195). Their problems were different from those of the colleges of further education, which were seen as having a crucial role in the teaching of new skills to young people who could no longer look for craft apprenticeships in old industries that were stagnant or in decline.

Social and Cultural Life

By the 1930s Lancashire had become one of the major attractions of the grand tour of depressed areas, featuring largely in George Orwell's exploration of the northern working class, *The Road to Wigan Pier* (published in 1937) and in J. B. Priestley's *English Journey* (1934). Orwell seems to have sought out the least salubrious lodgings, a combined tripe shop and lodging house in Wigan, in and from which he viewed the working people around him with the horrified fascination of an explorer. His landlord and lady were the Brookers, whining, self-pitying and stagnant: 'part of what industrialisation has done for us' and 'on the day when there was a full chamber-pot under the breakfast table I decided to leave' (Orwell 1937: 17). But Orwell was able to enter into many aspects of the lives of those around him. He sympathized with people being moved out of their old homes to Corporation estates out of town which had something ruthless and soulless about them: restrictions on pets or gardens, few small shops or pubs and high travel costs to work. The incomers missed 'the frowzy warmth of the slums'. Alice Foley was brought up in an old weaver's house in Bolton with neither bath nor hot water supply and an outside privy shared with another family. After her father's death the family moved to a house with bath and indoor toilet in 1915 and were later allocated a new council house at Dean on the edge of the countryside. Alice was ecstatic with the new house and garden, her mother less so. 'Eh, Alice' she said, 'what did thi' fotch mi here for; there's nowt but cocks an' hens' (Foley 1973: 79).

Orwell also found that, unlike London, few people slept in the streets though many lived in very poor housing and that marriage was not discouraged by the unemployment regulations nor by the fact that working-class men did nothing in the home to help their wives. He was perceptive about the attractions of the National Unemployed Workers' Movement, which brought men together against the Means Test, compared with the regulated atmosphere of the Unemployed Centres, which were meant to occupy the unemployed. The diet of working people was poor and monotonous, largely out of ignorance and a preference for the worst foods: white bread, tinned peas, tinned fish and tinned milk. Partly as a consequence health was generally poor, bad teeth were common and Orwell believed there had been physical degeneracy since the First World War, though this seems improbable. What reconciled people to the misery of their situation was the possibility of cheap luxuries: local theatres with variety turns, the cinema, radio, sweets, fish and chips, cheap flash clothes, sport and gambling, the billiard hall and above all football and the football pools (Orwell 1937). During the 1930s Liverpool became the major centre for pools, with Vernons and Littlewoods employing large numbers of girls there and using their profits to establish mail order and retail chain stores across the country (Mowat 1968: 500).

Priestley, as a Yorkshireman, was less shocked by the north, though admittedly in Manchester he stayed at the Midland Hotel, where he was spared the sight of full chamber pots. He too described decline. In Liverpool he contrasted the silence of the docks and the few stragglers who had been fortunate enough to find work, with the luxury of the Adelphi Hotel where he stayed:

> I wanted to eat and drink and have a party, chiefly because I could not get it out of my head that here I was, perched on a little lighted apex and that going down on every side were very long dark slopes.
>
> (Priestley 1934: 237)

In Manchester as in Liverpool, he found fog and decline.

> Still, when I was a boy, Manchester had the best newspaper and the best orchestra in the country, which is saying something: its citizens, who could read the Manchester Guardian in the morning and listen to the Hallé under Richter in the evening, were not badly off. . . . They had too, at that time, the best repertory theatre in the kingdom.
>
> (Priestley 1934: 238)

He commented on the Lancashire accent, the 'official accent of music hall humour', and on Gracie Fields, 'a sort of essence of Lancashire femininity'; but did not mention her male counterpart George Formby, whose eternal gormlessness contrasted so strongly with her essential shrewdness. Perhaps Orwell might have qualified his view of the dominance of the male in Lancashire had he been a cinema-goer. Priestley for his part was more interested in the difference between his own Yorkshire folk and those of the cotton county.

> We in Yorkshire considered the Lancastrians as people, real folk (not like the vapouring creatures from the South Country), but inclined to be frivolous and spendthrifts so that we shook our heads at the thought of their annual goings on in Blackpool.
>
> (Priestley 1934: 240)

As he wrote, the great days of hearty Wakes were becoming increasingly difficult for many working people, for example the plain weavers of the Blackburn district, where Priestley found only resigned poverty. Nevertheless the seaside resorts kept their markets. Blackpool, the greatest, continued to grow as a resort until the 1930s, when the building of boarding houses came to an end. It demonstrated flexibility, not only building on the mass Wakes entry of working people from the north and Midlands already apparent before 1900 but also attracting holidaymakers from further afield in Britain. Sea, beach, Tower and Winter Gardens were supplemented by the growth of the South Shore amusement park and the Golden Mile and, in 1939, the opening of the Derby Baths; the Illuminations extended the season into October and a Christmas season began to develop in the 1930s. Landladies also adapted to changing demand. Before the First World War they had provided 'apartments' and their customers provided their own food, which was cooked by the landlady. During the inter-war years full board became increasingly common before further shifts in the 1960s brought the self-catering flatlet, a return to earlier practices but easier for proprietors (Walton 1978). In 1900 there were about 3 million visitors; by the late 1960s, in the face of growing international competition, there were some 8 million a year (Pevsner 1979a: 68).

Neither Orwell nor Priestley was very interested in those working- and middle-class groups who prospered in the 1930s. They found what they sought, the problem of Lancashire, which was, in Priestley's view, a problem for England that could be solved only by a national plan. Those in full work or with regular incomes were more concerned with their own lives. They were the people who were able to move out to more pleasant suburbs, follow the fashion in dress, take more distant holidays and even buy a motor cycle or car and explore the still uncrowded roads.

Even the less fortunate had a wide range of recreations though they were principally for men. Angling, mainly on the canals, was not much reduced by unemployment and became more competitive with pegged, prize matches. Depression also encouraged professional boxing in which Manchester was prominent in the 1930s with Jackie Brown and Jock McAvoy. One Manchester boxer, Len Johnson, could perhaps have risen to greater heights but he was denied a chance at the British welterweight title in 1932 because he was Black. Cricket was a great spectator sport. Attendances at Lancashire League matches were over 300,000 in 1922 and unemployment does not seem to have reduced the numbers of people playing. For county cricket the post-war years were marked by a change in social character; in the decade beginning in 1910 there were fourteen débuts for Lancashire by public school gentlemen, similar to earlier decades, but in the 1920s this fell to three. The demise of middle-class leadership and participation in the region's life extended even to this hallowed ritual. Lancashire supporters had a great season in 1928 when the club won a hat-trick of titles but the 1930s saw a slide into mediocrity despite the advent of Hopwood, Paynter and Washbrook (Brooke and Goodyear 1991: 19–23). Nor was football seriously incommoded by unemployment either in the numbers playing or those merely watching. These were great days for the northern soccer clubs with Everton and Liverpool, Manchester City and United, Bolton Wanderers, Blackburn Rovers, Blackpool, Preston North End and Burnley fighting it out in the Cup and First Division. Schools and firms supplemented the amateur soccer leagues aided by the work of the National Playing Fields Association and some municipal recreation grounds were even open for Sunday football. Rugby league and union continued on their socially separate ways; the league game in particular benefited from the sturdy descendants of immigrants, hardened by the heavy industries of their native towns (Plate 5.6). (See Mason 1989 for social analysis of sport during the period.)

Sport was largely a refuge from real life but recreation and politics came together in the great expansion of rambling made possible by the railways. Since before the turn of the century there had been a middle-class campaign to open the moors and mountains to public access but in the 1920s and 1930s the Peak District became the focus of a working-class movement that rejected the orderly persuasive tactics of the Ramblers' Federation in favour of mass demonstrations and trespasses. This process culminated in a march on Kinder Scout on 24 April 1932, organized by the Lancashire branch of the British Workers' Sport Federation, an offshoot of the Communist Party, during which one of the eight gamekeepers trying to prevent trespass was injured. Five of the trespassers were sentenced to periods of imprisonment, there was great publicity and indignation on both sides but no further progress towards access was made before the Second World War. (See *Rucksack* vol. 9 no. 8 Autumn 1979; vol. 10 no. 8 June 1982; *Manchester Evening News* 22 April

---

Plate 5.6 The Rugby League Challenge Cup Final, 1969. Salford get the ball away in front of a massive Wembley crowd but Castleford ran out winners at eleven points to six.

1932.) Curiously Kinder Scout, the 1932 battleground, had been offered as a gift to Manchester City Council as a park by its then owner Mr James Watts in 1901 but it was declined because of the great cost of railing it off (*Manchester City News* 14 August 1926).

Before the First World war middle-class girls had played tennis and golf and some young working-class women had begun to break out of the confined circles of home, work and church or chapel through involvement in the socialist and suffrage movements and the cycling and rambling clubs that were becoming popular. After the war schools extended more athletic and sporting activities to girls; some of the larger cotton firms introduced sports and gymnastics for their female employees in association with the Women's League for Health and Beauty. In 1930 Allied Press organized a beauty competition for mill girls with eighteen girls selected by their districts as 'Cotton Queens' competing at Blackpool for the title 'Cotton Queen of Great Britain'. The winner, Frances Lockett of Hyde, was greeted on her return home by a crowd of at least 20,000 at the Town Hall (Middleton 1932: 178–9). For a few years the annual competition caused great excitement in the cotton towns but it failed in its attempt to revive the cotton industry.

Revival came with the national plan, advocated by Priestley, but in preparation for war and during the war itself. Initially the north-west gained comparatively little from re-armament but as the pace quickened, employment boomed and wages increased. By the spring of 1940 some engineering firms were paying the unheard of wage of £7 or £8 per week to skilled engineers and the cotton industry was thriving. Metropolitan-Vickers in Manchester worked forty-eight hours without a break to dispatch eight special radar transmitters as Germany invaded the Low Countries and also made, with AVRO, the Manchester and, later, Lancaster bombers. By the end of the war Ford had 17,000 employees at Manchester making aero engines and the Royal Ordnance Factory at Chorley employed 35,000 at its peak, bringing in labour from Manchester, Liverpool and Blackpool to its 1,000 acre site and 1,500 separate buildings. Fleetwood's fishing fleet had decreased from 159 in 1927 to 96 in 1938 but the war brought great profits for the Icelandic trawlers with catches worth from £10,000 to £20,000 (Calder 1969: 117, 325, 415, 446–7). Rationing may well have improved the diet of many people and the black-out, the cancellation of Bank Holidays and giving up of the Wakes, restricted entertainments and chronic shortages of beer and cigarettes were rather a nuisance than an intolerable burden.

Of course the terror of war outweighed its economic benefits. In August 1939 two-thirds of the children in the Lancashire conurbations of Liverpool, Wallasey, Bootle, Birkenhead, Manchester and Salford were evacuated, the highest proportion in the country (Calder 1969: 37–8). Half of the Manchester children returned in the first year, before the bombing (Harrisson 1990: 38). The bombers came in late August 1940 when over 150 attacked Merseyside on four consecutive nights in the first major attack on a British city. The raid on the fourth night started 160 fires in Liverpool's commercial centre. Merseyside suffered three major raids in November and December 1940 and raids in March and April 1941 culminated in six consecutive nights of heavy bombing at the beginning of May which left 1,900 dead and 1,450 seriously injured. An angry and dispirited people took refuge in flight. Maghull, which had prepared for 1,750 seeking refuge, found itself with 6,000 refugees on one night, almost doubling its population of 8,000, and opened every church, school and hall to accommodate them (Calder 1969: 153–4, 213). For a time the Merseyside docks worked only a quarter of their normal tonnage. Only London suffered more attacks than Liverpool (Plate 5.7). Excluding the August raids of 1940, German statistics recorded seventy-one major raids on London between 7 September 1940 and 16 May 1941, with 18,800 tons of bombs dropped. During the same period Liverpool and Birkenhead suffered eight major raids with 1,957 tons dropped, rather more than Birmingham, which was in third place. Manchester was less heavily attacked with three major raids and 578 tons dropped (Collier 1957: 506). Its great trial came in December 1940 and January 1941 with three major raids that destroyed much of the central business area by fire and damaged the cathedral (see Figure 5.1 for the *Luftwaffe* view of part of Manchester). Liverpool lost 2,596 civilians killed and had 4,148 injured; Manchester's losses were 577 dead and 583 seriously injured.

Other towns in the region escaped comparatively lightly but the peaceful morning of Christmas Eve 1944 was shattered by an air-launched flying bomb attack on Manchester from off the east coast. Only one flying bomb reached its target, falling in Didsbury, but seven fell elsewhere in Lancashire, six in Cheshire and two in north Derbyshire. Oldham suffered the greatest casualties with thirty-two dead (P. J. C. Smith 1988; Calder 1969: 562).

The territorial element in recruiting was not as marked as in the First World War and casualties in the armed forces were neither at those horrific levels nor as concentrated on particular districts but a steady flow of sad telegrams brought the same messages of death and captivity. Like other parts of the United Kingdom the region became accustomed to the presence of servicemen from other countries, Americans in particular in the Warrington area.

The post-war world was drab but there was cause for optimism. Unemployment had given way to labour shortage with displaced persons welcomed into the mills. The Labour government's policies reflected the mood for change that had swept the north-west like other regions. Nationalization of the mines promised peace and prosperity in that industry, the National Health Service offered an improvement to the region's high mortality rates, especially of children, and the Education Act 1944 appeared to open opportunities long denied. But the low unemployment rate which persisted until the 1970s masked the continuing industrial decline of the region.

In 1964 Geoffrey Moorhouse repeated Priestley's earlier visit and, like

him, commented on the decline of Manchester, the need for change and the necessity for a development plan. Manchester's air was becoming cleaner as a result of the 1952 smokeless zone and the Piccadilly Plaza hotel had just opened but the US consulate had closed in 1963 and the *Guardian* had dropped Manchester from its title and moved its editorial chair to London. Liverpool, though more exciting with its surge of pop groups using the port's Hamburg and New York connection, especially the Beatles, was, he suggested, more brutish, tense and cosmopolitan than Manchester. Old religious differences still influenced politics; the city did not get a Labour-controlled council until 1955 and even then the old Catholic Labour element was ill at ease with the militant secularism which was an increasing force (Moorhouse 1964: 125–8, 131–4).

The popular music that Moorhouse commented on was both a cause and effect of a greater change. Adolescent gangs had been a feature of Manchester and Liverpool life early in the twentieth century but they were male and violent, confined to the poorest quarters of those cities. The 1950s saw the rise of a new adolescent culture which was more broadly based, more prosperous and less violent. It also embraced both sexes. Musically it found its first expression in traditional jazz but from the mid-1950s the emphasis shifted to rock music, following the tour of Bill Haley and the Comets, and pop music in emulation of American singers, Elvis Presley in particular. Its early British exponents closely copied American models with varying degrees of success but·in Liverpool something new emerged. The city had for many years nurtured music hall traditions, producing comedians of the calibre of Tommy Handley, Robb Wilton and Arthur Askey. It also had a continuous stream of new American records brought in by the 'Cunard Yanks', seamen on the transatlantic run. Perhaps too the cross-cultural character that the city derived from its immigrant communities and the excitement of port life made it particularly open to outside influences. In 1960 Gerry and the Pacemakers (Plate 5.8) made 'You'll never walk alone' the Merseyside anthem with one performance at a boxing stadium. A little later Billy Fury from Bootle, backed by the Manchester Dakotas, became a national figure. In the early 1960s the example of the many Liverpool groups travelled up the Mersey to Manchester, where there was a surge of groups including the Hollies, but all paled beside the Beatles. From 1963 to 1969 this group, managed by another Liverpudlian, Brian Epstein, dominated popular music, drawing a world audience of 200 million for a satellite television appearance in 1967 and regularly filling the top places in the ratings at home and abroad. Their music made them cult figures, exemplars and models to young people, who foll-

Plate 5.7 Liverpool, the morning after. The Liver birds seem to have their backs turned to the devastation caused by the bombing. Here it is mainly destruction of commercial property that is seen but the people also suffered greatly.

BB 12 k (GB 4) Einzelobjekte:

102 Kanal-Drehbrücke üb. Manchester-Seekanal (Bild)

104 Straßenbrücke über Manchester-Seekanal

190 Tankanlage und Raffinerie in Barton, am Südufer des Manchester Ship Canal, etwa 2,5 km oberhalb der Schleusen von Barton.

191 Große und kleine Barton Schleuse

192 Kläranlagen der Manchester Corporation, Wasserwerke in Manchester-Davyhulme

193 Großmühle und Silo in Manchester-Trafford Park (Bild)

194 Kraftwerk in Manchester-Barton (Dampf u. Wasser) (Bild)

195 Stahlwerke in Manchester-Trafford Park (Bild)

196 Metropolitan Vickers El. Co. Ltd. in Manchester-Trafford Park, Elektr. Maschinen, Schweißapparate (Bild)

197 Flugzeughallenfabrik in Manchester-Trafford Park

198 Treibstofflager in Manchester-Trafford Park (Bild)

199 Kläranlagen der Salford Corporation Wasserwerke-Salford

245 Seifenfabrik

Bahnanlage, Güterschuppen

Hafenanlage, Kai, Landestation

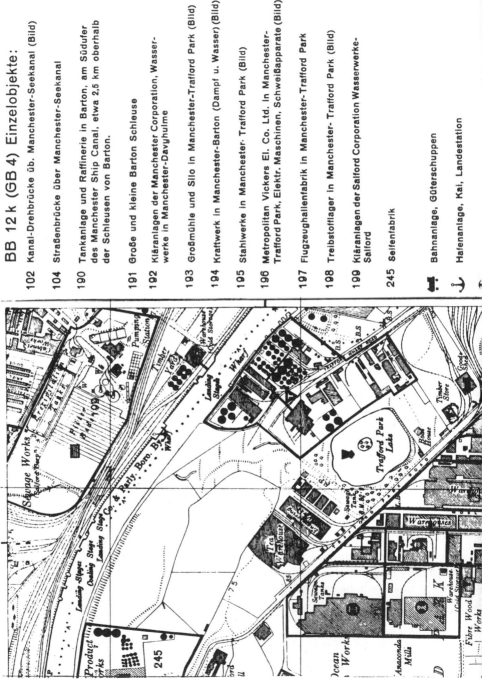

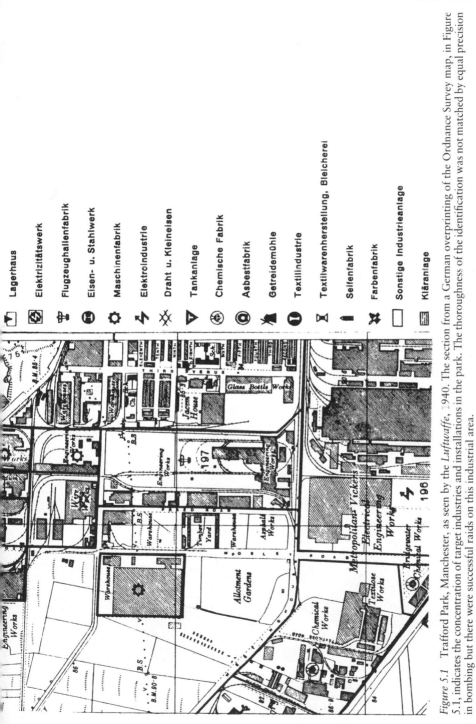

Lagerhaus

Elektrizitätswerk

Flugzeughallenfabrik

Eisen- u. Stahlwerk

Maschinenfabrik

Elektroindustrie

Draht u. Kleineisen

Tankanlage

Chemische Fabrik

Asbestfabrik

Getreidemühle

Textilindustrie

Textilwarenherstellung, Bleicherei

Seifenfabrik

Farbenfabrik

Sonstige Industrieanlage

Kläranlage

Figure 5.1 Trafford Park, Manchester, as seen by the *Luftwaffe*, 1940. The section from a German overprinting of the Ordnance Survey map, in Figure 5.1, indicates the concentration of target industries and installations in the park. The thoroughness of the identification was not matched by equal precision in bombing but there were successful raids on this industrial area.

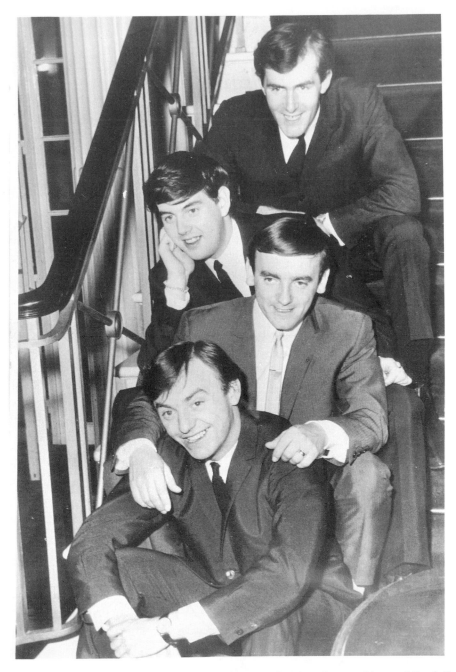

Plate 5.8 Gerry and the Pacemakers. Suited and smart, the group that gave Liverpool Football Club its anthem, and enthused the emergent Beatles, pose for posterity. They were pioneers of the new musical style and idiom that made Liverpool a mecca for pop fans.

owed their lives avidly and explored, through them or in emulation of them, dress and hair styles, sexual morality, political attitudes, the drug culture, peace and transcendental meditation. Their glamour extended to Liverpool itself, the city of Penny Lane and Strawberry Fields. Their musical talents are indisputable. Perhaps what was unique about them was their ability to take American musical models, change them and root them in their own experiences in a wry, half-mocking idiom that was wholly Liverpudlian but had universal appeal (Norman 1981).

The cheap luxuries that Orwell described in the 1930s gave way to greater technical sophistication after the Second World War. Television renamed the region Granadaland and L. S. Lowry and *Coronation Street* established an image of it tinged with false nostalgia like the Treadlepin Fold or Daisy Nook of Brierley and Waugh in the late nineteenth century. The great Wakes migrations to Blackpool (Plate 5.9) and Morecambe were replaced by foreign holidays, cinemas closed in favour of bingo, the Whit Walks faltered (Plates 5.10 and 5.11), and only sport retained its mass audience. In cricket the late 1940s was the era of Cyril Washbrook and the 1950s saw the arrival of Brian Statham but the 1960s were disappointing. In 1964 the committee resigned en bloc but in 1968 the signing of overseas players, especially Clive Lloyd, ushered in a period of success in the Gillette Cup and the John Player Sunday League (Brooke and Goodyear 1991: 23–30). In football, this was the age first of Matthews and Finney, then of Charlton, Best and Law. There were tragedies. In 1946 thirty-three people died when crush barriers collapsed at Burnden Park, Bolton, and in 1958 the whole region mourned the destruction of Manchester United's young and brilliant team in an air crash at Munich. Ominously in 1963–4 steel scaffolding was erected at Everton to keep spectators from the pitch. The violence that had seeped away from religious affiliation had found a new attachment. Moorhouse commented in 1964 that 'Liverpool football crowds have always been tougher than most' and wrote, prophetically, 'If ever we have an English football crowd rioting . . . the chances are that it will be at Anfield or Goodison Park' (Moorhouse 1964: 153–6).

In the countryside the dreams of the ramblers of the 1930s became reality when in 1950 the Peak District was designated the first national park in England. By 1970 seventy-six square miles of moorland was open under access agreements but by 1976 there was concern over the pressure on the Park and peripheral areas in Derbyshire were being asked to develop attractions that would ease it (Derbyshire County Council 1976). It was no longer necessary nor possible to plan a Peak excursion by rail: the car had transformed the most remote Peak wilderness into Manchester and Sheffield's back yard.

Politics and Society

The Conservatives maintained their hold on the north-west during the 1920s and 1930s though it was shaken in the elections of 1923 and 1929. After 1929 their only serious rival was Labour, which swept the region, as it did the rest of the country in 1945. The Conservatives slowly rebuilt their lead during the 1950s but lost it in the elections of the 1960s, the period ending with the two parties finely balanced (Table 5.13).

Between 1918 and 1970 only three constituencies returned a Labour MP at every election – Ince, Westhoughton and Wigan. For the Conservatives Wallasey, Chester, Knutsford, Macclesfield, Northwich and the Fylde, which had two seats from 1945, maintained a parallel record. After 1923 the Liberals were clearly a spent force and it could be argued that only the National Government of Ramsay MacDonald held back Labour domination of the region until after the Second World War. That domination was itself short lived, the 1950s were Conservative and the 1960s Labour, but the swing at elections was enough to stop either party claiming regional dominance.

Within the overall figures the performance of Manchester and Liverpool was important (Table 5.14). Elsewhere in the region the Conservatives were generally strong in the Cheshire countryside, in central Lancashire at Darwen and Clitheroe, in the suburban districts such as Altrincham, Crosby and Cheadle (both after 1945), Wallasey, Wirral, and the Fylde, and in the seaside resorts of Blackpool and Southport. They also maintained a strong presence in constituencies such as Stockport and Stretford, Runcorn, High Peak and Middleton. After 1945 Labour could usually depend on the coal and cotton towns and as the middle classes left the inner suburbs of the cities they too became largely Labour. Overspill development reduced inner city populations but may well have strengthened Labour voting in the areas of reception, though Wythenshawe was Conservative from its establishment in 1945 until 1964 when it fell to Labour.

The advance of Labour, interrupted in 1924 and 1931 by national events, and the great decline of the Liberals reflected both national shifts in political attitude and the collapse of the economic and social culture that had given the north-west its distinctive character. Socialism had entered the region before 1914 but with limited success though the representation of

Plate 5.9 Post-war Blackpool. The wheel (Plate 4.13) has given way to the Tower, there are more commercial attractions and the illuminations have extended the season. Blackpool carries into the late twentieth century an ability to separate not only Lancashire folk but also people from around the world from their money.

St George's Church

Table 5.13 Parliamentary elections 1918–70

Year[a]	Coalition			Cons.	Lib.	Lab.	I.N.[b]
	Con.	Lib.	Lab.				
1918	44	9	1	10	1	14	1

	Con.	Lib.	Lab.	Nat.Lib.	Ind.	I.N.[b]	Nat.Ind.	Nat.Lab
1922	49	3	19	7	1	1		
1923	28	29	21		1	1		
1924	56	5	17		1	1		
1929	30	6	42		1	1		
1931	69	2	5	2			1	1
1935	57	1	18	2			1	1
1945	26		55	1				
1950	38		42					
1951	42	1	37					
1955	44	1	33					
1959	42	1	35					
1964	30		48					
1966	23	1	54					
1970	38		40					

Notes:
[a] 1918–35 80 seats; 1945 82 seats; 1950–70 78 seats.
[b] I.N. = Irish Nationalist.
Source: F. W. S. Craig 1969; 1971.

labour had taken deeper root: both Liberals and, to a lesser extent, Conservatives adopted some working-class candidates. The paternalism that had been such a marked feature of later-nineteenth-century industrial and urban life had become weaker with joint-stock ownership and amalgamations and with the increasing social and geographical distance of second, third and fourth generation millowning families. The churches and chapels too had begun to feel the competition of secular recreations and hobbies – cycling and hiking, sport, the theatre of Ibsen and Shaw, the widening access to secular music, both popular and classical.

The start of the long decline of cotton in 1921 following the sacrifices of the war was a serious blow not only for the mill people but also for all those who had provided services for the millowners, the mills and their employees. The blow was compounded by the reflotations and recapitalizations of 1919 and 1921 under which 49 per cent of the spinning industry and 14 per cent of weaving had gone through financial reconstruction (Bowker 1928: 39). Not all firms passed into new hands but in many the old links between owners and

Plate 5.10 A Commissioner's church. St George's, Hyde, was built in 1831–2 to give the Church of England a voice in a growing industrial town where the oldest chapel was unitarian. The nave and chancel were funded by a grant of £4,310 from the Church Building Commissioners and a public subscription of £700 paid for the west tower. It is typical of the churches built with government support to bring the established religion to the unruly masses.

Table 5.14 Election results, Manchester and Liverpool

| | Manchester[a] | | | Liverpool[b] | | | |
	Con.	Lib.	Lab.	Con.	Lib.	Lab.	I.N.[c]
1918	8		2	10			1
1922	7		3	10			1
1923	1	5	4	7	2	1	1
1924	6		4	8		2	1
1929	3	2	5	6		4	1
1931	10			10		1	
1935	6		4	8		3	
1945	1		9	3		8	
1950	3		7	5		4	
1951	4		6	5		4	
1955	4		5	6		3	
1959	4		5	6		3	
1964	2		7	2		7	
1966	2		7	2		7	
1970	2		7	2		7	

Notes:
[a] 10 seats to 1951, 9 after
[b] 11 seats to 1945, 9 after
[c] I.N. = Irish Nationalist.
Source: Craig 1969; 1971.

operatives were broken and many towns lost families of benefactors. Even where the mill remained a family concern, reduced profits diminished the flow of municipal and charitable gifts that had been common in the late nineteenth century; although the more successful limited companies did engage in welfare activities, such as the provision of sports grounds and clubs, these were mill based. The paternalistic millowners had not only augmented municipal provision in parks, public baths, schools, hospitals and libraries but also built and maintained churches and chapels, founded and supported football, rugby and cricket clubs and, through personal knowledge and influence, assisted favoured working-class families in a variety of ways. Their progressive disappearance left a gap, especially in the smaller mill towns, and no comparable class of local entrepreneurs rose to fill it.

The unemployment that followed industrial decline dealt a further blow to paternalism. Between 1920 and 1937 relief for the unemployed shifted from a patchwork of national insurance and local Poor Law provision to a

Plate 5.11 Whit walks and the united sing. The Commissioners' churches did their work well. Here, in the 1960s, in front of Hyde Town Hall, the church and chapel folk mass for the united sing after their Whit walks round the town. From the early nineteenth century across the region the day was marked by bands, banners and processions, by new clothes and treats for the children and family reunions. Dispersal and secularism had reduced these great festivals to very modest proportions by the mid-1970s.

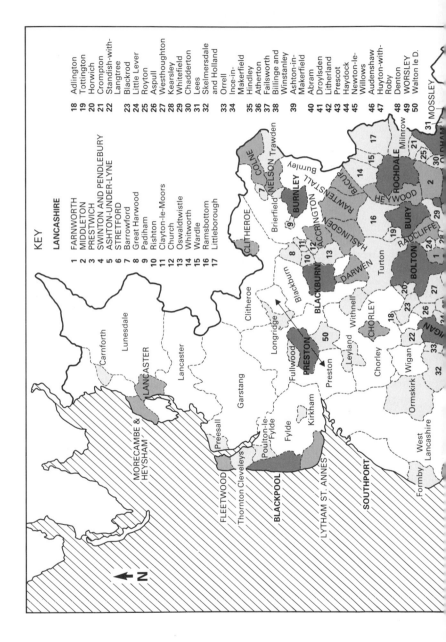

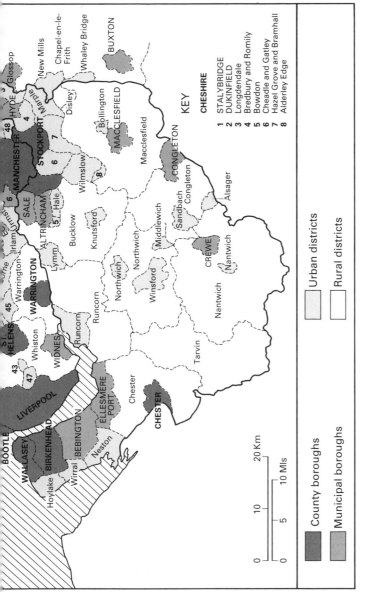

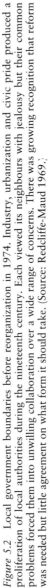

Figure 5.2 Local government boundaries before reorganization in 1974. Industry, urbanization and civic pride produced a proliferation of local authorities during the nineteenth century. Each viewed its neighbours with jealousy but their common problems forced them into unwilling collaboration over a wide range of concerns. There was growing recognition that reform was needed but little agreement on what form it should take. (Source: Redcliffe-Maud 1969.)

system of central administration with local offices. The years between were marked by confusion and protest. Working people, unemployed through no fault of their own, were perplexed by the complexities and inequalities of provision, unhappy about the low and changing rates of relief and bitterly offended by the 'means test'. This inquisitorial process, intended to establish proof of need, was supervised by local dignitaries whose involvement did much to undo what almost a century of paternalism had sought to do. Working people increasingly looked to Westminster for remedies and to their own political power to secure them (Mowat 1968).

On the industrial front north-western workers, like their peers across the country, were now enrolled in national unions which fought national campaigns. Disillusion at the economic decline that began in 1921 was followed by the bitterness of defeat in the General Strike and by resentment over the equivocal nature of the end of two Labour governments in the 1920s which simmered beneath the surface of the Conservative victories of 1931 and 1935. Increasingly, the politics of the region now conformed to national patterns; by 1945 the old paternalism and the political attitudes it encouraged were fading and religious affiliation was beginning to decline as a major influence, although in Liverpool an Orange procession could still bring out 5,000 marchers in 1963 (Moorhouse 1964: 134).

The Reform of Local Government

The towns that had so proudly flourished their new charters in the nineteenth century now faced hard times. The prosperity that had enabled the councils to make such strides in tackling the problems of over-rapid growth had ebbed and they faced the need for higher standards with reduced means (see Figure 5.2 for the geography of local government in the 1960s). Table 5.15 shows the region's comparative poverty, and demonstrates how the industrialization, urban development and civic pride of the region in the nineteenth century had left behind a legacy of poor boroughs. Out of the country's twenty-eight lowest rateable values, thirteen were in the region and, of those thirteen boroughs, eight had lost 232,000 people since 1921, the other five gaining only 45,000. Indeed of the poorest boroughs, Oldham, Blackburn and Burnley had reached their population peaks in 1911. Once again it was the coal, cotton and shipbuilding boroughs, with the addition of Salford, that made up the bottom level with Liverpool, also losing population, just above them and Manchester, saved by its great commercial centre, standing fourth in the region's table of rateable value. Only Chester, Blackpool and Southport were among the top twenty nationally with rateable values over £50.

Table 5.15 Population, area and rateable value of local authorities in descending order: mid-1968 ranked out of the 45 administrative counties in England

	Population		Area		Rateable Value (£)	
	Number	Rank	Sq. Miles	Rank	Per Head	Rank
Lancashire	2,428,040	1	1,614	6	34.3	28
Cheshire	1,056,370	5	971	21	41.9	11
Derbys.	667,660	11	975	20	34.2	29
County Boroughs						
Ranked out of the 79 County Boroughs in England and Wales						
Liverpool	688,101	2	43.5	5	39.7	50
Manchester	602,790	3	42.6	6	47.0	25
Bolton	153,700	28	23.9	18	36.2	59
Blackpool	147,850	30	13.5	49	56.0	8
Birkenhead	142,480	31	13.5	48	35.2	65
Stockport	140,660	32	13.2	50	38.6	53
Salford	139,830	33	8.1	68	35.9	62
Oldham	109,100	40	10.0	62	31.3	77
Preston	103,600	44	9.9	63	44.5	36
St Helens	102,470	45	13.9	45	36.1	61
Wallasey	101,990	46	9.2	66	36.9	55
Blackburn	100,370	49	12.6	53	34.3	67
Rochdale	86,350	56	14.9	40	32.4	73
Bootle	80,240	60	5.2	79	36.1	60
Southport	79,940	61	15.1	38	50.8	16
Wigan	79,410	62	7.9	69	39.5	51
Burnley	76,880	63	7.3	72	32.2	74
Warrington	71,830	67	7.1	76	44.8	34
Bury	65,960	72	11.6	55	32.7	72
Chester	60,620	74	7.3	74	56.0	7

Note: The highest rateable value was that of Brighton at £72.3 per head, the lowest at number 79 that of Halifax at £29.6 per head. London was excluded from the Redcliffe-Maud Inquiry and so does not appear in the tables.

Source: Redcliffe-Maud 1969: 331–41.

Essentially the 1966 Royal Commission set out to create new local government units that were large enough, both in population and area, to cater for the needs of the late twentieth century. There was agreement that the old division between town and country, enshrined in earlier local government, was no longer desirable when planning and housing, common services such as water and sewerage and the provision of public transport crossed so many boundaries. Equally the growth of education and of the public health and welfare services seemed to demand larger catchment areas to make economic sense. The Commission therefore recommended a North-West Province that embraced six unitary authorities and two two-tier metropolitan authorities, as Table 5.16 shows.

Merseyside was to consist of four metropolitan districts and SELNEC of nine. Thus both Lancashire and Cheshire were to disappear as administrat-

Table 5.16   The north-west province

Unit	Area (sq. m)	Est. population (000s)		Rateable value 1968	
		1968	1981	total (£000s)	per head (£)
Cumberland and N. Westmorland	1,901	304	322	10,561	34.7
Furness and N. Lancs	1,039	299	315	10,611	35.5
The Fylde	119	289	348	14,709	50.9
Preston-Leyland-Chorley	249	309	389	11,319	36.6
Blackburn	282	272	276	8,749	32.2
Burnley	150	222	210	6,689	30.1
Merseyside Met.	614	2,063	2,250	80,639	39.1
SELNEC Met.	1,048	3,232	3,530	124,553	38.5

Source: Redcliffe-Maud 1969: I. 204.

ive counties with the whole of Lancashire, Cumberland and Westmorland included in the province along with most of Cheshire and parts of Derbyshire and the West Riding of Yorkshire.

The proposals did not meet with unqualified approval. There was bitter resentment in areas that were threatened with the loss of their ancient county attachments and those who had fled the great towns and cities for outer suburbia saw themselves being dragged back to the high rates and difficult problems they had hoped to leave behind. Moreover the Redcliffe-Maud belief that the greatly expanded authorities would stimulate greater awareness of and interest in local government seemed to many to be a chimera. It might be possible to know local councillors under the old system but in the greatly expanded wards and distant councils of the new one that personal relationship was threatened.

In the event the final reorganization of 1974 was a watered-down version (see Figure 5.3). The Provincial Councils were never set up. Furness joined Westmorland and Cumberland in Cumbria. Lancashire and Cheshire remained, albeit truncated, and the counties kept their two tiers of authorities, though the second-tier ones were greatly enlarged and brought together some strange bedfellows. The two great metropolitan counties of Merseyside and Greater Manchester, thankfully no longer SELNEC, established their metropolitan boroughs. The north-west Derbyshire mill towns stayed in Derbyshire and Tintwistle found itself in the High Peak instead of Cheshire. Many other people had to come to terms with new affiliations. Cheshire gained Warrington, Widnes and part of Whiston from Lancashire; Lancashire took Barnoldswick, Earby, Bowland and part of Skipton from Yorkshire but lost the areas north of the sands to Cumbria; Greater Manchester absorbed the Yorkshire townships of Saddleworth (Department of the Environment 1974). The local pride and prejudice that had, perhaps, reached a peak in the later nineteenth century was dissolving in a welter of regional and sub-regional bodies.

Figure 5.3 The new structure of local government, 1974. There was opposition to the Red-cliffe-Maud recommendations even in their watered-down version but the power of central government was able to override municipal prejudice. Reform had been long needed but few people expressed joy at their new affiliations and many regretted the closeness and intimacy of their old authorities. (Source: J. J. Bagley 1956/76 and *VCH. Cheshire*, II.)

Abbreviations for manuscripts, depositories and sources

BL   British Library (previously British Museum)
CRO   Cheshire Record Office
   DCH   Cholmondeley of Cholmondeley MSS
   DCR   Crewe of Crewe MSS
   DTW   Tollemache (Cheshire Estates)
   DDX   Miscellaneous deposited documents
   EDV/3 Diocese of Chester, Visitation Records
   Pr   Diocese of Chester, Probate Records
   NVA   Local valuation records
JRUL   John Rylands University Library
LRO   Lancashire Record Office
   Pr   Diocese of Chester, Probate Records
   DDK   Stanley family (Earl of Derby) MSS
   DDF   Farington of Worden MSS
   DDHE Hesketh of Rufford MSS
   DP   Documents purchased
PRO   Public Record Office
   E 179   Exchequer, King's Remembrancer, Lay Subsidy Rolls
   E 190   Exchequer, King's Remembrancer, Port Books
Barber MSS. In private hands. Enquiries to Dr C. B. Phillips
Shaw MSS. (1902) Unpublished MS in the hands of Dr J. H. Smith
Whitfield School Log Book, unpublished MS at Whitfield School, Derbyshire

Bibliography

Abram, W. A. (ed.) (1884) *The Rolls of the Burgesses at the Gilds Merchant of the Borough of Preston 1397–1682*, Record Soc. Lancs. & Chesh., IX.

Addy, J. (ed.) (1987) *The Diary of Henry Prescott, LL.B., deputy registrar of Chester diocese*, Record Soc. Lancs. & Chesh., CXXVII.

Aiken, J. (1795) *A Description of the Country from Thirty to Forty Miles round Manchester*, London.

Aikin, Revd J. (1774) The bills of mortality for the town of Warrington for the year 1773, *Philosophical Transactions*, LXIV.

Albert, W. (1972) *The Turnpike Road System in England 1663–1840*, Cambridge.

Aldridge, N. (1986) The mechanics of decline: immigration and economy in early-modern Chester, *English Towns in Decline 1350–1800*, ed. M. Reed, Leicester.

Aldridge, N. (1987) Demographic shifts in the urban network of Cheshire, 1560–1660, *Les Petites villes en Europe Occidentale . . .*, Lille, France.

Allen, G. C. (1951) *British Industries and their Organization*, London.

Amalgamated Cotton Mills Trust Ltd (1920) *Concerning Cotton*, London.

Anderson, D. (1975) *The Orrell Coalfield, Lancashire, 1740–1850*, Buxton.

Anderson, M. (1971) *Family Structure in Nineteenth Century Lancashire*, Cambridge.

Anonymous (*c.* 1890) *Industries of Lancashire*, London.

Anonymous (1892) *The Century's Progress: Lancashire*, London.

Archer, J. H. G. (ed.) (1985) *Art and Architecture in Victorian Manchester*, Manchester.

Arlott, J. (ed.) (1954) *John Speed's England*, 4 vols, London.

Arkell, T. (1982) Multiplying factors for estimating population totals in the hearth tax, *Local Population Studies*, XXVIII.

Arkell, T. (1991) Interpreting the Hearth Tax Lists 1662–1674, unpublished Local Population Studies Society Conference Paper, Chester.

Armitage, P. W. (1984) Education in Blackburn hundred in the sixteenth century, unpublished MEd thesis, University of Manchester.

Armstrong, A. (1988) *Farmworkers*, London.

Armytage, G. J. and **Rylands, J. P.** (eds) (1909) *Pedigrees Made at the Visitation of Cheshire 1613*, Record Soc. Lancs. & Chesh., LVIII.

Ashmore, O. (1958) Household inventories of the Lancashire gentry 1550–1700, *Trans. Hist. Soc. Lancs. Cheshire*, CX.

Ashmore, O. (1969) *The Industrial Archaeology of Lancashire*, Newton Abbot.

Ashmore, O. (1972) The diary of James Garnett of Low Moor, Clitheroe 1858–65, part 2, *Trans. Lancs. & Chesh. Ant. Soc.*, CXIII.

Ashmore, O. (1982) *The Industrial Archaeology of North-West England*, Manchester.

Ashmore, O. and Bolton, T. (1975) Hugh Mason and the Oxford mills and community, Ashton-under-Lyne, *Trans. Lancs. & Chesh. Ant. Soc.*, LXXVIII.

Ashton, T. S. (1934) *Social and Economic Investigations in Manchester 1833–1933*, London.

Ashton, T. S. (1939) *An Eighteenth Century Industrialist: Peter Stubbs of Warrington 1756–1806*, Manchester.

Ashton, T. S. and Sykes, J. (1929) *The Coal Industry of the Eighteenth Century*, Manchester.

Aspin, C. (1969) *Lancashire, the First Industrial Society*, Helmshore.

Astle, W. (1932) *The History of Stockport*, Stockport.

Awty, B. G. (1957) Lancashire nail makers, 1579–1646, *Lancashire Record Office Report for 1957*, [Preston].

Awty, B. G. (1958) Charcoal ironmasters of Lancashire and Cheshire, 1600–1785, *Trans. Hist. Soc. Lancs. & Chesh.*, CIX.

Awty, B. G. (1977) Force forge in the seventeenth century, *Trans. Cumberland and Westmorland Antiq. & Arch. Soc.*, new series, LXXVII.

Axon, W. E. A. (1893) The Library of Richard Brereton of Ley, 1557, *Trans. Lancs. & Chesh. Antiq. Soc.*, XI.

Aylmer, G. E. (1973) *The State's Servants*, London.

Bagley, J. J. (1956) *A History of Lancashire with Maps and Pictures*, Beaconsfield, 3rd edn 1964; 6th edn 1976.

Bagley, J. J. (1971) *Historical Interpretation 2: Sources of British History 1540 to the Present Day*, Harmondsworth.

Bagley, J. J. (1985) *The Earls of Derby 1485–1985*. London.

Bailey, F. A. and Barker, T. C. (1969) The seventeenth-century origins of watchmaking in south-west Lancashire, *Liverpool and Merseyside*, ed. J. R. Harris, London.

Bailey, P. (ed.) (1986) *Music Hall: The Business of Pleasure*, Milton Keynes.

Baines, E. (1824–5) *History, Directory and Gazetteer of the County Palatine of Lancaster*, 2 vols, repr. 1968 Newton Abbot.

Baines, E. (1835) *The History of the Cotton Manufacture in Great Britain*, repr. 1966, London.

Baines, E. (1836) *History of the County Palatine of the Duchy of Lancaster*, 4 vols, London.

Baines, E. (1843) *The Social, Educational and Religious State of the Manufacturing Districts*, repr. 1969, London.

Baines, T. (1867) *Lancashire and Cheshire Past and Present*, 4 vols, London.

Bamford, S. (1839–41) *Passages in the Life of a Radical*, repr. 1967, London.

Bamford, S. (1848–9) *Early Days*, repr. 1967, London.

Banks, A. G. and Schofield, R. B. (1968) *Brindley at Wet Earth Colliery*, Newton Abbot.

Barker, T. C. (1951) Lancashire coal, Cheshire salt, and the rise of Liverpool, *Trans. Hist. Soc. Lancs. & Chesh.*, CIII.

Barker, T. C. (1960) *Pilkington Brothers and the Glass Industry*, London.

Barker, T. C. and Harris, J. R. (1954) *A Merseyside Town in the Industrial Revolution: St Helens 1750–1900*, repr. 1959 Liverpool.

Barker, W. H. (1927) Towns of south-east Lancashire, *Jour. Manchester Geographical Soc.*, XLIII.

Bartholomew, J. G. (ed.) (1907) *Atlas of the World's Commerce*, London.

Baskerville, S. W. (1980) The establishment of the Grosvenor interest in Chester 1710–1748, *Jour. Chester Arch. Soc.*, LXIII.

Baskerville, S. W. (1987) The political behaviour of the Cheshire clergy 1705–1752, *Northern History*, XXIII.

Bateman, J. (1883) *The Great Landowners of Great Britain and Ireland*, London, repr. 1971, Leicester.

Beckett, J. V. (1981) *Coal and Tobacco: The Lowthers and the Economic Development of West Cumberland 1660–1760*, Cambridge.

Beckett, J. V. (1986) *The Aristocracy in England 1660–1914*, London.

Beetham, M. (1985) Healthy reading: the periodical press in late Victorian Manchester, *City, Class and Culture*, ed. A. J. Kidd and K. W. Roberts, Manchester.

Bell, S. P. (ed.) (1974) *Victorian Lancashire*, Newton Abbot.

Beloff, M. (1968) *The Plateglass Universities*, London.

Bennett, J. H. E. (ed.) (1906) *The Rolls of the Freemen of Chester, Pt I: 1392–1700*, Record Soc. Lancs. & Chesh., LI.

Bennett, J. H. E. and Dewhurst, J. C. (1940) *Quarter-Sessions Records ... for the County Palatine of Chester 1559–1760*, Record Soc. Lancs. & Chesh., XCIV.

Beresford, M. W. and Finberg, H. P. R. (1973) *English Medieval Boroughs*, Newton Abbot.

Bindhoff, S. T. (1982) *The House of Commons 1509–1558*, London.

Blackburn (1928) *The Division of the Diocese of Manchester and the Creation of the Diocese of Blackburn*, Blackburn.

Blackwood, B. G. (1966) The Lancashire cavaliers and their tenants, *Trans. Hist. Soc. Lancs. & Chesh.*, LXVII.

Blackwood, B. G. (1978) *The Lancashire Gentry and the Great Rebellion 1640–1660*, Chetham Society, 3rd series, XXV. [Readers should note that where * appears after the name the reference includes Lancashire north of the sands.]

Blackwood, B. G. (1983) Parties and issues in the civil war in Lancashire, *Trans. Hist. Soc. Lancs. & Chesh.*, CXXXII.

Blundell, M. (1952) *Blundell's Diary and Letter Book*, Liverpool.

Blundell, N. (1968) *The Great Diurnal of Nicholas Blundell of Little Crosby, Lancashire, vol 1, 1702–1711*, ed. J. J. Bagley, Record Soc. Lancs. & Chesh., CX.

Blundell, N. (1970) *The Great Diurnal of Nicholas Blundell of Little Crosby, Lancashire, vol 2, 1712–1719*, ed. J. J. Bagley, Record Soc. Lancs. & Chesh., CXII.

Blundell, N. (1972) *The Great Diurnal of Nicholas Blundell of Little Crosby, Lancashire, vol 3, 1720–1728*, ed. J. J. Bagley, Record Soc. Lancs. & Chesh., CXIV.

Bobbin, T. (John Collier) (1862) *Works*, Manchester.

Borsay, P. (1977) The English urban renaissance: the development of provincial urban culture *c.* 1680–*c.* 1760, *Social History*, V.

Bossy, J. (1975) *The English Catholic Community 1570–1850*, London.

Bott, O. and Williams, R. (1975) *Man's Imprint on Cheshire*, Chester.

Bowker, B. (1928) *Lancashire under the Hammer*, London.

Bowman, W. (1960) *England in Ashton-under-Lyne*, Ashton-under-Lyne.

Bradley, J. (1904) *Reminiscences in the Life of Joshua Bradley*, Oldham.

Brewer, J. and Styles, J. (eds) (1980) *An Ungovernable People*, London.

Bridbury, A. R. (1955) *England and the Salt Trade in the Later Middle Ages*, London.

Brierley, B. (1881–1886) *Tales and Sketches of Lancashire Life*, Manchester.

Brigg, M. (ed.) (1982) *The Journals of a Lancashire Weaver*, Record Soc. Lancs. & Chesh., CXXII.

Briggs, A. (1959) *Chartist Studies*, London.

British Library (1808–12) (formerly British Museum) *A Catalogue of the Harleian MSS in the British Museum*, 4 vols continuous pagination, London.

British Railways Board (1963) *The Re-shaping of Britain's Railways*, London.

Brockbank, W. and Kenworthy, F. (1968) *The Diary of Richard Kay, 1716–51*, Chetham Soc., 3rd series, XVI.

Brooke, R. and Goodyear, D. (1991) *A Who's Who of Lancashire County Cricket Club 1865–1990*, Derby.

Bullen, A. (1984) *The Lancashire Weavers' Union*, Rochdale.

Burdett, P. P. (1777) *A Survey of the County Palatine of Chester ... 1777*, ed. J. B. Harley and P. Laxton, Liverpool.

Burgess, S. (1989) The market town of Northwich, unpublished BA thesis, University of Manchester.

Burke, E. (1871) *Burke's Landed Gentry*, London.

Burke (1949) *Peerage and Baronetage*, London.

Burke, T. (1910) *Catholic History of Liverpool*, Liverpool.

Burn, R. (1780) *The Justice of the Peace and Parish Officer*, 4 vols, London.

Bythell, D. (1969) *The Handloom Weavers*, Cambridge.

Calder, A. (1969) *The People's War: Britain 1939–45*, London.

Calvert, A. F. (1915) *Salt in Cheshire*, 2 vols, London.

Camden, W. (1610) *Britain*, ed. P. Holland, London.

Campbell, M. (1942) *The English Yeoman*, New Haven.

Campbell, W. A. (1971) *The Chemical Industry*, London.

Cardwell, D. (ed.) (1974) *Artisan to Graduate*, Manchester.

Carlson, R. E. (1969) *The Liverpool and Manchester Railway Project 1821–1831*, New York.

Carter, C. F. (ed.) (1962) *Manchester and its Regions*, Manchester.

Carter, D. P. (1973) The Lancashire Lieutenancy, 1625–1640, unpublished MA thesis, University of Manchester.

Catling, H. (1970) *The Spinning Mule*, Newton Abbot.

Central Office of Information (1966) *Britain: An Official Handbook*, London.

Challinor, R. (1972) *The Lancashire and Cheshire Miners*, Newcastle upon Tyne.

Chaloner, W. H. (1940) The reminiscences of Richard Lindop, farmer (1778–1871), *Trans. Lancs. and Chesh. Antiq. Soc.*, LV.

Chaloner, W. H. (1950a) *The Social and Economic Development of Crewe 1780–1923*, Manchester, repr. 1973.

Chaloner, W. H. (1950b) Charles Roe of Macclesfield (1715–1781): an eighteenth-century industrialist, part 1, *Trans. Lancs. and Chesh. Antiq. Soc.*, LXIII.

Chaloner, W. H. (1952) Charles Roe of Macclesfield (1715–1781): an eighteenth-century industrialist, part 2, *Trans. Lancs. and Chesh. Antiq. Soc.*, LXIII.

Chaloner, W. H. (1960) Salt in Cheshire 1600–1870, *Trans. Lancs. and Chesh. Antiq. Soc.*, LXXI.

Chaloner, W. H. (1961) Wm Furnival, H. E. Falk and the Salt Chamber of Commerce: some chapters in the economic history of Cheshire, *Trans. Hist. Soc. Lancs. & Chesh.*, CXII.

Chandler, G. and Saxton, E. B. (1960) *Liverpool under James I*, Liverpool.

Chandler, G. and Wilson, E. K. (1965) *Liverpool under Charles I*, Liverpool.

Chapman, A. (1986) Jeremy Shackerley (1626–1655?): Astronomy and patronage in civil war Lancashire, *Trans. Hist. Soc. Lancs. & Chesh.*, CXXXV.

Chapman, S. D. (1976) Workers' housing in the cotton factory colonies 1770–1850, *Textile History*, VII.

Chapman, S. J. (1904) *The Lancashire Cotton Industry*, Manchester.

Chapman, S. J. (1905) *The Cotton Industry and Trade*, London.

Charlton, H. B. (1951) *Portrait of a University*, Manchester.

Cheshire Times, Northwich.

Clapp, B. W. (1965) *John Owens, Manchester Merchant*, Manchester.

Clark, P. and Slack, P. (eds) (1976) *English Towns in Transition*, London.

Clarke, P. F. (1971) *Lancashire and the New Liberalism*, Cambridge.

Clarkson, L. A. (1971) *The Pre-Industrial Economy in England 1500–1700*, London.

Clay, C. G. A. (1984) *Economic Expansion and Social Change: England 1500–1700*, 2 vols, Cambridge.

Clayton, J. (1923) *The Registers of the Parish of Radcliffe: Burials 1558–1783*, Lancs. Parish Reg. Soc., LXI.

Clemens, P. G. E. (1976) The rise of Liverpool, 1665–1750, *Econ. Hist. Rev.*, 2nd series, XXIX.

Clemesha, H. W. (1912) *A History of Preston in Amounderness*, Manchester.

Clow, A. and Clow, N. L. (1952) *The Chemical Revolution*, London.

Coates, B. E. (1965) The origin and distribution of markets and fairs in medieval Derbyshire, *Derbys. Arch. Jour.*, LXXV.

Cockburn, J. S. (1977) *Crime in England*, London.

Collier, B. (1957) *The Defence of the United Kingdom*, London.

Cooke, J. H. (1904) *Bibliotheca Cestriensis*, Warrington.

Coppock, J. T. (1976) *An Agricultural Atlas of England and Wales*, London, revised edn.

Corfield, P. J. (1976) Urban development in England and Wales in the sixteenth and seventeenth centuries, *Trade, Government and Economy in Pre-Industrial England*, ed. D. C. Coleman and A. H. John, London.

Corfield, P. J. (1982) *The Impact of English Towns 1700–1800*, London.

Cotton Factory Times 8 August 1890, 5 June 1891, Ashton-under-Lyne.

Coward, B. (1983) *The Stanleys, Lords Stanley and Earls of Derby 1385–1672*, Chetham Soc., 3rd series, XXX.

Cragg, G. R. (1977) *The Church in the Age of Reason*, Harmondsworth.

Craig, F. W. S. (1969) *British Parliamentary Election Results 1918–1949*, Glasgow.

Craig, F. W. S. (1971) *British Parliamentary Election Results 1949–1970*, Chichester.

Craig, F. W. S. (1974) *British Parliamentary Election Results 1885–1918*, London.

Craig, F. W. S. (1976) *British Electoral Facts 1885–1975*, London.

Craig, F. W. S. (1977) *British Parliamentary Election Results 1832–1885*, London.

Craig, R. (1963) Some aspects of the trade and shipping of the river Dee in the eighteenth century, *Trans. Hist. Soc. Lancs. & Chesh.*, CXIV.

Credland, W. R. (1898) *Days Off*, Manchester.

Crofts, J. E. W. (1967) *Packhorse, Waggon and Post*, London.

Crook, W. H. (1931) *The General Strike*, North Carolina.

Crossley, F. H. (1940) The post-reformation effigies and monuments of Cheshire, *Trans. Hist. Soc. Lancs. & Chesh.*, XCI.

Cruikshank, M. (1981) *Children and Industry*, Manchester.

Crump, W. B. (1939) Saltways from the Cheshire wiches, *Trans. Lancs. & Chesh. Antiq. Soc.*, LIV.

Cunard (1917) *The Cunard Building*, Liverpool.

Cust, R. and Lake, P. (1981) Sir Richard Grosvenor and the rhetoric of magistracy, *Bulletin of the Institute of Historical Research*, LIV.

Darcy, C. P. (1976) *The Encouragement of the Fine Arts in Lancashire 1760–1860*, Chetham Soc., 3rd series, XIV.

Davies, C. S. (1960) *The Agricultural History of Cheshire 1750–1850*, Chetham Soc., 3rd series, X.

Davies, C. S. (1961) *A History of Macclesfield*, Manchester.

Davies, H. (1974) A shot in the dark, *Victorian Ashton*, ed S. Harrop and E. A. Rose, Ashton-under-Lyne.

Davies, T. (1976) *Bolton May 1926*, Bolton.

Defoe, D. (1724–6) *A Tour through the Whole Island of Great Britain*, 1971 edn, Harmondsworth.

Department of Economic Affairs (1965) *The North-West: A Regional Study*, London.

Department of the Environment (1974) *Local Government in England and Wales, A Guide to the New System*, London.

Derbyshire County Council (1976) *Derbyshire Structure Plan*, Derby.

Dickinson, J. (1855) The coal mines of Lancashire, Cheshire and north Wales. *Memoirs of Manch. Lit. & Phil. Soc.*, 2nd series, XII.

Diggle, J. W. (1889) *The Lancashire Life of Bishop Fraser*. London.

DNB *Dictionary of National Biography*.

Dodd, J. P. (1965) South Lancashire in transition: a study of the crop returns for 1795–1801, *Trans. Hist. Soc. Lancs. and Chesh.*, CXVII.

Dodgson, J. McN. (1970) *The Place Names of Cheshire*, English Place Name Society, XLIV–XLVII, 1970–72.

Doe, V. (ed.) (1978; 1979; 1981) *The Diary of James Clegg of Chapel en le Frith*, Derbys. Record Soc. II, III, IV.

Dore, R. N. (1966) *The Civil Wars in Cheshire*, Chester.

Dore, R. N. (1987) The sea approaches: the importance of the Dee and Mersey in the civil war in the north-west, *Trans. Hist. Soc. Lancs. & Chesh.*, CXXXVI.

Dore, R. N. and Morrill, J. S. (1967) The allegiance of the Cheshire gentry in the great civil war, *Trans. Lancs. Chesh. Antiq. Soc.*, LXXVII.

Dottie, R. G. (1983) The recusant riots at Childwall in May 1600: a reappraisal, *Trans. Hist. Soc. Lancs. & Chesh.*, CXXXII.

Driver, E. (1909) *Cheshire, its cheese makers, their homes, landlords and supporters*, Bradford.

Duckham, H. and Duckham, B. F. (1973) *Great Pit Disasters*, Newton Abbot.

Dunn, F. I. (1987) *The Ancient Parishes, Townships and Chapelries of Cheshire*, Chester.

Dyer, A. D. (1979) The market towns of southern England, 1500–1700, *Southern History*, I.

Dyke, E. (1949) Chester's earliest directories 1781 & 1782, *Jour. Chester Arch. Soc.*, XXXVII.

Earwaker, J. P. (1888) Notes on early booksellers ... of Manchester, *Trans. Lancs. & Chesh. Antiq. Soc.*, VI.

Earwaker, J. P. (ed.) (1884, 1893) *Lancashire and Cheshire Wills and Inventories*, Chetham Soc., new series, III and XXVIII.

Economic Research Section (1936) *Re-adjustment in Lancashire*, Manchester.

Edwards, D. G. (1982) *Derbyshire Hearth Tax Assessments 1662–1670*, Derbys. Rec. Soc., VII.

Elliot, G. (1973) Field systems of north-west England, in *Studies of Field Systems in the British Isles*, ed. A. R. H. Baker and R. A. Butlin, Cambridge.

Engels, F. (1845 Germany; 1892 England) *The Condition of the Working Class in England*, 1969 edn London.

Evans, S. (1985) The Century Guild connection, *Art and Architecture in Victorian Manchester*, ed. J. H. G. Archer, Manchester.

Everitt, A. E. (1967) The marketing of agricultural produce, *The Agrarian History of England and Wales, vol IV, 1500–1640*, ed. J. Thirsk, Cambridge.

Farnie, D. A. (1979) *The English Cotton Industry and the World Market 1815–1896*, Oxford

Farnie, D. A. (1980) *The Manchester Ship Canal and the Rise of the Port of Manchester 1894–1975*, Manchester.

Farnie, D. A. and Yonekawa, S. (1988) The emergence of the large firm in the cotton spinning industries of the world 1883–1938, *Textile History*, XIX.

Faucher, L. (1844) *Manchester in 1844: Its Present Condition and Future Prospects*, repr. 1969 London.

Fedden, R. and Joekes, R. (1973) *The National Trust Guide*. London.

Fell, A. (1908) *The Early Iron Industry of Furness and District*, Ulverston.

Fiennes, C. (1947) *The Journeys of Celia Fiennes*, ed. C. Morris, London.

Finke, U. (1985) The art treasures exhibition, *Art and Architecture in Victorian Manchester*, ed. J. H. G. Archer, Manchester.

First Report of the Commissioners appointed to inquire as to the best means of establishing an efficient constabulary force in the counties of England and Wales (1839), London.

Fishwick, H. (1887) *The History of the Parish of Bispham*, Chetham Soc., new series, X.

Fishwick, H. (1891) *The History of the Parish of St Michaels-on-Wyre*, Chetham Soc., new series, XXV.

Fitton, R. S. and Wadsworth, A. P. (1958) *The Strutts and the Arkwrights*, Manchester.

Fleetwood-Hesketh, P. (1955) *Murray's Lancashire Architectural Guide*, London.

Fleischman, R. K. jun. (1985) *Conditions of Life Among the Cotton Workers of Southeastern Lancashire 1780–1850*, New York.

Fletcher, T. W. (1961) Lancashire livestock farming during the great depression, *Agricultural History Review*, IX, repr. in Perry (1973).

Fletcher, T. W. (1962) The agrarian revolution in arable Lancashire, *Trans. Lancs. & Chesh. Antiq. Soc.*, LXXII.

Flinn, M. W. (1984) *History of the British Coal Industry, vol. 2, 1700–1830*, Oxford.

Floud, P. (1961) The English contribution to the chemistry of calico printing before Perkin, *CIBA Review*, 1961/1.

Fogarty, M. P. (1945) *Prospects for the Industrial Areas of Great Britain*, London.

Foley, A. (1973) *A Bolton Childhood*, Manchester.

Foster, C. F. (1992) *Four Cheshire Townships in the Eighteenth Century*, Northwich.

Fowler, A. (1986) Trade unions and technical change, the automatic loom strike 1908, *Looking Back at Hyde*, ed. A. Lock, Ashton-under-Lyne.

Fowler, A. and Wyke, T. (1987) *The Barefoot Aristocrats*, Littleborough.

Fox, L. (ed.) (1956) *English Historical Scholarship in the Sixteenth and Seventeenth Centuries*, London.

France, R. S. (1938) A history of plague in Lancashire, *Trans. Hist. Soc. Lancs. & Chesh.*, XC.

France, R. S. (1985) *Guide to the Lancashire Record Office*, Preston.

Frangopulo, N. J. (1962) *Rich Inheritance*, Manchester.

Frangopulo, N. J. (1977) *Tradition in Action: The Historical Evolution of the Greater Manchester County*, Manchester.

Freeman, T. W., Rodgers, H. B. and Kinvig, R. H. (1966) *Lancashire, Cheshire and the Isle of Man*, London.

Fryer, P. (1984) *Staying Power: The History of Black People in Britain*, London.

Fussell, G. E. (1954) Four centuries of Cheshire farming systems, *Trans. Hist. Soc. Lancs. & Chesh.*, CVI.

Garnett, M. E. (1988) The great re-building and economic change in south Lonsdale, *Trans. Hist. Soc. Lancs. & Chesh.*, CXXXVII.

Garnett, R. G. (1972) *Co-operation and the Owenite Socialist Communities in Britain 1825–1845*, Manchester.

Garrard, J. (1983) *Leadership and Power in Victorian Industrial Towns 1830–1880*, Manchester.

Gautrey, A. J. (1980) Births and baptisms at Rostherne, 1697–1705, *Trans. Hist. Soc. Lancs. & Chesh.*, CXXIX.

GEC (1900–9) *Complete Baronetage*, 6 vols, Exeter.

GEC (1910–40) *Complete Peerage*, 13 vols in 14, London.

Gibson, F. A. (1922) *A Compilation of Statistics of the Coal Mining Industry of the UK*, Cardiff.

Gilboy, E. (1934) *Wages in Eighteenth-Century England*, Connecticut.

Girouard, M. (1979) *The Victorian Country House*, London.

Glass, D. V. and Eversley, D. E. C. (1966) *Population in History*, London.

Glassey, L. K. J. (1979) *Politics and the Appointment of Justices of the Peace, 1675–1720*, London.

Glassey, L. K. J. (1987) The origins of political parties in late seventeenth-century Lancashire, *Trans. Hist. Soc. Lancs. & Chesh.*, CXXXVI.

Goose, N. (1985) The ecclesiastical returns of 1563: a cautionary note, *Local Population Studies*, XXXIV.

Gordon, C. (1975) *The Foundations of the University of Salford*, Altrincham.

Gormley, J. (1982) *Battered Cherub*, London.

Gourvish, T. R. (1986) *British Railways 1948–1973*, Cambridge.

Govett, L. A. (1890) *The King's Book of Sports*, London.

Graham, J. A. and Phythian, B. A. (1965) *The Manchester Grammar School 1515–1965*, Manchester.

Great Britain (1875) *Return of Owners of Land 1873*, Parliamentary Papers, 1874, LXXII, Parts 1 and 2, Cmd 1097.

Greenall, R. (1974) The making of the borough of Salford, *Victorian Lancashire*, ed. S. P. Bell, Newton Abbot.

Griffin, A. R. (1977) *The British Coalmining Industry*, Hartington.

Groombridge, M. J. (1952) The City gilds of Chester, *Jour. Chester Arch. Soc.*, XXXIX.

Gurr, D. and Hunt, J. (1985) *The Cotton Mills of Oldham*, Oldham.

Hadfield, C. and Biddle, G. (1970) *The Canals of North-West England*, Newton Abbot.

Haigh, C. A. (1969) *The Last Days of the Lancashire Monasteries and the Pilgrimage of Grace*, Chetham Soc., 3rd series, XVII.

Haigh, C. A. (1975) *Reformation and Resistance in Tudor Lancashire*, London.

Haigh, C. A. (1977) Puritan evangelism in the reign of Elizabeth I, *English Historical Review*, XCII.

Hall, J. (1883) *A History of the Town and Parish of Nantwich*. Manchester, repr. 1972.

Halley, R. (1872) *Lancashire: Its Puritanism and Non-conformity*. Manchester.

Hardie, D. W. F. (1950) *A History of the Chemical Industry in Widnes*. [? Liverpool].

Harland, J. (1856) *The Farm and Household Accounts of the Shuttleworths of Gawthorpe Hall . . .*, Chetham Soc., old series, XXXV.

Harrison, M. (1985) Art and philanthropy, *City, Class and Culture*, ed. A. J. Kidd and K. W. Roberts, Manchester.

Harrison, W. (1587) *The Description of England*, ed. G. Elden, New York, repr. 1968.

Harrison, W. (1886) The development of the turnpike system in Lancashire and Cheshire, *Trans. Lancs. & Chesh. Antiq. Soc.*, IV.

Harrisson, T. (1990) *Living through the Blitz*, Harmondsworth.

Harrop, S. (1985) *Old Birkdale and Ainsdale*, Southport.

Harvey, J. H. (1976) Two early nurseries: Knowsley, Lancashire and Knutsford, Cheshire, *Jour. Chester Arch. Soc.*, LIX.

Hasler, P. W. (1981) *The House of Commons 1558–1603*, London.

Hatcher, J. and Barker, T. C. (1974) *A History of British Pewter*, London.

'Hetherington' [1894] *John Hetherington & Sons Ltd*, [Manchester].

Heginbotham, H. (1877) *Stockport Ancient and Modern*, 2 vols, London, 1877–1892.

Heltzel, V. B. (ed.) (1962) Henry Peacham, *The Complete Gentleman*, repr. Ithaca, NY.

Henderson, J. M. (1979) The corporation of Chester and its members 1603–1625, unpublished BA thesis, University of Manchester.

Henning, B. D. (1983) *The House of Commons 1660–1690*, London.

Hewitt, M. (1958) *Wives and Mothers in Victorian Industry*, repr. 1975, Connecticut.

Higgins, G. P. (1976) The government of early Stuart Cheshire, *Northern History*, XII.

Higson, J. (1859) *Historical and Descriptive Notices of Droylsden*, Manchester.

Hill, S. (1907) *Bygone Stalybridge*, Stalybridge.
HMC (1894) Historical Manuscripts Commission, *The Manuscripts of Lord Kenyon*, 14th Report, appendix IV.
Hodson, J. H. (1978) *Cheshire 1660–1780; Restoration to Industrial Revolution*, Chester.
Hodson, J. H. and Smith, J. H. (1981) *Three Sundays in Wilmslow 1851–1871*, Wilmslow.
Holland, H. (1808) *General View of the Agriculture of the County of Cheshire*, London.
Hollingsworth, T. H. (1969) *Historical Demography*, London.
Holt, A. (1926) *The Story of Mossley*, repr. 1974, Mossley.
Holt, G. O. (1978) *A Regional History of the Railways of Great Britain, vol. 10, The North-West*, Newton Abbot.
Holt, J. (1795) *General View of the Agriculture of the County of Lancashire*, London.
Horne, H. O. (1947) *A History of Savings Banks*, Oxford.
Howson, J. S. and Rimmer, A. (1872) *Chester as it was*, London.
Hudson, D. (1972) *Munby, Man of Two Worlds*, London.
Hurst, D. (1978) *Reminiscences*, Tintwistle.
Hurst, J. G. (1948) *Edmund Potter and Dinting Vale*, Manchester.
Hutchins, B. L. and Harrison, A. (1911) *A History of Factory Legislation*, London.
Hutton, R. (1980) The failure of the Lancashire cavaliers, *Trans. Hist. Soc. Lancs. & Chesh.*, CXXIX.
Huxley, G. (1965) *Lady Elizabeth and the Grosvenors*, London.
Huxley, G. (1967) *Victorian Duke*, London.
Hyde, F. E. (1971) *Liverpool and the Mersey*, Newton Abbot.
Ingram, G. (1990) Art and art gallery provision in Birkenhead 1900–1928, unpublished MA thesis, University of Liverpool.
Irving, J. (1890) *The Annals of our Time*, London.
Jackson-Stopes, G. (1986) *The Treasure Houses of Britain*, London.
James, R. W. (1957) *To the Best of our Skill and Knowledge*, Chester.
Jenkins, T. D. (1973) The validity of factory returns 1835–1850, *Textile History*, IV.
Jewkes, J. and Gray, E. M. (1935) *Wages and Labour in the Lancashire Cotton Spinning Industry*, Manchester.
Johnson, A. M. (1972) Politics in Chester during the Civil War and Interregnum, in *Crisis and Order in English Towns 1500–1700*, ed. P. Clark and P. Slack, London.
Jones, W. J. (1967) *The Elizabethan Court of Chancery*, London.
Jones, W. J. (1979) Palatine performance in the seventeenth century, in *The English Commonwealth 1547–1640*, ed. P. Clark, A. G. R. Smith and N. Tyacke, London.
Jordan, W. K. (1962) *The Social Institutions of Lancashire*, Chetham Soc., 3rd series, XI.
Joyce, P. J. (1980), *Work, Society and Politics*, Brighton.
Kargon, R. H. (1977) *Science in Victorian Manchester*, Manchester.
Kellett, J. R. (1969) *Railways and Victorian Cities*, repr. 1979, London.
Kelly (1896, 1906, 1914, 1923, 1939) *Kelly's Directories of Cheshire*, London.
Kelly (1913, 1924) *Kelly's Directories of Lancashire*, London.

Kenny, S. A. (1975) The evolution of the Lancashire cotton industry 1750–1900, unpublished MA thesis, University of Manchester.

Kenyon, G. H. and **Kenyon, C. G.** (1971) *William Kenyon: An International Group*, Dukinfield.

Kerridge, E. (1967) *The Agricultural Revolution*, London.

Kerridge, E. (1969) *Agrarian Problems in the Sixteenth Century and After*, London.

Kerridge, E. (1985) *Textile Manufacture in Early Modern England*, Manchester.

Kidd, A. J. and **Roberts, K. W.** (eds) (1985) *City, Class and Culture*, Manchester.

'Kinder' (1892) *Kinder Printing Company: Its Strange History*.

King, D. (1656) *Vale–Royall of England*, London.

King, W. (1976) The economic and demographic development of Rossendale *c.* 1650–1800, unpublished PhD thesis, University of Leicester.

Lamb, R. (1866) *Free Thoughts on Many Subjects by a Manchester Man*, 2 vols, London.

Lancashire Ind. Devt Assoc. (LIDA) (1949) *Report no. 3 Merseyside*, Manchester.

Lancashire Record Office (1960) Annual Report.

Lane, J. and **Anderson, D.** (undated) *Mines and Miners of South Lancashire*, Wigan.

Langton, J. (1979) *Geographical Change and Industrial Revolution*, Cambridge.

Laslett, T. P. E. (1983) *The World we have Lost*, London, 3rd edn.

Laslett, T. P. E. and **Wall, R.** (1972) *Household and Family in Past Time*, London.

Laughton, J. (1986) The township of Rainow in the late seventeenth century, unpublished Local History Certificate dissertation, University of Manchester.

Lawton, G. O. (1979) *Northwich Hundred Poll Tax 1660 and Hearth Tax 1664*, Record Soc. Lancs. & Chesh., CXIX.

Lawton, R. (1962) Population trends in Lancashire and Cheshire from 1801, *Trans. Hist. Soc. Lancs. & Chesh.*, CXIV.

Lawton, R. and **Cunningham, C. M.** (1970) *Merseyside Social and Economic Studies*, London.

Leatherbarrow, J. S. (1947) *The Lancashire Elizabethan Recusants*, Chetham Soc., new series, CX.

Lee, J. M. (1963) *Social Leaders and Public Persons: A Study of County Government in Cheshire since 1888*, London.

Lee, J. M., Wood, B., Solomon, B. and **Walters, P.** (1974) *The Scope of Local Initiative: A Study of Cheshire County Council 1961–1974*, London.

Leland, J. (1535) *The Itinerary of J. Leland . . . 1535–1543*, ed. L. T. Smith, London, 5 vols, 1907–1910.

Levine, D. (1987) *Reproducing Families*, London.

Leycester, P. (1953) *Charges to the Grand Jury at the Quarter Sessions 1660–1677*, ed. E. M. Halcrow, Chetham Soc., 3rd series, V.

Liddle, J. (1982) Estate management and land reform politics: the Hesketh and Scarisbrick families and the making of Southport, 1842–1914, in *Patricians, Power and Politics in Nineteenth-Century Towns*, ed. D. Cannadine, Leicester.

Little, L. (1984) The Duke's dock in Liverpool, *Trans. Hist. Soc. Lancs. & Chesh.*, CXXXIII.

Liverpool University (1981) *The University of Liverpool Celebrates its Centenary, 1881–1981*, Liverpool.

Livesey, J. (1912) Acton church seating arrangements, *Trans. Hist. Soc. Lancs. & Chesh.*, LXIV.

Long, P. R. (1968) The wealth of the magisterial class in Lancashire *c*. 1590–1640, unpublished MA thesis, University of Manchester. [Readers should note that where * appears after the name the reference includes Lancashire north of the sands.]

Lowe, N. (1972) *The Lancashire Textile Industry in the Sixteenth Century*, Chetham Soc., 3rd series, XX.

Lowerson, J. (1989) Golf, *Sport in Britain*, ed. T. Mason, Cambridge.

Lyddon, D. and **Marshall, P.** (1975) *Paper in Bolton*, Altrincham.

McCaig, D. V. (1977) A survey of the domestic vernacular architecture of Cheshire, unpublished MA thesis, University of Manchester.

MacDonald, S. (1985) The Royal Manchester Institution, *Art and Architecture in Victorian Manchester*, ed. J. Archer, Manchester.

McKendrick, N., Brewer, J. and **Plumb, J. H.** (1982) *The Birth of a Consumer Society*, London.

McKisack, M. (1971) *Medieval History in the Tudor Age*, London.

Machin, R. (1977) The great re-building, a re-assessment, *Past and Present*, 77.

Magrath, J. R. (ed.) (1903) *The Flemings in Oxford, vol I, 1650–1680*, Oxford Historical Society, XLIV.

Malet, H. (1961) *The Canal Duke*, London.

Malet, H. (1977) *Bridgewater, the Canal Duke*, Manchester.

Manchester Guardian Commercial Year Book (1921, 1924) Manchester.

Manchester Guardian (1936) *Pictorial Geography of Lancashire*, Manchester.

Manchester Region History Review III (1989).

Manchester University, *Annual Reports of Council to Court*, Manchester.

Mannex, P. & Co. (1854) *History, Topography and Directory of Mid-Lancashire*, Preston.

Mannex, P. & Co. (1868) *Directory of North and East Lancashire*, Preston.

Manning, B. S. (1975) The peasantry and the English revolution, *Jour. Peasant Studies*, II.

Marshall, J. D. (1961) The Lancashire rural labourer in the early nineteenth century, *Trans. Lancs. & Chesh. Antiq. Soc.*, LXVI.

Marshall, J. D. (ed.) (1967) *The Autobiography of William Stout of Lancaster, 1665–1752*, Chetham Soc., 3rd series, XIV.

Marshall, J. D. (ed.) (1977) *The History of Lancashire County Council 1889 to 1974*, London.

Marshall, J. D. and **Davies-Shiel, M.** (1969) *The Industrial Archaeology of the Lake Counties*, Newton Abbot.

Mason, T. (ed.) (1989) *Sport in Britain*, Cambridge.

Meacham, S. (1977) *A Life Apart: The English Working Class 1890–1914*, London.

Meadowcroft, I. (1976) Aspects of Gorton, unpublished Local History Certificate thesis, University of Manchester.

Mercer, W. B. (1963) *A Survey of the Agriculture of Cheshire*, London.

Middlebrook, M. (1971) *The First Day on the Somme*, London.

Middleton, T. (1932) *History of Hyde*, Hyde.

Midwinter, E. (1969a) *Social Administration in Lancashire 1830–1860*, Manchester.

Midwinter, E. (1969b) The administration of public education in late Victorian Lancashire, *Northern History*, IV.

Midwinter, E. (1971) *Old Liverpool*, Newton Abbot.

Mills, W. Haslam (1917) *Sir Charles Macara bart*, Manchester.

Mingay, G. E. (1963) *English Landed Society in the Eighteenth Century*, London.

Mingay, G. E. (ed.) (1989) *The Agrarian History of England and Wales, vol VI, 1750–1850*, Cambridge.

Ministry of Agriculture, Fisheries and Food (MAFF) (before 1919 Board of Agriculture) (1911) *Agricultural Statistics 1911*, London.

MAFF (1972) *Agricultural Statistics 1970–1971, England and Wales*, London.

MAFF (1982) *Agricultural Statistics United Kingdom 1980 and 1981*, London.

Mitchell, B. R. (1988) *British Historical Statistics*, Cambridge.

Mitchell, S. I. (1982) Food shortages and public order in Cheshire 1757–1812, *Trans. Lancs. & Chesh. Antiq. Soc.*, LXXX.

Mitchell, S. I. (1984) The development of urban retailing 1700–1815, *The Transformation of English Provincial Towns*, ed. P. Clark, London.

Moorhouse, G. (1964) *Britain in the Sixties: The Other England*, Harmondsworth.

Morgan, N. (1990) *Vanished Dwellings*, Preston.

Morrill, J. S. (1973) Puritanism and the church in the diocese of Chester, *Northern History*, VIII.

Morrill, J. S. (1974) *Cheshire 1630–1660*, London.

Morrill, J. S. (1976) *The Cheshire Grand Jury 1625–1659*, Leicester.

Morrill, J. S. (1979) The northern gentry and the Great Rebellion, *Northern History*, XV.

Mortimer, J. (1897) *Industrial Lancashire*, Manchester.

Mowat, C. L. (1968) *Britain Between the Wars, 1918–1940*, repr. of 1955 edn, London.

Muir, R. and Platt, E. M. (1906) *A History of Municipal Government in Liverpool*, London.

Mullett, M. (1973) The politics of Liverpool 1660–1668, *Trans. Hist. Soc. Lancs. & Chesh.*, CXXIV.

Mullett, M. (1983) Conflict, politics and elections in Lancaster, *Northern History*, XIX.

Mullineux, F. (1973) Coal mining in Lancashire, *The Great Human Exploit*, ed. J. H. Smith, Chichester.

Musson, A. E. (1965) *Enterprise in Soap and Chemicals*, Manchester.

Musson, A. E. and Robinson, E. (1969) *Science and Technology in the Industrial Revolution*, Manchester.

Mutch, A. (1980) Rural society in Lancashire 1840–1914, unpublished PhD thesis, University of Manchester.

Namier, L. B. and Brooke, J. (1964) *The House of Commons 1754–1790*, London.

Neal, F. (1988) *Sectarian Violence: The Liverpool Experience 1819–1914*, Manchester.

Nef, J. U. (1932) *The Rise of the British Coal Industry*, 2 vols, London.

Newman, P. R. (1979) Catholic royalists of northern England, 1642–1645, *Northern History*, XV.

Newton, E. (1917) *The House of Lyme*, London.

Nicholas, R. (1945) *The City of Manchester Plan*, Norwich and London.

Nixon, F. (1969) *Industrial Archaeology of Derbyshire*, Newton Abbot.

Norman, P. (1981) *Shout: The True Story of the Beatles*, London.

Norris, J. H. (1965–6) The water-powered corn mills of Cheshire, *Trans. Lancs. & Chesh. Antiq. Soc.*, LXXV and LXXVI.

Nutall, D. (1967) A history of printing in Chester, *Jour. Chester Arch. Soc.*, LIV.

Offner, A. (1981) *Property and Politics 1870–1914*, Cambridge.

Ormerod, G. (1882) *The History of the County Palatine and City of Chester*, ed. T. Helsby, 3 vols, London.

Orwell, G. (1937) *The Road to Wigan Pier*, London.

Orwin, C. S. and **Whetham, E.** (1964) *History of British Agriculture 1846–1914*, London.

Owen, D. (1977) *Canals to Manchester*, Manchester.

Owen, W. (1784) *New Book of Roads*, London.

Owen, W. (1786) *New Book of Fairs*, London.

Palliser, D. M. and **Jones, L. J.** (1982) The diocesan population returns for April 1563 and 1603, *Local Pop. Studies*, XXX.

Parkinson, C. N. (1952) *The Rise of the Port of Liverpool*, London.

Parkinson, R. (ed.) (1845) *The Life of Adam Martindale, written by himself*, Chetham Soc., old series, IV.

Parssinen, T. M. (1983) *Secret Passions, Secret Remedies*, Manchester.

Pass, A. J. (1988) *Thomas Worthington: Victorian Architecture and Social Purpose*, Manchester.

Pearson, S. (1985) *Rural Houses of the Lancashire Pennines, 1560–1760*, London.

Percival, T. (1774) Observations on the state of population in Manchester and other adjacent places, *Philosophical Transactions*, LXIV.

Percival, T. (1775) Observations on the state of population in Manchester and other adjacent places, *Philosophical Transactions*, LXV.

Perry, P. J. (1970) Landlords and agricultural transformation, *Agricultural History Review*, XVIII, repr. in Perry (1973).

Perry, P. J. (1973) *British Agriculture 1875–1914*, London.

Pevsner, N. (1979a) *The Buildings of England: Lancashire, 1, The Industrial and Commercial South*, repr. of 1969 edn, Harmondsworth.

Pevsner, N. (1979b) *The Buildings of England: Lancashire, 2, The Rural North*, repr. of 1969 edn, Harmondsworth.

Pevsner, N. and **Hubbard, E.** (1971) *The Buildings of England: Cheshire*, Harmondsworth.

Phillips, A. D. M. (1980) Mossland reclamation in nineteenth-century Cheshire, *Trans. Hist. Soc. Lancs. & Chesh.*, CXXIX.

Phillips, C. B. (1985) Stockport: a small market town, unpublished paper to Lancashire and Cheshire Antiquarian Society.

Phillips, C. B. and **Smith, J. H.** (1985) *Stockport Probate Records, 1578–1619*, Record Soc. Lancs. & Chesh., CXXIV.

Piccope, G. J. (ed.) (1860, 1861) *Lancashire and Cheshire Wills and Inventories from the Ecclesiastical Court at Chester*, Chetham Soc., old series, LI and LV.

Pickstone, J. V. (1985) *Medicine and Industrial Society*, Manchester.

Pigot, J. & Co. (1828) *New Commercial Directory of Lancashire and Cheshire*, Manchester.

Pilkington, J. (1789) *A View of the Present State of Derbyshire*, Derby.

Place, G. W. (1989) Parkgate and the royal yachts: passenger traffic between the north-west and Dublin in the eighteenth century, *Trans. Hist. Soc. Lancs. & Chesh.*, CXXXVIII.

Pollard, S. (1963) Factory discipline in the industrial revolution, *Econ. Hist. Rev.*, 2nd series, XVI.

Pollard, S. and Robertson, P. (1979) *The British Shipbuilding Industry 1870–1914*, London.

Poor Law Commissioners (1836) *First Annual Report*, London.

Pope-Hennessey, J. (1955) *Lord Crewe 1858–1945*, London.

Porter, R. E. (1976) The marking of agricultural produce in Cheshire during the nineteenth century, *Trans. Hist. Soc. Lancs. & Chesh.*, CXXVI.

Potter, B. (1891) *The Co-operative Movement in Great Britain*, London.

Pound, J. F. (1981) The validity of the freemen's lists: some Norwich evidence, *Econ. Hist. Rev.*, 2nd series, XXXIV.

Powell, J. (1976) Mottram in Longendale, unpublished Local History Certificate dissertation, University of Manchester.

Prentice, A. (1851) *Historical Sketches and Personal Recollections of Manchester from 1792 to 1832*, London.

Prentice, A. (1853) *History of the Anti Corn-Law League*, 2 vols, London.

Pressnell, L. S. (1956) *Country Banking in the Industrial Revolution*, London.

Priestley, J. B. (1934) *English Journey*, repr. 1977 Harmondsworth.

Prince, J. C. (1844) *Hours with the Muses*, London.

PRO (1914) *List and Indexes*, XL.

PRO (1963) *Guide to the Public Record Office*, 2 vols, London.

Proceedings and Papers of the Historic Society of Lancashire and Cheshire, vols I and II.

Quintrell, B. W. (1981) *Lancashire JPs at the Sheriffs' Table, 1578–1694*, Record Soc. Lancs. & Chesh., CXXI.

Quintrell, B. W. (1982) Government in perspective: Lancashire and the Privy Council, 1570–1640, *Trans. Hist. Soc. Lancs. & Chesh.*, CXXXI.

Quintrell, B. W. (1983) Lancashire ills, the King's will and the troubling of Bishop Bridgeman, *Trans. Hist. Soc. Lancs. & Chesh.*, CXXXII.

Radcliffe, W. (1828) *The Origin of the New System of Manufacture Commonly Called Power-Loom Weaving*, Stockport.

Raffald, E. (1772) *The Manchester Directory for the Year 1772*, Manchester.

Raines, F. R. (ed.) (1845) *Notitia Cestriensis*, Chetham Soc., old series, VIII, XIX, XXI, XXII, 1845–1850.

Ramsay, G. D. (1942) The distribution of the English cloth industry in 1561–2, *Eng. Hist. Rev.*, LVII.

Reach, A. B. (ed. D. Aspin, 1972) *Manchester and the Textile Districts in 1849*, Helmshore.

Reader, W. J. (1970) *Imperial Chemical Industries: A History*, vol. 1, *The Forerunners*, Oxford.

Redcliffe-Maud, Lord (1969) *Report of the Royal Commission into Local Government in England, 1966–69*, London.

Redford, A. (1926, 2nd edition 1964) *Labour Migration in England 1800–1850*, Manchester.

Redford, A. (1939) *The History of Local Government in Manchester, vol. I, Manor and Township*, London.

Richards, R. (**1947**) *Old Cheshire Churches*, Liverpool.

Richardson, D. (1976) Profits in the Liverpool slave trade: the accounts of William Davenport, 1757–1784, *Liverpool, the African Slave Trade, and Abolition*, ed. R. Anstey and P. E. H. Hair, *Trans. Hist. Soc. Lancs. & Chesh.*, occasional series, II; enlarged repr. Liverpool 1989.

Richardson, R. C. (1972) *Puritanism in North-West England*, Manchester.

Riden, P. (1978a) The population of Derbyshire in 1563, *Derbys. Arch. Jour.*, XCVIII.

Riden, P. (1978b) Eighteenth-century blast furnaces: a new checklist, *Jour. Historical Metallurgy Soc.*, XII.

Riden, P. (1987) *A Gazeteer of Charcoal-Fired Blast Furnaces in Great Britain in use since 1660*, Cardiff.

Rideout, E. H. (1927) *The Growth of Wirral*, Liverpool.

Ridgway, M. H. (1966) Chester goldsmiths from early times to 1726, *Jour. Chester Arch. Soc.*, new series, LIII.

Robson, D. (1966) *Some Aspects of Education in Cheshire in the Eighteenth Century*, Chetham Soc., 3rd series, XIII.

Rodgers, H. B. (1956) The market area of Preston in the sixteenth and seventeenth centuries, *Geographical Studies*, III, i.

Rogers, C. D. (1975a) *The Lancashire Population Crisis of 1623*, Manchester.

Rogers, C. D. (1975b) The development of a teaching profession in England, 1574–1700, unpublished PhD thesis. University of Manchester.

Rogers, G. (1981) Social and economic change on Lancashire landed estates in the nineteenth century, unpublished PhD thesis, University of Lancaster.

Rogers, G (1986) Lancashire landowners and the great agricultural depression, *Northern History*, XXII.

Rose, A. G. (1963–4) Early cotton riots in Lancashire 1769–1779, *Trans. Lancs. & Chesh. Antiq. Soc.*, LXXIII and LXXIV.

Rose, E. A. (1975) Methodism in Cheshire to 1800, *Trans. Lancs. & Chesh. Antiq. Soc.*, LXXVIII.

Rose, E. A. (1982) Methodism in south Lancashire to 1800, *Trans. Lancs. & Chesh. Antiq. Soc.*, LXXXI.

Rose, M. E. (1985) Culture, philanthropy and the Manchester middle classes, *City, Class and Culture*, ed. A. J. Kidd and K. W. Roberts, Manchester.

Rowley, C. (n.d.) *Fifty Years of Work without Wages*, London.

Royal Commission (1919) *Royal Commission on Agriculture 1919–20: Minutes of Evidence, 1919*, vols II and III, Cmd 365 and 391, London.

Rubinstein, D. (1974) *Victorian Homes*, Newton Abbot.

Rubinstein, D. and **Simon, B.** (1969) *The Evolution of the Comprehensive School 1926–1966*, London.

Rucksack, Journal of the Ramblers' Association.

Rylands, J. P. (1897) *Lancashire and Cheshire wills and Inventories 1563–1807*, Chetham Soc., new series, XXXVII.

Sachse, W. L. (ed.) (1938) *The Diary of Roger Lowe of Ashton in Makerfield, Lancs. 1663–74*, London.

Salt, K. (1983) The Chester coopers in the late sixteenth and early seventeenth centuries, unpublished BA thesis, University of Manchester.

Sandberg, L. G. (1974) *Lancashire in Decline*, Columbus.

Sanderson, M. (1967) Education and the factory in industrial Lancashire, *Econ. Hist. Rev.*, 2nd series, XX.

Saxelby, C. H. (1953) *Bolton Survey*, Bolton.

Scard, G. (1981) *Squire and Tenant: Rural Life in Cheshire 1760–1900*, Chester.

Schofield, E. M. and Schofield, M. M. (1989) 'A good fortune and a good wife': the marriage of Christopher Hasell of Liverpool, merchant, 1765, *Trans. Hist. Soc. Lancs. & Chesh.*, CXXXVIII.

Schofield, M. M. (1946) *Outlines of an Economic History of Lancaster 1680–1860*, Part I, [Lancaster].

Schofield, M. M. (1961) Benjamin Satterthwaite's letter book, *Trans. Hist. Soc. Lancs. & Chesh.*, CXIII.

Schofield, M. M. (1986) Shoes, ships and sealing wax: eighteenth-century Lancashire exports to the colonies, *Trans. Hist. Soc. Lancs. & Chesh.*, CXXXV.

Schofield, M. M. (1989) The slave trade from Lancashire and Cheshire ports outside Liverpool *c.* 1750–*c.* 1790, repr. in *Liverpool, the African Slave Trade, and Abolition*, ed. R. Anstey and P. E. H. Hair, *Trans. Hist. Soc. Lancs. & Chesh.*, occasional series, II.

Schubert, H. R. (1957) *History of the British Iron and Steel Industry from c. 450 BC to AD 1775*, London.

Scott, J. and Smith, J. H. (1979) *The Joseph Hague Trust*, Glossop.

Scott, J., Smith, J. H. and Winterbottom, D. (1973) *Glossop Dale, Manor and Borough*, Glossop.

Sedgewick, R. (1970) *The House of Commons 1715–1754*, London.

Seth, R. (1967) *Stories of Great Witch Trials*, London.

Sharpe, J. A. (1984) *Crime in Early Modern England*, London.

Shaw, W. (1906) *The Knights of England*, 2 vols, London.

Shercliffe, W. H., Kitching, D. A. and Ryan, J. M. (1983) *Poynton: a Coal-Mining Village, 1700–1939*, Stockport.

Shipley, S. (1989) Boxing, *Sport in Britain*, ed. T. Mason, Cambridge.

Shorter, A. H. (1971) *Paper Making in the British Isles*, Newton Abbot.

Simon, A. (1953) *The Simon Engineering Group*, Stockport.

Simon, B. (1960) *Studies in the History of Education 1780–1870*, London.

Simon, D. (1938) *A Century of City Government 1838–1938*, London.

Simon, E. D. and Inman, J. (1935) *The Rebuilding of Manchester*, London.

Smiles, S. (1864) *James Brindley and the Early Engineers*, London.

Smith, A. (1955) Schools in the Salford hundred of Lancashire in the seventeenth century, unpublished MEd thesis, University of Manchester.

Smith, B. (1969) The Glossopdale new industrial co-operative society 1867–1914, unpublished Cert. Ed. thesis, Manchester College of Education.

Smith, D. M. (1969) *Industrial Britain: The North-West*, Newton Abbot.

Smith, F. (1923) *The Life and Work of Sir James Kay-Shuttleworth*, London.

Smith, J. H. (ed.) (1975) *I Remember*, Glossop.

Smith, J. H. (1979a) Ten acres of Deansgate in 1851, *Trans. Lancs. & Chesh. Antiq. Soc.*, LXXX.

Smith, J. H. (ed.) (1979b) *Glossop in 1851*, Glossop.

Smith, J. H. (1980) The development of the English felt and silk hat trades, 1500–1912, unpublished PhD thesis, University of Manchester.

Smith, J. T. (1970a) The evolution of the English peasant house to the late seventeenth century, *Jour. British Archaeological Association*, 3rd series, XXXIII.

Smith, J. T. (1970b) Lancashire and Cheshire houses: some problems of architectural and social history, *Archaeological Journal*, CXXVII.

Smith, M. R. (1988) The Wigan Pewterers 1620–1700, unpublished BA (Econ.) thesis, University of Manchester.

Smith, P. J. C. (1988) *Flying Bombs over the Pennines*, Swinton.

Smith, Sir Thomas (1583) *De republica Anglorum*, London, facsimile repr. Menston, 1970.

Smith, W. (1588) see Ormerod (1882).

Smith, W. J. (1977) The cost of building Lancashire loomhouses and weavers' workshops; the account book of James Brandwood of Turton, 1794–1814, *Textile History*, VIII.

Smith, W. J. (1987) *Saddleworth Buildings*, Saddleworth.

SPNW (1974) *Strategic Plan for the North-West*, London.

Speake, R. (1970) The historical demography of Warton parish before 1801, *Trans. Hist. Soc. Lancs. & Chesh.*, CXXII.

Speed, J (1611) *Theatre of the Empire of Great Britaine*, London.

Spencer, W. M. (ed.) (1968) *Colne Parish Church Burial Register 1790–1812*, Colne.

Spufford, M. (1984) *The Great Re-Clothing of Rural England*, London.

Stephens, W. B. (1969) The overseas trade of Chester in the early seventeenth century, *Trans. Hist. Soc. Lancs. & Chesh.*, CXX.

Stephens, W. B. (ed.) (1970) *History of Congleton*, Manchester.

Stewart, W. A. C. (1989) *Higher Education in Post-War Britain*, London.

Stewart-Brown, R. (ed.) (1934, 1935) *Cheshire Inquisitions* post mortem *Stuart Period 1603–1660*, Record Soc. Lancs. & Chesh., LXXXIV and LXXXVI.

Stone, L. (1965) *The Crisis of the Aristocracy 1558–1641*, London.

Stone, L. (1978) *The Causes of the English Revolution 1558–1641*, London.

Sturmey, S. G. (1955) Owner-farming in England and Wales, 1900–1950, *Manchester School of Economic and Social Studies*, XXIII.

Sutton, C. W. (1915) Survey of the manor of Penwortham in 1570, *Chetham miscellanies, new series, III*, Chetham Soc., new series, LXXIII.

Swain, E. (1984) Button making in seventeenth-century Macclesfield, unpublished BA thesis, University of Manchester.

Swain, J. T. (1986) *Industry before the Industrial Revolution*, Chetham Soc., 3rd series, XXXIII.

Sykes, A. J. (1925) *Concerning the Bleaching Industry*, Manchester.

Sylvester, D. and Nulty, G. (1958) *The Historical Atlas of Cheshire*, Chester.

Symonds, J. V. (1983) *The Mills of New Mills*, New Mills.

Tait, J. (1924) *Taxation in Salford Hundred 1524–1802*, Chetham Soc., new series, LXXXIII.

Tate, W. E. (1946) *A Handlist of Lancashire Enclosure Acts and Awards*, Preston.

Tate, W. E. (1978) *A Domesday of English Enclosure Acts and Awards*, ed. M. E. Turner, Reading.

Taylor, F. (1942) *The Parish Registers of Aughton 1541–1764*. Lancs. P.R. Soc., LXXXI.

Taylor, R. (1975) The coastal salt industry of Amounderness, *Trans. Lancs. & Chesh. Antiq. Soc.*, LXXVIII.

Taylor, R. F. (1966) Pudding Pie Nook, Wrea Green, *Trans. Hist. Soc. Lancs. & Chesh.*, CXVII.

Thirsk, J. (1959) Sources of information on population 1500–1760, *Amateur Historian*, IV.

Thirsk, J. (1967) *The Agrarian History of England and Wales, vol. IV, 1500–1640*, Cambridge.

Thirsk, J. (1978) *Economic Policy and Projects*, Oxford.

Thirsk, J. (1985) *The Agrarian History of England and Wales, vol. V, 1640–1760*, 2 parts, Cambridge.

Thirsk, J. (1987) *England's Agricultural Regions and Agrarian History, 1500–1750*, London.

Thomas, K. (1971) *Religion and the Decline of Magic*, repr. 1973 and 1984, Harmondsworth.

Thomas, W. J. and Perkins, R. J. (1962) Land utilisation and agriculture, *Manchester and its Region*, ed. C. F. Carter, Manchester.

Thompson, F. M. L. (1963) *English Landed Society in the Nineteenth Century*, repr. 1971, London.

Thompson, J. (1886) *The Owens College: Its Foundation and Growth*, Manchester.

Timmins, J. G. (1977) *Handloom Weavers' Cottages in Central Lancashire*, Lancaster.

Tippett, L. H. C. (1969) *A Portrait of the Lancashire Textile Industry*, Oxford.

Transactions of the Manchester Statistical Society.

Transactions of the Manchester Geological Society.

Tripp, B. H. (1956) *Renold Chains: A History of the Company and the Rise of the Precision Chain Industry*, London.

Tunnicliffe, W. (1787) *A Topographical Survey of the Counties of Stafford, Chester and Lancaster*, Nantwich, repr. Manchester, 1982.

Tupling, G. H. (1927) *The Economic History of Rossendale*, Chetham Soc., new series, LXXXVI.

Tupling, G. H. (1936) An alphabetical list of the markets and fairs of Lancashire recorded before the year 1701, *Trans. Lancs. & Chesh. Antiq. Soc.*, LI.

Tupling, G. H. (1949) The early metal trades and the beginning of engineering in Lancashire, *Trans. Lancs. & Chesh. Antiq. Soc.*, LXI.

Turnbull, G. (1979) *Traffic and Transport: An Economic History of Pickfords*, London.

Turnbull, G. (1951) *A History of the Calico Printing Industry of Great Britain*, Altrincham.

Turner, M. E. (ed.) (1978) W. F. Tate, *A Domesday of English Enclosure Acts and Awards*, Reading.

Turner, M. E. (1980) *English Parliamentary Enclosure*, Folkestone.

Turner, P. J. (1974) The commission of the peace in Cheshire 1536–1603, unpublished MA thesis, University of Manchester.

Turner, R. C. (1987) Peel Hall, an artisan mannerist puzzle in Cheshire, *Trans. Hist. Soc. Lancs. & Chesh.*, CXXXVI.

Turner, W. (1957) *The Warrington Academy*, Warrington.

Twemlowe, J. A. (ed.) (1935) *Liverpool Town Books, vol. II, 1571–1603*, Liverpool.

Twigg, G. (1989) Salt working in early-modern Nantwich, paper at Keele University seminar.

Tynan, K. (1908) *Father Mathew*, London.

Unwin, G. (1924) *Samuel Oldknow and the Arkwrights*, Manchester, repr. 1968.

Varley, B. (1957) *The History of Stockport Grammar School*, Manchester.

Varley, J. (ed.) (1941, 1944) *A Middlewich Chartulary*, Chetham Soc., new series, CV and CVIII.

VCH. Cheshire. *The Victoria History of the Counties of England: A History of the County of Chester*, 3 vols.

VCH. Derbys. *The Victoria History of the Counties of England: A History of the County of Derbyshire*, 2 vols, 1905–7.

VCH. Lancs. *The Victoria History of the Counties of England: A History of the County of Lancashire*, 8 vols, 1906–1914.

Vidler, A. R. (1974) *The Church in an Age of Revolution*, Harmondsworth.

Vigier, F. (1970) *Change and Apathy: Liverpool and Manchester during the Industrial Revolution*, Cambridge, Mass.

Vincent, J. (ed.) (1984) *The Crawford Papers*, Manchester.

Wadsworth, A. P. and Mann, J. de L. (1931) *The Cotton Trade and Industrial Lancashire 1600–1780*, Manchester.

Walker, F. (1939) *The Industrial Geography of South-West Lancashire before the Industrial Revolution*, Chetham Soc., new series, CIII.

Walker, H. (1989) Lawn Tennis, *Sport in Britain*, ed. T. Mason, Cambridge.

Walker, J. S. F. and Tindall, A. S. (1985) *Country Houses of Greater Manchester*, Manchester.

Walker, W. (1990) Duxbury in decline: the fortunes of a landed estate, 1756–1932, *Trans. Hist. Soc. Lancs. & Chesh.*, CXL.

Wallis, P. J. (1969) A preliminary register of old schools in Lancashire, *Trans. Hist. Soc. Lancs. & Chesh.*, CXX.

Walton, J. K. (1978) *The Blackpool Landlady*, Manchester.

Walton, J. K. (1987) *Lancashire: A Social History 1558–1939*, Manchester.

Walvin, J. (1975) *The People's Game: A Social History of British Football*, London.

Wanklyn, M. D. G. (1976) Landed society and allegiance in Cheshire and Shropshire in the first civil war, unpublished PhD thesis, University of Manchester.

Ward, J. (1905) *Moston Characters at Play*, Manchester.

Wark, K. R. (1971) *Elizabethan Recusancy in Cheshire*, Chetham Soc., 3rd Series, XIX.

Waters, C. (1986) Manchester morality and London capital: the battle over the Palace of Varieties, *Music Hall: The Business of Pleasure*, ed. P. Bailey, Milton Keynes.

Watkin, E. (1891) *Alderman Cobden of Manchester*, Manchester.

Watkin, W. T. (1886) *Roman Cheshire*, Liverpool.

Watson, J. B. (1963–4) The Lancashire gentry and the public service 1529–1558, *Trans. Lancs. & Chesh. Antiq. Soc.*, LXXII.

Watson, R. C. (1957) Traditional Fylde houses, *Trans. Hist. Soc. Lancs. & Chesh.*, CIX.

Watts, J. (1866) *Facts of the Cotton Famine*, London, 2nd impr. 1968.

Waugh, E. (1881) *Factory Folk during the Cotton Famine*, Manchester.

Weaver Trustees' (1896) *Minutes*, Northwich.

Webb, B. (1926) *My Apprenticeship*, London.

Webb, S. and Webb, B. (1906) *History of Local Government, vol. 1, The Parish and the County*, repr. 1963, London.

Webb, S. and **Webb, B.** (1913) *The History of Trade Unionism*, London.
Webb, S. and **Webb, B.** (1920) *English Local Government: The Story of the King's Highway*, London.
Webb, W. (1623) see Ormerod (1882).
Webster, C. (1967) Richard Townley, 1629–1707 and the Townley group, *Trans. Hist. Soc. Lancs. & Chesh.*, CXVIII.
Wedge, T. (1794) *General View of the Agriculture of the County Palatine of Chester*, London.
Weeks, W. S. (1924–6) Clitheroe in the seventeenth century, *Trans. Lancs. & Chesh. Antiq. Soc.*, XLI–XLIII.
Weinbaum, M. (1943) *British Borough Charters 1307–1660*, Cambridge.
Weld, J. (1913) *History of Leagram*, Chetham Soc., new series, LXXII.
Western, J. R. (1965) *The English Militia in the Eighteenth Century*, London.
Weston, S. (1971) The Grosvenor family and Chester politics 1747–1784, unpublished BA thesis, University of Manchester.
Whetham, E. (1978) *The Agrarian History of England and Wales, VIII, 1914–1939*, Cambridge.
White, F. & Co. (1860) *History, Gazetteer, and Directory of Cheshire*, Sheffield.
White, H. P. (1980) *The Continuing Conurbation: Change and Development in Greater Manchester*, Salford.
Wigan (1981) *Those Dark Satanic Mills*, Wigan.
Wilkinson, D. J. (1983) The commission of the peace in Lancashire 1603–1642, *Trans. Hist. Soc. Lancs. & Chesh.*, CXXXII.
Willan, T. S. (1936) *River Navigation in England 1600–1750*, Oxford; repr. 1964.
Willan, T. S. (1937) Chester and the navigation of the Dee 1600–1750, *Jour. Chester Arch. Soc.*, XXXII.
Willan, T. S. (1938) *The English Coasting Trade 1600–1750*, Manchester.
Willan, T. S. (1951) *The Navigation of the River Weaver*, Chetham Soc., 3rd series, V.
Willan, T. S. (1959) *Studies in Elizabethan Foreign Trade*, Manchester.
Willan, T. S. (1976) *The Inland Trade*, Manchester.
Willan, T. S. (1980) *Elizabethan Manchester*, Chetham Soc., 3rd series, XXVII.
Willan, T. S. (1983) Plague in perspective: the case of Manchester in 1605, *Trans. Hist. Soc. Lancs. & Chesh.*, CXXXII.
Williams, B. (1976) *The Making of Manchester Jewry 1740–1875*, Manchester.
Williams, G. (1989) Rugby union, *Sport in Britain*, ed. T. Mason, Cambridge.
Williams, J. (1989) Cricket, *Sport in Britain*, ed. T. Mason, Cambridge.
Williams, P. (1979) *The Tudor Regime*, London, repr. 1983.
Wilson, C. (1954) *The History of Unilever, vol. 1*, London.
Wilson, K. P. (1969) *Chester Customs Accounts 1301–1565*, Record Soc. Lancs. & Chesh., CXI.
Withersby, J. P. (1990) Linen men: a farmer/trader economy in Lancashire, unpublished MPhil thesis, University of Liverpool.
Wood, G. H. (1910) *The History of Wages in the Cotton Trade*, London.
Wood, K. (1984) *The Coal Pits of Chowbent*, Blackburn.
Woodward, D. W. (1968) The Chester leather industry 1558–1625, *Trans. Hist. Soc. Lancs. & Chesh.*, CXIX.
Woodward, D. W. (1970) *The Trade of Elizabethan Chester*, Hull.

Woolrych, A. H. (1961) *Battles of the English Civil War*, London.

Worthington, T. L. (1893) *The Dwellings of the Poor and Weekly Wage Earners in and around Towns*, London.

Wrightson, K. (1980) Two concepts of order, *An Ungovernable People*, ed. J. Brewer and J. Styles, London.

Wrightson, K. (1982) *English Society 1580–1680*, London.

Wrigley, A. (1949) *Rakings Up*, Rochdale.

Wrigley, E. A. and **Schofield, R. S.** (1981) *The Population History of England 1541–1871*, London.

Wrigley, F. and **Winder, T. H.** (1899) *The Registers of the Parish Church of Whittington*, Lancs. P. R. Soc., III.

Wyatt, G. (1990) Nantwich and Wybunbury, 1680–1819: a demographic study of two Cheshire parishes, *Trans. Hist. Soc. Lancs. & Chesh.*, CXXXIX.

Yates, W. (1786) *A Map of the County of Lancashire, 1786*, reprinted, with an introduction by J. B. Harley, by the Historic Society of Lancs. & Cheshire, 1968 [Liverpool].

Yearsley, I. (1962) *The Manchester Tram*, Huddersfield.

Youd, G. (1962) The common fields of Lancashire, *Trans. Hist. Soc. Lancs. & Chesh.*, CXIII.

Index

This index contains all personal names. Township, parish, and borough names have all been indexed and these headings subsume specific buildings, streets, and small urban districts within them. Halls, great houses, estates, mills, and farms are brought together under these headings and not listed separately by name. Space has forced the compression of subject headings, and readers are reminded of the sub-division of chapters set out on the contents page.